Enigma Books

Also published by Enigma Books

Hitler's Table Talk: 1941–1944
In Stalin's Secret Service
Hitler and Mussolini: The Secret Meetings
The Jews in Fascist Italy: A History
The Man Behind the Rosenbergs
Roosevelt and Hopkins: An Intimate History
Diary 1937–1943 (Galeazzo Ciano)
Secret Affairs: FDR, Cordell Hull, and Sumner Welles
Hitler and His Generals: Military Conferences 1942–1945
Stalin and the Jews: The Red Book
The Secret Front: Nazi Political Espionage
Fighting the Nazis: French Intelligence and Counterintelligence
A Death in Washington: Walter G. Krivitsky and the Stalin Terror
The Battle of the Casbah: Terrorism and Counterterrorism in Algeria 1955–1957
Hitler's Second Book: The Unpublished Sequel to *Mein Kampf*
At Napoleon's Side in Russia: The Classic Eyewitness Account
The Atlantic Wall: Hitler's Defenses for D-Day
Double Lives: Stalin, Willi Münzenberg and the Seduction of the Intellectuals
France and the Nazi Threat: The Collapse of French Diplomacy 1932–1939
Mussolini: The Secrets of His Death
Mortal Crimes: Soviet Penetration of the Manhattan Project
Top Nazi: Karl Wolff—The Man Between Hitler and Himmler
Empire on the Adriatic: Mussolini's Conquest of Yugoslavia
The Origins of the War of 1914 (3-volume set)
Hitler's Foreign Policy: 1933–1939—The Road to World War II
The Origins of Fascist Ideology 1918–1925
Max Corvo: OSS Italy 1942–1945
Hitler's Contract: The Secret History of the Italian Edition of *Mein Kampf*
Secret Intelligence and the Holocaust
Israel at High Noon
Balkan Inferno: Betrayal, War, and Intervention, 1990–2005
Calculated Risk: World War II Memoirs of General Mark Clark
The Murder of Maxim Gorky
The Kravchenko Case: One Man's War On Stalin
Operation Neptune
Paris Weekend
Shattered Sky
Hitler's Gift to France
The Mafia and the Allies
The Nazi Party, 1919-1945: A Complete History
Encyclopedia of Cold War Espionage, Spies, and Secret Operations
The Cicero Spy Affair
A Crate of Vodka
NOC
The First Iraq War: Britain's Mesopotamian Campaign, 1914-1918

Becoming Winston Churchill
Hitler's Intelligence Chief: Walter Schellenberg
Salazar: A Political Biography
The Italian Brothers
Nazi Palestine
Code Name: Kalistrat
Pax Romana
Lenin and His Comrades
Working with Napoleon
The Decision to Drop the Atomic Bomb
Target Hitler
Truman, MacArthur and the Korean War
The Eichmann Trial Diary
American Police: A History, Vol. 1
American Police: A History, Vol. 2
Cold Angel
Alphabet of Masks
Stalin's Man in Canada
Hunting Down the Jews
Mussolini Warlord
Election Year 1968
Spy Lost
Deadly Sleep

Adolf Hitler

Hitler at War

Meetings and Conversations
1939-1945

Edited and with an Introduction by Robert L. Miller

Enigma Books

Printed in Canada
Library of Congress Cataloging-in-Publication Data

[Available on request]

Contents

Introduction

This selection is based on documents from several published archives, and historical reconstructions in an effort to provide an accurate picture of the plans, thoughts, and objectives of Adolf Hitler at various key moments of the Second World War. The archival texts are reprinted in their entirety with minimal commentary and bibliographical suggestions. The military conferences, on the other hand, include the notes by German historian Helmut Heiber and American military historian David Glantz. The full account of each meeting offers the best insights into Hitler's thinking and reactions to major events as he issued fateful orders that were immediately carried out by his adjutants.

The selected documents are roughly divided into two broad areas: the early part of the war from September 1, 1939 to June 22, 1941, when Nazi Germany invaded the Soviet Union, and the period from the attack on the Soviet Union to the collapse of the Third Reich in May 1945.

The first section includes mostly political and diplomatic conferences with foreign leaders and diplomats. The final period from July 1941 to April 1945 is mostly centered on military operations concerning the war in Russia. A large sub-section is assigned to the Italian crisis from July to September 1943, triggered by the invasion of Sicily and the overthrow of Mussolini. Those dramatic events constituted a major blow to Germany's prestige, sowing doubt in the minds of the German people, along with the many Nazi collaborators and sympathizers in Europe and elsewhere.

This documentary record of the meetings and conversations held by the Nazi dictator from September 1, 1939 to April 27, 1945, is a selection and remains necessarily incomplete. The transcribed daily military conferences alone, of which only a little more than 1,000 pages remain, represents a mere ten percent of the estimated total. The bulk of that archive was burned by the SS in May 1945. At times additional documents have been authenticated and added to the existing collection.

Hitler was far more explicit than one may expect in his conversations with various personalities. While several important texts help us understand the evolution of the politician and the war leader over a relatively short period, many important areas remain unknown. The twelve-year Third Reich reached its apex in the summer of 1942, when the overextended Wehrmacht was stopped in its advance into the Caucasus and at Stalingrad on the Volga River. The defeat at El Alamein in November 1942 ended the winning streak of Rommel's Afrika Korps at that same moment. With the surrender of von Paulus at Stalingrad in February 1943, the Supreme Warlord, while forever in denial, had to know that full victory was no longer within his grasp.

In the fall of 1942 Hitler ordered that stenographers keep an accurate record of the daily military conferences that he chaired at OKW headquarters. The purpose of that record was to document the discussions and decisions made for posterity, given the strategic and tactical disagreements that had surfaced within the High Command.

As Gerhard Weinberg explains in his preface to *Hitler and His Generals*:

> As he was being told that the German army was unable to punch through Red Army resistance in the western Caucasus on the road to Tuapse, while at the same time the German forces heading toward the main oilfields at Grozny and Baku, as well as those heading for Stalingrad, were making very slow progress—if any—Hitler blew up. He temporarily took over command of Army Group A in the Caucasus himself; he replaced the chief of staff of the German army; and he considered replacing his immediate assistants in the High Command of the Armed Forces [Oberkommando der Wehrmacht—OKW].*

---

* H. Heiber and D. Glantz, Eds. Introduction by Gerhard L. Weinberg, *Hitler and His Generals. Military Conferences 1942-1945* (New York: Enigma Books, 2003), p. 13.

The workings of a global conflict of almost unlimited proportions have Hitler directing operations on a daily, and hourly, basis. In innumerable meetings, long nightly monologues, critical military conferences, the character, motivations, thoughts, and actions of the one man who wanted the war at all costs, emerge providing a chilling picture of the ruthless manner in which the German army was ordered to fight the war.

During those conversations, and conferences, the inner workings of the Nazi regime, the leadership of the German Army, the strategic and tactical vision behind the war in victory and defeat, and the ways by which Hitler used and exploited his allies and collaborators are revealed. The picture becomes more complicated as the documents move from the discussion of a peace offer to Great Britain and France in September 1939, just two weeks after the war started, to a tense conversation with American Under Secretary of State Sumner Welles in February 1940 about Germany's objectives, while Hitler was at the same time persuading Mussolini to enter the war. These were followed by the invasion of Denmark and Norway, the triumph over France, the failure of the meetings with Franco, Pétain, and Mussolini who couldn't be stopped from marching head-on into catastrophe in Greece. The revealing conversations with the Grand Mufti of Jerusalem, Matsuoka, Molotov, Mannerheim, and Ciano would also follow.

With the invasion of Russia in June 1941, most of Hitler's time until the end of the war in April 1945 would be focused on the Eastern front, while the attention paid to other theaters was probably less than ten percent, judging from the volume of the documentation available. The daily military conferences where Hitler directed the war and vented his frustrations to his entourage of generals and admirals, whom he despised as useless uniformed aristocrats, are among the most illuminating of his thinking and style.

Mussolini and a few Nazi leaders, such as Göring and possibly Goebbels, were hoping to persuade Hitler to seek a separate peace with Stalin. Those conversations took place in secret and we only have vague allusions about a possible outcome. The Allied leaders, mainly Churchill and FDR, had anxiously observed the Nazi Soviet Non-Aggression Pact of August 1939, making the two dictatorships virtual allies in the carving up of Poland. After the German attack on the Soviet Union in 1941 the Allies remained very much aware of the danger of a possible repeat of the Treaty of Brest-Litovsk, when Russia dropped out of the First World War in 1918. But none of those dreaded scenarios materialized, although serious doubts persisted—at least up to the Teheran Conference in November 1943.

The rest of Hitler's time was spent with his inner circle and Nazi party officials, notably Martin Bormann, the Nazi Party secretary, Joseph Goebbels, armaments minister Albert Speer, Heinrich Himmler, and others. Of those confidential discussions where presumably the Holocaust and the extermination programs in Poland and Russia were discussed there is little or no trace, only a few allusions.

As for Hitler's ability as a strategist and military leader, Gerhard Weinberg again provides valuable insight into the widely held belief that the Nazi leader was in fact a military genius:

> The record shows him as a mean and suspicious individual who made decisions on the basis of preposterous beliefs about such countries as the Soviet Union and the United States.[*]

The single-minded reliance on his prejudices led Hitler to believe that those ideas were reality, when in fact they were for the most part figments of his imagination. Ideological thinking rather than *realpolitik* ultimately led Germany to disaster.

Robert L. Miller

---

[*] Ibid. p. 16

Hitler at War

Meetings and Conversations
1939-1945

Part I

1939

Attempts to quickly end the hostilities as soon as the war broke out on September 1, 1939, with the attack on Poland and the declarations of war by Great Britain and France began almost immediately. By the date of this conversation Swedish businessman and friend of Hermann Göring's, Birger Dahlerus had already traveled to London to broker a truce, and possibly a negotiated peace between Nazi Germany and the British and French Allies. Those efforts were destined to fail, while the tone and outcome of this encounter provides a sense of the atmosphere prevailing during the early weeks of the war. As of September 17 Poland was defeated and invaded from the East by Soviet troops in accordance with the provisions of the Secret Protocol of Nazi Soviet Non-Aggression Pact of August 24, 1939.

*****

Memorandum of the conversation between the Führer and M. Dahlerus in the presence of Field Marshal Göring

Berlin, September 26, 1939.

[Birger Dahlerus, a Swedish civil engineer and manufacturer, whose efforts as an unofficial intermediary between Britain and Germany during the weeks before the outbreak of war are described in his book, translated as *The Last Attempt* (London, 1947). Sir George Ogilvie-Forbes, Counselor, British Legation in Norway, September 1939-February 1940. Dahlerus testified Mar. 19, 1946, before the International Military Tribunal at Nuremberg that his meeting with Ogilvie-Forbes took place in Oslo, not Stockholm, on Sept. 24, 1939. *Trial of the Major War Criminals*, vol. XXXIV, p. 473. Dahlerus had been in contact in Berlin with Ogilvie-Forbes, who was Counselor of the British embassy until the outbreak of war. See also: Leonard Mosley, *On Borrowed Time* (New York: Random House, 1969); Gerhard L. Weinberg, *Hitler's Foreign Policy 1933-1939* (New York: Enigma Books, 2010).]

M. Dahlerus pointed out, by way of introduction, that the British, were such great egoists that they were now deliberating, in view of the difficulties of the present situation, how they could extricate themselves from the whole affair. He had told Forbes in Stockholm that, after the speeches of Churchill and Chamberlain, negotiations between the British and the German governments were probably out of the question. Forbes denied this and, on the contrary, took the view that the British government could very well conduct such negotiations with Germany if only a formula were found which assured to the peoples of Europe their territorial integrity and their freedom by means of a treaty among the great European Powers. Poland was considered lost, so they took the position that it was now a matter of at least saving their own skins.

The Führer replied that the worst of it was that the British had always considered everything pure bluff and immediately interpreted all restraint and patience on his part as weakness. Because he (the Führer) had for years put up with certain things from the Poles, because there was not always immediate resort to shooting, England had come to the false conclusion of mistaking for weakness the considerateness and forbearance of the Führer. The British were now trying something similar with their declaration of a 3-year war. If Germany declared that this threat was a matter of indifference to her that, too, would be considered bluffing. But they should not let themselves be deceived about the Führer; he would soon wage the war toward the West, also, in such a way as to stun the British. He had destroyed Poland in 3 weeks. The British should stop and think what could happen to them in 3 months. The Führer then stressed the fact that he had always come out for friendship with England, but that today an abysmal hatred for England was gradually spreading among the German people. The British were now foolishly also dropping leaflets which bore witness to their absolute ignorance of the German frame of mind. Particularly when they attacked a person like the Führer, to whom Germany looked up full of gratitude, this produced a state of mind in the German people which made agreement with England more and more difficult. The British would by this method finally drive things so far that a rapprochement with England would be impossible because the people would not want it. If the British, instead of a 3-year war, contemplated a 7-year war, or one even longer, Germany would survive it, too, and in the end turn England completely into a heap of ruins.

M. Dahlerus again spoke of the possibility of peace arising out of the egoism of the British. The Führer replied that the British, if they wanted peace, would certainly have to be absolutely clear about the actual facts. Germany had won a victory in Poland which was without precedent in history. In 14 days he had completely destroyed a country of 36 million inhabitants which had an army of 45 divisions, in part well equipped, and whose soldiers had fought bravely. In these circumstances, the Führer had no intention of allowing anyone to interfere in the solution of the Polish question. Moreover, the Russians also had a weighty word to say in the matter. They, too, had occupied large portions of Poland. The Führer pointed out in this connection that in view of the campaign of lies directed against him and Germany because of an alleged German lust for conquest, he was now completely disinteresting himself in all regions that did not affect Germany's interests. It was a matter of complete indifference to him whether another country appropriated territory anywhere outside the German sphere of interest.

M. Dahlerus then inquired whether in the opinion of the Germans there would be any object at all in the British declaring themselves ready for peace discussions. The Führer replied that a condition for peace discussions would be to allow him an entirely free hand with regard to Poland. If the British still wanted to salvage something of Poland he could only advise them to hasten the peace discussions. Beyond this he was

entirely prepared to join in guaranteeing the status quo of the rest of
Europe. He had at the time not joined in guaranteeing Czechoslovakia
because he had intended to do so only when all her neighbors were prepared to do so. At that time Poland had herself appropriated areas of
Czechoslovakia. If the British desired peace in Europe they should make it
clearly understood. Germany would in any case be prepared for it, for she
needed peace in order to cultivate the newly acquired areas in the East that
had formerly belonged to the German cultural sphere. This would require
at least 50 years.

The Führer intended to reincorporate into the Reich the former
German and former Austrian sections of Poland, as well as strategically
important territories. Besides this there was to be a "reshuffling" not only
by reuniting once more inside the Reich by large-scale resettlement the
scattered Germany minority groups, but also by effecting an adjustment
between the thickly populated west, with a population density of 140
persons per square kilometer a condition that could not last and the thinly
populated east with a density of only 35 people per square kilometer. To
carry out these great plans would require 50 to 100 years, particularly if
one considered the tremendous backwardness and demoralization of
Poland, in comparison with which the remaining Czechia looked like a
veritable paradise. It was insolence for such a debased country as Poland
to dare to turn against a country like Germany. M. Dahlerus mentioned in
this connection a statement of Lipski, who had declared that the Poles
would not yield to Germany, for he knew Germany very well and within a
week a revolution would surely break out and force Germany to back
down. The Führer then described further his awful impressions of Poland
during his trips to the front. The Vistula, supposed to be Poland's great
river, was silted up everywhere and navigable only by rowboat. And now
for this wretched country millions of Englishmen and Germans were to lay
down their lives!

M. Dahlerus stated in this connection that it depended on only one
thing: how the British could save face. The Führer pointed out that the
Poles had deceived the British, that they had had absolutely no basis for
opposing Germany, as they had led the British to believe. M. Dahlerus
then brought up the question of the Jews. The British were considering
where the Jews were to stay, whereupon the Führer replied that if he
should reorganize the Polish state, an asylum could also be created for the
Jews. Someone had to see that there was order in the East and convert the
condition of complete disorganization into an orderly one. In addition to

this there would be the above-mentioned reshuffling of peoples: Germans would be settled in the thinly populated areas in order at least to increase the population density from 35 persons per square kilometer to 80. The aim was to create a sensible regional distribution of nationalities as well as a sensible economic structure in the Polish area.

M. Dahlerus again brought up the question of peace and said that the main problem for the British was to find a formula by which peace would be assured in the future. At the Führer's suggestion that the British should then send somebody to Germany who took him, the Führer, seriously and did not believe that he was only bluffing, M. Dahlerus replied that the dispatching of an Englishman would probably require an armistice. He could imagine, for example, that General Ironside might be sent from England on a strictly secret mission. The Führer replied that before an armistice could be concluded, an unofficial exchange of views must first have taken place in order to examine the prospects of its conclusion. Moreover, everything depended on whether the British actually desired peace. If the British actually wanted peace, the Führer continued, they could have it in 2 weeks without losing face. A prerequisite for this, to be sure, was that they reconcile themselves to the fact that Poland could not again arise. Russia, too, had something to say about the matter and was not inclined to give up again the areas she occupied. The fate of Poland would not be decided at the conference table, for the decision had already fallen elsewhere. It was now a question of the future of Europe, which could only be assured if the Polish problem, which had already been decided, were completely set aside and thought given only to Europe. The question arose as to what the British wanted in Europe. He, the Führer, was prepared to guarantee them security for their own country, as he had previously done when he had concluded the Naval Treaty with England, which he had not terminated until the British took a hostile attitude. For France he was prepared to give a guarantee forthwith. The West Wall was the unalterable western border of Germany. He had repeatedly offered guarantees for Belgium and Holland. He was prepared to incorporate all these things in a European treaty. He could only repeat once more that Germany did not wish any conquests in the west or in the Balkans; in the Balkans she had only commercial interests.

M. Dahlerus again asked about the preliminaries for an armistice in the event that somebody from England came to Berlin. The Führer expressed himself very skeptically regarding England's real desire for peace as well as the possibilities of sending somebody to Germany. Perhaps it would be

best, on the whole, for France, or else a neutral, to take the first step. The
Duce, for instance, could take over this role. M. Dahlerus replied that the
Duce was not considered sufficiently neutral; the Queen of the Netherlands
had been thought of. Field Marshal Göring summed up the possibilities for
an exchange of views, saying that a representative of Germany and a
representative of England should first meet in Holland and probe the possibility of agreement. Only if such possibilities became evident should the
Queen of the Netherlands be approached, who would then officially invite
the representatives of both countries to armistice discussions. It would not
be a bad idea if an officer, such as General Ironside, were selected by the
British for the first unofficial conference.

The Führer again brought up the question of whether the British really
desired peace or whether they were not again indulging in some vain hopes
of a German defeat, now that things in Poland had turned out so very
differently from what they had imagined. Germany did not want to
"swallow any Poles"; she wanted only security for the Reich, and borders
which would provide the necessary possibilities for her provisioning and
for the reshuffling of peoples. The Field Marshal pointed out that the question of Poland was now settled in any case, not only by Germany but also
by Russia and that, in his opinion, some way could be found to prevent the
whole of Europe from being destroyed because of so backward a nation.
He believed, moreover, that the experience of the past weeks did not fail to
make an impression on the British and that many of them were now much
more reasonable than formerly, before the commencement of hostilities
with Poland The Führer expressed doubts as to whether the meeting in
Holland could be kept secret and asked whether Chamberlain could undertake anything like that at all, since the British Parliament wanted war. Of
course, if the British reflected that Germany, with a bad government and
only 87 divisions had held out against the whole world for 4 years, they
would have to realize the hopelessness of vanquishing the Germany of
today, with her good, energetic government, and 156 divisions. Thus far,
to be sure, neither France nor England had made any really serious attack.

M. Dahlerus interjected here that that was precisely the proof that the
British no longer wanted war. The best hope of peace was British egoism.
The Führer replied that the British could have peace if they wanted it, but
they would have to hurry, for not for long would leaflets alone be dropped.
The mood of the German troops in the west, particularly after contact with
the victorious troops coming from the east, was one of extraordinary
eagerness for combat, and the Field Marshal had already had to give very

strict orders in order to impose a certain restraint on the operations of the victory-conscious air arm in the west. A dangerous eagerness had appeared. In this connection the Field Marshal also referred to the economic side of the German preparations.

The Führer supplemented his remarks by saying that he was referring to the complete conversion of the economy to wartime requirements. The world would be amazed when once it perceived what Germany was producing in the way of airplanes, arms, ammunition, submarines, and E-boats. So if peace was wanted, one would have to hurry somewhat. A way could then perhaps be found. At the same time, of course, the honor of a victorious army would by all means have to be respected. He, the Führer, could simply not expect certain things of his generals and of the German nation, which was a nation of soldiers, and had to repeat that he was skeptical with regard to the British will to peace and the possibilities of realizing the will. M. Dahlerus replied in conclusion that he would nevertheless do his best and would go to England the very next day in order to send out feelers in the direction indicated.

SCHMIDT Minister

*****

Conversation between the Führer and Count Ciano in the presence of the Foreign Minister, on October 1, 1939, at the Reich Chancellery

[Galeazzo Ciano (1903-1944) was Italy's foreign minister from 1936 to 1943. He was also Mussolini's son-in-law and a main promoter of the Axis who later turned against Nazi Germany and voted against Mussolini in 1943. He was executed by a fascist firing squad in February 1944. See Galeazzo Ciano, *Diary 1937-1943* (New York: Enigma Books, 2003); Ciano's own memorandum of this conversation is printed in English translation in Ciano's Diplomatic Papers, edited by M. Muggeridge (London, 1948), pp. 309-316. The original Italian version appears in *L'Europa verso la catastrofe* (Milan, 1948), pp. 466-477.]

Berlin, October 1, 1939.

The Führer expressed his pleasure over the opportunity to have a personal conversation with Count Ciano. It would not have been possible for him to leave Berlin during the few days that he was spending in the capital, and he was therefore grateful to Count Ciano for having come to Berlin. Count

Ciano in turn thanked the Führer for the opportunity for this conversation. Difficulties similar to those experienced by the Führer prevented the Duce from leaving the capital. The Italian government had scheduled a number of Cabinet meetings at which important economic and military measures were to be adopted and the presence of the Duce was required. Moreover, a meeting between the Führer and the Duce at the present moment would be a sensation which might better be reserved for an occasion when definitive and conclusive decisions would be taken.

The Führer replied that he wished, through Count Ciano, to give the Duce a picture of the past development of events and of the present situation. He had put this conversation off until the conclusion of the first phase of the present conflict, that is, until the annihilation of the Polish forces. Only now was it possible to form a conclusive picture of his future plans and of the disposition of his forces. Much as he (the Führer) had been convinced that Poland would be defeated in very short order, a war always contained certain unpredictable elements, and he (the Führer) had therefore waited for the end of the first act of the conflict to inform the Duce of the plans for the future. Militarily, as he had said, the first act of the conflict was ended as of this day; German troops had begun marching into Warsaw last night and thus were occupying Poland's capital. The fortress of Modlin had likewise surrendered, and surrender negotiations had been in progress with Admiral von Unruh on the Hela Peninsula since this evening. From the military standpoint, therefore, the Polish question had been conclusively settled.

Poland could have been conquered even more swiftly if Germany had been willing to sacrifice more lives. But there had been no intention of sacrificing even a single man unnecessarily in the East, since there was better to use every one in the West. Warsaw had not made the heroic stand that was being spoken of everywhere. The first bombardment of the city and the first attack had taken place on September 25. On the 26th this attack had been carried further, and on the 27th the city had capitulated. There had been no bombardment before September 25, only a siege of the city. One could not speak, therefore, of any heroic stand. The Warsaw garrison was already demoralized after a short time, just as was true of the Polish Army in general.

The Führer then gave a summary of the relative numerical strength, of the forces and of the losses sustained. Germany had entered the battle with 121 divisions, to which must be added a certain number of border defense divisions. Of the 70 divisions allocated to the East, only a part had been actually committed against the enemy. The combat and operational losses of materiel were extremely moderate and amount to only one eighth of the advance estimate. Casualties were far fewer than had been expected. As of September 26, 5,200 dead, 22,000 wounded, and a few thousand missing had been counted. Of the latter, strayed groups had turned up again at various places. It had to be assumed, however, that some had been ambushed and massacred by the Poles. It could be expected that the total of fatal casualties would reach 6,000. In consequence of these relatively light losses, it had been possible to form immediately a great number of replacement divisions, the activation of which had been scheduled for later on, so that Germany could at the moment count on 152 divisions of 20 to 22,000 men each, to which a large number of corps troops must be added.

Even as early as September 10, while the operations in Poland were in full progress, the transfer of troops back to the West had begun. The reason for the light German losses was to be found in the new and modern individual training of the infantry. The favorable results of the campaign were attributable not only to the new infantry tactics but also to the use of heavy infantry weapons, as well as to the effective employment of armor and the Luftwaffe. Poland, by the way, seemed to have received operational advice from the French, but it had been far from convincing and effective. The bravery of some elements of the Polish Army could not be denied. The Poles had been poorly equipped and led, however, and the non-Polish, contingents had gone into battle very unwillingly, falling back as soon as they had lost their leaders. Nevertheless, the Polish Army must, be described as a modernly equipped Army which, given better leadership and training, would doubtless have accomplished more.

Poland had 35 regular divisions. In addition to this, there were 36 regiments of cavalry (about 11 cavalry divisions) which had in some instances undertaken very foolish attacks, Poland, moreover, also had at her disposal 15 second-line reserve divisions with relatively good equipment. Then there were supposed to have been another 15 third-line divisions which probably had for the most part fought in civilian clothing. What happened on the Western front was a farce. The attacks of the French which received so much sensational publicity in the enemy press were solely of token character. Nowhere had the enemy come near the German defense lines. Patrols had pushed forward only in areas where the German fortifications were 15 to 20 kilometers behind the border. At no point had the German combat outposts been pushed back, artillery fire had also been extremely moderate. Valuable installations and open cities had been bombarded by neither side. Today was the first time that a shell had fallen on a German bunker, without, however, causing any appreciable damage.

Thus Germany could regard the battle in the West so far as of no consequence whatsoever. It had been easy for her to hold her combat outposts. Moreover, neither France nor England had either the manpower or the materiel for any large-scale attack on the Western front. To be sure, the state of relative quiet there would not last forever. The war on the seas had in the main consisted of the so-called blockade, to which Germany had replied with submarine warfare. Notwithstanding the "chivalrous methods" she had pursued, Germany had by September 28 sunk 290,000 tons. The moment Germany gave the submarine war a more serious character, enemy losses would, of course, mount very considerably. German submarines would then no longer consent to first stopping the enemy ships, then searching them carefully, and finally even assuring themselves that the lifeboats were in order, as they were now doing, but they would simply torpedo the ships without warning. Nevertheless, even with the present methods they had sunk the aircraft carrier Courageous and, from our observations, another one, the Ark Royal, the sinking of which Churchill would not admit only because no neutral ships had been present as witnesses, as there had been in the former instance. In addition, two destroyers had also been sunk.

In the air war in the West, the British had thus far made a bombing attack on Wilhelmshaven. Of 24 bombers, 11 had been shot down. The day before yesterday the British had attacked two German destroyers. Of six attackers, five were shot down. Otherwise, Germany had been spared any bombing attacks. Merely leaflets had been dropped at night, from an altitude of 5 to 6 thousand meters which were remarkable for their stupidity and innocuousness. They were stupid because their authors had believed that they could precisely at this present moment incite the German people to defection from their government; if dropped in larger quantities, they could at most be regarded as additional paper supply.

Count Ciano observed at this point that the people would never allow themselves to be separated from a leader who was always the winner. The Führer continued that on the Western front itself everything was being shot down that came into view. Thus 14 planes, 12 British and 2 French, had been shot down yesterday. The ratio of total losses of planes was 1 to 9 in favor of Germany. One German fighter wing alone had brought down 44 planes, while losing only 4 of its own. In principle, therefore, Germany was in a position to withdraw her troops from the East, allow them a short rehabilitation period, richly deserved after the formidable long-distance marches; the time could also be used for the reconditioning of materiel, and then they could be shipped to the West. Germany was therefore prepared and able at all times to become active in the West. This announcement by the Führer made an obvious impression on Count Ciano. He inquired once more to make sure he had understood correctly that Germany was prepared at all times to become active in the West, and the Führer confirmed this.

The Führer further remarked that Germany was not in fact interested in forcing a war in the West if such a war could be avoided. After the Polish victories it was unnecessary to continue the war for reasons of military prestige. Nor were there other reasons for doing so. But if peace was not attainable, then Germany would give the war in the West another character. On the subject of the agreements with Russia, the Führer observed that their purpose was to define the spheres of interest in the newly acquired territories. In a generally difficult time it was not in Germany's interest to have a hostile neighbor at her back, and so she had reached agreements with Russia that were absolutely clear-cut and completely ruled out any possibility of misunderstanding or conflict in the future. In the territory east of the line which was known to Count Ciano, the shaping of the political and economic organization was an exclusively Russian matter, while west of the line Germany pursued her own interests with the same exclusiveness.

It was important for the Duce to know that Germany had two things in mind in this territory west of the line: first, to wipe out the Versailles Treaty boundaries and establish a new boundary that was acceptable to Germany from the ethnographic, historical, and economic standpoint; and second, to give the remaining territory of Polish nationality a political organization that would rule out for all time to come any threat to the Reich from that direction. Furthermore, both Russia and Germany wanted to prevent any element of intrigue apt to sow discord between Germany and Russia from arising out of this settlement at any time in the future. The Führer declared that in every other respect he wanted the German Reich to be encumbered as little as possible with the responsibility for the existence of the Polish residual state. The permanent form that this residual state was to have would be wholly determined by the effort of pacification and of restoring orderly political and economic conditions. The timing of the execution of this plan depended on whether the war was ended or would go on now. Naturally, no final decisions on this matter could be taken until hostilities were concluded.

Count Ciano asked for a more precise definition of the form envisaged by the Führer for organizing the Polish residual state. The Führer declared that the Polish residual state had to be so organized that it would no longer constitute a military threat to Germany, could not engage in political intrigues between Germany and Russia, and would absolutely ensure protection of Germany's economic and political interests. Count Ciano asked whether it would be a sovereign state or a protectorate controlled by Germany.

The Führer replied that he could not yet say anything final on that point. In principle, he wished to burden Germany as little as possible with the Polish residual state. On his visits to the front he had found Poland in so run-down and rotten a condition that he wanted to have as little to do with it as possible. He believed that the Western nations, if they could see it with their own eyes, would not fight another day for this totally bankrupt country. It would take from 50 to 100 years to colonize the areas that were to be annexed to Germany. Finally, Germany was pursuing the additional objective of a thorough cleanup of the nationality problem in the course of which the various ethnic elements scattered over the entire territory would be consolidated into larger nationality groups. In this connection, a climatically and topographically suited area was to be set aside for the resettlement of the Southern Tyrolese. Similarly, he planned to settle German minority groups from Hungary and the entire East in this new territory, in order to put an end, for all time, to any friction that might arise from the existence of German minorities.

Count Ciano asked how large the Polish residual state was likely to be. The Führer replied that this was difficult to say at the moment, because much depended on the ethnographic reorganization and because there were still many national minorities on Polish territory which had preserved their identity in the face of all oppression. Thus there was still a German minority of 570,000 in the country around Lodz.

Count Ciano thereupon asked what the probable population of the Polish rump state would be the Führer gave an estimate of a minimum of 8 to 10 millions. He remarked in conclusion that the ideas which he had just expressed could, of course, be carried out only after peace was restored. Count Ciano asked whether the Führer would mention these ideas in his speech before the Reichstag as the conditions for peace. The Führer replied that as a matter of fact he did intend to state them before the Reichstag with all appropriate caution. He had told them to Count Ciano at this time so that the Duce could be informed in advance, but for the rest would ask that they be treated in strict confidence. Apart from this, the Führer continued, there were also other important European problems which had emerged in connection with the present conflict and which could not be settled unilaterally, but only in a generally calm atmosphere by means of a conference or by general agreements.

In his Reichstag speech in the coming week he would emphasize Germany's readiness for such solutions but did not believe that this would make a deep impression on the enemy. He was doing it only in order to place the enemy in the wrong. If the enemy obstinately rejected any thought of a peaceful settlement, he (the Führer) was determined to settle the score with him in another way. He would then conduct the war in an entirely different manner from that imagined by the British and French. He believed, moreover, that the Duce could accomplish an important mission by rallying the neutral world, which was suffering great hardship by reason of the present state of war, and desired peace. If the Duce assumed the leadership of the neutral world, its influence would thereby be greatly increased. Apart from this, however, it was necessary to realize that not only the future of Germany, but also that of Italy, would be at stake in a final showdown between Germany, on the one hand, and England and France, on the other. The Führer expressed his unshakable conviction that in this showdown Germany would emerge triumphant, since the military situation today was quite different from that of 25 years ago. A defeat of Germany, however, would at the same time mean the end of Italy's great aspirations in the Mediterranean.

The German Foreign Minister referred in this connection to the Moscow agreements and their economic advantages for Germany. He said that he wondered whether, in these circumstances, it was not perhaps better, on the whole, if the showdown with the Western Powers took place now, since it was bound to happen sometime in any event. The Führer elaborated this by saying that many people in Germany were of the opinion that it would be best coldly to settle accounts with the British and French right now, and added that if Italy were at Germany's side now as a military ally he would not doubt for a second that the present moment was the most favorable for the showdown with the Western Powers: for he was convinced that if Germany and Italy went into the battle together, England and France would be so completely crushed that many of the still unsettled problems would be solved once and for all.

The Führer in this connection came to speak of the dangers of the air war, stating that the best protection from enemy air attacks lay not so much in the anti-aircraft guns, which could not, of course, be very effective at night, as in the enemy's fear of reprisals. Count Ciano asked whether the Führer would confine himself to a cautious expression in his Reichstag speech of the ideas he had just presented or whether he would in addition undertake an initiative for peace, or have others, Italy, for instance, do so. The Führer replied that he would confine himself to his Reichstag speech and await what Mussolini had to say after the speech, in the light of the reaction to it in other countries.

Count Ciano, referring to the Führer's suggestion that the Duce could accomplish a great mission if he put himself at the head of the neutral world, replied that Italy had not hitherto undertaken anything of the kind. Nor had she taken any outright neutral position, having merely declared that she would not take any military initiative in the West. This had been done at a time when Germany wanted to go to war in the East and the Führer had announced his intention of localizing the conflict. Had Italy resorted to armed intervention at once, she would have thwarted this intention because the conflict would then immediately have become generalized. Italy had never made a neutrality declaration and had no intention of doing so. She was, however, convinced that it would be advantageous to rally those countries that were the chief targets of British and French propaganda. Because of the close tie between Germany and Italy, these countries would thereby be drawn away from England and France and automatically brought closer to the Axis. Italy was of the opinion, moreover, that her present attitude was more advantageous to Germany than direct military intervention would have been. If she had taken such a step, Italy would have exposed herself to direct attacks from the air and the sea by the French and British, especially in the colonies.

The Führer replied that, in his opinion, England would not have signed her final treaty with Poland if she had not previously learned what Italy's attitude would be. However, this had not in any way altered the military situation in Poland and besides it must be admitted that Italy's attitude had in point of fact worked out favorably. Count Ciano denied that England had had previous information on Italy's attitude, but did not go into the matter further; he merely pointed once more to the advantages that had resulted for Germany from Italy's attitude. At the close of the first phase of the conflict, the score was 1:0 in favor of Germany. If Italy had intervened actively, the result would not have been as favorable, for even if Italy had not been dealt a mortal blow by England and France, she would, neverthe-less, have been struck very severely. This would have entailed serious psychological disadvantages.

Count Ciano then went on to speak of the formation of the neutral bloc, and stated that Italy, if she was not to tie her own hands for all time, could not easily, for geographic and other reasons, take a neutral position. It was difficult for Italy to remain neutral to the end, and an effort was therefore being made in Italy to be prepared against all eventualities. At the Alpine border, in Africa and elsewhere in the Empire, Italy was already tying down 800,000 French troops, 300,000 in Tunisia alone. The Italian forces in Libya had been increased by 150,000 men, and Italy no longer had to fear a French attack there. Italy's weak point was the deficiency in anti-aircraft artillery, coupled with the fact that the armament industry was concentrated on the Tyrrhenian coast, in Genoa, La Spezia, and Livorno, and could therefore be reached in 30 to 40 minutes flying time by French bombers from Corsica. Italy, however, had not reconciled herself to remaining neutral if the war should go on. She had, as he had said before, worked extremely hard to build up her preparedness. Moreover, her relations with England and France could hardly be called correct. All rumors to the contrary were made up entirely of thin air. To be sure, he (Ciano) had on several occasions before the crisis talked to the French and British ambassadors on the subject of Italian mediation. Since then, however, their meetings had become considerably less frequent. Only current "administrative" matters were taken up in them. There had been no political consultation of any kind with the Western Powers. The Führer replied that it was quite clear to him personally that Italy's attitude, con-sidering the course which events had taken, had worked out to advantage. It induced the French to proceed with caution. The Duce's last speech, which had been addressed to Party representatives near Bologna, had by its veiled threats caused Paris to exercise even greater caution. Count Ciano mentioned in this connection that wide circles in France, including many generals, for example: General Colson, would greatly welcome Italy's active intervention and considered the Duce's attitude vis-à-vis France a clever move.

The Führer remarked that the German people also looked upon the whole matter as a very subtle bit of teamwork between Italy and Germany. The conversation then turned to the reception that the Italian mediation proposal had had in France. It turned out that Daladier had not expressed himself at all on the Italian proposal. Only Bonnet, foreign minister at the time, took a more positive attitude. To be sure, he too stated that the British would on no account agree to the Italian proposal for an armistice that left the German troops where they were, and that France could therefore not accede to this proposal either. Bonnet, however, did inform Home at 2 o'clock in the morning, through the Italian ambassador in Paris, that he believed that France could agree to the Italian proposal if the German troops were withdrawn, at least symbolically, by the withdrawal of a single "flag or gun."

In the further course of the conversation the Führer came back once more to the subject of Russia. Germany wanted to live in peace with Russia, as she had often done in the past for a hundred years at a time. The realization of this wish would be aided by Russia's traditional fear of too close a contact with the West and its superior culture and standard of living. Thus, in this instance again, Russia, because of her old, traditional attitude, had been willing to limit her own advance to the West. Poland, on the contrary, had persisted in striking at Germany on every possible occasion. Already in the years 1936-1937, Poland had been active in this way.

The Reich Foreign Minister pointed out in this connection that the Polish Foreign Minister, on the occasion of the occupation of the Rhineland, had counseled a preventive war against Germany and had offered Poland's participation. In the further course of the conversation, Count Ciano inquired about the situation in the Balkans and spoke of the possibility of forming a group of neutral Balkan countries. He showed concern about Romania.

The Führer replied that Romania was in no danger so long as she remained really neutral. Should she, however, compromise her neutrality, she would probably be attacked from all directions. The Führer then spoke of his endeavor always to create clear-cut relationships. It was for that reason that he had clearly defined Germany's interests to both France and England. In his conversations with the Duce also, he always had been governed by this desire for clarity and had made it plain that the Mediterranean was exclusively Italy's sphere of interest. He had similarly pursued a policy of a clear-cut demarcation of spheres of interest with respect to Russia. This was the only way to restore stability and peace. The result had been concretely demonstrated by the relationship between Germany and Italy, which had indeed been possible only because of the clear-cut separation of interests. The Duce had recognized Germany's interests in Austria and Czechoslovakia, while Germany most liberally left the Mediterranean to Italy as her exclusive domain. Germany had rejoiced over all of Italy's successes, because each one, in the last analysis, also benefited the Axis as a whole.

The Führer then stated once more that if the conflict should be continued, both air and submarine warfare would be waged by Germany in an entirely different manner. Moreover, Germany did not believe that the Maginot Line, which consisted of groups of installations with large gaps in between, was invincible. In reply to Count Ciano's question regarding America's role, the Führer replied that America could only come to the aid of the West if she had sufficient tonnage at her disposal. Submarine warfare would here play an important role. Replying to Ciano's question as to whether Japan also should be included in the neutral bloc under the leadership of the Duce, the Führer said that Japan was surely waiting for England to receive the first severe blow, when she would be able, free and without hindrance, to gain her objectives in East Asia.

The Reich Foreign Minister pointed out in this connection that Japan at the moment had a middle-of-the-road government, but that in the event of German victories the spirit of the Japanese Army would come to the fore and establish a new government which, with the backing of the Japanese Navy, would enable Japan to take advantage of the greatest opportunity of her political existence. Referring to the announcements of the British that they would wage a 3-year war, the Führer declared that he was preparing for a 5-year war. Germany had shown in Poland how she waged war in practice, and he was certain that France and England would suffer severe blows from Germany.

Count Ciano replied that the armament of Germany's enemies obviously had a rather weak basis, because Italy, through a variety of devious channels had received requests for delivery of even the most elementary articles of equipment, such as field glasses and the like. Italy had, of course, refused to make such deliveries. The Führer stated that this information was corroborated by recently discovered documents which showed how trifling were the deliveries that England and France intended to make to Poland in October. Thus Poland was to receive twelve 48mm anti-tank guns, twenty 25mm guns and six tanks. Count Ciano also mentioned a conversation he had had with François-Poncet, to whom, wishing to frighten him, he had pointed out the fatal risks incurred by France. François-Poncet had admitted that the situation was difficult at the moment with respect to materiel. Referring to America, however, he had added that in the spring France would receive enormous deliveries of airplanes from America. France was counting on several thousand planes. Besides, France

always lost in the first 6 months, to win the more resoundingly in the
succeeding 6 months. To that Count Ciano had replied that there was no
telling whether the war would last more than 6 months, and perhaps there
would be no time left at all for any winning. In reply to another question
by Ciano, the Führer declared that in his Reichstag speech he would not
only speak of Poland in the manner previously stated, but would also
present his ideas regarding the settlement of general problems at a conference. The Führer explained in reply to another question from Ciano that he
had no detailed program for this as yet. He would only speak of disarmament, general security, and removal of trade barriers. In reply to a further
question by Ciano, the Führer stated that the date for the Reichstag session
was not yet fixed, as he wanted to visit Warsaw first. After a duration of
two-and-a-half hours, the conversation ended at about 9:15 p.m. Submitted
herewith, in accordance with instructions, to Foreign Minister von
Ribbentrop.

SCHMIDT Minister

*****

Visit of the Swedish explorer, Sven Hedin, to the Führer on October 16, 1939, from 12 o'clock noon to 1:15 p.m.

[Hedin's version of this conversation, together with his account of a
controversy growing out of his subsequent press interview with a British
reporter in Stockholm, is given in Sven Hedin, *German Diary, 1935-1942*
(Dublin, 1951), pp. 40-66. Sven Hedin (1865-1952) was a Swedish writer
and explorer who became an expert on Central Asia where he led many
expeditions. As an international personality he came in contact with the
Nazi leadership and met with Hitler several times. The Nazi leadership and
Goebbels in particular befriended Hedin and sought to use his prestigious
reputation for propaganda purposes. Although sympathetic toward
nationalism he was not a Nazi and later successfully interceded in favor of
Jews and other Nazi victims.]

Sven Hedin had stated in advance that although he had spoken with the
king of Sweden he was coming not on an official mission, but rather as an
old acquaintance. The conversation began by Sven Hedin's remarking to
the Führer on the tremendous burden the Führer was carrying. The Führer
replied that he was happy to be allowed to carry it. He was a man who

loved responsibility and who was glad that the solution of this great problem had been allotted to him. Sven Hedin said that he was afraid for Sweden. He thought that Sweden would soon have to help Finland, and he feared that Sweden would thereby place herself in opposition to Germany.

The Führer did not think that Finland would become involved in a war with Russia; the Russian demands would not go very far. If it should come to a conflict nevertheless, he did not believe that Sweden could help Finland. At Sven Hedin's question as to whether the Führer could not help Sweden, he said he would not attack her from the rear. The Führer added some comments here on his relationship to the Scandinavian countries, observing that in the long years of Germany's struggle for equality, he had not received the slightest help from the Scandinavian countries. The Baltic States had been created by the sacrifice of German lives, and Finland also had been rescued from bolshevism by von der Goltz. Nine hundred thousand Germans had fallen on the Eastern Front and their blood had helped to bring these countries into being. To be sure, he had not expected these countries to fight for Germany now, but they could at least have taken a stand in the League of Nations in favor of Germany, for this would never have hurt them. But they had always fundamentally opposed Germany.

The press in these countries had in the most shameless manner published distorted, mendacious, and inflammatory versions of conditions in Germany, so that one day he had made up his mind to revise the principles of Germany's foreign policy. The Führer went on to say that he was through with getting politically involved in matters that were no concern of Germany's. He no longer claimed any interests in the Mediterranean, and in Albania and Greece he had registered no interest. He had effected a delimitation of spheres of interest. In the German sphere of interest he would certainly fight and defend himself to the last. Where an aircraft carrier had been established against Germany i. e., Czechoslovakia, Poland he had destroyed it. He had written off the West; there was no problem there. Any advance there would only impair the nationality balance in Germany. He had written off the South and likewise the North, where he had experienced only ingratitude and antipathy, although he had never done them any harm. He could say that these countries had acted abominably in public statements and in their press. And to the Danes he had ceded the previously hard-won territories. Friendship was worth more to him than a few square kilometers. In the East, too, there was now a clear-cut division of interests.

He had freed Germany from bolshevism, and Germany was now invulnerable against bolshevism. The countries that, ... the whole .... [one page missing from the German text] had already lost the World War. Hedin said he thought the British Empire was finished. He described the situation in Asia where the proud British Empire was in retreat before the Japanese. He mentioned British capital there amounting to 300 million pounds, and referred to Hong Kong and England's inability to send her Home Fleet there. The Führer said that England was ruled by lunatics who thought that England was an island, which she no longer was.

England was in for some big surprises, Hedin asked: "What are you going to do?" The Führer said that anyone considering the situation had to say that this was the most preposterous affair in world history. He had repeatedly offered peace and friendship to that nation and received only slaps in return. The preservation of the British Empire was also to Germany's advantage; for, if England lost India, we had nothing to gain by it. Now he was convinced, however, that this war had to be fought to a finish. He could describe Chamberlain as nothing else than mad. Naturally, he would restore the Polish state, for he did not want that riff-raff, the Poles, within his own borders, but never again would Poland become a threat to Germany. He had no demands to make of the West aside from the colonies which were of no value to England herself.

He now compared at some length the relative strength of Germany and England, and concluded that Germany had enormous superiority. And in such circumstances England believed that Germany should beg for forgiveness!! Hedin wondered what the French really were fighting for. They were England's slaves and faced ruin. The Führer: "France will sacrifice her national strength." There were many Frenchmen who thought the same but they were not allowed to speak out. Hedin: If he succeeded in preventing the war, future generations would venerate Eastern Europe were at our disposal. Thanks to the abundant harvests of recent years, Germany had a 2 years' supply of grain on hand. Hedin said that it was senseless to blockade Germany, the Führer agreed. The others were much more vulnerable than we. He was glad to take on this fight and he grew envious at the thought that this fight otherwise would have to be carried on by someone else after him. Hedin inquired whether there was really no possibility of peace now.

The Führer replied: "So far as it is up to us, at any moment, but England does not want it. England must learn that she has to keep out of the German spheres of interest. She wasn't even decent enough to help the

Poles." Indeed, England had made long-distance flights through France for propaganda reasons, but the planes had carried gasoline instead of bombs. Our planes, however, were flying all the way to the Shetland Islands with heavy bomb loads and even then would engage in combat for hours. Hedin asked whether everything would be over quickly.

The Führer replied that he did not know. His first war plan was for 5 years, but he could go on fighting even 8 and 10 years. In a final show-down, we would triumph and England would be a field of ruins. The British were stupid enough to believe that they were safe from the German submarines, but they were thinking of submarines used in the World War, which had long since been improved upon. There were no weapons against our present submarines. If England wanted peace, she could have it. She was playing a role in Europe that no longer convinced anyone. In the Far East, the British were whining already. He could not say this publicly, but the only man in England that he would care to call a genius was Lloyd George. Eden was a foppish nonentity. Of all the British to whom he had spoken to date, Lloyd George had made the greatest impression upon him.

The Führer then gave a detailed account of the capture of Warsaw. Hedin asked whether he could not give him a message to the king of Sweden. The Führer asked Hedin to thank the king for his good intentions, adding that it was not really up to him, France and England did not want peace. In the North we had no other desire than to live in friendship with the countries there. England was to blame for everything that was happening there today. There was only one chance for England, and that was to recognize Germany's interests. These were very limited. In the East Russia was powerful; an advance to the Urals was ruled out. Collaboration between Germany and England would be a tremendous factor in behalf of the peace and would constitute the most potent element in the world. England was the greatest sea power, Germany the greatest land power. But England did not realize that Germany was the greatest land power. Perhaps she thought that France was. Poland's collapse had not come as a gift from Heaven. It had been accomplished by inspired generalship in the Prussian military tradition, equipment engineered superbly to the last technical detail, and painstaking, unremitting training.

Germany was the soundest power in the world, and no hothouse plant. Our military preparations had been cautious and pedantic, if anything, and the training of the soldier, thorough and careful. A battle might be won once in a while by accident, but a triumphal march, such as that of the Polish campaign, was no accident, but the fruit of enormously painstaking preparations. Sven Hedin said he had always, even in 1919, believed in a new dawn for Germany but the Führer's accomplishments were phenomenal indeed. And yet he was sometimes afraid of the peril that might threaten Germany from the United States or if Russia should betray Germany. The Führer said that he had pondered all possibilities. If the war had to come some time, it was best that it should have come now. Our lead in armaments was enormous, and we were far out in front in the field of inventions as well.

He spoke of the rebirth of the German Army out of the 100,000-man army. Hedin ought to take a look at the new aircraft factories. Against them those in England were a joke. He described the amateurish measures of the British, such as the evacuation of the children, etc.; he compared the air forces and pointed out that the German antiaircraft defenses were the best in the whole world. On taking leave, Hedin asked once more what Germany had to say to Sweden if she should get into difficulties over Finland: "Will Germany give Sweden her blessing in that fight?" The Führer replied: "We shall not attack Sweden from the rear." Hedin asked what could be done for the cause of peace, and the Führer replied that that was not up to us. Germany had not declared war! If the British changed he had no objection, but he had to insist on one condition: Czechoslovakia was not to be discussed. The settlement of Poland had to be left to him, but he was prepared to negotiate all other problems. The conversation was very cordial and amicable throughout.

HEWEL

Part II

1940

Memorandum by the Führer

Directive for the conversations with Mr. Sumner Welles

[A translation of the text of Hitler's directions for the conversations with Mr. Welles, dated February 29, 1940, is printed in Department of State, Documents on German Foreign Policy, 1918-1945, series D, vol. VIII, p. 817.]

February 29, 1940.

1. In general I request that on the German side reserve be exercised in the conversations, and that as far as possible Mr. Sumner Welles be allowed to do the talking.
2. In regard to Germany's relations with the United States, it may be stressed that the present situation is unsatisfactory to both nations.

The government of the Reich has done nothing for its part to bring about this development in the relations between the two countries; if by sending Mr. Sumner Welles to Berlin the American government is seeking to bring about a change in this regard, that would doubtless be in the interest of both peoples. 3. Germany's viewpoint with regard to the international situation and the war has been made known to the world through my speeches, In particular, the following points are to be stressed: Germany did not declare war on the Western Powers, but, on the contrary, they declared war on Germany, England and France had no justifiable reason at all for a wax against Germany. Just as on the basis of the Monroe Doctrine the United States would firmly reject any interference by European governments in Mexican affairs, for example, Germany regards the Eastern European area as her sphere of interest, concerning which she must come to an understanding with Russia alone, but never with England and France. After the end of the Polish campaign, Germany came to terms with Russia on Eastern questions and thus conclusively safeguarded her European position by this revision in the East which had become unavoidable. Then at the beginning of October, I again made one last offer of peace to England and France. Thereupon both these countries committed the biggest blunder they could possibly have made : they considered this offer a sign of weakness and rejected it with scorn. Germany drew the only possible conclusion from this: she accepted the challenge of England and France. Since then the war aim of England and France has been revealed more and more clearly. It consists, as is now openly stated, in the destruction of the German state and the dismemberment of the German people under a Versailles system even worse than before. Considering this development, Germany, as a state under attack, has nothing to say on the subject of peace. She is unshakable in her determination once and for all to break the will to annihilate [Germany] which now dominates British and French policy and to utilize the power of her 80 million people to this end. Not until the Anglo-French will to annihilate [Germany] has been broken can a new, really peaceful Europe be built. While in their unprecedented delusion England and France are more and more openly proclaiming as their war aim the annihilation of Germany and a new division of Europe into nations with rights and others without rights, even today Germany does not demand the annihilation of the British Empire and France; rather she regards the satisfaction of the vital interests of the great nations in their natural Lebensraum as a guarantee for the consolidation of Europe, in which there is room for small states which have proved their viability in the course of history as well as for the large ones. Germany is convinced that this goal can be attained only by a German victory

**Special mission to Europe of Sumner Welles,
Undersecretary of State.
Exchanges of views regarding the possibility of peace
and on postwar problems**.

[Sumner Welles (1892-1961) was Undersecretary of State and a major advisor to Franklin D. Roosevelt on diplomatic affairs. This exploratory mission to examine a possible peace in Europe early in the war was not expected to succeed. Welles resigned in 1943. See also: J. Simon Rofe, *Franklin Roosevelt's Foreign Policy and the Welles Mission* (New York: Palgrave Macmillan, 2007); Robert Dallek, *Franklin D. Roosevelt and American Foreign Policy 1932-1945* (New York: Oxford, 1979); Irwin F. Gellman, *Secret Affairs* (New York: Enigma Books, 2002).]

[Foreign Relations of the United States 1940, Vol. I]

Berlin, March 2, 1940

At eleven o'clock several Foreign Office officials, headed by Herr von Doernberg, came for me at my hotel to take me to my interview with Hitler at the new Chancery, which had been completed last year within a period of eight months. Workmen had worked there night and day in order to have it ready for the Chancellor's New Year's Day reception for the Diplomatic Corps so that they might have a taste of what the new Berlin was going to look like.

Kirk accompanied me at my request. He had never before been permitted to see the Führer except at a distance.

The façade of the new building on the Wilhelmstrasse reminds me of a factory building. My car drove into a rectangular court with very high blank walls. At one end was a flight of broad steps leading into the Chancery. Monumental black nudes flanked the portico to which the steps led. The whole impression of the court was reminiscent of nothing other than a prison courtyard. A company of soldiers was drawn up on each side to give me the Nazi salute as I entered.

At the head of steps I was greeted by Reichminister Meissner, the head of Hitler's Chancery. He spoke to me most cordially in English, as did all the other officials present.

We then formed a procession of some twenty couples headed by Meissner and myself, and with very slow and measured tread first traversed a tremendously long marble hall, of which the walls and floor are both of marble; then up a flight of excessively slippery red marble steps into a gallery which, also of red marble, has windows on one side and tapestries on the other. The gallery is lined on the tapestry side by an interminable series of sofas, each with a table and four chairs in front of them. From the gallery open off a series of drawing rooms. Finally, we deployed into one of these, and I was requested to sit down until the Chancellor was ready to receive me.

In a very few minutes Meissner came to announce that Hitler was ready to see me, and I went with Kirk into the adjoining room, a very long drawing-room furnished with comfortably upholstered sofas and chairs, and overlooking the garden of Bismarck's old residence, in which Hitler now lives.

Hitler received me near the door. He greeted me very pleasantly, but with great formality. Ribbentrop and Meissner [Schmidt, the interpreter] were the only two German officials present at the interview.

Hitler is taller than I had judged from his photographs. He has, in real life, none of the somewhat effeminate appearance of which he has been accused. He looked in excellent physical condition and in good training. His color is good, and while his eyes were tired, they were clear. He was dignified both in speech and in movement, and there was not the slightest impression of the comic effect from the moustache and hair which one sees in his caricatures. His voice in conversation is low and modulated. It had only once, during our hour and a half's conversation, the raucous stridency which is heard in his speeches and it was only at that moment that his features lost their composure and that his eyes lost their decidedly "gemutlich" look.

After we were seated, and Hitler placed me next to him, he looked at me to indicate I was to commence the conversation. I set forth the detailed purposes of my mission as I had already explained them to Ribbentrop. I made particular reference to the confidential nature of my interviews, and to the fact that I had no proposals to offer. In as eloquent terms as I could command, I then emphasized the President's hope that there might still be a way open for a stable, just and lasting peace, not a truce or a precarious breathing spell. I pointed out that if a war of annihilation now broke out, whether it was short or whether it was long, it would definitely preclude for the present the negotiation of a reasonable and just peace because of the human suffering it would create and of the human passions it would arouse, as well as because of the exhaustion of the economic and financial resources which still existed in Europe. From such a war as that, I said, who would be the victors? It seemed clear that all would be the losers. And in that sense not only would the belligerents be the losers, but also the neutrals, of which the United States was the greatest and the most powerful. We as a people now realized fully that such a war must inevitably have the gravest repercussions upon almost every aspect of our national structure.

The President of the United States had, in communications addressed to Chancellor Hitler himself, made it clear that if a just political peace could be found—and in the negotiation of such a peace we could not be directly involved—the United States would play its full part in cooperating towards two fundamental needs of a sane and ordered world-limitation and reduction of armaments and the establishment of a sound international trade relationship. If such bases could still be found, was it not worth every effort to seek the way of peace before the war of devastation commenced, and before the doors to peace were closed? I spoke, I said, only of a just peace, a peace which promised stability and security for the future. Personally, I said, I could not conceive of a lasting and real peace unless it envisaged as an essential component part a united, prosperous and con-tented German people, a German people satisfied with their own domain and their own security; but at the same time I could conceive of no lasting or real peace unless as an equally important factor Germany no longer was regarded by her neighbors as a threat to their independence or to their security, and unless Germany made it evident that she was, in fact, not striving for constantly increasing objectives—and objectives which im-plied aggression and a threat to the rights of free peoples.

The Chancellor knew, I said, that I had had the privilege of speaking with the Duce in Rome. That conversation, the Chancellor would appreciate, I must retain in complete confidence, but I felt at liberty to say that I had happily gained the impression from that conversation that the Duce believed the foundations of a just and lasting peace might still be laid. I hoped the Chancellor would find it possible to confirm that impression. I would be most grateful for any views he felt able to express.

The Chancellor then very quietly and moderately outlined his foreign policy during the past seven years. The outline pursued exactly the lines followed in my conversation of the day before by the Minister for Foreign Affairs. (It is noteworthy that in every conversation I had with every member of the German government, except Dr. Schacht, exactly the same historical survey prefaced the conversation. It is entirely clear that either the Chancellor or the Foreign Secretary had dictated the course which the conversations to be had with me by the members of the German government were to follow.)

Hitler, however, emphasized even more strongly than had Herr von Ribbentrop his desire to reach an amicable and lasting understanding with England. He stressed particularly the naval agreement of 1935 as an indication that Germany, under his government, had no intention of challenging British naval supremacy nor the security of the British Empire. When he came to the account of the negotiations with Poland which had resulted in the invasion of Poland by Germany in September, he turned to me and said, "I have never in my life made a more earnest nor a more sincere appeal than I did to the British ambassador, Sir Nevile Henderson, when I sent for him just prior to the break with Poland. He was sitting in the same place where you are now sitting, and I besought him to tell his government that Germany had no intention of attacking England nor of impairing directly or indirectly British interests, but that Germany could not permit a continued domination by the Western European powers of the smaller States of Eastern Europe, nor the continuation of a state of affairs which resulted in a continuous attack and a continuous threat upon German vital interests."

The Chancellor then concluded by saying, "That appeal, like every other approach made to England in seven years, was rejected with derision."

Hitler then said that I had referred to the problem of limitation and reduction of armaments. Time and again, he said, he had offered England and the other powers of the world the opportunity for a real and practicable reduction of armaments. He had guaranteed that Germany would maintain her standing army at 200,000 men; then at 300,000 men; he had expressed German willingness to outlaw certain types of munitions and implements of war. Never once, however, had these offers on his part received the slightest attention or, much less, consideration, as a basis of agreement. The Chancellor then said, "The present armament burden is crushing the life out of all peoples; it cannot continue much longer. The national economy of every nation will crash before much further time elapses."

He stated that he believed these were two practicable methods of securing a real disarmament. The first was for the great powers of Europe to agree upon their minimum ratios of military and of naval strength, outlawing all but a minimum of offensive armaments, and upon that basis further to agree that in the event of any threat to their security, or to the peace of Europe, these powers would pool their military and naval resources as a police power. He had formally made this proposal to Great Britain and to France. He had never received the slightest response.

The other alternative was for the powers to agree upon a progressive and gradual reduction in their respective military strength; with the gradual elimination at the same time of certain categories of offensive armament. This he believed would take a very long time, and was the less satisfactory of the two methods.

I had also mentioned the problem of a liberal, most-favored-nation international trade relationship as an objective towards which the nations of the world should strive. He felt quite in accord with me, he said, that that was a desirable goal and Germany, under more normal conditions, would gladly cooperate towards that end. He did not, however, believe that unrestricted international trade was the cure for all of the world's economic problems. He said, for example, that while Germany would doubtless profit by taking a considerable portion of America's agricultural surpluses, an industrial country like Germany could not take any considerable portion of industrial products from the United States, nor could the United States take any considerable portion of Germany's industrial exports. It was, consequently, necessary for Germany to intensify her trade relations with countries in Central and Southeastern Europe who desired to take Germany's industrial exports, which they themselves did not produce, in return for raw materials desired by Germany. At this point I interjected to say that the Chancellor appeared to overlook the fact that while the United States, it was true, was a large industrial producer as well as an exporter of agricultural surpluses, nevertheless, trade between the United States and Germany over a period of many generations had been highly profitable to both sides. The Chancellor, I said, must not forget that Germany produced many forms of industrial products which were produced either more cheaply or in more efficient form than similar products produced in the United States, and that such exports from Germany had always been profitably sold by Germany to the United States. The question, I said, was not one of a purely bilateral nature but involved necessarily the problem of profitable triangular trade which had always entered into the picture of Germany's trade relations with the United States. Furthermore for Germany to be able to sell profitably the bulk of her luxury manufactured products she had to find countries where the standard of living was relatively high. Surely I believed the standard of living in the countries of Southeastern Europe was not sufficiently high to make it possible for Germany to find there any profitable market for a very large percentage of her industrial production.

Hitler did not seem to comprehend this problem, and dropped the topic after remarking that a country with a population of 140 individuals to the square kilometer must increase its production if those individuals are to find the wherewithal to survive. I said that it seemed to me that there was no country in the world that would profit more immediately and more greatly than Germany from a restoration of liberal international trade relations, and that through such a restoration the 140 individuals to the square German kilometer of whom he had spoken would obtain an increased standard of living and derive there from an immediately greater purchasing power, particularly if their work was dedicated to constructive production, rather than to the sterile manufacture of munitions. Hitler then said that Germany's aims and objectives were simple and that he would outline them to me; he would classify them as (a) historical, (b) political and (e) economic.

From the historical aspect Germany had existed as an empire five hundred years before Columbus had discovered the western world. The German people had every right to demand that their historical position of a thousand years should be restored to them; Germany had no ambition and no aim other than the return by the German people to the territorial position which was historically theirs. Germany's political aims were coordinate. Germany could not tolerate the existence of a State such as Czechoslovakia which constituted an enclave created by Versailles solely for strategic reasons, and which formed an ever-present menace to the security of the German people; nor could Germany tolerate the separation from Greater Germany of German provinces by corridors, under alien control, and again created solely for strategic reasons. No great power could exist under such conditions. Germany, however, did not desire to dominate non-German peoples, and if such peoples adjacent to German boundaries did not constitute a military or political threat to the German people, Germany had no desire permanently to destroy, nor to prejudice, the independent lives of such peoples. From the economic standpoint, Germany must claim the right to profit to the fullest extent through trade with the nations close to her in Central and Southeastern Europe. She would no longer permit that the western powers of Europe infringe or impair Germany's preferential situation in this regard.

In brief, the German people intended to maintain the unity which he had now achieved for them; they intended to prevent any State on

Germany's eastern frontier from constituting again a military or strategic threat against German security and, finally, Germany intended to obtain recognition for her economic priority in Eastern and Southeastern Europe. Germany, further, would insist that the colonies stolen from her at Versailles be returned to her. Germany had not obtained these colonies through military conquest; she had obtained them through purchase or through pacific negotiation; she had never utilized her colonies for military purposes. She now required them in order to obtain for the German people raw materials which could not be produced in Germany, and as a field for German emigration. Such a demand, Hitler felt, was not only reasonable, but just. At no time during the course of our conversation did Hitler mention the subject of German-American relations, nor did he refer directly or indirectly to German relations with Soviet Russia and with Italy.

The Chancellor then passed to the subject of the war aims of the Allies. He asked me if I had heard or read the speech made in England the night before by Sir John Simon. I told him that I had not. He said that if I had read the speech, I would gain there from the same clear understanding that he had gained, namely, that the speech constituted a clear-cut definition of English aims, that is, the total destruction of Germany.

He said, "I am fully aware that the allied powers believe that a distinction can be made between National Socialism and the German people. There was never a greater mistake. The German people today are united as one man, and I have the support of every German. I can see no hope for the establishment of any lasting peace until the will of England and France to destroy Germany is itself destroyed. I fear that there is no way by which the will to destroy Germany can be itself destroyed, except through a German victory. I believe that German might is such as to ensure the triumph of Germany but, if not, we will all go down together (and here he added the extraordinary phrase) whether that be for better or for worse." He paused a moment and then said textually, rapidly and with impatience, "I did not want this war. It has been forced upon me against my will. It is a waste of my time. My life should have been spent in constructing, and not in destroying."

I said that the Chancellor would, of course, understand that it was the belief of my government that if some way could be found towards a stable and lasting peace which promised security to all peoples, no nation could [would?] have to "go down," let alone all of them. For that reason I earnestly trusted that such a way and such a peace might still be found.

Hitler looked at me, and remained quiet for a moment or two. He then said, "I appreciate your sincerity and that of your government, and I am grateful for your mission. I can assure you that Germany's aim, whether it must come through war or otherwise, is a just peace."

I replied by saying that I would remember the phrase the Chancellor had used. The interview then terminated.

Conversation between the Führer and Sven Hedin in the presence of Minister Meissner on March 4, 1940

[Documents on German Foreign Policy]

After a lengthy conversation on his personal experiences in his travels in Asia, Sven Hedin asked the Führer the same question he had put to the Foreign Minister a few days ago, 2 namely, whether Germany could not do something to put an end to the Russo-Finnish conflict by mediation between the two belligerent parties. The Führer replied by first reading an item from the Finnish press which had just come to his attention, approximately to the effect that the Finnish war was beginning to be inconvenient to Stalin and Hitler and that they were therefore seeking to settle the conflict. The Finns, however, had no intention of spontaneously making any sacrifices but would keep on fighting.

The Führer commented that the attitude of the Finns as indicated by this newspaper item was entirely senseless, but also showed how impossible German mediation in the conflict would be. If the Finns themselves rejected mediation, as they did in the newspaper report just cited, and wished to keep on fighting, there was really not the slightest justification for Germany to step in. Furthermore, Germany had to look after her own interests in the difficult struggle for existence in which she now found herself. An understanding had been reached with Russia on the basis of a clear division of interest in the East. This had freed Germany at the rear, and she could now in contrast to the World War, where she had had to carry on a war not only on two fronts but on many fronts concentrate her entire forces in the West.

As a result of the new relationship which she had established with Russia her sympathies were naturally also on the side of that country. Sven Hedin interjected here that some consideration should be given to the Finns, too, who were fighting so bravely. The Führer admitted that the Finns were brave, but their policy had been entirely senseless. It was absolutely sure that they would not stand up against the Russians in the long run. "Up to now the bad weather had been extremely advantageous to them. They should never have entered into a conflict with the Russians, for Stalin had after all asked nothing more of them than a secure access to an ice-free sea. Stalin was undergoing a change, anyway. He was no longer the international bolshevist, but showed himself as an absolute Russian nationalist and was in the last analysis following exactly the same natural policy of Russian nationalism as the Tsars. A constant and easily under-standable element of this policy had always been the striving for an ice-free port. Otherwise, except for a shifting of the Finnish-Russian border at the Karelian Isthmus which was necessary for the safety of Leningrad and would even be compensated for by cession of other territory north of Lake Ladoga Stalin had asked nothing more of the Finns. It would have been the wisest thing for the Finns to make an agreement with the Russians on this basis. Instead of this they had slipped into a war without exactly knowing why. The only way out was to be sought not in mediation by third parties but in a direct settlement between Finland and Russia.

Sven Hedin then came to speak of the Swedish attitude toward the Finnish conflict and mentioned, as he had already done in his conversation with the Reich Foreign Minister, the current in Swedish public opinion, constantly growing in strength, which advocated granting the Finns more Swedish aid than heretofore. Officially, Sweden would naturally remain neutral, but the flow of Swedish volunteers to Finland would probably increase to an extraordinary degree in the course of time, especially when the stream of refugees from Finland became much larger. How would Germany feel about this? Would she take steps against Sweden? The Führer answered in the negative, but pointed out that in his opinion even Swedish help would have no effect on the ultimate outcome of the Finnish-Russian war. The Scandinavian countries ought above all else to beware of intervention by England. The British cared nothing about Finland per se, and when the Finns had played their part in the British plan, the British smiling coldly would drop them. One thing was sure: If England got a foothold anywhere in Scandinavia, then Germany for her part would also intervene at once, since she could not permit such a threat to her flank.

In the further course of the conversation, the Führer tried to dispel certain misgivings of Sven Hedin to the effect that the Russians might possibly advance beyond Finland to Sweden and Norway; Sven Hedin remarked that it could be disagreeable for Germany, too, if Russia gained control of the Swedish iron mines from which Germany obtained a large part of her iron ore. The Führer stated in this connection that he did not believe that Stalin had such expansionist aspirations; he again stressed Stalin's policy of Russian nationalism with its drive for an ice-free port and emphasized that once this goal had been achieved there need be no fear of further expansion. He was also not concerned about a possible advance by the Russians into the Baltic, which was being discussed so much abroad as an alleged threat to the German position there. In the age of the airplane, the Baltic was no longer an operations area for navies. Even the North Sea had lost this character for the British Navy as a result of German air supremacy in that area.

When Sven Hedin asked once more that something be done for the poor Finns by means of mediation between Finland and Russia, the Führer refused with the observation that he predicted the Finns would certainly not thank him, but at most blame him subsequently for the loss of Hango or other areas. The Finns had every reason, by the way, to be grateful to Germany, for without the active interference of the German troops in 1918 Finland would never have come into being at all. Now, however, the only solution was a direct agreement with Russia.

SCHMIDT Minister

Conversation of the Führer with Colin Ross on March 12, 1940, from 12 noon to 1 p.m.

[Colin Ross was born in Vienna of Scottish ancestry in 1885. He was a student of Karl Haushofer and earned a PhD from the University of Heidelberg. Known as world traveler and journalist as well as an outspoken Nazi and admirer of Adolf Hitler, Ross was a dedicated anti-Semite and this conversation centers on the subject regarding the United States. He committed suicide with his wife at the home of his friend, Nazi youth leader Baldur Von Schirach.]

Present : Senior Counselor Hewel.

Colin Ross opened his remarks by telling the Führer that during his recent world travels he had concerned himself mainly with three problems: 1) How can the United States of America be kept out of the war? 2) How can Japan be kept in our camp, or rather, how can the threat of her entry into the war be turned into a strong political asset for us? 3) How can we make the best ideological use of the German-Russian Pact throughout the world?

With regard to this last point he [Colin Ross] then pointed out that heretofore Germany had been looked upon as the bulwark against Bolshevism, that is to say, as defender of the bourgeois world against Bolshevism. Actually, through her pact with Russia, she had neutralized Bolshevism and paved the way to a more understanding attitude on the part of socialist movements in the world. Upon a request by the Führer, Colin Ross then reported that at the time of the Czech crisis a European war would have been extremely popular in America. There, was actual disappointment that France and England had not struck, and hundreds of thousands of Americans would have gladly gone to Europe to take part in the war. But when England and France did not do anything, a feeling of disgust with old Europe developed in America so that there is today a greater lack of interest in Europe than there was a year ago. It was in this atmosphere that he [Colin Ross] undertook his propaganda trip and was able to have success with his lectures. He reported that an imperialist tendency was prevailing today in the United States. To the Führer's question whether this imperialist tendency did not strengthen the desire for the Anschluss of Canada to the United States and thus produce an anti-English attitude, Colin Ross replied that this was not the case, since Canada's Anschluss to the United States was not an acute problem. The Americans expected that sooner or later the Anschluss would come about automatically, and even today the border between the two countries represented hardly an obstacle. The Americanization of the southern, most important, part of Canada "was advanced to such a degree that there was no question of a division as we in Europe knew it. The greatest technical difficulty in a union of Canada and the USA was raised by the Province of Quebec which had remained completely French in nationality. The Americans feel that in case of a union this could serve as a precedent for the formation of other compact communities, such as the German one. Although the American is gradually abandoning his belief that a national community can be created by education, independent of race and nationality (theory of the melting pot), nevertheless, any organization on the basis of nationality within the great American political community is still repugnant to him.

Colin Ross explained as follows the strange fact that hatred against Germany is extremely strong in America, even though, for geopolitical reasons England ought to be considered as the enemy of the United States: For a very long time, America has been governed by a kind of Anglo-Saxon aristocracy which looks upon those of different race—including the Germans as something inferior and at the same time sinister, and which knows how to always keep down those immigrants of different races. An additional factor is the monstrous power of Jewry, directing with a really fantastic cleverness and organizational skill the struggle against everything German and National Socialist. This organization, the ramifications of which extend into the remotest corners, has succeeded in defaming everything that is "fascist" to such a degree, that no one in America dares to defend it openly, although the idea of National Socialism often meets with a distinct sympathy and understanding; that is to say, in public opinion and particularly in society, National Socialism has been branded as culturally destructive, barbaric, and cruel.

The American, who essentially has very little *Zivilcourage,* obeys this unwritten law slavishly. Colin Ross cited numerous examples from among his own acquaintances, showing how people with the greatest good will toward us were taking an anti-German position in public, partly because of indolence, partly because of the fear of boycott in business or social life. Even good Germans and people with National Socialist sympathies, for instance, subscribed to the Jewish fund, because they would suffer economic and social defamation if they did not do so. Hatred tainting the fear of everything German was also based on the fact that the Americans knew the English in their good as well as in their bad aspects. They fought against them and the English have lost one position after the other; on the other hand, the Americans have done business with them and are convinced that they do not have to be afraid of England. But they don't know Germany; to them, Germany represents something strange and sinister which they therefore oppose.

Colin Ross then talked about Roosevelt whom he believes to be an enemy of the Führer for reasons of pure personal jealousy and also on account of his personal lust for power. His [Roosevelt's] principal objective is to be re-elected and he employs every possible means for this purpose. After his re-election he would undoubtedly have at his disposal so much power in his country that he then would be able to lead the American people into war, whenever he wanted. He had come to power the same year as the Führer and he had to watch the latter carrying out his great plans, while he, Roosevelt, hemmed in by a tremendous domestic resistance, had not reached his goals. He too had ideas of dictatorship which in some respects were very similar to National Socialist ideas. Yet precisely this realization, namely, that the Führer had attained his goal, while he had not, gave to his pathological ambition the desire to act upon the stage of world history as the Führer's rival.

Colin Ross then attempted to present some ideas in order to familiarize the Führer with those elements in the life of the United States which are good and strong and akin to us. The German share in the life and work of America, as well as the proportion of German blood, is very considerable and can't be disputed away. He then mentioned something about his lectures and characterized them as successful with regard to their effect. He furthermore discussed anti-Semitism which is very strong in America and which is a matter of course in certain circles, again, however, it is balanced by the American's indifference referred to previously. To exercise influence upon these matters from Germany is hardly possible. To see that as many Jewish emigrants as was possible should get to America was really the best method since opposition against undisputed Jewish domination of the sphere of culture and communications as well as of business was bound to arise sometime or other. In this connection, he spoke of the necessity of coming out with a positive solution of the Jewish question.

The moment Germany would promote a constructive solution of this question, as for instance, by assigning a large area for settlement by Jews, anti-Semitism in America would awaken from its dormant stage and the Americans who in their hearts want to get rid of the Jews would support wholeheartedly this attempt to solve the Jewish question. The Führer showed great understanding for this argument, but said the Jewish question really was a space question which was difficult to solve, particularly for him, since he himself had no space at his disposal. Neither would the establishment of a Jewish state around Lublin ever constitute a solution as even there the Jews lived too close together to be able to attain a somewhat satisfactory standard of living. "Wherever more than 70 people per one square kilometer were living together life was difficult and hemmed in, and the world crisis which we were facing today was caused by the urge of nations to pour out of over-populated spaces and into those of sparse population. Since the beginnings of history, those migrations of peoples have been accompanied by great ruthlessness and cruelty which could not be helped. He, too, would welcome a positive solution of the Jewish question, if only he could indicate a solution; this, however, was not possible under present conditions when he had not even sufficient space for his own people.

In conclusion, Colin Ross stated that after long study he had reached the following conclusion. If Germany succeeded in convincing the Americans that it was in accordance with our German and National Socialist principles that the Western Hemisphere belonged to the Americans (since in the contemporary world large spaces were being formed on the basis of geopolitics such as, for example, the Soviet Union as ruler over the western Asiatic space, the union of the Chinese and Mongols in East Asia under Japanese leadership, and the union of Central Europe under German leadership), then the Americans could develop very much understanding for our struggle since they would, after all, derive a clear profit from it. He had worked out a map on which he had marked in, from north to south, the English spheres of influence against the United States. If an American should see this map and should, moreover, hear that in Germany's view the Western Hemisphere should belong to the Americans, America automatically would take a position directed against England. It. was his great desire to be active and to work in this direction and he was waiting for an instruction by the Führer in order to continue his work in this special field of his. Colin Ross also told of the difficulties he had had in America, of the interpellation made in the House of Representatives and of the sentence passed against him by the Dies Committee at a time when he had already left America. He told the Führer that he was now forced to take up the fight against this, which was also in the interest of the many German friends over there who had suffered defamation at the hands of the same elements in America. He requested the support of the Foreign Ministry in this mutter. The Führer instructed me to tell the Foreign Minister to take steps so that Herr Colin Ross may receive every possible assistance from the Foreign Ministry. The Führer invited Herr Colin Ross to lunch for Thursday. After Herr Colin Ross had taken his leave, the Führer remarked that Colin Ross was a wry intelligent man who certainly had many good ideas.

HEWEL

Hitler-Mussolini Conference—Brenner Pass, March 18, 1940

[From S. Corvaja, *Hitler and Mussolini. The Secret Meetings*
(New York: Enigma Books, 2005).]

On Sunday, March 17, at 1:30 in the afternoon, Mussolini and Ciano, with a small group of functionaries including Anfuso, left for the Brenner Pass. Before pulling out of the station, the German ambassador, ill at ease, told Ciano that the Führer wished to have a private meeting with the Duce before the conference. This was the signal for the purge of anti-Axis elements from the Italian government, and Hitler wanted to resolve the issue alone with Mussolini. The Duce was calm during the trip; he let his imagination run as he planned the positioning of the ships, armies, and air fleets on the left wing of the Axis deployment. Ciano read the cables from various capitals which commented favorably on the Brenner meeting. Optimists related the meeting to the Sumner Welles mission, with whom Ciano had met twice just the day before. Was peace at hand? The hopeful question was on everyone's mind.

At 10:00 a.m. on March 18, Mussolini's train stopped about 300 meters from the border. Half an hour later, slightly behind schedule, Hitler's train pulled in. The weather was awful, with a strong wind and driving snow. The Duce was waiting for the Führer on the platform. After the usual long and warm handshake, the two dictators entered the Italian train. Hitler told the Duce, with all the diplomacy he was capable of, how in Berlin there was considerable anxiety regarding the unfriendly attitude displayed by Count Ciano toward Germany. He added that Ribbentrop was asking clearly for the resolution of the "Attolico case." The Wilhelm-strasse also felt deeply uneasy when it had to contact the Italian embassy. Had Ciano himself not requested the removal some time before of Ambassador Ulrich von Hassell because he was considered "an uncooperative man, hostile to the friendship between the two peoples founded on the identity of political regimes and a common policy?"

Ciano wrote in his Diary about the departure of von Hassell when he was replaced by Georg von Mackensen on February 4, 1938: "I feel not the slightest remorse in having been instrumental in replacing this individual, who served his country and the German-Italian friendship so poorly." Under the circumstances, Attolico would also have to pack his bags, said Ribbentrop, who had the gall to propose two names as candidates to the new ambassador's post to Berlin: either Roberto Farinacci or Dino Alfieri. Ciano politely reserved his answer until he had time to consult with the Duce.

With Paul Schmidt as interpreter, Hitler then began his monologue, after spreading a map on the table showing the positions of 207 German divisions already in place or about to be deployed. This was a powerful psychological weapon to use on Mussolini, who followed intently the deployment of the tremendous wall of steel and fire ready to be let loose on any new enemy of the Reich. Hitler began by justifying his attack on Poland with the "fact" that Germans living in border areas were subjected to persecution and unspeakable atrocities by the Poles.

Naturally, this attack was made possible by the satisfactory agreement reached with Russia, and, he added with a slight argument toward the Duce (who had criticized the move), that "since there was no conflict of interest between the two countries," he, Hitler, had determined that it was essential to maintain forever good relations with the Soviet Union, since "Stalin had thrown Judeo-Bolshevism overboard to re-launch Slav nationalism." In the near future, a German-Russian agreement would be possible with Italian participation to keep the peace in the Orient and the Balkans.

With respect to the "blitzkrieg" (which he, Hitler, was convinced he had invented), the Führer explained that it was a modern use of mechanized divisions together with light bombers, especially the famed Stukas, which had performed beyond all expectation. "Entire centers are blown away in a few hours. The Luftwaffe has been a surprise, not just for the enemy, but also for us. A wonderful surprise. That augurs well for the future." Hitler then analyzed the relations between Britain and France, carefully showing the moral superiority of the Third Reich when compared to the decadent democratic nations.

Then he came to the crux of the meeting. As persuasively and patronizingly as possible, he said that he had not come all the way down to the Brenner to ask for something of his Italian friend, but only to explain how things stood. If Italy was content with a secondary role in the Mediterranean, then she had no need to make any moves; but if Italy aspired to play the role of a great power, then she would always find her path blocked by France and Britain. It was up to the Duce to make the final decision, based upon the objective analysis he had undertaken. The Führer emphasized once again that Italy's and Germany's fates were now irrevocably joined. The defeat of Germany would mean the end of the Italian Empire. But he was a realist and did not wish to push the Duce to do anything that would go against the interests of the Italian people because, "contrary to what the British do, we don't expect anyone else to pull the chestnuts out of the fire." Hitler concluded that the German divisions were poised to attack in the west without saying how and when. "What will you do?" he asked the Duce.

Humbled like a poor relation, Mussolini answered that he too hated the French and the British; he agreed with the Führer that Italy would have to enter the war. The date was the big problem because the depleted condition of the Italian treasury did not allow for a long war. If the expected German offensive in the west could be delayed for three to four months, then Italy could complete some of its preparations. In this way, Italy could participate in the offensive and not just look on from the sidelines at its ally's battles.

Hitler answered that he would not alter his plans to suit Italy.

> I suggest, Duce, an attack that would be less difficult and costly than a direct assault against France over the Alps. I propose that about twenty Italian divisions line up alongside the German army near the Swiss border, facing the Rhone Valley in an attempt to outflank the Italian-French border.

Mussolini showed enthusiasm for this idea but insisted that Italy's role would be to give a coup de grace to the Allies "strong enough to break their legs." However, if the German advance were to be slow, Italy would have to wait.

Hitler, now convinced that his future offensive depended on speed, didn't even consider the possibility of a slower advance, and he formally accepted Mussolini's declaration to come into the war in due course. Having reached this agreement in principle, the dictators had a quick lunch and then parted company with the promise of meeting again soon to celebrate the inevitable victory.

At 1:10 p.m., Mussolini's train journeyed back to Rome. Ciano noted that Mussolini had found Hitler to be as adamant as Ribbentrop had led them to believe. The Duce thought Hitler would hesitate longer before ordering the offensive, and he advised the Führer to make more use of his air force and navy. The meeting had not changed any of Italy's plans. Mussolini reported by cable to the king the next day:

> Yesterday's conversation was very important, more than I had antici-pated. Hitler impressed me as being in good spirits and excellent physical condition and, in spite of some minor hesitations, certain of victory. I do not think there will be an immediate ground offensive. As soon as more news arrives from Berlin, I'll send you a report. I wish to offer to Your Majesty my devoted respects.

The press reports from the meeting said very little: "The Duce and the Führer have held, at the Brenner Pass, in the Duce's railroad car, a two-and-one-half-hour meeting with the participation of Count Ciano and von Ribbentrop." The entire German press expressed satisfaction at the friendly atmosphere of the discussions. The *Deutsche Allegemeine Zeitung* commented on the coincidence of the submarine attack at Scapa Flow and the Brenner meeting:

> Our soldiers are taking the war where England does not expect it. Our foreign policy prevents war where England would want it to be. In Berlin, we note that both Germany and Italy are in agreement in preventing the extension of the war to the Middle East and the Balkans. Rumors reported yesterday relating to the possible Russian and German guarantee, joined also by Italy, for peace in those regions continue to be discussed in many circles and are thought by many to be related to the Brenner meeting. It is possible that Hitler and Mussolini have discussed this issue at length.

The Italian embassy in Berlin had a much less enthusiastic assessment:

> Tuesday, March 19, the Führer returned from the Brenner Pass but did not want anyone from the embassy staff to be present at his arrival. An obvious condemnation of Attolico's policies. Everyone thinks we are on the threshold of peace; they all praise Mussolini and fail to recognize that, because of Italy, the war is about to become even more intense. Even the few people who know the situation but who are not blinded by the ideas of Ribbentrop and Hitler, think that the Duce, by changing his attitude so radically, may be trying some mysterious move. These same people are absolutely convinced that Italy has no intention of going to war anytime soon. Our military officers show signs of alarm. They had thought we were exaggerating when we told them our fears after Ribbentrop's visit to Rome. Now these same people have seen some evidence and are becoming very uneasy. They show us on paper why it is impossible for Italy to go to war. The Germans know this. They don't believe in our entry into the war and don't even want it. Other indications show that Ribbentrop's March 10 visit to Rome was meant to secure Italy's neutrality just before the Reich's next offensive.

Ciano knew all the secrets of the Brenner meeting, and everyone wanted him to reveal what had really happened. The next day, March 19, he met quietly with Sumner Welles at the Acquasanta Golf Club outside Rome to tell him there were no new developments: "An internal Axis event that leaves everything unchanged."

The U.S. undersecretary was pleased to note, as Ciano relates:

> There is no immediate threat of a military clash. Roosevelt will thus have the time to ponder Welles's conclusions and possibly make some move for

peace. Welles also spoke of a possible meeting between Mussolini and Roosevelt at the Azores: a complicated project with uncertain results.

Ciano was less reticent than usual with the American diplomat in order to position himself, in the eyes of the Western powers, as someone in the know, someone who could play an important role. In fact, hoping to create a back channel to Roosevelt, he told Welles:

> Please give the president the following message. Tell him that I have the greatest personal admiration for him and the utmost faith in what he can accomplish for civilization in Europe. Tell him that as long as I remain Italian foreign minister, Italy will not enter this war at Germany's side and that I will do all I can to influence Mussolini in this direction. Tell him that I wish above all to have the opportunity for Italy to cooperate with the United States to reestablish the peace the President is hoping for.

But when the fateful moment arrived, Ciano did not keep his promise and resigned from the post of foreign minister. Neither he nor Mussolini had understood the long-term strategy of President Roosevelt, who had already decided to enter the war on the side of the Allies with a series of small steps to provoke a German reaction.

Memorandum by an official of the Foreign Minister's Secretariat at Montoire-sur-Le-Loir, October 22, 1940

Conversation between the Führer and the vice-president of the French Council of Ministers, Pierre Laval, in the presence of the Reich foreign minister, at the railway station of Montoire-sur-Le Loir in the work coach of the Führer, on October 22, 1940

[Pierre Laval (1883-1945), French politician and prime minister in the 1930s, was instrumental in the creation of the Vichy regime after the fall of France in 1940. As Vice Prime Minister in Marshal Pétain's government he became the main supporter of French collaboration with Nazi Germany. He was tried and executed for treason in 1945. See Robert O. Paxton, *Vichy France* (New York: A. Knopf, 1972); Adm. William Leahy, *I Was There* (New York: McGraw Hill, 1950); William Langer, *Our Vichy Gamble* (New York: Knopf, 1947).]

M. Laval first thanked the Führer for the opportunity of having this conference. He had thought at first that he would speak only with the Foreign Minister and had learned only a little while before that the Führer would receive him. He intended to speak to the Führer with absolute frankness and to stress the hope which he placed in German-French cooperation. He regretted that he had not visited the Führer several years ago, for the sad events which had befallen France could perhaps then have been avoided. He had stated before the National Assembly that France's declaration of war on Germany was the greatest crime that had ever been committed in the course of French history. Even before the war had been an advocate of German-French cooperation and of a methodical organization of Europe and could therefore pursue the same political policy again now without any restraint. His only regret was that he had to do so at a moment when France was so severely prostrated. He was of the opinion that the policy of France must be based on cooperation with the Reich. Germany had won the victory. If she so desired, she could misuse it, for France was not capable of the slightest reaction and would have to bear any hardships. He, Laval, doubted, however, whether in such a case (i.e., if she misused her victory) Germany would be able to assure for herself all the moral and material advantages that she rightly expected from her incomparable victory.

He was not neglecting any opportunity, moreover, to point out repeatedly to Marshal Pétain, who shared his views, that sincere and unreserved cooperation with Germany was France's only salvation.

The Führer replied that he had considered it advisable to hold the conference with M. Laval at a time when other important international conferences of decisive moment were held or about to be held. It was obvious that this first conference could not go into any great detail on German-French relations, which after all could not be treated exhaustively in a couple of hours, but would rather have to seek a clarification of fundamentals. This was necessary, not only because a basic clarification was the prerequisite for the treatment of details, but because it was important for the further steps which he (the Führer) was about to undertake.

One point had to be emphasized: The war between France and Germany was really, as far as its beginning was concerned, a totally unjustifiable crime. As late as September 2, 1939, he had tried to prevent this war, for which he could not see any reason. Germany had not made any demands either on England or on France that justified any action so monstrous as a declaration of war. Nevertheless war tad been declared and

Germany had waged it in her manner. If it were now concluded, it would now be possible to consider a definitive settlement of the problems to be solved. Against the wish of the Führer, however, the war was still going on. When it would end was perhaps not entirely certain, but its military outcome was absolutely beyond doubt. He (the Führer) said this even at the risk of being called an optimistic prophet, pointing out in that connection that much of what he had prophesied had come true.

The bad weather which was favoring England might indeed delay the final settlement, pat could in no wise change its outcome, just as the bad weather during the past winter had merely delayed settlements which the Führer wished to bring about as early as last fall, without affecting their consummation in the slightest. It was clear that the Führer intended to end the war as quickly as possible, for he is not waging the war for the sake of war but only in order that he may resume his peaceful work as soon as possible, since each additional week cost, further sacrifices of a material nature.

It should ho obvious to Laval that someone had to take the responsibility for the costs of the war and bear their consequences. Each additional month increased the totally unproductive expenditures of the war. It could not be expected, however, that these war costs would in be charged to a country which had not wanted the war and had neither started it nor lost it.

The Führer then called attention to certain currents in France which were nourished by the hope that if the war should last for some time there would be a change in the military situation that would benefit France. The future would show that these hopes were completely unfounded and that the expectation based on them was absolutely false.

Militarily the war would be decided either by a series of lightning blows by Germany or by the gradual destruction of the will and the ability of the British to resist. The Führer expressed his firm conviction that the time would come when Germany would enforce peace in one way or another. He had no doubt that there would then be a revision in the calculation of those circles in France which imagined that in 4, 6, or 8 months the situation of their country might be improved, or which perhaps assumed that from a certain moment on England would not in any circumstances conclude peace with Germany at the expense of others.

For Germany the question of who was finally to bear the costs of the war was decisive. The blood that had been sacrificed could not be compensated for, since the dead would not arise again and the cripples would not be healed. For the material sacrifices, however, she had to demand compensation. Germany's goal in the matter of material compensation was determined by military and purely material factors. From the military point of view France was the first country conquered and consequently an enemy to be held primarily liable. From the material point of view it was a matter of helping to cover the essential needs of the German people in the same way. Germany was not seeking a peace inspired by arrogance or vengeance, but was acting under the hard compulsion of necessity. It was also conceivable that the destruction of England would offer him other opportunities as well.

Basically he (the Führer) personally approached this question without passion, for he had tried for many years, unfortunately without success, to bring about cooperation between Germany and France. In the future, too, he would choose this way of cooperation between the two countries, provided that the necessary conditions for it were present.

Laval replied that he had already emphasized in the statements he had made in the beginning that in his opinion France's declaration of war on Germany was a crime committed against France. The war had also been far from popular in France; the French had not known why they should fight. He saw proof of the correctness of this view inter alia in the figure of 2,000,000 prisoners of war. A country which was capable of fighting and had also shown in the course of its history how it could fight gave proof by this number of prisoners that its people did not want the war. He (Laval) understood perfectly well that the time had not yet come for speaking about the details of a joint German-French policy. He therefore understood the Führer's wish that today's conversation be limited to fundamentals. He willingly conceded, to continue along the line of the Führer's thought, that the war had been totally unjustified and that the former French governments had made a mistake in not seizing every possible opportunity for a rapprochement with Germany. He also realized that there could be no final settlement between Germany and France as long as the war was still going on.

About the outcome of this struggle he did not have the slightest doubt: England would be defeated, and as a Frenchman he could only add that he desired the defeat of the British with all his heart. England had done everything to plunge France into the war and had then done nothing to support her in this struggle. Since the conclusion of the armistice she had proceeded against France in such a way that this desire for her defeat by Germany had become stronger and more sincere than ever. He (Laval) also realized that someone had to bear the costs of this struggle, that they increased from month to month, and that consequently it was desirable in the interest of all to bring about as early an end of the conflict as possible. He also readily understood that Germany, which had neither desired the war nor lost it, could not bear the costs. He hoped, however, that in the discussion of the details of this German-French cooperation he would have an opportunity to defend the interest of his country. The Führer had referred to certain currents in France which were quietly hoping that a prolongation of the war would bring about an improvement in the situation of France. He could only say that to him such thoughts seemed very foolish. Besides, he would like to point out that it would be unjust and wrong to assume that all the French were of this opinion.

The Popular Front people, who could not reconcile themselves to the new regime in France, the Jews, and many rich people who hoped that the pleasant life of prewar days would sooner or later be resumed, probably held this view. But even among the representatives of this trend there were many of perfectly good will who suffered only because of the occupation of their fatherland and saw no glimmer of hope for the future in any other direction. He could state with at certainty, however, that if this conference and the further conventions that would perhaps follow should show that the idea of German French cooperation was possible and if France should be offered honorable peace or such a peace could be accepted by Germany this Anglophile tendency in France would disappear. He knew his o country very well and could therefore state that certain, incidental very discreet, manifestations of the same tendency were of no significance. If the Führer would take the hand extended to him by France" and Germany would cooperate with France, the French people would all, with the exception of a few who never learn, be strongly in favor of it.

In this connection Laval called the conversation with the Führer an act of great political importance that would arouse strong hopes in France. He was aware that before the war the Führer had frequently offered France cooperation and during the war had repeatedly offered her peace. Although France had permitted herself to be led astray at that time, she could now return to the right road and had in fact already found her way back to it. If, as the Führer had just stated, Germany did not desire a peace of vengeance—which for that matter Laval had never expected she would— everything was possible. If the Führer, in view of France's long historical development—and he had previously shown that he was able to appreciate it—would grant France an honorable place, in keeping with her history and genius, in the new order in Europe created by him (the Führer), everything could be achieved.

The Führer said in this connection that it could be stated unquestionably that a positive form of some kind or other for German-French relations could not be definitely established as long as the war was not actually over. As long as the war was still undecided, the question of who would pay the costs remained open, and if Germany should happen to find an opportunity at some later time to make a reasonable settlement elsewhere, no one could expect that she would fight on merely in order to spare France. This had to be stated in all soberness and thereon the future relations between the two countries ultimately depended. He (the Führer) had learned that Laval personally was no friend of the English and desired their defeat. Many Frenchmen, however, naturally took a different view and cherished other hopes.

The Führer emphasized that he was determined, if necessary, to mobilize everything humanly conceivable against England. It would perhaps become evident even in the very near future that this was not merely empty talk. The question of whether France intended to take a positive attitude toward this general mobilization against England or thought that an attitude of waiting promised greater advantages for the future was of extreme importance for the relations between the two countries. The question was also decisive for the reason that the general extension of the front against England would obviously be determined or at least essentially affected by consideration of French interests or disregard of these interests, depending on the attitude France took. He (the Führer) believed that basically even the best peace between Germany and France, which would necessarily have to be concluded at the expense of England, could only be a peace that took general account of certain German interests in Europe and Africa, and furthermore would in general have to lead to a more European concept of the representation of the legitimate interests of a number of nations in Africa. In principle it was conceivable to him that France not only would not have to endure the suffering which she herself inflicted on Germany in 1918 and which she would, according to certain publications, inflict on Germany again in case of victory, but would receive consideration commensurate with her importance, both in Europe and in Africa. But if the war should last longer and Germany should find a settlement in another direction, the Reich would also be forced to indemnify itself in some other way.

The Führer added that of course he did not expect M. Laval to make any general statement in reply to these explanations. He only asked <u>him</u> to convey the substance of the conversation to Marshal Pétain. Perhaps it would then be possible to hold a personal conference between the Marshal and the Führer. He (the Führer) would have a conversation with Franco tomorrow, and if Marshal Pétain accepted his invitation to a personal conference, it might perhaps take place thereafter.

Laval said immediately that the Marshal would accept any invitation of the Führer and that he could therefore accept it in his name at once.[8] For the rest, he (Laval) agreed with the Führer on almost all points. He spoke only for himself personally, however, and his only interest was to secure a peace that was least bad for his country. He saw only one possibility for that: the defeat of England. If the war should go on and a German-English settlement should be concluded, and if France's attitude should have been unclear, German-French relations would naturally be affected thereby.

The Führer had spoken of certain documents and publications revealing the suffering that France would inflict on her if Germany were defeated. He did not know which publications and documents the Führer had in mind in that connection and could only say that the sinister influence and pernicious interference of England in French affairs found expression there too.

In reply the Führer merely stated that the sensitivity of French racial pride could be spared only if peace were concluded at the expense of England.

It was then proposed that the conference between the Führer sand Marshal Pétain should be held the day after tomorrow—October 24—at the same place.

During the entire conversation Laval took close written notes of the Führer's statements, the French translation of which he had dictated for recording almost verbatim.

SCHMIDT

Unsigned Memorandum

Record of the conversation between the Führer and the Caudillo in the Führer's parlor car at the Hendaye railroad station on October 23, 1940

[General Francisco Franco (1892-1975) led the military revolt and the Nationalists in the Spanish Civil War with the support of Germany and Italy from 1936 to 1939. He came close to entering the war in 1940 but was dissuaded by doubts concerning Germany's final victory. See Stanley Payne, *Franco and Hitler* (New Haven: Yale University Press, 2008); and Stanley Payne and Jesus Palacios, *Franco* (Madison: Wisconsin U.P. 2014). The memorandum was probably prepared by Paul Otto Schmidt, cf. Schmidt's *Statist auf diplomatischer Bühne 1928-45* (Bonn, 1949), pp. 500-502.]

At the beginning the Caudillo expressed his satisfaction at now being able to make the personal acquaintance of the Führer and to render to him Spain's thanks for everything that Germany had previously done for his country. Spain has always been spiritually allied with the German people without any reservation and in complete loyalty. In the same sense, Spain has at every moment felt herself united with the Axis. In the Civil War the soldiers of the three countries had fought together and a profound unity had risen among them. Likewise, Spain would in the future attach herself closely to Germany, for historically there were between Spain and Germany only forces of unity, and none of separation,

In the present war as well, Spain would gladly fight at Germany's side. The difficulties which were to be overcome in that case were well known to the Führer. A war would necessitate preparations in the economic, military, and political spheres. Within the framework of her limited capabilities, Spain had begun these preparations but was of course coming up against difficulties that were being made for her by anti-Axis elements in America and Europe. Therefore Spain must mark time and look kindly toward things of which she thoroughly disapproved.

Franco then came to speak of Spain's growing provisioning difficulties and in this connection mentioned that the United States and Argentina apparently were precisely following orders from London, for there had been cases in which the channel through the English embassy immediately removed difficulties in both the above-mentioned countries. The difficulties already existing would be more intensified by the bad harvest In spite of this, Spain, mindful of her spiritual alliance with the Axis Powers, had assumed the same attitude toward the war as had Italy in the past autumn.

The Führer replied that he was glad to see the Caudillo personally for the first time in his life after he had so often been with him in spirit during the Spanish Civil War. He knew precisely how difficult the struggle in Spain had been, for he himself since 1918-19 had had to go through similar grave conflicts, until he had helped the National Socialist movement to victory. Spain's enemies had been his enemies too. The struggle which was raging in Europe today would be decisive for the fate of the Continent and of the world for a long time to come. Militarily, this struggle as such was decided. Germany had established a front against the British Isles from the North Cape to the Spanish border and would no longer allow the English a landing on the Continent. Military operations were now taking place right in the English motherland. In spite of that, England still had certain hopes: Russia and America. With Russia, Germany had treaties. Aside from this, however, he (the Führer) immediately after conclusion of the French campaign had undertaken a reorganization of the German Army so that, beginning with March of the coming year, the latter would appear in the following strength: of a total of 230 divisions, 186 were assault divisions. The rest consisted of defense and occupation troops. Of the 186 assault divisions, 20 were armored divisions equipped with German material, while 4 additional armored brigades possessed captured material in part. In addition to this there were 12 motorized divisions. With this army strength Germany was ready for any eventuality. He (the Führer) believed that England was wrong in placing her hope on Russia. If the latter country were aroused at all from her inactivity, she would, if anything, be on the German side. It was therefore a matter of miscalculation on the part of England.

With respect to America, there was no need to be afraid of an active intervention during the winter. There would therefore be no change in the present military situation. At least 18 months to 2 years would pass before America's military power was fully armed. There would arise nevertheless a considerable danger if America and England established themselves in the islands lying off Africa in the Atlantic Ocean. The danger was the greater because it was not certain whether the French troops stationed in the colonies would under all circumstances remain loyal to Pétain. The greatest threat existing at the moment was that a part of the colonial empire would, with abundant material and military resources, desert France and go over to de Gaulle, England, or the United States.

Meanwhile, the war of Germany against England was continuing. The difficulty was that the operations had to be carried on across an ocean on which Germany did not have naval control. She had only air supremacy, and of course over the Channel the weather for exercising this had, so far, been extremely unfavorable. Since the middle of August there had not even been 5 fair days, and the major attack against England had as yet not been able to begin since an attack against the British naval forces, on the part of Germany, could only be carried out from the air; according to previous experiences when atmospheric conditions were good, the British fleet had always been forced to yield to such attack. On the basis of meteorological forecasts which predicted with certainty a period of fair weather for 7 to 8 days, a great ah- attack had been started on a fixed day. After half a day it had to be broken off again, to be sure, because of a sudden change in the weather.

So far Germany had won very great victories. But for this very reason, he (the Führer) wanted to guard against suffering a failure by some thoughtless move. In this connection, the Führer mentioned as an example of his tactics, the events of the great offensive in France. Originally he had had the plan of striking the great blow as early as last October, but had constantly been hindered from doing this by the weather. He had suffered at not being able to act but he had been really determined not to begin the offensive in bad weather, but on the contrary had preferred to wait until the weather conditions became better. When the meteorologists had then reported to him that on May 10 the normal period of clear summer weather would begin, he had, on May 8, issued the order for attack. The result of this attack was known, and in the battle against England he would act precisely as in the case of the French offensive. He would begin the great attack only when the weather conditions permitted absolute success. In the meantime England, and especially London, was being bombarded day and night. On London alone, 300,000 to 500,000 kilograms of bombs had been dropped. Many harbor installations, factories, and armament works were thus being shattered; England's approaches were being mined; and an increasing U-boat activity was contributing to the further isolation of the island. At the moment the number of U-boats being finished was 10. In the spring it would rise to 17; in July to 25; and after that up to 34 per month. He hoped the concentrated activity of the air arm, minelayers and destroyers, U-boats, and speed boats would do so much damage and harm to England that in the end attrition would set in. In spite of this, he was lying in wait in order to carry out the great blow during fair weather even if this could not happen until spring. It is self-evident that the time during which such vast masses of troops were lying inactive would continue to be exploited.

Naturally Germany had an interest in ending the war in a short time if possible, since every additional month cost money and sacrifice. In the attempt to bring about the end of the war as soon as possible to render the entry of the United States into the war more difficult, Germany had concluded the Tripartite Pact. This Pact was compelling the United States to keep her Navy in the Pacific Ocean and to prepare herself for a Japanese attack from that direction. In Europe as well, Germany was attempting to expand her base. He could confidentially report that several other nations had announced their intention of joining the Tripartite Pact.

To guarantee her petroleum supply, Germany has sent pursuit squadrons and armored troops to Romania upon the request of the Romanian government and in agreement with it.

The great problem to be solved at the moment consisted in hindering the de Gaulle movement in French Africa from further expanding itself and thereby establishing in this way bases for England and America on the African coast. A danger in this direction actually existed. The Pétain government was in the deplorable condition of having to liquidate a war for which it was not responsible, for the consequences of which, however, its opponents blamed it. It was now a matter of preventing de Gaulle from receiving an increase in power from this difficult position of the French government, something which moreover would lead France to complete collapse. Finally, the attempt had to be made to bring France herself to a definite stand against England. This indeed was a difficult undertaking because there were still two tendencies in France: a fascist one represented by Pétain and Laval, and an opposition one which wanted to carry on a double-dealing game with England. Moreover, it was particularly difficult to stir the French to a clear stand because they did not know how the peace would look. On the other hand, nothing could be said about the peace as long as the war was not completely ended, for one of Germany's opponents certainly had to pay for the war. Were England soon overpowered, Germany would then be ready without further ado to grant France easier peace terms. Should the war continue, however, and should the English as a result offer Germany a compromise, she (Germany) would certainly not continue to fight only to spare France. Moreover Germany needed France as a base as long as she was fighting against England. Yesterday he had, in all frankness, informed Vice President Laval of this view, and he would on the morrow speak with Pétain in precisely the same manner.

The purpose of this conference in Hendaye was the following: If succeeded in effecting quite a large front against England, then the struggle would be substantially easier for all the participants and could be ended sooner. In setting up this front the Spanish desires and the French hopes were obstacles in the path. Were England no longer participating in the war and if there were no de Gaulle, one would not have to think of relinquishing demands on France. France would then have to submit and, in case she did not want to cooperate, she could be occupied by the military within 12 days without any difficulty.

More difficult would be the solution of the administrative problems and the economic problems. To occupy North Africa would of course be difficult and would not be possible without a strong military effort. The French knew that they had to sacrifice something in the peace treaty. They expected to lose the German colonies and Alsace-Lorraine; they knew that border rectifications would be undertaken and that Nice, Corsica, and Tunis would be lost to them. In the latter case, they would of course be very downcast over the loss and would prefer to make an arrangement which would, in another fashion, assure access to the raw materials there. Such an arrangement would be a fraud, however, for he who no longer had the country would no longer at the suitable moment be given the raw materials.

There was the danger that, if the French were explicitly told that they would have to get out of certain African areas, the African possessions would perhaps desert France even with the concurrence of the government of Vichy. In order to meet this danger, he had worked up a general formula which he had explained yesterday to M. Laval. In doing this he had not involved himself in any concrete statements regarding the territorial changes which were to take place after the war. He had merely assured M. Laval that changes in France's African holdings were unavoidable and told him that it was up to France herself, by cooperating in defeating England, to create her own possibilities of compensation for territorial losses—these could not yet be indicated—so that ultimately through such compensations France would retain a highly valuable colonial empire. He would present the same ideas tomorrow to Marshal Pétain and in this connection wished the Caudillo to consider the following: If cooperation with France proved possible, then the territorial results of the war may perhaps not be so great. Yet the risk would be smaller and success more readily attainable. In his personal view it was better in so severe a struggle to aim at a quick success in a short time, even if the gain would be smaller than to wage long drawn-out wars. If with France's aid German mid win faster, she was ready to give France easier peace terms in return. Moreover the Führer was convinced that Germany, Italy and Spain would emerge from the war as allies, and there would still be opportunities for rectification later. As a concession, even the German demands on France were being partially abandoned since a rapid end to the war would constitute a greater success for all the participants than a victory after a longer struggle, even though Germany could still continue the war for an unlimited time. But on top of the military burden was the economic burden, and it might be the greatest success could not be reckoned an economic gain.

The purpose of his trip to Hendaye was to examine the possibility cooperating with France on this basis, without running the danger that the French might suddenly inform us that their African possessions had separated from them. To be sure, it was not clear whether ... [the record of this conversation is incomplete.]

*****

Memorandum by an Official of the Foreign Minister's Secretariat

MONTOIRE, October 24, 1940.

Conference between the Führer and Marshal Pétain in the presence of the Foreign Minister and the Vice President of the Council of Ministers Pierre Laval, in the Führer's special train, at the railway station of Montoire-Sur-Le-Loir, on October 24, 1940

[Marshal Philippe Pétain (1856-1951), a hero of World War I, became the head of the French government in June 1940 and agreed to the armistice with Germany. He was tried and condemned to death for treason but the sentence was commuted to life in prison. See Charles Williams, *Pétain* (New York: Palgrave Macmillan, 2005).]

The Führer began by expressing his regret over having to receive Marshal Pétain under such distressing circumstances. He would have been glad if he had had the opportunity before of making the Marshal's acquaintance. Today's talk would at the same time be a reply to the letter which the Marshal addressed to the Führer sometime ago.

The Marshal replied that he was very gratified by the Führer's welcome, despite the painful atmosphere pervading the whole situation. He was especially impressed by the Führer's understanding for the difficult position in which he (the Marshal) found himself. His position was truly a tragic one. He had at all times been an opponent of the war with Germany. In consequence, past French governments had sent him as ambassador to Spain. When the crisis approached in 1939, he had twice requested to be allowed to return to France and to resume his functions in the War Council. He did so because the information reaching him indicated that France was on the point of plunging into a disastrous adventure. That was a very painful time for him and when he finally learned that France had declared war on Germany, he was barely able to restrain his grief. This declaration of war he considered an act of great folly. He, who had been throughout against this war, was now called upon to atone for the errors of past governments. M. Laval had reported to him the conversation he had with the Führer day before yesterday. He understood that the subject of that conversation was the question of cooperation between the two counts. He was sorry that such cooperation had not been begun before, in the years before this war. But there was perhaps still time to regain what had been lost. The English were affording the best opportunity that. As France's allies their conduct toward that country had been exceedingly bad since the Armistice. France would not forget the events of Oran and the attack on Dakar This latter action, upon England's instigation, had been headed by a bad Frenchman, a French general who had denied his country. Today's France no longer tolerated things of this kind and this officer accordingly was promptly condemned to death, to the confiscation of his property, and perpetual banishment from France. Justice had thus taken its course against him.

The English, however, were continuing their attacks on France, principally against her colonial empire and especially in Africa. France had effectively resisted at Dakar. He (Pétain) had sent an officer to the African colonies with the mission of restoring the disaffected to the cause of France. In this respect, and since the Führer had done France the honor of speaking of cooperation, a field might be found where its realization between the two countries was a practical possibility. He did not wish to go into details, but he could give assurance for his own person that as far as matters depended on him everything would be done in order to secure these colonial territories for France.

Replying to the remarks of Marshal Pétain, the Führer sketched very briefly a picture of the present and the future, as he saw it. He was aware that Marshal Pétain did not belong among those men who had favored declaring war on Germany. If this were not the case this talk could never have taken place. Putting this to the side, there remained the historical fact that the war had been imposed upon Germany in spite of the Führer's ceaseless efforts to avert a new bloody conflict and although Germany was not pressing France with any demands. The war had been conducted by France for motives which he (the Führer) recently analyzed for [Vice-] President Laval. He had no doubt but that in the event of a German defeat, France would have inflicted upon Germany sufferings far worse than in 1918. He was happy that fate had permitted him to lead his nation and its armed forces in this war, and so avert all misfortune from the German people. He believed moreover that this development might perhaps prove fortunate for the future. He was dealing with France as a man like Marshal Pétain, had not wanted the war and now wished to preserve a clear view of the future, transcending the present situation.

One thing however was obvious: it would not do for a nation to declare war without any objective causes and later on be relieved of any responsibility for the consequences of that action. It was therefore natural that France should be made to share in bearing the costs of the war in so far as they could be compensated for in territorial and material terms. If he (the Führer), together with his ally Mussolini, was considering the question as to the direction the final political orientation was to take, he was doing so now at a moment when the war was already decided from a military point of view.

He was addressing himself to the soldier of great stature, which he knew Marshal Pétain to be, in expounding from the military standpoint the basis of this view. The military operations thus far had resulted in destroying England's continental position. He was resolved to carry this struggle forward to the annihilation of the island center of the British Empire. Military operations against England could now be affected only by meteorological conditions, similarly as in the autumn of 1939 the immediate final decision planned by the Führer in the west had to be postponed owing to bad weather. This delay, however, which lasted 7 months, did not in any way change the final outcome of those operations. And while it was entirely conceivable that weather conditions might compel Germany to put off a direct assault on England for weeks or months, England would in the meantime be attacked from the air on a mounting scale and would be hurt increasingly on the sea front through the continuously increasing U-boat activity and the intensified mining of ports. British propaganda since the beginning of the war was operating with partly silly and partly outrageous lies. He (the Führer) could assure Marshal Pétain that there was not a true word to British reports of German losses in submarines and aircraft. The German Luftwaffe unremittingly continued its fight over England, and the losses of U-boats since the beginning of the war totaled 28. Besides, the U-boat construction program, calling at the present for 10 ships a month, would constantly expand and provide 14 in December 1940; 17 in March-April; 24 next July-August; and 30 to 34 at the beginning of 1942.

England was being bombarded in steady day and night attacks, and, including London, 5,000 to 8,000 tons of explosives had been dropped. Weather conditions permitting, the all-out attack on England would be launched at once.

England had lost her continental position and also her insular position had become untenable. Only she refused to admit this. She was still putting her hope in America and Russia.

America, however, considering her present state of armaments, could play no significant role prior to 1942. By that time England would either be occupied or turned into a waste of rubble. The notion of an American landing on the Continent, viewed from the military standpoint, was completely illusory.

Russia was bound to Germany by treaties. But all treaties aside, he (the Führer), in order to elucidate his views, would give Marshal Pétain the following figures:

By March, 1941, Germany would have 230 divisions, including 186 combat divisions of outstanding quality. Of these combat divisions, 20 were armored divisions with German equipment. To these must be added 4 armored brigades with partly German partly captured equipment, and 12 motorized divisions.

Aircraft production next winter would be more than double the previous production. Beginning next April, the Luftwaffe would be numerically stronger than it was on May 10 of this year, and its fighter and pursuit units would be supplied with new equipment. Together with her ally, Germany constituted a military power which could not be attacked, let alone defeated, by any coalition in the world. The hope entertained by the English that Germany might disintegrate internally was childish, as was their talk of Germany's economic difficulties. This was the picture of the military situation today as it presented itself to the sober-minded observer, without indulging in fantasy. Despite this favorable military situation he entertained the sincere desire to end the war as quickly as possible, for he saw war not a condition worth pursuing, let alone as a desirable permanent state. Every additional month of the war increased perhaps not so much the number of victims as the material costs which at a later date would bear heavily on the nations. There existed no undertaking less profitable than war. This conviction motivated his (the Führer's) endeavor to shorten the war by every conceivable means of a military, political, and economic nature. In so doing he was aware that prolongation of the war not only inflicted a burden primarily on Ger-many but was to the disadvantage of all of Europe, and that it would increase exorbitantly the final reckoning that would have to be faced some day. This final account would have to be settled, on the one hand, by satisfying the vital demands of some peoples in Europe, which had not been met or out of which they had been cheated in the past. On the other hand, this final account would also call for payment of the material costs of the war. It was his personal opinion that England was chiefly to blame for the war and that England accordingly would have to bear the chief burden of the costs of the war. Each month by which England's collapse was brought nearer would bring the war to an earlier end and relieve the Continent of its troubles, difficulties, and sacrifices. Each month by which the war was prolonged raised the total of Europe's victims, deferred the time of restoring orderly and tolerable living conditions, and increased the guilt that would have to be atoned. He therefore believed European countries having an interest in terminating the conflict ought accordingly to form a natural continental community. He was acting at the present time to organize a European and in part extra-European community against Britain, the enemy of the Continent. He had exchanged ideas with the French government with a view to ascertaining whether France was prepared to join and cooperate with this community. It was imperative to study the possibilities of ending this war that might result from such a cooperation between Germany and Italy, on the one side, and France on the other.

Marshal Pétain, in his reply, broached the question of the Franco-English war aims which, if he understood the Führer correctly, were supposed to have culminated in the dismemberment of Germany. He had never seen such a plan and if it had been drawn up at all, it had never been put before him. Nevertheless it was clear that the associated powers of France and England would have to assume responsibility for the damages caused by the war they had declared. He hoped however, that the future peace treaty would be no treaty of oppression, because such a treaty would prevent the growth of harmonious relations among the nations. He held, besides, that distinctions ought to be made in apportioning responsibility, so as to give encouragement to those who, filled with better intentions, wished to make a new start.

The Führer's plan was designed to accomplish the encirclement of England on all seas and all countries facing her shores. If the community, which the Führer had spoken of, could be achieved, it would probably mean a quick end for England.

He (Pétain), however, was in no position at this time to define the exact limits of French cooperation with Germany. All he could do was to express himself in favor of the principle of such cooperation. Vice-President Laval had already given similar assurances in his first talk with the Führer, which he (Pétain) now expressly confirmed. As regards the conditions of cooperation, however, he could enter no binding under-takings without consulting the French government. Upon his return he would inform the French government that he had agreed to the principle of cooperation with Germany without making any further commitments, but that it opened for France a window, as it were, on her colonial empire.

Laval emphasized the importance of the declaration just made by Pétain, which was in full accord with the spirit of the conversation conducted between the Führer and himself (Laval) the day before yesterday. In accepting the principle of cooperation with Germany, Marshal Pétain had pointed to the larger military possibilities open to France in Africa, where England was the aggressor. But generally, in taking further action, it would be necessary to take account of the state of public opinion in France. The talk between the Führer and Laval had given rise to hopes for a better future, which would be tremendously enhanced by today's conversation between the Führer and Pétain. Until now the French had faced a wall, as it were, with out and without hope. The fact that the Führer had assented to having that talk and had offered cooperation with Germany, make a deep and favorable impression on French public opinion and go far in counteracting English propaganda. But if France to commit herself today as to the conditions of that cooperation, would not advance the relationship to Germany but on the contrary have a detrimental influence. Besides, Marshal Pétain had signed a law by which—and Laval held that this had gone to an extreme—the right to wage war was made dependent on a vote in the Parliament. If Pétain wished to declare war on England, he would have to convoke Parliament, that is, a Parliament dating from the past era, which he felt not the least inclination to do, for obvious reasons. But there existed other possibilities for giving effect to cooperation with Germany. France could offer resistance, which would have certain repercussions in the country itself as also in England, and this could in the final account accomplish the same results as those produced by actual cooperation.

In any event, what Marshal Pétain desired to achieve, as he had already indicated, was to obtain the least onerous peace for France. If Germany, in contradistinction to France's attitude in 1918, and after a victory much more brilliant than France's victory in the World War, now even extended the offer of cooperation, France not only accepted but acknowledged such an offer with gratitude. In the beginning, however, as Marshal Pétain had pointed out, it was necessary to proceed slowly and with caution.

Pétain gave eloquent expression to his admiration for the German armament program. He characterized as fantastic the organization that was necessary to carry out the program, and displayed particular interest in the procurement of the raw materials required for its execution, which must involve "astronomical" figures since these raw materials, which were not available in unlimited amounts, were at the same time being used by other countries as well. To be sure, Germany could resort to substitutes in her own country and the territories subject to her control. The Führer interjected at this point that up to the day when war broke out he had spent 92 billion reichsmarks for the armament of Germany. Marshal Pétain then asked what the cost of the new armament program would be since raw materials had become still more costly, and guessed that the cost would now be twice what it had been for the first German armament effort. However, thanks to the monetary system introduced by Dr. Schacht and Germany's autarkic organization much would prove easier than before, especially with respect to financial matters.

In conclusion he also expressed his admiration for the Führer personally. He had never known anyone possessing so much self-confidence and confidence in his people, and accomplishing such gigantic achievements as did the Führer.

The Führer pointed out that first of all he had mobilized the total energy of the Gorman nation, employing it in work days of not merely 8 hours, but sometimes running to 9,10, and even 11 hours. The Foreign Minister remarked at this point that this was the real secret of the Führer's success, Schacht's monetary system was much less important; this observation was received by both Laval arid Pétain with understanding mirth.

The Führer next spoke about Germany's raw materials position. She had coal in abundance. Her iron production, too, was sufficient to meet requirements and the supply was assured by the construction of large works and blast furnaces, among which the largest was the Salzgitter works with a capacity of 40 million tons of ore and 10 million tons of iron. In addition, Germany had called into being the world's largest light metal industry to make up for copper. Certain textile staple fibers replaced cotton and a fabric of remarkable quality was being produced from the fibers of potato plants.

The conversation then turned to the American aircraft industry. The Führer mentioned in this connection that for the 60,000 workers in America in 1939, Germany employed 480,000 in that industry in that year. Today the figure in Germany was doubled.

Laval emphasized America's unreliability as a supplier of war material and cited in this connection a talk with Bullitt, in which Bullitt admitted to him as late as last March that America had no more than 130 planes herself. Asked when the Allies could in that case count on substantial support from the American aircraft industry, Bullitt had vaguely mentioned 1940 or 1941; this had led Laval to conclude that all the statements of the past French governments about American aid were wholly based on illusions and compounded of dreams and lies. America had only a small number of skilled workers, not enough manufacturing models and no plants. France had been prepared to invest considerable funds in such plants in America and had failed to achieve any results; and when he (Laval) was hearing all this new talk about the supposed American aid to England, he felt that the English were being taken in just as much as the French had been last summer.

The Führer finally mentioned the difficulties of building up an industry and spoke of his experiences in this regard in Germany, and then he summed up the result of the conversation as follows:

Marshal Pétain says that he is prepared in principle to consider cooperation with Germany as outlined by the Führer. The conditions of this cooperation would be established and settled in detail and from case to case. Marshal Pétain anticipates from this a more advantageous outcome of the war for France. The Führer declares that he is in agreement.

Laval had the Führer's comprehensive statement taken down for himself in a word for word French translation. This brought the conversation to its conclusion.

SCHMIDT

*****

Record of the conversation between the Führer and the Duce in the presence of the Reich Foreign Minister and the Italian Foreign Minister at the Palazzo Vecchio in Florence on October 28, 1940

[Mussolini had decided to attack Greece that same day without advising Germany of his plans. Hitler disapproved. The Greek campaign turned into a disaster and only German intervention was able to overcome Greece's resistance. It ultimately undermined the Fascist regime in Italy and signaled the eventual downfall of Mussolini in July 1943.]

The Führer opened the conversation by saying that he had come to Florence to inform the Duce of his conversations with Laval, Franco, and Pétain, and in order to speak with him on the question of Greece. He mentioned on the latter point that Germany could make available for the military operations against Greece, especially for the protection of Crete against occupation by the English, a division of airborne troops and a division of parachute troops, for which North Africa would be the proper starting base.

Turning to the conversations of the past few days, the Führer remarked that the relations of the two Axis Powers to each other had not been changed by them and would not be changed. He referred to the difficult situation that could arise for the African territories lying opposite Gibraltar if the English, possibly as the vanguard of America, established themselves in Morocco. It was possible that because this territory did not belong to them, they would hand it over to the United States. The defense of these North African territories, however, depended on France. If Morocco broke off from France, the Spaniards would surely not be in a position with their own resources to conquer the French Zone of the Sultanate. On the contrary, if the English committed strong forces there, there would even be the danger that the Spaniards would also forfeit Spanish Morocco. Besides, he (the Führer) had often wondered whether there were not some secret connection between Pétain and de Gaulle. After the French defense of Dakar, however, it looked as though there were actually deep-seated opposition between a Vichy government and de Gaulle. He had also gained the impression from the films of the naval battle of Oran that this had been a serious battle, although he had at first entertained doubts on this score. In his conversation with Pétain the latter had in strong terms expressed his aversion for de Gaulle.

According to reports from Ambassador Abetz, the intellectuals, bourgeoisie, Jews and Communists in France were on the side of de Gaulle, while the petty bourgeois and workmen, who had always been the enemies of England anyway, were for Pétain.

The important thing now was to prevent the secession of Morocco from France, for since Spain could not on her own resources take a stand against it, such a procedure would force the Axis powers, despite insufficient preparation, to press for Spain's immediate entry into the war since that country was needed as a bridge to Africa in order to conquer Gibraltar, protect Spanish Morocco, and if possible anticipate the English there with such celerity that they could not seize any more air bases. Since the Axis powers did not have naval supremacy, in carrying out these operations they would have to rely largely on the Luftwaffe. In these circumstances it was clear that it would be best for the Axis powers if the North African were defended by the French themselves. The French air forces stationed there were commanded by a French officer who was thoroughly hostile to England and in the French navy, also, the sentiment was anti-British. The Army would stick to Pétain as long as it believed it could still save something for France. As soon, however, as a necessity of a cession of certain regions of North and West Africa leaked out, they would secede, and the young officers in particular would mutiny. Some inducement therefore had to be held out to the French to defend their territory themselves.

There was no doubt that France expected considerably harder peace terms than the modest demands made to her by Italy and Germany, but had had quite other things in store for the latter in the event of a victory over Germany. He also reminded Pétain and Laval very plainly of France's plans to dismember Germany. As recently as May 11 of this year, the French military weekly spoke of partitioning Germany. In these circumstances the modest peace terms of Germany and Italy were a tremendous concession to France. If these two countries acted today against France in the way France herself had planned to act against Germany, they would, for instance, demand the independence of Normandy. France therefore did not deserve a peace so comparatively favorable as that contemplated by Italy and Germany, and she must first prove herself worthy of it by rendering special service, namely, by making herself available in the fight against England. In addition there were continual concessions that France required on specific points, as, for instance, in the question of those French prisoners of war who were interned in Switzerland, or more properly speaking, were quartered in empty Swiss hotels at a charge of 12 Swiss francs per day and whose return to France the Pétain government desired. Germany was not averse to complying with this request, since she had no interest in having France pay out such large sums to Switzerland. But on this question just as on the question of occupation costs, she would make concessions only on a quid pro quo basis, in return for corresponding services rendered by France. The occupation costs were undoubtedly fixed high, but in this way they functioned as means of pressure on France, since she was interested in as speedy end to the war as possible.

He (the Führer) would not ask France for any direct military aid. Germany and Italy had enough resources of military power. France was only to make available bases for the Luftwaffe and commit parts of her fleet, above all, submarines, particularly from West African ports, against the English.

He thought the principal effect of the integration of France into the front against England, however, would be in the psychological field. For actually the whole of Europe, including the former ally, would thereby be solidly arrayed against England. He considered that the psychological effects of this fact on Great Britain would be all the greater since the English in their desperate military situation could still maintain their domestic front only psychologically, by all kinds of mendacious maneuvering, and it might therefore hit them in a particularly sensitive spot.

The Führer then described in detail the uninterrupted air attacks on England and particularly London, indicated the quantities of bombs that had already been dropped, mentioned the new tactics of letting long-range fighters and fighter planes serve as bombers, since both before and after release of the bombs they could defend themselves successfully against the English fighter planes. He also pointed out the devastating effects of a new German air bomb with a 2,000 kg. bursting charge.

In order to determine the possibilities of integrating France into the European front, he had begun discussions with the French government and had spoken first of all with Laval. He personally considered Laval a typical democratic politician, who at heart probably did not believe a word of what he had told him (the Führer), but would be prepared only under the pressure of necessity to cooperate with Germany. He had held it up to Laval that France for no cause had declared war against Germany, had lost, and now had to pay. The German troops would remain in France until the war was over, by receiving the old raw materials nostrum of supplying through economic cooperation, raw material to country poor in them. The Führer had however rejected this idea at once, remarking that this was a problem of Lebensraum and that all the ownership rights had to be settled anew in Africa, and that in this connection France would be given a free hand to compensate herself with English possessions. Spain's wishes had to be satisfied too, however. The redistribution of colonial possessions would have to be made in such a way that all concerned obtained their rights and that Europe and Africa would grow into a community of interests, like North and South America.

Laval had given him to understand that if France could hope to retain the main part of her colonial empire she would be prepared to help drive the English from their possessions. The Führer here added a short comment on the bad impression that he had gained of conditions in France on his journey through that country. Farming had impressed him as being very neglected, unlike what he had seen that morning from the train in Italy, which had seemed to him like a cultivated garden.

He then spoke about his conversation with Franco. The latter certainly had a stout heart, but only by an accident had he become Generalissimo and leader of the Spanish state. He was not a man who was up to the problem of the political and material development of his country. The Spaniards, moreover, seemed to have no feeling for the limits to their own strength and would be easily inclined to begin undertakings which they then could not carry through. In the negotiations with Germany they had, on the one hand, requested her to assume very concrete obligations, such as, for instance, the delivery of grain, gasoline, etc., but had always been very vague about what *they* would do. Thus they had, for example, reserved entirely for their own decision the important question of the time of Spain's entry into the war. If on the other hand, they complained that nothing precise and concrete had been promised them in response to their colonial demands, this was so if only because in case such assurances became known, the danger of secession of Morocco would be very great. Since Franco had declared, however, that he needed such assurances to justify to his people Spain's entry into the war, publication of these assurances was surely to be expected and particularly because reticence was hardly one of the outstanding qualities of Spanish official quarters.

In this connection the Führer repeated the promise already made to the Duce in the last conversation at the Brenner Pass, that he would on no account conclude peace with France if the claims of Italy were not completely satisfied. not completely satisfied. Naturally he could not give Spain such an assurance, for then Africa would secede from France and it would take severe battles to reconquer it and to protect the Spanish Zone.

The Foreign Minister then explained the technical development of the negotiations with the Spaniards and the present situation, and presented the Spanish text of the secret protocol which the Spaniards had promised ultimately to sign. At the same time he described in particular the difficulties that Serrano Suñer had made with regard to point 5, that is, the formula envisaged for the solution of the colonial problem.

The Führer then spoke of his conversation with Marshal Pétain who, in contrast to Laval, had given the impression of a very decent, reliable character. The words of the Marshal to the effect that he had always been opposed to the English and to the entry of France into the war, he (the Führer) had believed at once. Pétain, who had previously seen to it that the English observer was ousted from the French Defense Council, had, as he had indicated, been shunted over to Spain as ambassador by the French government, and had not been allowed, despite several requests, to return to France and resume his old seat on the Defense Council.

The Führer mentioned that he had told Pétain essentially what he had told Laval and had only emphasized the military aspect of the situation more strongly. Pétain, who was certainly no opportunistic politician, had expressed himself with the greatest indignation about de Gaulle, and called his behavior a blot on the honor of the French officers' corps; this blot had been erased at once by the death sentence against de Gaulle. Pétain had pointed out that it was difficult at the moment for France to declare war upon England. He had cited psychological reasons for this and referred to the constitutional necessity for convening the Chambers, which surely would lead to internal political difficulties for the Vichy government. He had been prepared, however, to defend energetically at once the French position in Africa and had spoken of the possibility that a further action against England might perhaps develop from it. He (the Führer) had told Pétain nothing about the arrangements with Spain and had stated, moreover, that the modalities of collaboration were to be determined by the Armistice Commission or commissions to be established.

If France were brought into the anti-English front, then French West and North Africa would be secured, new bases against England acquired, and Gibraltar could be taken with a very small force: and with her help, the one gateway of the Mediterranean could be sealed off while the other exit, the Suez Canal could be just as effectively closed by means of new German [mines?] already mentioned in the last conversation, which had proved in practice to be very effective and heretofore not clearable.

This procedure in the west together with the action in the Balkans particularly in Romania would have a favorable influence on Russia

With this the conversation turned to the subject of Russia. The Führer pointed out pointed out that Italy and Germany were natural allies, while the partnership with Russia had sprung purely from considerations of expediency. Just as mistrustful as Stalin was toward him (the Führer) so was he also toward Stalin. Molotov would now come to Berlin (this communication was received by the Duce and Count Ciano with evident surprise and great interest) and it would perhaps be possible to divert the activity of the Russians to India. There was a danger that they would again turn to their old goal, the Bosporus, and they had to be kept away from it. It had become necessary to point out to them that they might not step beyond certain definite boundaries....to speak. [the foregoing line is illegible.]

This country [Finland], which owed her existence to Germany, had in Geneva and elsewhere in the past never shown herself very grateful and had often taken a position opposed to Germany. She had, however, defended herself with extraordinary bravery in the war against Russia and it would therefore also be difficult for Germany, as a matter of sentiment, to stand by idly in the event of a second Russian attack upon Finland. Germany had, moreover, great material interests in the Norwegian territory around Kirkenes adjacent to Finland. There were iron ore deposits there of 85-90 percent iron content, which were needed as an admixture to the Swedish iron ores for producing high-grade steels. Germany had, therefore, already stationed two mountain divisions and one SS Death's Head Brigade in the Norwegian territory in question, and had built airports and roads. Nevertheless the safest way to Kirkenes lay through Finland, and so on the basis of a special agreement, transports for the German Army in Norway had been routed in this way. Mainly involved were antiaircraft gun supplies, munitions shipments, and food for a year. Germany delivered to the Finns the arms which she still owed them on of former agreements. Five shiploads of arms, moreover, stated to be for Finland and seized in Bergen—they surely were originally sent to Bergen for other purposes—had been released. Germany could also never admit that Petsamo had become Russian.

With regard to Romania, the Führer observed that he had not been able to send more troops to that country than Antonescu was willing to receive. He had seen to it, however, that these troops were not dispersed in small detachments throughout the country, but stayed together as regiments at least as units ready for action.

In this connection stressing again the Russian danger to the Bosporus, the Führer spoke once more of the visit of Molotov to Berlin on November 10 and 11, and stated that it must be made clear to the Russians that there was little sense in their seeking expansion in areas where they would collide with Italy's or Germany's interests and finally gain nothing but an outlet to inland seas. It would doubtless be better for them to expand in other directions. Stalin was shrewd enough to realize this and then, if possibly a world front against England was formed from Japan via Russia to Europe, the effect upon the island empire, which was in desperate straits and still living only on hopes and psychological considerations, would be shattering.

The Führer then described again the military measures against England, which would be carried out even if a landing were not possible. If England were bombarded from the air for 100 days as destructively as Germany was now planning and in part already doing both day and night, the moral effect upon the English would be extremely severe and their last hopes would be destroyed. Moreover, the effectiveness of the submarine force would become more and more noticeable since Admiral Dönitz had developed a new system of committing 8 or 9 submarines against a single convoy. In this way very important results had very recently been achieved against England's supplies. The Italian submarines conducted themselves very bravely. Crews and material were excellent, according to the reports of the German Admiralty. They still had only to get used to the special methods of fighting in the northern waters as well as to the Dönitz system in order to be completely successful. If England's last hopes were dashed by both air and submarine operations, a worse collapse than France's would come.

The Duce replied that he inferred from the communications of the Führer that the latter wished to bring about a coalition of all Europe against England. He (the Duce) entirely approved of this plan and believed that it was necessary in order to guarantee ultimate victory. On the specific questions that the Führer had raised, the Duce took the following position: Italy had a particular interest in France. The country which had wanted and lost the war had to pay the costs, particularly since in many speeches the Führer had repeatedly sought in vain an understanding with France. The Duce recalled in this connection publications of Charles Maurras, who had advocated a dismemberment of Germany, as in the Peace of Westphalia into 23 single states, whereupon the Führer remarked that this might still be the program of France after the present war. Continuing, the Duce stated that the Pétain government was undoubtedly the best government in France for Germany and Italy and that it was therefore in their interest to support it. In order to attain this goal, France had to be told precisely what was desired of her. The Duce again emphasized the moderation of the Italian demands: Nice, Corsica, Tunis and Somaliland.

If France appeared amenable to the wishes of Germany and Italy for integration into the anti-English front, she must be given the means to defend the colonial territories remaining to her. She had to cooperate in a passive way and when peace was concluded, be indemnified for possible losses of colonial territory. The question arose whether a settlement with France should be made at once or reserved for the future.

The Führer replied to the effect that the final settlement could wait until the war was ended. So long as the fight against England continued, the German Army had to stay in France, and so long as the war lasted, France must retain the feeling that she was interested in getting it over quickly. It was difficult, for example, to satisfy so soon some of the French wishes mentioned earlier. Germany absolutely needed the prisoners of war as laborers and it was already necessary to have a pledge in one's hand against certain eventualities, for one could never be too cautious toward France.

The Duce remarked that even now many Frenchmen did not grasp that they had been conquered and spoke of a *fausse défaite*.

The Führer supplemented this remark by referring to Laval's statement to the effect that the number of two million French prisoners showed that the French people had not desired the war and had therefore not wanted to fight.

Regarding further handling of cooperation with France, the Führer proposed negotiations between the Foreign Minister, Count Ciano, and Laval, at a place in Germany yet to be determined, so that France might from the very outset get the impression of unity between Germany and Italy.

In reply to another question from the Duce as to how the Pétain government could be supported, the Führer replied that this could best be done by giving Pétain the assurance that Germany and Italy had only moderate demands to make on France and did not intend, moreover to destroy the French Empire but even wished to give France the opportunity for compensation at England's expense. If France knew this, this would mean the end of de Gaulle. Pétain's position would be eased if he were not given too concrete assurances, for then Pétain could give only general answers to all-too-curious questioners from his own ranks. Moreover, certain small concessions could be granted him step by step such as the return of the French prisoners of war interned in Switzerland, for whom France had to pay 140 million French francs per day, or 12 Swiss francs per head to Switzerland; the liberation from captivity of an old French general, whose return to France Pétain was especially anxious to effect; the reduction of the occupation costs and the return of the government to Paris or Versailles.

In reply to a question by the Duce as to what should be done with Spain the Führer replied that the Spaniards claimed for themselves French Catalonia, a rectification of the Pyrenees frontier, Oran, French Morocco,

enlargement of the territory of Rio de Oro to the twentieth degree of lati-
tude and an enlargement of Spanish Guinea. The Foreign Minister
observed that the Spanish demands were as unreasonable as the German
and Italian demands were modest, and he referred again to the protocol
which had been previously submitted, and stressed its extremely confidential nature. Only six statesmen and their closest assistants knew of it. He
then once more informed the Duce regarding the significance of the
colonial formula in point 5 of the protocol and the difficulties that Serrano
Suñer had made in this connection.

To a question from the Duce as to what the Spaniards should be given,
the Führer replied that they could not get any more than a substantial enlargement of Spanish Morocco. At the same time he stressed the fact that
Germany had to have bases on the African coast and that he would prefer
to lay claim to one of the islands off the coast of Africa for this purpose. If
this were not possible, bases would have to be found on the African coast.

As far as Spanish accession to the Tripartite Pact and the German-
Italian Alliance was concerned, it could not be announced until the military preparations for the protection of Spain were concluded. At a remark
from the Duce to the effect that the announcement of possible agreements
between Italy, Germany, and Spain might be very dangerous to Pétain's
position, the Foreign Minister again stressed the need for secrecy, but
emphasized that if something should nevertheless leak out, it would be
better if nothing too definite had been awarded the Spaniards and they had
merely received vague promises. The Spaniards themselves had told him
that because of their current food imports from the British Empire, they
were perhaps even more interested than the Axis Powers in keeping it
secret, They also knew that upon its becoming known that they had joined
the Axis, Churchill would not hesitate to attempt the seizure of the Spanish
islands and bases in the Atlantic.

To a question from the Duce as to the exact time of the intervention of
the Spaniards in the military operations, the Führer replied that Franco had
been very vague here and had stated only that he would intervene when the
military preparations were completed. The Führer then spoke again of
Gibraltar and stated that, according to studies by German experts, the
operation, if well prepared and executed with lightning speed, could go off
well with very few troops and certain prospects of success. According to
the Spaniards they had already put the Canary Islands in a condition of
defense. They would moreover, be supported by heavy batteries, by dive
bombers, long-range guns, and special troops.

To a question from the Duce as to whether it would not be well if the English found out that they could no longer put hope in Spain the Führer replied that, in his opinion, the announcement of Spain's joining the Axis must be postponed until it was absolutely certain that the English could not land in Spain and on the islands. The Duce mentioned in this connection that it would perhaps also be advantageous to the internal situation in Spain if the firm alignment with the Axis Powers could be announced. The Führer then proposed that the three Foreign Ministers make all the preparations with Spain that were necessary for her entry into the war, as well as settle all other details still pending, and that a meeting then take place in Florence between the Führer, the Duce, and Franco, at which the participation of Spain in the Tripartite Pact and the German-Italian Alliance could be announced with full publicity.

With regard to Russia, the Duce remarked that bringing her into the general front would be very advantageous. The very visit of Molotov would mean a violent blow to England and the foes of the Axis. It would perhaps be advisable to publicize the fact of this visit even before the American presidential election. The Foreign Minister replied that negotiations had already begun with the Russian government, which had requested that this visit be kept strictly secret.

The Duce observed in conclusion that Germany and Italy were therefore, as always, in accord on all points, to which the Führer agreed. Shortly before the close of the conversation, the Führer again stressed the fact that he did not construe the entry of Russia into the common front, as meaning that an alliance would be concluded with Russia but, as the Foreign Minister stressed, that a special form of agreement with Russia and the partners to the Tripartite Pact would be found. The Führer also mentioned that Romania, Hungary, and Slovakia wished to accede to the Tripartite Pact while Bulgaria was apparently afraid of the Turks. The Foreign Minister called the breaking of the alliance with England by the Turks a very desirable goal and stated, in reply to a question from the Duce as to how this goal was to be attained, that in case of an agreement between the Axis Powers and Russia, Turkey would probably be very much more accessible, and that finally it would also be possible to bribe the Turkish statesmen. The conversation was continued at a luncheon for four and in a series of separate conversations between the Führer and the Duce, the Foreign Minister and the Duce, as well as the Foreign Minister and Count Ciano in the course of the afternoon.

SCHMIDT

*****

Hitler and Molotov: November 12, 1940

Memorandum of the conversation between the Führer and the Chairman of the Council of People's Commissars and People's Commissar for Foreign Affairs, Molotov, in the presence of the Reich Foreign Minister, the Deputy People's Commissar, Dekanosov, as well as of Counselor of Embassy Hilger and Herr Pavlov, who acted as interpreters, on November 12, 1940

[Vyacheslav Molotov (1890-1986) was Soviet prime minister, then foreign minister under Stalin. His visit to Berlin encouraged Hitler to finalize his plans to attack Russia in 1941. See Gabriel Gorodetsky, *Grand Delusion*, (New Haven: Yale, 1999); Roger Moorhouse, *The Devil's Alliance* (New York: Basic Books, 2014).]

After some words of welcome, the Führer stated that the idea that was uppermost in his mind in the conversations now taking place was this: In the life of peoples it was indeed difficult to lay down a course for development over a long period in the future and the outbreak of conflicts was often strongly influenced by personal factors; he believed, nevertheless, that an attempt had to be made to fix the development of nations, even for a long period of time, in so far as that was possible, so that friction would be avoided and the elements of conflict precluded as far as humanly possible. This was particularly in order when two nations such as the German and Russian nations had at their helm men who possessed sufficient authority to commit their countries to a development in a definite direction. In the case of Russia and Germany, moreover, two very great nations were involved which need not by nature have any conflict of interests, if each nation understood that the other required certain vital necessities without the guarantee of which its existence was impossible. Besides this, both countries had systems of government which did not wage war for the sake of war, but which needed peace more than war in order to carry out their domestic tasks. With due regard for vital needs, particularly in the economic field, it should really be possible to achieve a settlement between them, which would lead to peaceful collaboration between the two countries beyond the life span of the present leaders.

After Molotov had expressed his entire agreement with these arguments, the Führer continued that it was obviously a difficult task to chart developments between peoples and countries over a long period. He believed, however, that it would be possible to elaborate clearly and precisely certain general points of views quite independently of personal motives and to orient the political and economic interests of peoples in such a manner as to give some guarantee that conflicts would be avoided even for rather long periods. The situation in which the conversation of today was taking place was characterized by the fact that Germany was at war, while Soviet Russia was not. Many of the measures taken by Germany had been influenced by the fact of her belligerency. Many of the steps that were necessary in the course of the war had developed from the conduct of the war itself and could not have been anticipated at the outbreak of war. By and large, not only Germany but also Russia had gained great advantages. On further consideration, the political collaboration during the one year of its existence had been of considerable value to both countries.

Molotov stated that this was quite correct.

The Führer declared further that probably neither of the two peoples had realized its wishes 100 percent. In political life, however, even a 20-25 percent realization of demands was a good deal. He believed that not every wish would be fulfilled in the future either, but that the two greatest peoples of Europe, if they went along together, would, in any case gain more than if they worked against each other. If they stood together, some advantage would always accrue to both countries. If they worked against each other, however, third countries would be the sole gainers.

Molotov replied that the argument of the Führer was entirely correct and would be confirmed by history; that it was particularly applicable to the present situation, however.

The Führer then went on to say that proceeding from these ideas he had again quite soberly pondered the question of German-Russian collaboration, at a time when the military operations were in effect concluded.

The war had, moreover, led to complications which were not intended by Germany, but which had compelled her from time to time to react militarily to certain events. The Führer then outlined to Molotov the course of military operations up to the present, which had led to the fact that England no longer had an ally on the continent. He described in detail the military operations now being carried out against England, and he stressed the influence of atmospheric conditions on these operations. The English retaliatory measures were ridiculous, and the Russian gentlemen could convince themselves at first hand of the fiction of alleged destruction in Berlin. As soon as atmospheric conditions improved, Germany would be poised for the great and final blow against England. At the moment, then, it was her aim to try not only to make military preparations for this final struggle, but also to clarify the political issues which would be of importance during and after this showdown. He had, therefore, reexamined the relations with Russia, and not in a negative spirit, but with the intention of organizing them positively, if possible, for a long period of time. In so doing he had reached several conclusions:

1. Germany was not seeking to obtain military aid from Russia;

2. Because of the tremendous extension of the war, Germany had been forced, in order to oppose England, to penetrate into territories remote from her and in which she was not basically interested politically or economically;

3. There were nevertheless certain requirements, the full importance of which had become apparent only during the war, but which were absolutely vital to Germany. Among them were certain sources of raw materials which were considered by Germany as most vital and absolutely indispensable. Possibly Herr Molotov was of the opinion that in one case or another they had departed from the conception of the spheres of influence which had been agreed upon by Stalin and the Reich Foreign Minister. Such departures had already occurred in some cases in the course of Russian operations against Poland. In a number of cases, on calm consideration of the German and Russian interests, he (the Führer) had not been ready to made concessions' but he had realized that it was desirable to meet the needs of Russia half-way, as, for instance, in the case of Lithuania. From an economic point of view, Lithuania had, it is true, had a certain importance for us, but from a political point of view, we had understood the necessity of straightening out the situation in this whole field in order thereby to prevent in the future the spiritual revival of tendencies that were capable of causing tension between the two countries of Germany and Russia. In another case, namely, that of the South Tyrol, Germany had taken a similar position. However, in the course of the war, factors had arisen for Germany which could not have been anticipated at the outbreak of the war, but which had to be considered absolutely vital from the standpoint of military operations.

He (the Führer) now had pondered the question how, beyond all petty momentary considerations, further to clarify in bold outline the collaboration between Germany and Russia and what direction future German-

Russian developments should take. In this matter the following viewpoints were of importance for Germany:

1. Need for Lebensraum [Raumnot]. During the war Germany had acquired such large areas that she would require one hundred years to utilize them fully.

2. Some colonial expansion in Central Africa was necessary.

3. Germany needed certain raw materials, the supply of which she would have to safeguard under all circumstances. And

4. She could not permit the establishment by hostile powers of air or naval bases in certain areas.

In no event, however, would the interests of Russia be selected. The Russian empire could develop without in the least prejudicing German interests. (Molotov said this was quite correct.) If both countries came to realize this fact, they could collaborate to their mutual advantage and could spare themselves difficulties, friction, and nervous tension. It was perfectly obvious that Germany and Russia would never become one world. Both countries would always exist separate from each other as two powerful elements of the world. Each of them could shape its future as it liked, if in so doing it considered the interests of the other. Germany herself had no interests in Asia other than general economic and commercial interests. In particular, she had no colonial interests there. She knew, furthermore, that the possible colonial territories in Asia would probably fall to Japan. If by any chance China, too, should be drawn into the orbit of the awakening [erwachenden] nations, any colonial aspirations would be doomed to disappointment from the start in view of the masses of people living there.

There were in Europe a number of points of contact [Berührungsmomenten] between Germany, Russia, and Italy. Each one of these three countries had an understandable desire for an outlet to the open sea. Germany wanted to get out of the North Sea, Italy wanted to remove the barrier of Gibraltar, and Russia was also striving toward the ocean. The question now was how much chance there was for these great countries really to obtain free access to the ocean without in turn coming into conflict with each other over the matter. This was also the viewpoint from which he looked upon the organization of European relations after the war. The leading statesmen of Europe must prevent this war from becoming the father of a new war. The issues to be settled had, therefore, to be settled in such a manner that, at least in the foreseeable future, no new conflict could arise.

In this spirit, he (the Führer) had talked with the French statesmen and believed that he had found among them some sympathy for a settlement which would lead to tolerable conditions for a rather long period and which would be of advantage to all concerned, if only to the extent that a new war did not again have to be feared immediately. Referring to the preamble of the Armistice Treaty with France, he had pointed out to Pétain and Laval that, as long as the war with England lasted, no step might be taken which would in any way be incompatible with the conditions for ending this war against Great Britain.

Elsewhere, too, there were problems such as these, but ones which arose only for the duration of the war. Thus, for instance, Germany had no political interests whatsoever in the Balkans and was active there at present exclusively under the compulsion of securing for herself certain raw materials. It was a matter of purely military interests, the safeguarding of which was not a pleasant task, since, for instance, a German military force had to be maintained in Romania, hundreds of kilometers away from the supply centers.

For similar reasons the idea was intolerable to Germany that England might get a foothold in Greece in order to establish air and naval bases there. The Reich was compelled to prevent this under any circumstances.

The continuation of the war under such circumstances was of course not desirable. And that is why Germany had wanted to end the war after the conclusion of the Polish campaign. At that time England and France could have had peace without personal sacrifices; they had, however, preferred to continue the war. Of course, blood also creates rights, and it was inadmissible that certain countries should have declared and waged war without afterward paying the cost. He (the Führer) had made this clear to the French. At the present stage of developments, however, the question was which of the countries responsible for the war had to pay more. At any rate, Germany would have preferred to end the war last year and to have demobilized her army in order to resume her peacetime work, since from an economic point of view any war was bad business. Even the victor had to incur such expenses before, during, and after the war that he could have reached his goal much more cheaply in a peaceful development.

Molotov concurred in this idea, stating that in any case it was vastly more expensive to attain a goal by military measures than by peaceful means. The Führer pointed out further that under the present circumstances Germany had been forced by wartime developments to become active in areas in which she was politically disinterested but had at most economic interests. Self-preservation, however, absolutely dictated this course. Nevertheless, this activity of Germany—forced upon her in the areas in question—represented no obstacle to any pacification of the world which would later be undertaken, and which would bring to the nations working toward the same end that for which they hoped.

In addition, there was the problem of America. The United States was now pursuing an imperialistic policy. It was not fighting for England, but only trying to get the British Empire into its grasp. They were helping England, at best, in order to further their own rearmament and to reinforce their military power by acquiring bases. In the distant future it would be a question of establishing a great solidarity among those countries which might be involved in case of an extension of the sphere of influence of this Anglo-Saxon power, which had a more solid foundation, by far, than England. In this case, it was not a question of the immediate future; not in 1945, but in 1970 or 1980, at the earliest, would the freedom of other nations be seriously endangered by this Anglo-Saxon power. At any rate, the Continent of Europe had to adjust itself now to this development and had to act jointly against the Anglo-Saxons and against any of their attempts to acquire dangerous bases. Therefore, he had undertaken an exchange of ideas with France, Italy, and Spain, in order with these countries to set up in the whole of Europe and Africa some kind of Monroe Doctrine and to adopt a new joint colonial policy by which each of the powers concerned would claim for itself only as much colonial territory as it could really utilize. In other regions, where Russia was the power in the foremost position, the interests of the latter would, of course, have to come first. This would result in a great coalition of powers which, guided by sober appraisal of realities, would have to establish their respective spheres of interest and would assert themselves against the rest of the world correspondingly. It was surely a difficult task to organize such a coalition of countries; and yet, to conceive it was not as difficult as to carry it out.

The Führer then reverted to the German-Russian efforts. He understood thoroughly Russia's attempts to get ice-free ports with absolutely secure access to the open sea. Germany had enormously expanded her Lebensraum in her present eastern provinces. At least half of this area, however, must be regarded as an economic liability. Probably both Russia and Germany had not achieved everything they had set out to do. In any case, however, the successes had been great on both sides. If a liberal view were taken of the remaining issues and due regard were taken of the fact that Germany was still at war and had to concern herself with areas which, in and for themselves, were of no importance to her politically, substantial gains for both partners could be achieved in the future, too. In this connection the Führer again turned to the Balkans and repeated that Germany would at once oppose by military action any attempt by England to get a foothold in Salonika. She still retained unpleasant memories from the last war of the then Salonika Front.

To a question of Molotov's as to how Salonika constituted a danger, the Führer referred to the proximity of the Romanian petroleum fields, which Germany wished to protect under all circumstances. As soon as peace prevailed, however, the German troops would immediately leave Romania again.

In the further course of the conversation, the Führer asked Molotov how Russia planned to safeguard her interests in the Black Sea and in the Straits. Germany would also be prepared at any time to help effect an improvement for Russia in the regime of the Straits.

Molotov replied that the statements of the Führer had been of a general nature and that in general he could agree with his reasoning. He was also of the opinion that it would be in the interest of Germany and the Soviet Union if the two countries would collaborate and not fight each other. Upon his departure from Moscow, Stalin had given him exact instructions, and everything that he was about to say was identical with the views of Stalin. He concurred in the opinion of the Führer that both partners had derived substantial benefits from the German-Russian agreement. Germany had received a secure hinterland that, as was generally known, had been of great importance for the further course of events during the year of war. In Poland, too, Germany had gained considerable economic advantages. By the exchange of Lithuania for the Voivodeship of Lublin, all possible friction between Russia and Germany had been avoided.

Finland Question: Molotov questions German good faith.

The German-Russian agreement of last year could therefore be regarded as fulfilled, except for one point, namely, Finland. The Finnish question was still unsolved, and he asked the Führer to tell him whether the German-Russian agreement, as far as it concerned Finland, was still in force. In the opinion of the Soviet government, no changes had occurred here. Also, in the opinion of the Soviet government the German-Russian agreement of last year represented only a partial solution. In the meanwhile, other issues had arisen that also had to be solved.

Molotov then turned to the matter of the significance of the Tripartite Pact. What was the meaning of the New Order in Europe and in Asia, and what role would the U.S.S.R. be given in it? These issues must be discussed during the Berlin conversations and during the contemplated visit of the Reich Foreign Minister to Moscow, on which the Russians were definitely counting. Moreover, there were issues to be clarified regarding Russia's Balkan and Black Sea interests with respect to Bulgaria, Romania, and Turkey. It would be easier for the Russian government to give specific replies to the questions raised by the Führer, if it could obtain the explanations just requested. It would be interested in the New Order in Europe, and particularly in the tempo and the form of this New Order. It would also like to have an idea of the boundaries of the so-called Greater East Asian Sphere.

The Führer replied that the Tripartite Pact was intended to regulate conditions in Europe as to the natural interests of the European countries and, consequently, Germany was now approaching the Soviet Union in order that she might express herself regarding the areas of interest to her. In no case was a settlement to be made without Soviet Russian cooperation. This applied not only to Europe, but also to Asia, where Russia herself was to cooperate in the definition of the Greater East Asian Sphere and where she was to designate her claims there. Germany's task in this case was that of a mediator. Russia by no means was to be confronted with a fait accompli.

When the Führer undertook to try to establish the above-mentioned coalition of powers, it was not the German-Russian relationship which appeared to him to be the most difficult point, but the question of whether a collaboration between Germany, France, and Italy was possible. Only now that he believed this problem could be solved, and after a settlement in broad outlines had in effect been accepted by the three countries, had he thought it possible to contact Soviet Russia for the purpose of settling the questions of the Black Sea, the Balkans, and Turkey.

In conclusion, the Führer summed up by stating that the discussion, to a certain extent, represented the first concrete step toward a comprehensive collaboration, with due consideration for the problems of Western Europe, which were to be settled between Germany, Italy, and France, as well as for the issues of the East, which were essentially the concern of Russia and Japan, but in which Germany offered her good offices as mediator. It was a matter of opposing any attempt on the part of America to "make money on Europe." The United States had no business either in Europe, in Africa, or in Asia.

Molotov expressed his agreement with the statements of the Führer regarding the role of America and England. The participation of Russia in the Tripartite Pact appeared to him entirely acceptable in principle, provided that Russia was to cooperate as a partner and not be merely an object. In that case he saw no difficulties in the matter of participation of the Soviet Union in the common effort. But the aim and the significance of the Pact must first be more closely defined, particularly because of the delimitation of the Greater East Asian Sphere.

In view of a possible air raid alarm the talk was broken off at this point and postponed until the following day, the Führer promising Molotov that he would discuss with him in detail the various issues which had come up during the conversation.

SCHMIDT
BERLIN, November 16, 1940.

*****

Hitler and Molotov: November 13, 1940

Memorandum of the conversation between the Führer and the Chairman of the Council of People's Commissars Molotov in the Presence of the Reich Foreign Minister and the Deputy People's Commissar for Foreign Affairs, Dekanosov, as well as of Counselor of Embassy Hilger and Herr Pavlov, who acted as interpreters, in Berlin on November 13, 1940

The Führer referred to the remark of Molotov during yesterday's conversation, according to which the German-Russian agreement was fulfilled "with the exception of one point: namely, of Finland."

Molotov explained that this remark referred not only to the German-Russian agreement itself, but in particular to the Secret Protocols too.

The Führer replied that, in the Secret Protocol, zones of influence and spheres of interest had been designated and distributed between Germany and Russia. In so far as it had been a question of actually taking possession, Germany had lived up to the agreements, which was not quite the case on the Russian side. At any rate, Germany had not occupied any territory that was within the Russian sphere of influence.

Lithuania had already been mentioned yesterday. There could be no doubt that in this case the changes from the original German-Russian agreement were essentially due to Russian initiative. Whether the difficulties—to avoid which the Russians had offered their suggestion—would actually have resulted from the partition of Poland, could be left out of the discussion. In any case, the Voivodeship of Lublin was no compensation, economically, for Lithuania. However, the Germans had seen that in the course of events a situation had resulted which necessitated revision of the original agreement.

The same applied to Bucovina. Strictly speaking, in the original agreement Germany had declared herself disinterested only in Bessarabia. Nevertheless, she had realized, in this case too, that revision of the agreement was in certain respects advantageous for the other partner.

The situation regarding Finland was quite similar. Germany had no political interest there. This was known to the Russian government. During the Russo-Finnish War Germany had meticulously fulfilled all her obligations in regard to absolutely benevolent neutrality.

Molotov interposed here that the Russian government had had no cause for criticism with regard to the attitude of Germany during that conflict.

In this connection the Führer mentioned also that he had even detained ships in Bergen which were transporting arms and ammunition to Finland, for which Germany had actually had no authority. Germany had incurred the serious opposition of the rest of the world, and of Sweden in particular, by her attitude during the Russo-Finnish War. As a result, during the subsequent Norwegian campaign, itself involving considerable risks, she had to employ a large number of divisions for protection against Sweden, which she would not have needed otherwise.

The real situation was as follows: In accordance with the German-Russian agreements. Germany recognized that, politically, Finland was of primary interest to Russia and was in her zone of influence. However, Germany had to consider the following two points:

1. For the duration of the war she was very greatly interested in the deliveries of nickel and lumber from Finland, and
2. She did not desire any new conflict in the Baltic Sea which would further curtail her freedom of movement in one of the few merchant shipping

regions which still remained to her. It was completely incorrect to assert that Finland was occupied by German troops. To be sure, troops were being transported to Kirkenes via Finland, of which fact Russia had been officially informed by Germany. Because of the length of the route, the trains had to stop two or three times in Finnish territory. However, as soon as the transit of the troop contingents to be transported had been completed, no additional troops would be sent through Finland. He (the Führer) pointed out that both Germany and Russia would naturally be interested in not allowing the Baltic Sea to become a combat zone again. Since the Russo-Finnish War, the possibilities for military operations had shifted, because England had available long-range bombers and long-range destroyers. The English thereby had a chance to get a foothold on Finnish airports.

In addition, there was a purely psychological factor which was extremely onerous. The Finns had defended themselves bravely, and they had gained the sympathies of the world-particularly of Scandinavia. In Germany too during the Russo-Finnish War, the people were somewhat annoyed at the position which, as a result of the agreements with Russia, Germany had to take and actually did take. Germany did not wish any new Finnish War because of the aforementioned considerations. However, the legitimate claims of Russia were not affected by that. Germany had proved this again and again by her attitude on various issues, among others the issue of the fortification of the Aaland Islands. For the duration of the war, however, her economic interests in Finland were just as important as in Romania. Germany expected consideration of these interests all the more, since she herself had also shown understanding of the Russian wishes in the issues of Lithuania and Bucovina at the time. At any rate, she had no political interest of any kind in Finland, and she fully accepted the fact that that country belonged to the Russian zone of influence.

In his reply Molotov pointed out that the agreement of 1939 had referred to a certain stage of the development which had been concluded by the end of the Polish War, while the second stage was brought to an end by the defeat of France, and that they were really in the third stage now. He recalled that by the original agreement, with its Secret Protocol, the common German-Russian boundary had been fixed and issues concerning the adjacent Baltic countries and Romania, Finland, and Poland had been settled. For the rest, he agreed with the remarks of the Führer on the revisions made. However, if he drew up a balance sheet of the situation that resulted after the defeat of France, he would have to state that the

German-Russian agreement had not been without influence upon the great German victories.

As to the question of the revision of the original agreement with regard to Lithuania and the Voivodeship of Lublin, Molotov pointed out that the Soviet Union would not have insisted on that revision if Germany had not wanted it. But he believed that the new solution had been in the interest of both parties. At this point the Reich Foreign Minister interjected that, to be sure, Russia had not made this revision an absolute condition, but at any rate had urged it very strongly.

Molotov insisted that the Soviet government would not have refused to leave matters as provided in the original agreement. At any rate, however, Germany, for its concession in Lithuania, had received compensation in Polish territory.

The Führer interjected here that in this exchange one could not, from the point of view of economics, speak of adequate compensation.

Molotov then mentioned the question of the strip of Lithuanian territory and emphasized that the Soviet government had not received any clear answer yet from Germany on this question. However, it awaited a decision.

Regarding Bucovina, he admitted that this involved an additional territory, one not mentioned in the Secret Protocol. Russia had at first confined her demands to Northern Bucovina. Under the present circumstances, however, Germany must understand the Russian interest in Southern Bucovina. But Russia had not received an answer to her question regarding this subject either. Instead, Germany had guaranteed the entire territory of Romania and completely disregarded Russia's wishes with regard to Southern Bucovina.

The Führer replied that it would mean a considerable concession on the part of Germany, if even part of Bucovina were to be occupied by Russia. According to an oral agreement, the former Austrian territories were to fall within the German sphere of influence. Besides, the territories belonging to the Russian zone had been mentioned by name: Bessarabia, for example. There was, however, not a word regarding Bucovina in the agreements. Finally, the exact meaning of the expression "sphere of influence" was not further defined. At any rate, Germany had not violated the agreement in the least in this matter. To the objection of Molotov that the revisions with regard to the strip of Lithuanian territory and of Bucovina were not of very great importance in comparison with the revision which Germany had under taken elsewhere by military force, the

Führer replied that so-called "revision by force of arms" had not been the subject of the agreement at all.

Molotov, however, persisted in the opinion previously stated: that the revisions desired by Russia were insignificant.

The Führer replied that if German-Russian collaboration was to show positive results in the future, the Soviet government would have to understand that Germany was engaged in a life and death struggle, which, at all events, she wanted to conclude successfully. For that, a number of prerequisites depending upon economic and military factors were required, which Germany wanted to secure for herself by all means. If the Soviet Union were in a similar position, Germany on her part would, and would have to, demonstrate a similar understanding for Russian needs. The conditions which Germany wanted to assure did not conflict with the agreements with Russia. The German wish to avoid a war with unforeseeable consequences in the Baltic Sea did not mean any violation of the German-Russian agreements according to which Finland belonged in the Russian sphere of influence. The guarantee given upon the wish and request of the Romanian government was no violation of the agreements concerning Bessarabia. The Soviet Union had to realize that in the framework of any broader collaboration of the two countries advantages of quite different scope were to be reached than the insignificant revisions which were now being discussed. Much greater successes could then be achieved, provided that Russia did not now seek successes in territories in which Germany was interested for the duration of the war. The future successes would be the greater, the more Germany and Russia succeeded in fighting back to back against the outside world, and would become the smaller, the more the two countries faced each other breast to breast. In the first case there was no power on earth which could oppose the two countries.

In his reply Molotov voiced his agreement with the last conclusions of the Führer. In this connection he stressed the viewpoint of the Soviet leaders, and of Stalin in particular, that it would be possible and expedient to strengthen and activate the relations between the two countries. However, in order to give those relations a permanent basis, issues would also have to be clarified which were of secondary importance, but which spoiled the atmosphere of German-Russian relations. Finland belonged among these issues. If Russia and Germany had a good understanding, this issue could be solved without war, but there must be neither German troops in Finland nor political demonstrations in that country against the Soviet-Russian government.

The Führer replied that the second point could not be a matter for debate, since Germany had nothing whatsoever to do with these things. Incidentally, demonstrations could easily be staged, and it was very difficult to find out afterward who had been the real instigator. However, regarding the German troops, he could give the assurance that, if a general settlement were made, no German troops would appear in Finland any longer.

Molotov replied that by demonstrations he also understood the dispatch of Finnish delegations to Germany or receptions of prominent Finns in Germany. Moreover, the circumstance of the presence of German troops had led to an ambiguous attitude on the part of Finland. Thus, for instance, slogans were brought out that "nobody was a Finn who approved of the last Russo-Finnish Peace Treaty," and the like.

The Führer replied that Germany had always exerted only a moderating influence and that she had advised Finland and also Romania, in particular, to accept the Russian demands.

Molotov replied that the Soviet government considered it as its duty definitively to settle and clarify the Finnish question. No new agreements were needed for that. The old German-Russian agreement assigned Finland to the Russian sphere of influence.

In conclusion the Führer stated on this point that Germany did not desire any war in the Baltic Sea and that she urgently needed Finland as a supplier of nickel and lumber. Politically, she was not interested and, in contrast to Russia, had occupied no Finnish territory. Incidentally, the transit of German troops would be finished within the next few days. No further troop trains would then be sent. The decisive question for Germany was whether Russia had the intention of going to war against Finland.

Molotov answered this question somewhat evasively with the statement that everything would be all right if the Finnish government would give up its ambiguous attitude toward the U.S.S.R., and if the agitation against Russia among the population (bringing out of slogans such as the ones previously mentioned) would cease.

To the Führer's objection that he feared that Sweden might intervene in a Russo-Finnish War the next time, Molotov replied that he could not say anything about Sweden, but he had to stress that Germany, as well as the Soviet Union, was interested in the neutrality of Sweden. Of course, both countries were also interested in peace in the Baltic, but the Soviet Union was entirely able to assure peace in that region.

The Führer replied that they would perhaps experience in a different part of Europe how even the best military intentions were greatly restricted by geographical factors. He could, therefore, imagine that in the case of a new conflict a sort of resistance cell would be formed in Sweden and Finland, which would furnish air bases to England or even America. This would force Germany to intervene. He (the Führer) would, however, do this only reluctantly. He had already mentioned yesterday that the necessity for intervention would perhaps also arise in Salonika, and the case of Salonika was entirely sufficient for him. He had no interest in being forced to become active in the North too. He repeated that entirely different results could be achieved in future collaboration between the two countries and that Russia would after all, on the basis of the peace, receive everything that in her opinion was due her. It would perhaps be only a matter of six months or a year's delay. Besides, the Finnish government had just sent a note in which it gave assurance of the closest and friendliest cooperation with Russia.

Molotov replied that the deeds did not always correspond with the words, and he persisted in the opinion which he had previously expressed: that peace in the Baltic Sea region could be absolutely insured, if perfect understanding were attained between Germany and Russia in the Finnish matter. Under those circumstances he did not understand why Russia should postpone the realization of her wishes for six months or a year. After all, the German-Russian agreement contained no time limits, and the hands of none of the partners were tied in their spheres of influence.

With a reference to the changes made in the agreement at Russia's request, the Führer stated that there must not be any war in the Baltic. A Baltic conflict would be a heavy strain on German-Russian relations and on the great collaboration of the future. In his opinion, however, future collaboration was more important than the settlement of secondary issues at this very moment.

Molotov replied that it was not a matter of war in the Baltic, but of the question of Finland and its settlement within the framework of the agreement of last year. In reply to a question of the Führer he declared that he imagined this settlement on the same scale as in Bessarabia and in the adjacent countries, and he requested the Führer to give his opinion on that.

When the Führer replied that he could only repeat that there must be no war with Finland, because such a conflict might have far-reaching repercussions, Molotov stated that a new factor had been introduced into the discussion by this position, which was not expressed in the treaty of last year.

The Führer replied that during the Russo-Finnish War, despite the danger that in connection with it Allied bases might be established in Scandinavia, Germany had meticulously kept her obligations toward Russia and had always advised Finland to give in.

In this connection the Reich Foreign Minister pointed out that Germany had even gone so far as to deny to the Finnish President the use of a German cable for a radio address to America.

Then the Führer went on to explain that just as Russia at the time had pointed out that a partition of Poland might lead to a strain on German-Russian relations, he now declared with the same frankness that a war in Finland would represent such a strain on German-Russian relations, and he asked the Russians to show exactly the same understanding in this instance as he had shown a year ago in the issue of Poland. Considering the genius of Russian diplomacy, ways and means could certainly be found to avoid such a war.

Molotov replied that he could not understand the German fear that a war might break out in the Baltic. Last year, when the international situation was worse for Germany than now, Germany had not raised this issue. Quite apart from the fact that Germany had occupied Denmark. Norway, Holland, and Belgium, she had completely defeated France and even believed that she had already conquered England. He (Molotov) did not see where under those circumstances the danger of war in the Baltic Sea should come from. He would have to request that Germany take the same stand as last year. If she did that unconditionally, there would certainly be no complications in connection with the Finnish issue. However, if she made reservations, a new situation would arise which would then have to be discussed.

In reply to the statements of Molotov regarding the absence of military danger in the Finnish question, the Führer stressed that he too had some understanding of military matters, and he considered it entirely possible that the United States would get a foothold in those regions in case of participation by Sweden in a possible war. He (the Führer) wanted to end the European War, and he could only repeat that in view of the uncertain attitude of Sweden a new war in the Baltic would mean a strain on German-Russian relations with unforeseeable consequences. Would Russia declare war on the United States, in case the latter should intervene in connection with the Finnish conflict?

When Molotov replied that this question was not of present interest, the Führer replied that it would be too late for a decision when it became so. When Molotov then declared that he did not see any indication of the outbreak of war in the Baltic, the Führer replied that in that case everything would be in order anyway and the whole discussion was really of a purely theoretical nature.

Summarizing, the Reich Foreign Minister pointed out that

(1) the Führer had declared that Finland remained in the sphere of influence of Russia and that Germany would not maintain any troops there;

(2) Germany had nothing to do with demonstrations of Finland against Russia, but was exerting her influence in the opposite direction; and

(3) the collaboration of the two countries was the decisive problem of long-range importance, which in the past had already resulted in great advantages for Russia, but which in the future would show advantages compared with which the matters that had just been discussed would appear entirely insignificant. There was actually no reason at all for making an issue of the Finnish question. Perhaps it was a misunderstanding only. Strategically, all of Russia's wishes had been satisfied by her peace treaty with Finland. Demonstrations in a conquered country were not at all unnatural, and if perhaps the transit of German troops had caused certain reactions in the Finnish population they would disappear with the end of those troop transits. Hence, if one considered matters realistically, there were no differences between Germany and Russia.

The Führer pointed out that both sides agreed in principle that Finland belonged to the Russian sphere of influence. Instead, therefore, of continuing a purely theoretical discussion, they should rather turn to more important problems.

After the conquest of England the British Empire would be apportioned as a gigantic world-wide estate in bankruptcy of 40 million square kilometers. In this bankrupt estate there would be for Russia access to the ice-free and really open ocean. Thus far, a minority of 40 million Englishmen had ruled 600 million inhabitants of the British Empire. He was about to crush this minority. Even the United States was actually doing nothing but picking out of this bankrupt estate a few items particularly suitable to the United States. Germany, of course, would like to avoid any conflict which would divert her from her struggle against the heart of the Empire, the British Isles. For that reason, he (the Führer) did not like Italy's war against Greece, as it diverted forces to the periphery instead of concentrating them against England at one point. The same would occur during a

Baltic war. The conflict with England would be fought to the last ditch, and he had no doubt that the defeat of the British Isles would lead to the dissolution of the Empire. It was a chimera to believe that the Empire could possibly be ruled and held together from Canada. Under those circumstances there arose world-wide perspectives. During the next few weeks they would have to be settled in joint diplomatic negotiations with Russia, and Russia's participation in the solution of these problems would have to be arranged. All the countries which could possibly be interested in the bankrupt estate would have to stop all controversies among themselves and concern themselves exclusively with the partition of the British Empire. This applied to Germany, France, Italy, Russia, and Japan.

Molotov replied that he had followed the arguments of with interest and that he was in agreement with everything that he had understood. However, he could comment thereon less than the Führer, since the latter had surely thought more about these problems and formed more concrete opinions regarding them. The main thing was first to make up their minds regarding German-Russian collaboration, in which Italy and Japan could be included later on. In this connection nothing should be changed that had been started; rather, they should only contemplate a continuation of what had been begun.

The Führer mentioned here that the further efforts in the sense of the opening up of great prospects would not be easy and emphasized in this connection that Germany did not want to annex France as the Russians appeared to assume. He wanted to create a world coalition of interested powers which would consist of Spain, France, Italy, Germany, Soviet Russia, and Japan and would to a certain degree represent a coalition—extending from North Africa to Eastern Asia—of all those who wanted to be satisfied out of the British bankrupt estate. To this end all internal controversies between the members of this coalition must be removed or at least neutralized. For this purpose the settlement of a whole series of questions was necessary. In the West, i.e., between Spain, France, Italy, and Germany, he believed he had now found a formula which satisfied everybody alike. It had not been easy to reconcile the views of Spain and France for instance, in regard to North Africa; however, recognizing the greater future possibilities, both countries finally had given in. After the West was thus settled, an agreement in the East must now be reached. In this case it was not a matter of relations between Soviet Russia and Turkey only, but also of the Greater Asian Sphere. The latter consisted not only of the Greater East Asian Sphere, but also of a purely Asiatic area oriented toward the south, that Germany even now recognized as Russia's sphere of influence. It was a matter of determining in bold outlines the boundaries for the future activity of peoples and of assigning to nations large areas where they could find an ample field of activity for fifty to a hundred years.

Molotov replied that the Führer had raised a number of questions which concerned not only Europe but, beyond that, other territories too. He wanted to discuss first a problem closer to Europe, that of Turkey. As a Black Sea power, the Soviet Union was tied up with a number of countries. In this connection there was still an unsettled question that was just now being discussed by the Danube Commission. Moreover, the Soviet Union had expressed its dissatisfaction to Romania that the latter had accepted the guarantee of Germany and Italy without consultation with Russia. The Soviet government had already explained its position twice, and it was of the opinion that the guarantee was aimed against the interests of Soviet Russia, "if one might express oneself so bluntly." Therefore, the question had arisen of revoking this guarantee. To this the Führer had declared that for a certain time it was necessary and its removal therefore impossible. This affected the interests of the Soviet Union as a Black Sea power.

Molotov then came to speak of the Straits, which, referring to the Crimean War and the events of the years 1918-19, he called England's historic gateway for attack on the Soviet Union. The situation was all the more menacing to Russia, as the British had now gained a foothold in Greece. For reasons of security the relations between Soviet Russia and other Black Sea powers were of great importance.

In this connection Molotov asked the Führer what Germany would say if Russia gave Bulgaria, that is, the independent country located closest to the Straits, a guarantee under exactly the same conditions as Germany and Italy had given one to Romania. Russia, however, intended to agree beforehand on this matter with Germany and, if possible, with Italy too.

To a question by Molotov regarding the German position on the question of the Straits, the Führer replied that the Reich Foreign Minister had already considered this point and that he had envisaged a revision of the Montreux Convention in favor of the Soviet Union.

The Reich Foreign Minister confirmed this and stated that the Italians also took a benevolent attitude on the question of this revision.

Molotov again brought up the guarantee to Bulgaria and gave the assurance that the Soviet Union did not intend to interfere in the internal order of the country under any circumstances. "Not a hairs-breadth" would they deviate from this. Regarding Germany's and Italy's guarantee to Romania, the Führer stated that this guarantee had been the only possibility of inducing Romania to cede Bessarabia to Russia without a fight. Besides, because of her oil wells, Romania represented an absolute German-Italian interest, and, lastly, the Romanian government itself had asked that Germany assume the air and ground protection of the oil region, since it did not feel entirely secure from attacks by the English. Referring to a threat of invasion by the English at Salonika, the Führer repeated in this connection that Germany would not tolerate such a landing, but he gave the assurance that at the end of the war all German soldiers would be withdrawn from Romania.

In reply to Molotov's question regarding Germany's opinion on a Russian guarantee to Bulgaria, the Führer replied that if this guarantee was to be given under the same conditions as the German-Italian guarantee to Romania, the question would first arise whether Bulgaria herself had asked for a guarantee. He (the Führer) did not know of any request by Bulgaria. Besides, he would, of course, have to inquire about the position of Italy before he himself could make any statement.

However, the decisive question was whether Russia saw a chance to gain sufficient security for her Black Sea interests through a revision of the Montreux Convention. He did not expect an immediate answer to this question, since he knew that Molotov would first have to discuss these matters with Stalin.

Molotov replied that Russia had only one aim in this respect. She wanted to be secure from an attack by way of the Straits and would like to settle this question with Turkey; a guarantee given to Bulgaria would alleviate the situation. As a Black Sea power Russia was entitled to such security and believed that she would be able to come to an understanding with Turkey in regard thereto.

The Führer replied that this would conform approximately with Germany's views, according to which only Russian warships might pass freely through the Dardanelles, while the Straits would be closed to all other warships.

Molotov added that Russia wanted to obtain a guarantee against an attack on the Black Sea via the Straits not only on paper but "in reality" and believed that she could reach an agreement with Turkey in regard thereto. In this connection he came back again to the question of the Russian guarantee to Bulgaria and repeated that the internal regime of the country would remain unaffected, whereas on the other hand Russia was prepared to guarantee Bulgaria an outlet to the Aegean Sea. He was again addressing to the Führer—as the one who was to decide on the entire German policy—the question as to what position Germany would take with regard to this Russian guarantee.

The Führer replied with a counter-question as to whether the Bulgarians had actually asked for a guarantee, and he again stated that he would have to ask the Duce for his opinion.

Molotov stressed that he was not asking the Führer for a final decision, but that he was asking only for a provisional expression of opinion.

The Führer replied that he could not under any circumstances take a position before he had talked with the Duce, since Germany was interested in the matter only secondarily. As a great Danubian power, she was interested only in the Danube River, but not in the passage into the Black Sea. For if she were perchance looking for sources of friction with Russia, she would not need the Straits for that.

The talk then turned again to the great plans for collaboration between the powers interested in the British Empire's bankrupt estate. The Führer pointed out that he was not, of course, absolutely sure whether these plans could be carried out. In case it was not possible, a great historical opportunity would be missed, at any rate. All these questions would perhaps have to be examined again in Moscow by the Foreign Ministers of Germany, Italy, and Japan together with Herr Molotov, after they had been appropriately prepared through diplomatic channels.

At this point in the conversation the Führer called attention to the late hour and stated that in view of the possibility of English air attacks it would be better to break off the talk now, since the main issues had probably been sufficiently discussed.

Summarizing, he stated that subsequently the possibilities of safeguarding Russia's interests as a Black Sea power would have to be examined further and that in general Russia's further wishes with regard to her future position in the world would have to be considered.

In a closing remark Molotov stated that a number of important and new questions had been raised for Soviet Russia. The Soviet Union, as a powerful country, could not keep aloof from the great issues in Europe and Asia.

Finally he came to speak of Russo-Japanese relations, which had recently improved. He anticipated that the improvement would continue at a still faster pace and thanked the Reich government for its efforts in this direction.

Concerning Sino-Japanese relations, it was certainly the task of Russia and Germany to attend to their settlement. But an honorable solution would have to be assured for China, all the more since Japan now stood a chance of getting "Indonesia."

SCHMIDT
BERLIN, November 15, 1940.

Part III

1941

Fuschl, January 21, 1941

Record of the conversation between the Führer and the Duce in the presence of the foreign minister and Count Ciano, as well as Field Marshal Keitel, General Jodl, General von Rintelen, and the Italian Generals Guzzoni and Marras, on January 21, 1941

[This conference was preceded by a strictly military discussion of Field Marshal Keitel with General Guzzoni on Jan. 19. The record of this meeting, together with the OKW record of Hitler's remarks on Jan. 20, is printed as document No. 134-C, *Trial of the Major War Criminals,* vol. XXXIV, pp. 462-471; English translation in *Nazi Conspiracy and Aggression* (Washington, Government Printing Office, 1946), vol. vi, pp. 939-946.]

Coming in the midst of the Italian debacle in Greece and North Africa, it should be noted how those embarrassing situations were not even hinted at by Hitler in his discussion with Mussolini.

In the course of the conversation, the Führer gave a comprehensive presentation of the military situation at the present moment. He stated that the German forces assembling in the Romanian area far exceeded the numbers that would be used for direct operations in Greece. At the request of the Bulgarians a military force would be made ready to intercept a possible attack by the Russians from the north in the region of Constanţa. A second military force would be assembled in Romania in order to prevent a possible concentric attack by the Russians from the north and east, aimed at Galaţi. The transportation of these forces placed a considerable burden on the railroad lines required for that purpose; and yet the entire number of troops which had been transported would not make an appearance in Greece. The crux of the matter was that these forces would be transported through Hungary by shoving them into the normal schedules of the Hungarian railroads and could only be committed in the course of the month of March. The bridge construction necessary for crossing the Danube would require 14 days to 3 weeks. As soon as the crossing of the Danube started, however, the English could be expected to attack the oil fields of Ploeşti. The aerial defense had therefore to be organized simultaneously with the assembling of the troops, since the distance from the English bases on Greek territory to the Romanian oil fields was only about 600 kilometers, that is, not greater than the distance from London to Berlin. Under these conditions, the beginning of open military action would have to be put off as long as possible in order, in the meantime, to make the defenses of the vulnerable points as effective as possible.

With regard to Albania, the Führer remarked that if a German force were sent there and did not take part in the military action, it would represent a significant psychological burden. It was to be expected, moreover, that the English would attack if German troops participated in the fighting. If the German plans were revealed too early, an English attack on the bridge of Cernavodă and on the preparations for crossing by the German troops had to be expected, with the result that construction of the bridge would be again delayed. The best tactics in these circumstances would therefore be to carry out the concentration of the German troops as far as possible without enemy interference, to cross the Danube as late as possible, and to begin the attack as early as possible after the crossing.

The layout of the whole plan was determined by Russia's attitude. Germany could not at the moment withstand a serious Russian threat in view of the 34 Russian divisions concentrated on the Romanian frontier. A relief at other places on the German-Russian frontier was not possible until May. The Russians were absolutely clear about this state of affairs. In no circumstances did they want a consolidation of Balkan affairs under Italian leadership.

Germany's difficulties lay in the fact that she had to maintain an army at a great distance from her own territory and was dependent on other countries, being agreeable as regards transportation and supply.

The question whether it was possible to clear out the English bases in the Aegean Sea was hard to answer. By occupying Crete the English had in any case acquired a very broad base. An additional factor was that the new American long-range bombers could travel a distance of 4,500 kilometers, provided only that adequate airfields were available for the heavy machines. Practice had shown, for one thing, that airfields could not be destroyed. The situation was such, therefore, that there could be no real relief before the end of March, but that attacks on the Romanian oil regions were entirely possible. As regards Turkey, the Führer remarked that she would not dare to intervene against Germany. It would be worse, however, if Turkey were to make some airfields available to the English.

Turning to the situation in the West, the Führer remarked that he would launch an attack upon England only if its success were absolutely certain, because if it failed no second attempt could be made in view of the gigantic machinery involved. In case of a failure, England would at once be able to release forces which she could, on the one hand, use in her production, and on the other hand, dispatch to other theaters of war. Whether an attack on the British Isles would be carried out depended on whether or not conditions demonstrated that the odds were high on the probability for success. It was Germany's aim to do everything to carry out such an attack, but all the factors coming into consideration had to be very soberly weighed against each other. The weather played an essential role. If there were fine weather for 5 days in succession, the English fighter force could be completely destroyed.

After referring to the huge battery positions which Germany had constructed on the north French coast, the Führer stated that the decision in the air would depend on the quality of the machines which the opposing air forces would put into action next spring Germany was putting up many new types, whose superiority or inferiority in relation to the new enemy planes was yet to be demonstrated. The German fliers fought courageously, but the English, too, were very brave, for they knew that they were fighting for the existence of a world empire.

The Führer then discussed the German front, which extended from Norway to Biarritz. Kirkenes was important because of its ore exports; Trondheim and other ports, as submarine construction centers and bases; and the North Sea coast down to the Atlantic coast of France, as bases for

German airplanes and U-boats.

The Sicilian Strait could, in his estimation, be blockaded from the air, but that was only a poor substitute for the possession of Gibraltar and the African shore lying opposite it, whereby, for example, the rail communications between Morocco and Algiers would be disrupted, and the Axis position in North Africa in general could be strengthened to such a point that all blackmail by the French would cease at once. In the present situation one had to give in to the French on many points in order to prevent a declaration of independence by French North Africa which involved the danger of a French attack upon Tripoli.

In this connection the Führer underlined how important it was for the Duce to make another appeal to Franco. What was at stake was not only the occupation of Gibraltar and the strategic advantages of the African territory across from it, but also the possibility of establishing German submarine bases on the Spanish Atlantic coast, which would be less exposed to English air attacks than the French submarine ports. A period of 20 days was necessary before the German units would stand before Gibraltar, ready for commitment. Difficulties would arise in regard to transporting them and maintaining their ammunition supply because only one railroad line, with a different gauge, was available on the Spanish side; it might be possible, however, in the further course of the operation, to get France to permit the use of the other railroad line to Spain.

He (the Führer) saw no danger in an intervention by the United States. Only the existence of the Russian colossus, which tied up important forces, was disagreeable, just as was the opaque attitude of the French. For economic reasons Germany would prefer to discharge 60 divisions, in order to use them in production.

After a remark about the length of time needed for the training of officers and men for the special tasks of present-day warfare, especially in the Luftwaffe and the tank arm, the Führer stressed the fact that the present war would at a certain moment become exclusively an air war. In view of this, huge quantities of planes and antiaircraft batteries were needed, particularly because antiaircraft guns had to be replaced at a faster rate than ordinary artillery, and also because keeping them supplied with ammunition was more difficult. Production, therefore, had to be concentrated primarily on the antiaircraft arm. The supplying of antiaircraft ammunition was assuming progressively tremendous proportions. If certain parts of Germany were bombed night after night, the demand for antiaircraft ammunition mounted at an extraordinary rate. Naturally Germany was returning the English air attacks eightfold. She was in a much more favorable position with respect to England not only in regard to the number of planes available, but also because of the much shorter distances involved (less use of fuel, larger amounts of explosives). In the last large-scale attacks, explosives were dropped on England at the rate of one ton per plane, in addition to countless incendiary bombs.

Going on to the subject of the battle in North Africa, the Führer remarked that the appraisal of the situation there was essentially a matter for the Italian commanders; he emphasized, however, how extremely important it was that the Italians should hold the position because it might possibly be needed as a point of departure for clearing up the Morocco question. So long as this question remained unsettled, Germany could not take any serious step against the French government. All she could do was to threaten the French Cabinet through the Paris press. At Vichy the reins were in the hands of the reaction and the Church. Both were foes of Germany. Pétain made declarations of loyalty because he could make no other declarations. It was necessary to be very cautious toward the French. Therefore he (the Führer) was also opposed to releasing more ships to them for their African possessions. According to reports received in Germany, the French, to be sure, had withdrawn their forces in Morocco to the west and had only about 20,000 troops stationed at the border of Tripolitania. In the internal political field there was a certain competition among the individual leading generals, Pétain, Weygand, Noguès, Huntziger, etc. In their inward negative attitude toward Germany, however, they were all united.

Regarding the German-Russian relationship the Führer remarked that Germany was bound to Russia through treaties. Her security, however, was based not on the treaties, but on the troops at her disposal. So long as Stalin, who was shrewd and cautious, lived, Russia would certainly not attempt anything against Germany. But it was not yet known who his successor would be. Therefore Germany had to be strong. The treaties with the Russians all suffered from a one-sided interpretation of their provisions by the Soviet Union. The Führer illustrated this remark with the example of Lithuania, which at first lay in the German sphere of influence, but then was claimed by the Russians as the result of a somewhat one-sided interpretation of the treaty; likewise, Russia's interpretation of the guarantee agreements with the Baltic States as implying the complete absorption of these states represented something unique.

Russia had offered a mutual assistance pact to Bulgaria, too, but had significantly added the somewhat singular sounding assurance that she did not intend to undertake anything against the Bulgarian king. It was necessary, therefore, to be very cautious in dealings with the Russians. They were constantly looking for points in the treaties on which new demands could be based. In their treaty agreements, therefore, like Jewish lawyers, they preferred vague formulations and liked to base their arguments on ambiguous definitions that were capable of various interpretations. In their trade agreements they operated on a big scale, but only a part of these had thus far been realized. Russia was a gigantic state that one could not leave out of sight and which constituted an important factor in all combinations. No operation of a military nature could be undertaken without considering Russia. There was nothing to be feared from the army, but in the era of aviation the danger of an attack by the Russian air force was not to be underestimated. If the Romanian oil fields, for instance, were attacked not only by the English but also by the Russians, they would in a very short time be turned into smoking heaps of rubble. In Finland the Russians would not undertake anything warlike, for they hoped to become masters of the country through peaceful penetration. Precisely in this point, however, the Finns had considerable power of resistance.

The danger spots of the present situation were Russia and Algeria. The second point, however, would at once be eliminated as an element of danger if Gibraltar came into the hands of the Axis.

The Führer then brought up the subject of Tripolitania. He pointed out that there would be no object in keeping German units there inactive for months. The blocking forces of antitank troops which were to be sent to western Tripolitania, brought with them their experience of the war against France. They had their baptism of fire behind them and were well trained. And precisely the training of tank troops was a lengthy affair. Even crews whose training had already been completed required from 4 to 6 months of practice to become efficient on new types.

The Führer then discussed at length the problems connected with the armored troops and their employment, particularly the question of transportation and repairs, as well as the psychological qualifications of the crews. The blocking force that was to be sent would have to be sent into action. It must not be a parade unit. For psychological and propaganda reasons that could not be borne. It should not be said of the German units as was said of the English in France1 namely, that they let the other partner do the fighting, while they themselves looked on. The unit to be sent to western Tripolitania would therefore have to arrive there at a time when fighting was still climatically possible for German troops.

As for the three English divisions allegedly shipped from Alexandria to Salonika, the report had not yet been confirmed.

The foreign minister stated at this point that only Churchill wanted to push the Greek venture more actively, while large groups in England would prefer to do nothing.

Continuing, the Führer inquired about the situation in the Dodecanese. Shipment of gasoline to the islands, no doubt, was possible only by submarine. Anyway, there were a good number of bases for land and sea planes there. Only dive bombers could be used successfully against armed ships. Every time an English ship was damaged or sunk, wherever this might be, it was an advantage for Germany, for she wished to reduce the available tonnage as radically as possible. Dive bombers could fly from the Bulgarian bases to the Dodecanese and from there carry on their operations against English shipping. The Führer demonstrated in detail by means of examples that the sinking of shipping tonnage hit England in her most vulnerable spot. The English might perhaps grow accustomed to living in caves, to having no more windows in their houses, etc., but if the food supply were not assured, they would have to give up the fight. It was therefore important for Germany to sink as many ships as possible, especially refrigerator ships, because their replacement would take a long time.

The sinking of three refrigerator ships in the past few weeks disorganized the meat ration in all England for 14 days.

In conclusion the Führer expressed the firm conviction that Germany would become master of the British Isles.

At the close, the conversation turned once more to the subject of Turkey. The Duce expressed the view that Turkey would remain at peace, and the Führer agreed, saying that active intervention in the conflict was improbable if only because of the armament situation of that country. The Turks knew, moreover, that Constantinople was extremely vulnerable from the air. Incendiary bombs would be enough to destroy the whole city. Explosive bombs were not needed for the purpose. The foreign minister remarked that the Turks would positively not attempt anything and, in fact, would not have stirred if Bulgaria had not pursued such a feeble policy. Bulgaria had only herself to blame for the attitude of Turkey and Greece, and for the blackmail by the Russians..

As the last point in the conversation the Führer discussed Romania. General Antonescu, who was a real fanatic, had made a good impression on him.

Romania's difficulties stemmed primarily from the fact that the first team of the present regime had been murdered and the second team was not equal to the tasks. It would be impossible in the long run to maintain the separation between the Leader of the State and the Leader of the Legion. Hard, cold reason dictated that one or the other must go. The Führer further expressed himself in terms of great esteem con-cerning General Antonescu and mentioned that on his next to the last visit, he had been given quite plainly to understand in advance that he would not be allowed to criticize the Vienna Award. Nevertheless, out of fanatical patriotism, he delivered a 3-hour criticism of the new territorial order. The Duce remarked that, in his opinion, Antonescu ought to assume overall leadership. The foreign minister pointed out that he must not, however, rule in opposition to the Legion, but rather in cooperation with the good elements in the Legion, and that Horia Sima could be given a high govern-ment office, perhaps the Foreign Ministry. In any case it was necessary to avoid creating the impression that Antonescu was being forced upon the Legion from the outside. Minister von Killinger would also have a part in seeing to it that a movement to make Antonescu the leader sprang up within the Legion itself.

SCHMIDT

Hitler and Matsuoka
March 27, 1941

Record of the discussion between the Führer and Japanese Foreign Minister Matsuoka in the presence of the Reich Foreign Minister and Ambassadors Ott and Oshima.
March 27, 1941

Memorandum by an official of the Foreign Minister's Secretariat

Berlin, April 1, 1941

[Yosuke Matsuoka (1880-1946) was Foreign Minister of Japan in 1940-1941 and a strong supporter of the Axis and Tripartite Pact with Italy and Germany. After meeting with Mussolini in Rome, Matsuoka went to Berlin for two meetings with Hitler and Ribbentrop. Then the Japanese

Foreign Minister traveled to Moscow, where he signed the Japanese-Soviet Neutrality pact. See David Lu, *Agony of Choice: Matsuoka Yosuke and the Rise and Fall of the Japanese Empire* (Lanham, MD: Lexington Books, 2002).]

After some words of welcome the Führer inquired how Matsuoka had found the long tiresome journey from Japan to Germany. Matsuoka replied that he had stood the trip very well, since especially on the journey across Siberia he had been completely cut off from the outer world and had only been able to see from time to time a small Siberian provincial newspaper, in which practically no reports on current events appeared. It had been therefore much like being away on a holiday trip.

Then the Führer gave a review of the general situation. Germany had been forced into the war. She had not, however, been surprised by the war; for she had had the chance to observe for years the campaign of hate carried on by certain English, French, and American circles, and was accordingly prepared for anything. In spite of this basic preparation the outbreak of war had not been one of the goals of her policy. Germany had had political claims; she had hoped, however, to be able to satisfy them by reasonable methods. In the year 1939 the previously successful methods of securing a peaceful revision of intolerable conditions had been interrupted by the resistance of Poland and the consequences which arose therefrom.

If a person considered the present situation carefully and without illusions, he would have to concede that when the war began in the year 1939, there were in existence on the side of the opposition 60 Polish, 6 Norwegian, 18 Dutch, 22 Belgian, and 138 French divisions. In addition there were 12 or 13 British divisions on the Continent. Yet in scarcely a year and a half 60 Polish divisions had been eliminated with the occupation of Poland, 6 Norwegian divisions with the occupation of Norway, 18 Dutch divisions with the occupation of Holland, and 22 Belgian divisions with the occupation of Belgium, and of the 138 French divisions there remained only 8 weak brigades. All of the English units had been routed and driven out. These were losses which could not be recouped and the position of England was no longer recoverable. Thus the war had been decided, and the Axis powers had become the dominant combination. Resistance to their will had become impossible.

As Matsuoka knew Germany had only at the beginning of the war set out to construct a navy. Nevertheless all of the military operations which had necessitated the use of water routes, especially those in Norway, had been carried out without successful opposition by the English. The German U-boats, as well as the surface craft (auxiliary cruisers and battle-ships), had, in cooperation with the Luftwaffe, caused England losses which amounted in tonnage almost to three-quarters of the English and Allied losses during the World War. At first Germany had produced few U-boats. By far the greater number of them had therefore been used to train new crews for the numerous units which were being constructed by mass production. The real U-boat warfare was just beginning in the present and coming months. England would be damaged to an extent far sur-passing her present rate of losses and would no longer be able to threaten the German coasts and shipping routes in any way, Besides, Germany was tying down an increasing percentage of the English fleet in the North Sea and in the Atlantic. The same was being done by the Italian fleet and the German Luftwaffe in the Mediterranean.

In the air Germany had absolute supremacy, in spite of all the claims of the English to success. Matsuoka could test this assertion if he looked about in Berlin and compared present-day Berlin with present-day London. The attacks of the Luftwaffe in the coming months would actually grow much stronger. England would suffer even more severe losses in tonnage; and the effectiveness of the German blockade was demonstrated by the fact that in England rationing was much more severe than in Germany. In the meantime the war would go on in preparation for the final stroke against England.

The Führer then took up the situation in the Mediterranean and declared that Italy had had bad luck in North Africa because the necessary antitank guns had not been available against the British armored forces. Now the danger had been eliminated with the arrival of the first Panzer division in Tripolitania, which would soon be followed by a second division, A further British advance would be impossible; on the contrary, the Axis would in a short time pass over to a counterattack.

Unfavorable weather conditions had hindered Italian operations in the Balkans. In the next few days, however, the joint advance of Germany and Italy would eliminate all difficulties there. There was no military problem since Germany had at her disposal 240 "unemployed" divisions, of which 186 were first-class combat divisions. The losses in personnel and material which had been suffered campaigns just past, Germany was stronger in every respect than in 1939.

The Führer then spoke of his conviction that England had already lost the war. It was only a matter of having the intelligence to admit it. Then would occur the collapse of the individuals and of the government which had been responsible for the insane policy of England.

In her present critical situation England was looking for any straw to grasp. She was relying principally on two hopes:

First, on American help. Germany, however, had taken such help into her calculations in advance. It could appear in tangible form only in the year 1942 at the earliest, but even then the extent of such help would bear no relation to the increased productive capacity of Germany.

The second hope of England was Russia. Both the British Empire and the United States hoped that in spite of everything they would be able to bring Russia in on the side of England. They believed that they could attain this goal, if not this year, perhaps next, and thus produce a new balance of power in Europe.

In this connection it should be noted that Germany had concluded well-known treaties with Russia, but much weightier than this was the fact that Germany had at her disposal in case of necessity some 160 to 180 divisions for defense against Russia. She therefore did not fear such a possibility in the slightest and would not hesitate a second to take the necessary steps in case of danger. He (the Führer) believed, however, that this danger would not arise.

Concerning the German war aims in Europe, the Führer said that in any circumstances British hegemony would be destroyed, British influence would be excluded from Europe, and any attempt at American interference in Europe would be beaten back. In addition, an indispensable element of the new order on the European Continent would be the limitation of rights and duties to those who lived on the Continent, and the exclusion of all countries who wished only to interfere from the outside, especially England and America. In the present conflict the Axis Powers were being supported spiritually, morally, and, in part, materially by Japan. The Tripartite Pact had through the cooperation of Japan made possible, for example, the supplying of German auxiliary cruisers in East Asia. Most important of all, it had had the effect of making America hesitate to enter the war officially. On the other hand, through her effort in the conflict, Germany had brought her Japanese partner appreciable assistance for Japan's own future. Few situations could be envisaged which offered greater facilities land. Increasingly powerful English forces were being pinned down in the Mediterranean. Also on the oceans more powerful units were being required for convoy service. Cruisers and destroyers were no longer found to be sufficient, since these convoys were being attacked by the Germans with battleships. For in contrast with the World War, Germany possessed today on the long front from Narvik to the Spanish-French frontier numerous bases from which she could attack England and her approaches with naval forces. Thus England was tied down in Europe; the objective was the destruction of the British world empire,

America was confronted by three possibilities: She could arm herself, she could assist England, or she could wage war on another front. If she helped England, she could not arm herself. If she abandoned England, the latter would be destroyed and America would then find herself confronting the Powers of the Tripartite Pact alone. In no case, however, could America wage war on another front.

Thus there could never in human imagination be a better condition for a joint effort of the Tripartite Pact countries than the one which had now been produced. On the other hand it was also clear to him that in any historic act some risk had to be taken in the bargain. Seldom in history, however, had a risk been smaller than at present: While war was being fought in Europe and England was occupied there, and while America was only in the initial stages of her own armament, Japan was the strongest power in the East Asia area and Eussia could not intervene, since on her western border stood 150 German divisions. Such a moment would never return. It was unique in history. The Fiihrer admitted that there was a certain amount of risk, but it was extraordinarily slight at a moment in which Russia and England were eliminated and America was not yet ready. If this favorable moment passed by and the European conflict ended in some fashion with a compromise, France and England after a few years would recover. America would join them as a third enemy of Japan and Japan sooner or later would be confronted with the necessity of undertaking the defense of her Lebensraum in a struggle against these three Powers.

Even from the military point of view there had probably never in the memory of man been a situation so relatively favorable as at present, even though the military difficulties presented by a combined advance should not be underestimated.

It was especially favorable since between Japan and her allies there were no conflicts of interest. Germany, who would satisfy her own colonial claims in Africa, was as little interested in East Asia as Japan was in Europe. This was the best sort of preliminary condition for collaboration

with the Anglo-Saxons, on the contrary, never represented actual cooperation, but only a playing off of one against the other. Just as England never
tolerated the hegemony of one state in Europe, so in East Asia she played
off Japan, China, and Russia against each other, to further the interests of
her own world empire. Just as had England, so would the United States
conduct herself, if she inherited the world empire and set up American imperialism in place of British imperialism.

Also on personal grounds a better situation for joint action would
scarcely occur again. He (the Führer) had complete confidence in himself,
and the German nation stood united behind him as it had been behind no
one in its previous history. He had the necessary power of decision in
critical situations, and, finally, Germany had had an unparalleled series of
successes such as occurred only once in world history and was unlikely to
occur again.

In conclusion the Führer declared that his attitude toward Japan had not
been adopted in the year 1941. He had always been in favor of collaboration with that country. Ambassador Oshima knew that he (the Führer) had
worked resolutely for many years to that end. He was determined not to
depart from that line in the future. Especially favorable for collaboration,
as he had said, was the fact that there were no conflicts of interest between
Japan and Germany. For, in the long run, interests were stronger than
personalities and the will of a leader, and could always endanger anew the
cooperation of countries in case their interests were contradictory. In the
case of Germany and Japan, because of the nonexistence of such contra-
dictions, one could make long-term plans. This had been his firm conviction since his earliest youth. The Japanese, German, and Italian peoples
would achieve great successes if they drew the necessary conclusions from
the present unique situation.

Matsuoka thanked the Führer for his frank presentation, which seemed
to him to put the whole situation in a clearer light. He would think over
once more most carefully the arguments which the Führer had advanced,
although he had already deliberated at length on these subjects.

On the whole he agreed with the views expressed by the Führer. He
was especially of the opinion that any action which was determined upon
always carried with it a certain risk. Matsuoka declared—after referring to
the reports of Ambassador Ott and the Reich Foreign Minister, through
which the Führer would certainly be informed about the current situation
in Japan—that he would personally set forth the situation in the frankest
fashion. There were in Japan as in other countries, certain intellectual

circles which only a powerful individual could hold firmly under control^
He meant by that the sort of person who would like to capture the1 tiger
cub, but who was not prepared to go into the den and take it away from its
mother. He had used this line of thought in making: the same point in the
presence of two princes of the Imperial Family in a conference at headquarters. It was regrettable that Japan had not yet eliminated those
elements and that some of these people were even occupying influential
positions. Confidentially, he could state that in the interview at headquarters, after an earnest discussion, his point of view had prevailed. Japan
would take action, and in1 a decisive form, if she had the feeling that
otherwise she would lose a^ chance which could only occur once in a
thousand years; and in fact Japan would act without consideration of the
state of her preparations, since there were always some people who
claimed that preparations were insufficient. Matsuoka had also made this
point with the two princes. The hesitant politicians in Japan would always
delay and act partly from a pro-British or pro-American attitude.

Matsuoka declared that he had come out for the alliance long before the
outbreak of the European war. He had been very active at that time to this
end, but unfortunately he had had no success. After the outbreak of the
European war he personally had held the opinion that Japan should first
attack Singapore and bring to an end the British influence in that area and
should then join the Tripartite Pact, since he did not favor the idea that
Japan should join the alliance without having made some contribution
toward bringing about the collapse of England. While Germany had been
engaged in a titanic struggle against England for a year, Japan, up to the
conclusion of the alliance, had contributed nothing. He had therefore come
out very strongly for the plan of an attack on Singapore, but he had not
prevailed and, under the force of events, had then reversed his program
and had come around to the entry into the alliance first.

He had not the slightest doubt that the South Sea problem could not be
solved by Japan without the capture of Singapore. They would have to
press into the tiger's den and drag out the young by force.

It was only a question of the time when Japan would attack. According
to his idea the attack should come as soon as possible. Unfortunately he
did not control Japan, but had to bring those who were in control around to
his point of view. He would certainly be successful in this someday. But at
the present moment he could in these circumstances make no pledge on
behalf of the Japanese empire that it would take action.

He would after his interviews with the Führer and the Reich Foreign Minister, and after he examined the situation in Europe give his closest attention to these matters on his return He could make no definite commitment, but he would promise that he personally would do his utmost for the ends that had been mentioned.

Matsuoka then requested urgently that the representations which he had made be treated as strictly confidential, since, if they became known in Japan, those among his Cabinet colleagues who thought differently from him would probably become alarmed and would seek to get him out of office.

In connection with his efforts to bring about the treaty of alliance he had maintained strict secrecy up to the last minute and in order to deceive his opponents he had oftentimes intentionally given the impression of having a pro-American or pro-British attitude.

Shortly before the conclusion of the treaty of alliance it had been reported to him that the British ambassador1 was conducting a strong propaganda campaign among the Japanese to the effect that Japan was taking a very risky step in adhering to the Tripartite Pact. The American ambassador also had been active in the same direction. A few days after the conclusion of the treaty of alliance he had asked the American ambassador whether the reports about these propaganda activities were correct. The latter had admitted everything and had stated as well that every Japanese whom he had met, since the adherence to the treaty of alliance had become known, had expressed the opinion that Germany would win the war. In the opinion of the American ambassador that was false; Germany had no chance to win the war and therefore in the ambassador's opinion it actually was a very risky step for Japan if the alliance had been concluded in the expectation of a possible German victory.

Matsuoka continued that he had answered the American ambassador that only the good God knew who would finally win the war. He (Matsuoka) had, however, not concluded the alliance on the basis of the victory of this or the other power, but he had based his action on his vision of the new order. He had heard with interest the statements of the Führer on the subject of the new order and had been fully and completely convinced by them. If, however, he assumed entirely hypothetically that the fortune of war at some period would turn against Germany, he must tell the American ambassador that in such a case Japan would come at once to the assistance of her ally.

His vision of the new order had been set forth in the preamble to the Tripartite Pact. There was at stake an ideal, which had been handed down from one generation to another from time immemorial. For him personally the realization of that ideal was his life's aim, to which up to the present day he had dedicated his fullest efforts, in order to make on his own part a slight contribution toward its realization. The Berlin-Rome-Tokyo Tripartite Pact was also a contribution to such a realization. The consummation of this idea, so Matsuoka went on, would be realized under the slogan: "No conquest, no oppression, and no spoliation." This would not be understood in all quarters in Japan. If, however, Japan seemed likely to depart from this line he would be the first to attempt to prevent it.

In this connection, Matsuoka referred to still another principle of the preamble to the Tripartite Pact according to which every people must assume the place it deserved. Although if it were necessary, Japan, in the creation of the new order, would proceed by force, and although she must sometimes lead with a strong hand the peoples who would be affected by this new order, nevertheless she had always before her the slogan which he had previously quoted: "No conquest, no oppression, no spoliation."

In the further course of the conversation, Matsuoka referred to his conference with Stalin in Moscow. As an ally he owed an explanation on that subject to the Reich Foreign Minister and he would have given it in the course of the morning's conversation if the Reich Foreign Minister had not been called away early. Now he would give this information to the Führer.

He had first only wanted to make a courtesy call on Molotov on passing through Moscow. After some consideration, however, he had decided to instruct the Japanese ambassador to make discreet inquiry of the Soviet government whether the latter would be interested in an interview between Stalin and himself. However, before the Japanese ambassador had been able to carry out his instructions with the Soviet government, a proposal was made by the Russian government itself for a meeting between Stalin, Molotov, and Matsuoka. He had spoken with Molotov for about 30 minutes and with Stalin for an hour, so that, taking into account the necessary translations, he had conversed with Molotov for perhaps 10 minutes and with Stalin for 25 minutes.

He had told Stalin that the Japanese were moral Communists. This ideal had been handed down from father to son from time immemorial. At the same time, however, he had said that he did not believe in political and economic communism, and he rather assumed that his Japanese ancestors had much earlier given up any attempt in that direction and had turned to moral communism. In connection with what he called moral communism, Matsuoka cited several examples from his own family. The Japanese ideal of moral communism had been overthrown by the liberalism, individualism, and egoism introduced from the West. At the moment the situation in Japan in this field was extraordinarily confused. However, there was a minority which was strong enough to fight successfully for the restoration of the "Old Ego" of the Japanese. This ideological struggle in Japan was extremely bitter. But those who were fighting for the restoration of the old ideals were convinced that they would finally be victorious. The Anglo-Saxons were basically responsible for the entry of the new philosophy which he had mentioned, and, in order to restore the old traditional Japanese ideals, Japan was compelled to fight against the Anglo-Saxons, just as in China they were not fighting against the Chinese but only against Great Britain in China and capitalism in China.

Matsuoka then continued that he had discussed with Stalin his ideas about the new order and had stated that the Anglo-Saxons represented the greatest hindrance to the establishment of this order and that Japan therefore was compelled to fight against them. He had told Stalin that the Soviets on their part also were coming out for something new and that he believed that after the collapse of the British Empire the difficulties between Japan and Russia could be eliminated. He had represented the Anglo-Saxons as the common foe of Japan, Germany, and Soviet Russia.

Stalin had arranged to give him an answer when he passed through Moscow again on his return journey to Japan; he had, however, after some reflection stated that Soviet Russia had never gotten along well with Great Britain and never would.

Matsuoka in the further course of the conversation made several remarks about the status of the Tenno, the Tenno was the State, and the life and the property of every Japanese belonged to the Tenno, that is, to the State. That was, in a way, the Japanese version of the idea of the totalitarian state,

Further, Matsuoka expressed himself as marveling over the way in which the Führer with decisiveness and power was leading the German people, who stood completely united behind him through this great period of upheaval, a period without parallel in previous history. A people found such a Führer once in a thousand years. The Japanese people had not yet found their Führer. He would, however, certainly appear in time of need and with determination take over the leadership of the people.

SCHMIDT Minister

Record of the discussion between the Führer and Japanese Foreign Minister Matsuoka in the presence of the Reich Foreign Minister and Minister of State Meissner at Berlin, April 4, 1941

Memorandum by an official of the Foreign Minister's Secretariat.

Berlin, April 4, 1941

Matsuoka first thanked the Führer for the gifts which had been presented to him in the Führer's name, which he said he would treasure forever in an honored place as a perpetual remembrance of his stay in Berlin. At the same time he expressed his thanks for the friendly reception which he had received in Germany from the Führer, the Reich foreign minister, and the whole German people. As long as he lived he would never forget the sympathy which had been displayed toward him here on all sides. On his return to Japan he would exert himself with all his power to convince the Japanese people of the sincere friendship and esteem in which they were held by the German people.

Next Matsuoka reported concerning his conversations with the Duce and the pope.

With the Duce he had discussed the European situation in general and the state of the war, as well as the relationship of Italy to Germany and the future course of world development. The Duce had informed him (Matsuoka) of his views of the situation of the war in Greece, Yugoslavia, and North Africa and of the part which Italy herself had in these events. Finally the Chief of the Italian government had spoken of Soviet Russia and America. He had said that one must have a clear notion of the importance of one's opponents. The enemy No. 1 was America, and Soviet Russia came only in second place. By these remarks the Duce had given him to understand that America as enemy No. 1 would have to be very carefully observed, but should not be provoked. On the other hand one must be thoroughly prepared for all eventualities. Matsuoka had agreed in this line of thought.

With regard to Soviet Russia the Duce had spoken only briefly and to the same effect as had the Führer and the Reich foreign minister. In that connection also Matsuoka had agreed with him.

As the deepest impression which he was bringing back from his conversation with the Duce, Matsuoka mentioned the sense of complete unity between Italy and Germany, whose relations, in his firmly determined not to let this position be shaken. Matsuoka felt this previously, but his conviction after his conversation with the Duce was stronger than ever. On his return to Japan he would try to drive home this fact, especially with those Japanese who continued to believe that Italy could be persuaded by Great Britain, perhaps not to become detached from Germany completely, but at least to cease to fight with her whole heart for the common cause.

Count Ciano, with whom he was personally friendly, had informed him that he did not always completely understand the policy of the Führer, but that nevertheless he had implicit confidence in him and his decisions.

With the pope he had had an open and friendly conversation lasting for an hour and a quarter, which was concerned in a more theoretical fashion with the present situation and the future development of civilization. They had not spoken of the war, so that it would be hardly useful to describe the conversation any further to the Führer. At his departure Matsuoka had asked the pope whether or not the latter perceived any opportunity or chance for bringing about peace. After brief consideration the pope had said "No," and on his part asked Matsuoka whether or not he discerned any possibilities of peace. Matsuoka had also replied in the negative. The pope had added only that nevertheless he prayed daily for peace and he requested Matsuoka to do the same, which the latter promised to do. In addition the pope declared that if Japan saw any possibility of peace he would be glad to give his assistance.

Matsuoka further reported that he had told the pope that during the World War he had served in the Foreign Office in Tokyo as private secretary to the then prime minister, and that, in that capacity, he had sought to persuade the prime minister and Field Marshal Yamagata to establish communication with the Vatican for the purpose of bringing about peace. Both had been favorable in principle but they had not had the boldness to put the idea into actual operation.

Matsuoka added that he had been led to undertake these peace efforts principally in view of the personality of Cardinal Gasparri.

Further, he had sought to convince the pope that the United States and especially the American president were prolonging the war in Europe and in China. It was not a matter of proving whether America and her president were right or wrong. They would certainly have definite grounds for their policy. Entirely apart from the question of right or wrong, the fact would have to be recognized that they were prolonging the war in Europe and in China. In connection with China he had sought to convince the pope that Japan was not fighting against the Chinese or China herself, but only against Bolshevism, which was threatening to spread over China and the whole Far East. It was regrettable that America and England stood on the side of Bolshevism.

The Führer here interjected that both countries had stood on the side of Bolshevism in Spain as well.

Matsuoka then advanced the request that the Fiihrer should instruct the appropriate authorities in Germany to meet the desires of the Japanese Military Commission as fully as possible. Especially in the field of U-boat warfare, Japan required German help in the way of furnishing the latest operational experience and the newest technical improvements and discoveries. Japan would do everything in her power to avoid a war with the United States. In case his country determined on a stroke against Singapore, the Japanese navy must, of course, also make preparations against the United States, for in such a case America might possibly come out on the side of Great Britain. Personally, he (Matsuoka) believed that he could by diplomatic means prevent the entry of the United States into the war on the side of Great Britain. The Army and Navy must, however, prepare for the worst, i.e., for a war against America. They believed that such a war might last over 5 years and would be fought out as a guerrilla war in the Pacific Ocean and South Seas. For this reason the experience derived by Germany in her guerrilla war would be most important for Japan. It was a matter of how such a war could best be carried on and how all the technical improvements of the U-boats, down to individual parts, such as periscopes and the like, could be made useful by Japan.

Summing up, Matsuoka asked the Führer to see to it that the improvements and discoveries in the naval and military fields should be made available to the Japanese by the competent German authorities.

The Führer agreed to this and added that Germany also considered a war with the United States to be undesirable, but that it had already been included in his calculations. In Germany the viewpoint was that America's performance depended upon her transport capabilities, which in turn would be limited by the tonnage available. Germany's warfare against shipping tonnage represented an appreciable weakening not only of England but of America also. Germany had made her preparations so that no American could land in Europe. She would wage a vigorous war against America with the U-boats and the Luftwaffe, and with her greater experience, which the United States had still to achieve, would be more than a match for America, entirely apart from the fact that the German soldiers were, obviously, far superior to the Americans.

In the further course of the conversation the Führer declared that if Japan got into a conflict with the United States, Germany on her part would take the necessary steps at once. It made no difference with whom the United States first came into conflict, whether it was with Germany or with Japan. They would always be intent upon disposing of one country first, not with the idea of then coming to an agreement with the other country, but with the idea of disposing of it next. Therefore Germany would, as he had said, promptly take part in case of a conflict between Japan and America, for the strength of the allies in the Tripartite Pact lay in their acting in common. Their weakness would be in allowing themselves to be defeated separately.

Matsuoka again repeated his request that the Führer should give the necessary instructions, so that the competent German authorities would make available to the Japanese the latest inventions and improvements of interest to them, for the Japanese navy must make preparations at once for a conflict with the United States.

With regard to Japanese-American relations Matsuoka continued that in his own country he had always declared that if Japan continued in the same fashion as at present, a war with the United States sooner or later would be unavoidable. In his view this conflict might better occur sooner than later. Accordingly, so his argument had run, should not Japan decide to act with determination at the proper moment and take the risk of a war against America? Exactly by such means the war might perhaps be postponed for generations, especially if Japan secured domination in the South Seas. In Japan, however, many people refused to follow this line of thought. In those circles Matsuoka was considered to be a dangerous man with dangerous ideas. He declared, however, that if Japan proceeded further along the present course she would someday have to fight and that this might happen under more unfavorable circumstances than at present.

The Führer replied that he had much sympathy for Matsuoka's position, since he had found himself in similar situations (the occupation of the Rhineland, and the resumption of full military independence). He had also come to the conclusion that in a period when he was still young and vigorous he should make use of favorable circumstances and take upon himself the risk of a war which was eventually unavoidable. That he had been right in taking this position had been demonstrated by events. Europe was now free, He would not hesitate a moment to reply at once to any extension of the war, whether by Russia or by America. Providence favored those who did not let perils overtake them, but who confronted them courageously.

Matsuoka replied that the United States or rather the statesmen who were in control there, had lately undertaken a last maneuver dition that Japan should permit shipments of rubber and tin from these areas to proceed unhindered to their points of destination in America, America would, however, fight Japan the moment she felt that Japan intended to enter the war with the intention of assisting in the destruction of Great Britain. With the English-oriented education which many Japanese had received, this sort of argument naturally was not without effect on the Japanese.

The Führer declared in this connection that this attitude of America meant no more than that as long as the British Empire remained, the United States would cherish the hope of one day being able to proceed together with Great Britain against Japan, while with a collapse of the Empire they would be completely isolated as against Japan and could accomplish nothing against her.

The Reich foreign minister here interjected that the Americans in any circumstances would seek to uphold the English power position in East Asia; that, however, this attitude showed how much they feared joint action on the part of Japan and Germany.

Matsuoka continued that it seemed important to him to give the Führer the true story about the actual situation in Japan. Therefore he must inform him of the regrettable circumstances that he (Matsuoka), as Japanese foreign minister, in Japan itself did not dare to say a word about the plans which he had set forth to the Führer and the Reich foreign minister. In political and financial circles it would do him much harm. He had once, previously, before he had become Japanese foreign minister, made the mistake of telling a close friend something about his intentions. The latter had apparently spread the matter about, so that every kind of rumor arose, which, although he always otherwise spoke the truth, as foreign minister he was bound energetically to contradict. Also, in these circumstances, he could not state how soon he would be able to hold a conference with the Japanese prime minister or with the Emperor about the questions which had been discussed. He would first have to go into developments in Japan closely and carefully, in order to determine a favorable occasion on which to give Prince Konoye and the Emperor the true picture about his real plans. The decision would then have to follow in a few days, for otherwise the problems would be talked to pieces. If he were not able to put through his plans, it would be an indication that he lacked sufficient influence, power of persuasion, and tactical ability. But if he could put them through, it would show that he had attained great influence in Japan. He personally believed that he would be able to put them through.

On his return he would admit to the Emperor, the prime minister, the navy and war ministers, if they asked, that the matter of Singapore had been discussed. He would, however, declare that this had been done only in a hypothetical way,

In addition Matsuoka expressly requested that nothing be cabled on the subject of Singapore, since he feared that by use of telegrams something might slip out. In case of necessity, he would send a courier.

The Führer agreed and assured him that he could rely fully and completely on German discretion.

Matsuoka replied that he had confidence in German discretion, but he could not, unfortunately, say the same thing for Japan.

After some personal farewell greetings the conversation came to a close.

SCHMIDT

Memorandum, by an Official of the Foreign Minister's Secretariat

Record of the conversation between the Führer and Admiral Darlan in the presence of the Reich Foreign Minister at the Berghof on May 11, 1941

[Admiral Jean-François Darlan (1881-1942) was Chief of Staff of the French navy, 1937-1941. Under the Vichy regime he became deputy prime minister in February 1941, as well as minister of foreign affairs, of the interior, and national defense. He met with Hitler in May 1941, where he came very close to joining the Axis in a military collaboration. In April 1942 he was replaced by Pierre Laval, but remained in the Vichy government. On November 7, 1942, he was in Algiers when the Allies landed in French North Africa. Darlan remained in charge of the French Empire, but was assassinated by a young Gaullist on December 24, 1942.

See: William Langer, *Our Vichy Gamble* (New York: A. Knopf, 1947); Jean-Baptiste Duroselle, *Politique étrangère de la France: L'abîme: 1940–1944* (Paris: Imprimerie nationale, 1982, 1986); Henri Michel, *Darlan* (Paris: Hachette, 1993); Arthur L. Funk, *The Politics of Torch* (Lawrence: University Press of Kansas, 1974).]

Darlan first transmitted Marshal Pétain's greetings to the Führer and then thanked him for the great honor which the Führer had accorded <u>him</u> by this reception, which took place on the day commemorating Joan of Arc, i.e., the day honoring the French national heroine who drove the English out of France. Darlan also thanked the Führer for the concessions made with reference to the demarcation line and for the reduction in the occupation costs which Germany had granted.[1]

Moreover he (Darlan) welcomed this opportunity to stress once more the extent to which Marshal Pétain and he himself were convinced of the need for cooperation between France and Germany. Ever since the German army won its lightning victories, the strength and invincibility of the Wehrmacht had become obvious. Not only was the Führer the inspired creator of this instrument of power, but he also knew how to use it with unequaled strategic skill. Darlan stated in this connection that he himself, as a fighting man, had on a more modest scale created the French navy as an instrument of power and had also commanded it. Therefore he knew that the prerequisite for the effectiveness of such a weapon was the creation of a moral climate. In this task, too, the Führer had been exceptionally successful; he had completely transformed the spirit of the German nation and reorganized the relations of the separate parts of this nation with one another on the basis of National Socialist theory.

In a similar manner the new order could also develop the relations between the nations of Europe within the framework of a European hierarchy.

The Führer had conquered Europe. The formation of a European confederation of states therefore depended on him. He alone was qualified to bring about this development. To be sure, the permanence and continuity of such a European confederation required the voluntary and sincere cooperation of all its members. From this there also followed the unavoidable necessity of German-French collaboration.

He (Darlan) would direct French policy in this spirit, in agreement with Pétain. He was fully aware of the fact that France had been beaten and would have to assume the consequences of her defeat. France found a certain consolation in the fact that she had not been beaten by just any opponent, but by the Führer, who was more of a constructive than destructive spirit.

In the further course of his remarks Darlan then quoted a statement by Marshal Pétain, in which the latter expressed the wish for promoting the rapprochement between France and Germany but at the same time pointed out that at the moment France was unfortunately marching "in the dark"; he hoped that the Führer would light up the dark road along which France was moving, so that the French nation could get a clearer picture of its future,

In conclusion Darlan once more emphasized the confidence which Pétain and he himself had in the Führer and asked the latter to have the same confidence in the loyalty of Pétain and Darlan.

The Führer replied that he was a man who from personal disposition and a sense of responsibility had fought most for European understanding. Even now he did not understand why France and England had declared war on Germany. There were no practical or sensible reasons for it, unless the two countries wished to keep a great nation from existing. The declaration of war was made without any cause. For Germany had demanded nothing from either France or England. The tremendous disaster involved in a war such as the present one was out of all proportion to the colonial revision for which Germany was striving. Moreover, Germany had never presented these colonial demands in an urgent form or in a manner that would in any way have threatened the honor or the existence of France or England. On the other hand he (the Führer), a nationalist, had taken upon himself the grave sacrifice of waiving claim to a province, Alsace-Lorraine. He had hoped that this sacrifice would be acknowledged in such a manner that peace would thereby be assured for the future.

As late as September 1, 1939, he (the Führer) had implored French Ambassador Coulondre during a conversation with him that France should not make the mad decision to go to war.[1] The Polish conflict could easily have been localized. The German demands on Poland had been very moderate. The German city of Danzig was to have been returned to Germany, and for the rest a vote had been planned under international supervision. He (the Führer) had not declared his agreement to such international supervision because of weakness—the world had probably come to realize this in the meantime—but merely from his feeling of responsibility. The French ambassador had, however, taken an abruptly negative attitude and the British ambassador had even become insulting to the Führer. Thus, unfortunately, the armed conflict which was still going on, had come about. Not only Germany but also the other European nations were suffering as a result. France was doubly affected: by the suffering which she had had to undergo as the direct consequence of the war, and the difficulties which she was now experiencing because of the continuation of the conflict.

In the preamble to the armistice provisions it was stated that Germany's position must in no circumstances be injured or made more difficult as long as the war lasted. If the war had ended in June or July, all of the European nations would have benefited.

The Führer emphasized in this connection that he did not have the ambition to be a great military leader but was interested. rather, as the leader of his nation, in assuring the cultural and social advance of the German nation. Others had forced him to be a military leader. He would have been happy if the war had ended in June or July of last year, just as he had striven for peace after the Polish campaign. All nations would have benefited by such a peace. For no gain through war was in any proportion to the sacrifices imposed by war. In England, however, a few insane statesmen had wanted to continue the war. Therefore German policy was forced to take care of the needs arising out of the continuation of the war. The measures which were taken by Germany must therefore also be adapted to the war requirements. Germany was being forced to continue the war. She had tried, at the outbreak of the war in September 1939, to save the peace. The same was true after the Polish campaign. The action of the English, however, had compelled her to intervene in Norway and recently also in the Balkans. Lord Halifax had now openly stated that the English knew that Germany did not want to wage war in the Balkans and considered it a special victory on their part to have forced Germany into this war.[2] Therefore Germany had to safeguard for the future, too, the requirements growing out of the continuation of the war. Those who suffered were:

1. The German people, who had to shed their blood and sacrifice their men, time, and equipment;
2. The innocent European states which had been drawn into the conflict without any action on their part;
3. Those countries which themselves shared in the responsibility for the outbreak of the war; to this group belonged France.

If the English had not fanatically insisted on continuing the war, there would have been peace long since and all European countries could devote themselves to repairing the misfortunes of war and to reconstruction. It was not Germany's fault, at any rate, that this could not be done. The question now was whether, in the greater European interest of ending the war, one should not jointly oppose the incendiaries who constantly wished to feed the flames of war in Europe with new objects. Germany, at any rate, would fight until England was forced to her knees. This might possibly be the case in 3 months, but perhaps not for another year, or for 3 or 5 years; Germany, however, would never capitulate. In these circumstances the question arose whether other nations merely wished to watch this conflict as neutral observers, even though they could not escape its consequences.   The complaints presented by Admiral Darlan with reference to France could likewise be made by other countries. Only recently the English had tried to draw the Turks into the war; fortunately the members of the Turkish government had been clever enough to recognize this danger at once. As long as the war continued, suffering and hardships would continue to burden all of Europe.

On the other hand he (the Führer) knew that certain groups continued to nurse the hope that Germany would lose in the end after all. Even if this should happen, Europe would not gain, for nowadays the interests of Europe as a whole had to be considered, and in the eventuality mentioned one could rest assured that Europe's possessions in the world would be lost. At the same time Germany was not primarily threatened. Countries such as Holland, Belgium, and Portugal, with their large overseas possessions, and naturally France, too, with her colonial empire, and finally even England herself would be much more affected. For almost 20 years Germany's life had had a continental orientation. German chemistry would certainly do what was necessary to produce synthetically the materials necessary to the Reich, such as, for example, rubber and other raw materials. Moreover, Germany had assured herself a *Lebensraum* in Europe, so that she herself would be able to survive in any case. It was not a question, however, of what Germany would lose but of what Europe would lose. From that point of view he (the Führer) could not understand how anyone could rejoice if a European state, which was at present the strongest champion defending Europe's vital interests against non-European interests, should lose the war. An American imperialism was coming into being, and it should be recalled in this connection that France had at an earlier tune lost certain areas situated in America to the United States. Now it might happen that she would have to cede African territories to America as well. Those groups in France which still placed their hopes on England had to realize that the initiative no longer lay with Great Britain but with America. If little England had developed such a big appetite as to incorporate a quarter of the territories of the world into her empire, how big would be the land hunger of the much larger United States! In summary the Führer stated that:

    1. Germany was not to blame for the distress in Europe; the responsibility should be placed on English and French political leaders who started the war;

    2. Nor was it Germany's fault that the emergency in Europe continued.

    3. Germany was doing everything in her power to remove this aim, Germany did not by any chance want to rule and tyrannize Europe.

Being a nationalist he (the Führer) merely wished to be the leader of the German people and develop his own people culturally and above all socially. He was not interested in appearing as a great military leader; therefore he did not have any rank in the Army and wore no insignia of any kind, although he was the Supreme Commander. After peace was re-established he wished to be active only in a domestic colonization and as a social reformer. Thus he was actually fighting for peace, and he wondered what the others were doing to achieve this aim.

On the other hand it was natural that Germany should not be weakened in any way in her struggle and not miss her chances against England for reasons of being goodhearted. She and her ally alone were fighting the war against England. The sooner it could be ended, the sooner the European countries could be given relief. Today the German soldier was not giving his life for Germany alone, but was serving Europe as well by dying for peace. What were the others doing to end this period of suffering? It was obvious that the difficulties now prevailing with reference to the supply of food and consumer goods could not finally be removed until peacetime, after the millions who were now mobilized, about to be mobilized, or held prisoner in other countries, could be brought back into the process of production, where they would then produce consumer goods instead of shells. All measures which could be taken at the moment were merely emergency measures. France had to realize that real recovery could not begin until after England had finally been beaten. At present he (the Führer) could grant relief only within certain limits, i.e., only if Germany's position in the war benefited thereby, and in no circumstances if it were made difficult in any way. Therefore he always had to ask a compensation for any relief granted. He was no haggler, but acted in this manner only because the circumstances of the war forced him to do so.

Admiral Darlan thanked the Führer for his statements and agreed with his view that nothing definitive could be done until England was defeated.

He pointed out that since he joined the French government certain measures had been taken in agreement with Marshal Pétain, especially in the economic field, which clearly supported the spirit of French collaboration with Germany. In this connection he referred to the trucks sold in Tunisia and the airfields which were being made available in Syria. Compared to Germany's efforts this was little, to be sure, but Marshal Petain and he himself had agreed to these things in order to show to what extent they subscribed to German-French collaboration. They knew that they were exposing themselves to incurring the bad graces of England and perhaps even to an English attack on French territory. France was prepared to make the appropriate reply.

Marshal Petain thought it was important, however, to be able to tell the French, especially those in Syria, West Africa, and Morocco, whom he was asking to defend their territory against the English and also the Americans, that they were actually defending territory that would remain French. These French groups were constantly asking him why they should defend a territory which will after all be taken away from them later on. He (Darlan) understood that nothing definite could be said about these things until England was defeated. It would, however, greatly facilitate the work of the Marshal and his own work with the French people if the French government could somehow make it understandable to these overseas Frenchmen that they do not work for the "Roi de Prusse." Besides, it was the theme of English propaganda that it was of no use for the French to defend these territories because they would lose them in the end in any event.

Among the French at home, the question was raised time and again how one could cooperate with a Germany which had divided France into two parts, had imposed high occupation costs, and prevented the French government from governing the two parts uniformly. Every gesture which would ameliorate these difficulties in this respect and reduce the occupation costs would evoke a favorable reaction among the French people.

Regarding the question of food supply, Darlan remarked that by and large he considered it very salutary for the French to limit themselves in this respect, because before the war they had not given enough thought to the consequences of such a conflict. It was a good training in moral education but matters must not be pushed too far.

Furthermore, they were saying in France that it was difficult to collaborate with a country that was retaining so many French prisoners. Naturally there could be no talk of releasing all of the prisoners at once. It would probably be difficult for France to digest such a large number of returning soldiers. But a certain number of prisoners should, after all, be released. This too would create an exceedingly good impression in France.

In reply to the concern voiced by Darlan with respect to the French colonial empire, the Führer stated that he had already told Marshal Pétain that Germany had no intention of destroying the French colonial empire. Germany had also indicated as much on the occasion of the armistice negotiations; otherwise the armistice terms would have been quite different. Germany was merely demanding the return of the German colonies. This demand was known to France and did not affect the interests of her colonial empire. The demands of Germany's ally were also moderate. He had already told Laval that the colonial bill of this war would have to be paid by the English. Germany, at any rate, did not constitute a threat to the French colonial empire. She had incorporated huge areas east of the Reich, for the development of which she would need a century.

Moreover he (the Führer) was not a fanatic for space [Raumfanatiker], who strove to conquer as large a number of square kilometers as possible. He merely wished to guarantee the independence, existence, and economic well-being of Germany. It was up to France to keep her colonial empire and not to relinquish it to America.

With reference to the points raised by Darlan concerning metropolitan France the Führer remarked that the division of France into two parts was a military necessity. Germany needed a part of the French territory for the assembly of a strong army. She would be happy if she could again withdraw her troops. The Führer, however, had to be prepared for all eventualities, in case England should suddenly attack Portugal, or Spain and her colonies, and Tangiers; in the light of recent events in. the Balkans this did not appear impossible. Thirty-six to forty divisions had to be available for these purposes.

Moreover, the situation with respect to England might at a certain moment be clarified in such a manner that Germany would be able to strike the decisive blow against Great Britain. Admiral Darlan knew that Germany had maintained her preparations for this operation to a certain extent in order to be ready at any time. From all this it followed that the measures taken by German authorities in France were necessitated by the circumstances of the war. If the French government should be at war with England tomorrow, the points raised by Darlan would no longer present a problem. Furthermore, Germany still needed a certain guarantee with respect to France. Not the least important reason for Laval's falling into disfavor was his policy of collaboration with Germany. Until France undertook some decisive action in order to confirm her policy, the latter rested exclusively on Marshal Pétain, who was quite advanced in years, and on Admiral Darlan. If some madman should assassinate these leading personalities, the continuation of the French policy would no longer be guaranteed. With reference to the question of prisoners [of war] the Führer pointed out that the German prisoners were not released until 1920, although the war had ended long before that. For the duration of the war the prisoners not only meant a safeguard for Germany, but were also a safeguard for a France who was ready for an understanding. Their sudden return to France would probably, as Admiral Darlan had also indicated, create a serious crisis for the French government.

In the further course of the conversation the Führer also asked Admiral Darlan a few detailed questions: for example, what practical measures France would take in the defense of Dakar. Darlan replied that the Americans certainly had their eye on Dakar. Moreover, they were the ones who, according to reports received in France, had induced the British to attack Dakar in the autumn. To be sure, Dakar was not the only base that might be desirable to the Anglo-Saxons in this area. In addition there were the islands of the Azores, the Canary Islands, and the Cape Verde Islands. The latter were only of little interest, since they had insufficient anchorages, no drinking water or other supplies, and Dakar could take their place in every respect. The Canary Islands, on the other hand, had much better anchorages and supplies. Especially favorable was the situation of the Azores, the "turntable" of the Atlantic, with the two anchorages and the overseas cables converging from all directions.

Since the vigorous submarine campaign on the part of Germany the convoys to England had, moreover, been forced to use the southern route. Proof of this fact had again been provided just recently by a French merchantman, which was repeatedly stopped by British naval vessels between the Azores and the Canary Islands and had discovered on this occasion that the convoys from Canada and from the Cape of Good Hope assemble in the area between the Canary Islands and the Azores. The French ship, by the way, which had a British guard aboard, was liberated by French naval vessels. Thereupon the Führer remarked that England had not only lost every one of her European positions in this war, but would have to expect a terrible economic and social crisis internally, too, after the war was over. He had told Marshal Pétain at Montoire that naval warfare against England would not begin with full intensity until March and April. The figures of sinkings which the English themselves published, although they reported only 30 percent to 40 percent of their actual losses, confirmed this prediction.

The Führer then also spoke about Iraq. Germany was about to oppose the English in Iraq and was looking into the possibilities of doing this. He (the Führer) would be interested in hearing Darlan's opinion in the matter, especially with reference to the French forces stationed there. Darlan, who did not appear well informed about the particulars, replied that there were approximately two divisions of French troops in Syria, but that they did not have any modern equipment. Furthermore numerous airfields were available, some of which had been rendered useless by order of the Italians but could again be put in operation relatively quickly. He had given the list of these airfields to General Vogl.[3] Moreover, considerable stores of French aerial bombs were available. To be sure, France could not transfer any sizable reinforcements to Syria, since the English from their base at Cyprus would stop the transports.

He had no information concerning the forces available to the English in Iraq.

Otherwise Darlan repeated his offer to sell war material to Iraq through the intermediary of Minister Rahn, i.e., all rifles stocked up under Italian control as well as two-thirds of all stores of arms and ammunition. France needed the remaining third to equip her own troops in the event of an English attack. Finally, Darlan asked support for the French propaganda among the natives of Syria to the effect that France would in all circumstances retain the mandate over this area.

The Führer emphasized in his reply that Germany was as little responsible for the outbreak of the conflict in Iraq as for the spreading of the war to Greece and Yugoslavia. If Germany were behind the events in Iraq, she would certainly have made better preparations.

The Fuhrer then asked Darlan whether the French government would consent to letting the trucks purchased by Germany in Tunisia proceed to Tripoli with a load; since the unloading facilities of the harbors of Tripoli were being used to capacity, additional quantities of German equipment, which would be unloaded in French harbors and then transported to Tripoli with the help of these trucks, would in this manner be placed at Germany's disposal in North Africa. Darlan stated that, faithful to the policy on which he had embarked, he would answer this question in the affirmative;[4] however, he pointed out in this connection that the Italian delegation in Tunisia had also tried to buy trucks, which the French government, however, could in no circumstances relinquish unless it wished to provoke a revolution in the colony.

At the same time Italy was now also demanding airfields in Syria for her own planes. He did not know where Italy had learned about the German-French negotiations in this matter. General Vogl had at the time instructed him, Darlan, not to tell the Italians anything about it. In general, each time France made a concession to Germany the Italians demanded the same of the French, and this led to extraordinary difficulties. If, for example, Italy demanded trucks from France, he (Darlan) suggested that these vehicles be given to Germany and only then be handed over to Italy by the Germans. France was making concessions to Germany because she had been defeated by Germany; she had not been defeated by Italy, however, and therefore had no intention of making concessions.

The Führer replied that France should not make concessions to Germany as the victor but rather as the country which was fighting to end the war and therefore obtaining for France, too, the benefits of the efforts toward peace. Germany was fighting in North Africa to help her ally. Her own situation would be eased if this ally were to become strong enough to do its own fighting. Indirectly this would also benefit Germany.

Darlan replied that he ought to supplement his remark concerning France's concessions to Germany as the victor to the effect that Germany was the victor with whom France was engaged in conversations pertaining to close cooperation. France did not, however, consider it advisable to enter into conversations with Italy.

In conclusion Darlan asked the Führer to facilitate through granting concessions the task facing the present French government of getting the support of the majority of the French for the policy of collaboration. It should be kept in mind that official French propaganda had for 35 years done everything to orient French public opinion toward England and to educate it to admire everything English. Now public opinion had to be guided in the opposite direction. The concessions recently made by Germany had already reduced the number of Anglophiles in France. Therefore he was asking the Führer to grant France further concessions; they did not so much need to go very deeply as to be outwardly apparent (*des avantages plus spectaculaires que profonds*).[5]

After an interruption for tea the conversation was resumed with the help of a map of Syria. In addition to the above-mentioned persons, Minister von Hentig and Baron Benoist-Méchin took part in this conference.[6] The transport question was discussed and the observation made that the railroad leading to the so-called "duck's bill" of Syria, i.e., the strip of territory between Iraq and Turkey—which would be needed to transport the war materials to be delivered to Iraq—was in part on Turkish territory. The assumption was expressed that there existed a Turkish-Syrian treaty, on the basis of which the Syrian government could demand the transport of war material in sealed cars. The French stated that a more southerly route could not be used for these transports, since there was danger that the materials might fall into English hands.

On the basis of his travel experiences Minister von Hentig commented on the condition of the country in general, on the roads, some of which were very good in the dry season but were impassable hi the rainy season, as well as on the nature of the plains in the eastern areas, which offered the best possible conditions for landing planes. The French, who did not appear very well informed on the strength of the troops, stated that there were approximately two or three divisions of French troops in the country. They again pointed to the supply difficulties as long as Cyprus was not captured. At most an attempt could now be made to establish connections with Syria by loading the materials on small Turkish ships and utilizing Turkish territorial waters. "Complicity" by the Turks, however, was required in this case as also in others. After a discussion of further technical details of lesser importance the conversation was concluded and another conference with the Reich Foreign Minister in Fuschl was planned for the next day.

SCHMIDT

Record of the Duce's conversation with the Führer

The Führer's Headquarters,

August 25, 1941/XIX.

[Mussolini visited the Eastern Front in the Ukraine during the Barbarossa Offensive. This account is translated from a photostatic copy of an Italian version found in a collection of Italian Foreign Ministry documents brought to Lisbon during World War II. The originals were later returned to the Italian government. No official German text relating to this visit has been found. The Italian record below is the same as is printed in Galeazzo Ciano, *L'Europa verso la castastrofe* (Milan, 1948), pp. 609-675. Hitler's appointment book indicates that the visit lasted over 4 days, Aug, 25 to Aug, 28, when the Italian delegation started homeward at 8:00 p.m. ("Führer's Tagebuch 1934-1943," p. 77, deposited in the Library of Congress, Washington, D.C., Manuscripts Division, captured German documents).]

[Documents on German Foreign Policy]

I

In his first conversation with the Duce immediately after the latter's arrival at Headquarters, the Führer gave the Duce a general outline of the situation, together with a detailed account of the military developments.

The Führer began by acknowledging to the Duce that it had been a wise decision to liquidate Greece along with Yugoslavia before launching the Russian campaign. Greece and Yugoslavia were in reality two potential and active enemies of the Axis, and eliminating them in time proved a great advantage at the moment when it became necessary to take action against Soviet Russia in order to eliminate the grave Bolshevik menace and to achieve effective control of Europe.

The Führer then made a special point of acknowledging that for the first time since the beginning of the conflict, the German military intelligence service had failed. It had in fact not reported that Russia had a very well armed and equipped army composed for the most part of men imbued with a veritable fanaticism who, despite their racial heterogeneity, were now fighting with blind fury. The Bolshevik army as a whole could be viewed as made up of two large masses: one, the larger, consisting of peasants who fought with unreasoning obstinancy; and the other made up in the main of industrial workers who strongly believed in the words of Marx and fought with fanaticism. For opposite reasons, both were fighting to the last man; the former out of primitive ignorance, the latter because they were bewitched by the mystique of Communism.

The Führer added that he would not let himself be ensnared by the Soviets into continuing the battle inside cities by street fighting, for which the Russians were exceptionally well prepared. He had no intention of destroying the large cities, but would leave them to fall by themselves after he had won the battle of annihilation against the Soviet military forces emplaced around them. That was his plan for Leningrad, which had an urban area comprising about 4 million inhabitants. It would fall as soon as the total destruction of the Soviet forces ringing the city was accomplished. By avoiding street fighting, which yields no useful results, he would above all be able to save important forces.

The Führer had no doubt whatsoever as to the outcome of the struggle. He thought there was no point at the moment in dwelling on a consideration of what might at some future date become a line of resistance set up by the Soviets; he was inclined to believe that the Red military strength would inevitably collapse not later than October under the incessant blows that were being, and would be, inflicted upon them. A contributing factor, as time went on, would be the conquest, already begun and soon to be completed, of the major Soviet industrial centers and mining regions, for example the Don river basin. Whether this collapse would come soon, within a few months, or next spring, could be considered of secondary importance because already the means of victory were in Germany's hands. Inasmuch as the German losses to date, despite the fierceness of the struggle, had not exceeded the low figure of 68,000 men, and the war booty that had fallen into German hands was so immense, far exceeding the needs of the armed forces of the Reich, the Führer had decided to concentrate the production effort from now on exclusively on the construction of submarines, tanks, and antiaircraft artillery.

Regarding military plans for the future, the Führer told the Duce—in absolute secrecy—that after completion of the Russian campaign he intended to deal England the final blow by invading the island. To that end he was now marshaling the necessary resources by preparing the appropriate naval and land material needed for the landing. In the opinion of the Führer, that would mark the final act of the conflict. In dealing with that problem while the battle was still in progress in Russia. He had found justification for his feeling of distrust of the French, whom he was watching carefully and with respect to whom he intended to maintain a negative attitude. The French question would be taken up again at the end of the war.

Reverting to the Russian campaign, the Führer stated that the grain harvest in the Ukraine had in large part fallen into German hands. It should be borne in mind, however, that next year's Russian harvest must be used chiefly to supply the occupied countries. The Führer repeated his praise of the Finnish troops, who had fought admirably, and he had words of praise also for the Romanians, the Hungarians, and the Italians. Referring to these last, he said they had acquitted themselves in brilliant fashion in their first engagements.

The Führer's remarks were delivered in an orderly and precise manner, which conveyed an impression of absolute calm and serenity. It was for this reason, among others, that the Duce thought it appropriate to let the Führer develop his thoughts without interruption, and postpone to a subsequent conversation the specific questions he wanted to ask concerning the progress of the military operations and certain territorial problems.

II

In the course of the second conversation which the Duce had with the Führer on the evening of August 25, the Duce set forth his views on certain questions of major importance.

Turkey: Turkey, the Duce noted, was continuing to pursue a wavering policy between the Axis and England, and that policy was being closely watched. It might be profitable, he said, to make some new efforts to win Turkey over to our side by offering her some compensation and by using as a lever Turkey's sensitiveness about her military position. The Führer agreed with the Duce's thought. The attitude of Turkey naturally was influenced directly by the developments in the Russian campaign. Consideration might be given, however, to offering her perhaps a minor boundary rectification in Bulgarian territory and some future concession in Syria at the end of the war. The possibility of offering German armored forces could also be considered.

Crete: The Führer expressed to the Duce his desire to have an Italian division transferred to Crete to take the place of the German Alpine Corps, which he wished to send to the Russian front preparatory to operations in the Caucasus, The Duce gave his assent.

Spain: The Führer spoke in bitter terms about Spain, expressing his genuine and profound disappointment with that country had undergone prolonged training carried out with great enthusiasm and effectiveness. If Franco could have made up his mind in January or February, the big special 620 [mm.] heavy mortars (of which the Duce had seen two examples, the Thor and the Odin on his visit today to Brest Litovsk) would have been extremely effective against Gibraltar thanks to the crushing force of their 2,000 kg projectiles.

The Duce, while concurring with the Führer's thought, observed that for all practical purposes and given Spain's particular situation and special circumstances, it was pointless to bring further pressure to bear to induce her to take an active part. There was no question that she was already, and would increasingly be, impelled by her interests to support the Axis, and that therefore it would be useful to keep her in reserve at present and until the time came when the Spanish trump card could and would have to be played in our game.

France: With respect to France, the Duce outlined to the Führer the anomaly of the situation which had developed in the relations with that country. These were governed at present by the Armistice Agreement, but the Agreement no longer performed its function because its powers had been canceled by the development of events. It would therefore be necessary to talk to the French at a given moment, pro6ting incidentally from the fact that Pétain was in deep water as a result of the unending domestic and external difficulties with which he had to contend.

The Führer repeated to the Duce that the feelings he entertained toward the French were those of antipathy and distrust, and that he was fully aware of what the Duce had said concerning the anomaly of the relations between that country and the Axis Powers. He thought it advisable, however, to postpone any substantial and serious talks because it was essential, in order to strip the French of any hopes and illusions, to bring the campaign in Russia to a definitive conclusion.

Sweden: The Führer spoke in rather harsh terms about the Swedes, calling them cowards. Sweden maintained a treacherously hostile attitude toward Germany and raised endless difficulties to German requests for troop transit.

Switzerland: The Führer spoke in adverse terms also about Switzerland, which, while moving with great circumspection, entertained feelings of unadulterated aversion toward the Axis.

Japan: The Duce expressed his point of view concerning Japan, observing that that country had a complex and difficult domestic strongly animated by a nationalistic dynamism that caused her to gravitate to the Axis; in a certain sense her policy followed a straighter line than that of Spain. It was fairly probable that one day she would align herself with the Axis. It was therefore necessary to appraise her capabilities realistically and judge her present and future attitude.

United States: The Duce pointed out that the "Potomac meeting" had, in the last analysis, not caused Roosevelt's political stock to rise, and that, rather, it had even dropped somewhat since the declaration in question. However that might be, the attitude of the United States was now clear enough and, as matters stood, it was preferable to avoid any useless polemics.

The Führer gave a detailed analysis of the Jewish clique surrounding Roosevelt and exploiting the American people. He stated that he would not for anything in the world live in a country like the United States, which had a concept of life inspired by the most vulgar commercialism and had no feeling for any of the most sublime expressions of the human spirit, such as music.

The Mediterranean: The Führer stated that he was satisfied with the situation in the Mediterranean. The Duce agreed, noting that the new front opened up against Great Britain in Iran had relieved English pressure in the Mediterranean.

Italian participation in the campaign in Russia: The Duce expressed to the Führer his ardent desire for the Italian Armed Forces to participate in the operations against the Soviets on a larger scale. Italy, the Duce stated, has an abundance of manpower and could send an additional six, nine, and even more divisions. The Führer replied that he greatly appreciated that offer and thanked the Duce heartily. He added, however, that the great distance of the Russian front from Italy and the logistical difficulties would cause a serious problem with respect to transportation and the proper functioning of large masses of military forces. The Duce affirmed on his part that Italy could render a major contribution to the war effort against Russia, and suggested that further contingents of Italian troops be used to take the place of German troops sent on leave. The Führer took note of this proposal, which would be given further study, and touched upon the possibility of employing the Italian troops in the Ukraine, where the average winter temperature as a rule does not go lower than six degrees below zero [centigrade].

The Führer finally drove home one more point he had already made in his preceding conversation, namely that he did not intend to wage a war of destruction or for prestige; but a war of annihilation of the enemy armed forces in order to liberate Germany and Europe from the recurrent threat of conflict and create the necessary basis for constructing the new European order. He concluded by expressing his very keen desire, once the war was ended to come to Italy and spend some time in Florence, the city he preferred above all for the harmony of its art and the beauty of its natural surroundings, This project was enthusiastically received by the Duce, who immediately invited the Führer to come to Florence, once the war was over, and assured him of the affection and friendship with which the Italian people would welcome him again as their most honored guest.

*****

Memorandum by an official of the Foreign Minister's secretariat

Berlin, November 30, 1941.

Record of the conversation between the Führer and the Grand Mufti of Jerusalem on November 28, 1941, in the presence of Reich Foreign Minister and Minister Grobba in Berlin

[Fearing arrest in 1941 by the British, the Grand Mufti of Jerusalem Hadj Amin Al Husseini (1897-1974) had managed to escape from Teheran and Istanbul to Rome, where he met with Mussolini. Immediately after those meetings the Mufti traveled to Berlin for meetings with Hitler and Ribbentrop. The issue of the extermination of the Jews was brought up by Hitler in this meeting, where he made no secret of his intentions. See K. M. Mallmann and Martin Cüppers, *Nazi Palestine. The Plan to Exterminate the Jews in Palestine* (New York: Enigma Books, 2010).]

The Grand Mufti began by thanking the Führer for the great honor he had bestowed by receiving him. He wished to seize the opportunity to convey to the Führer of the Greater German Reich, admired by the entire Arab world, his thanks for the sympathy which he had always shown for the Arab and especially the Palestinian cause, and to which he had given clear expression in his public speeches. The Arab countries were firmly convinced that Germany would win the war and that the Arab cause would then prosper. The Arabs were Germany's natural friends because they had the same enemies as had Germany, namely the English, the Jews, and the Communists. They were therefore prepared to cooperate with Germany with all their hearts and stood ready to participate in the war, not only negatively by the commission of acts of sabotage and the instigation of revolutions, but also positively by the formation of an Arab Legion.

The Arabs could be more useful to Germany as allies than might be apparent at first glance, both for geographical reasons and because of the suffering inflicted upon them by the English and the Jews. Furthermore, they had close relations with all Moslem nations, of which they could make use in behalf of the common cause. The Arab Legion would be quite easy to raise. An appeal by the Mufti to the Arab countries and the prisoners of Arab, Algerian, Tunisian, and Moroccan nationality in Germany would produce a great number of volunteers eager to fight. Of Germany's victory the Arab world was firmly convinced, not only because the Reich possessed a large army, brave soldiers, and military leaders of genius, but also because the Almighty could never award the victory to an unjust cause.

In this struggle, the Arabs were striving for the independence and unity of Palestine, Syria, and Iraq. They had the fullest confidence in the Führer and looked to his hand for the balm on their wounds which had been inflicted upon them by the enemies of Germany.

The Mufti then mentioned the letter he had received from Germany, which stated that Germany was holding no Arab territories and understood and recognized the aspirations to independence and freedom of the Arabs, just as she supported the elimination of the Jewish national home.1

A public declaration in this sense would be very useful for its propagandists effect on the Arab peoples at this moment. It would rouse the Arabs from their momentary lethargy and give them new courage. It would also ease the Mufti's work of secretly organizing the Arabs against the moment when they could strike. At the same time, he could give the assurance that the Arabs would in strict discipline patiently wait for the right moment and only strike upon an order from Berlin,

With regard to the events in Iraq, the Mufti observed that the Arabs in that country certainly had by no means been incited by Germany to attack England, but solely had acted in reaction to a direct English assault upon their honor.

The Turks, he believed, would welcome the establishment of an Arab government in the neighboring territories because they would prefer weaker Arab to strong European governments in the neighboring countries, and, being themselves a nation of 7 millions, they had moreover nothing to fear from the 1,700,000 Arabs inhabiting Syria, Transjordan, Iraq, and Palestine.

France likewise would have no objections to the unification plan because she had conceded independence to Syria as early as 1936 and had given her approval to the unification of- Iraq and Syria under King Faisal as early as 1983.

In these circumstances he was renewing his request that the Führer make a public declaration so that the Arabs would not lose hope, which is so powerful a force in the life of nations. With such hope in their hearts the Arabs, as he had said, were willing to wait. They were not pressing for immediate realization of their aspirations; they could easily wait half a year or a whole year. But if they were not inspired with such a hope by a declaration of this sort, it could be expected that the English would be the gainers from it.

The Führer replied that Germany's fundamental attitude on these questions, as the Mufti himself had already stated, was clear. Germany stood for uncompromising war against the Jews. That naturally included active opposition to the Jewish national home in Palestine, which was nothing other than a center, in the form of a state, for the exercise of destructive influence by Jewish interests. Germany was also aware that the assertion that the Jews were carrying out the function of economic pioneers in Palestine was a lie. The work there was done only by the Arabs, not by the Jews. Germany was resolved, step by step, to ask one European nation after the other to solve its Jewish problem, and at the proper time direct a similar appeal to non-European nations as well.

Germany was at the present time engaged in a life and death struggle with two citadels of Jewish power: Great Britain and Soviet Russia. Theoretically there was a difference between England's capitalism and Soviet Russia's communism, actually, however, the Jews in both countries were pursuing a common goal. This was the decisive struggle; on the political plane, it presented itself in the main as a conflict between Germany and England, but ideologically it was a battle between National Socialism and the Jews. It went without saying that Germany would furnish positive and practical aid to the Arabs involved in the same struggle, because platonic promises were useless in a war for survival or destruction in which the Jews were able to mobilize all of England's power for their ends.

The aid to the Arabs would have to be material aid. Of how little help sympathies alone were in such a battle had been demonstrated plainly by the operation in Iraq, where circumstances had not permitted the rendering of really effective, practical aid. In spite of all the sympathies, German aid had not been sufficient and Iraq was overcome by the power of Britain, that is, the guardian of the Jews.

The Mufti could not but be aware, however, that the outcome of the struggle going on at present would also decide the fate of the Arab world. The Führer therefore had to think and speak coolly and deliberately, as a rational man and primarily as a soldier, as the leader of the German and allied armies. Everything of a nature to help in this titanic battle for the common cause, and thus also for the Arabs, would have to be done. Anything, however, that might contribute to weakening the military situation must be put aside, no matter how unpopular this move might be.

Germany was now engaged in very severe battles to force the gateway to the northern Caucasus region. The difficulties were mainly with regard to maintaining the supply, which was most difficult as a result of the destruction of railroads and highways as well as of the oncoming winter. If at such a moment, the Führer were to raise the problem of Syria in a declaration, those elements in France which were under de Gaulle's influence would receive new strength. They would interpret the Führer's declaration as an intention to break up France's colonial empire and appeal to their fellow countrymen that they should rather make common cause with the English to try to save what still could be saved. A German declaration regarding Syria would in France be understood to refer to the French colonies in general, and that would at the present time create new troubles in Western Europe, which means that a portion of the German armed forces would be immobilized in the west and no longer be available for the campaign in the east.

The Führer then made the following statement to the Mufti, enjoining him to lock it in the uttermost depths of his heart:

1.   He (the Führer) would carry on the battle to the total destruction of the Judeo-Communist empire in Europe,

2.   At some moment which was impossible to set exactly today but which in any event was not distant, the German armies would in the course of this struggle reach the southern exit from Caucasia,

3.   As soon as this had happened, the Führer would on his own give the Arab world the assurance that its hour of liberation had arrived. Germany's objective would then be solely the destruction of the Jewish element residing in the Arab sphere under the protection of British power. In that hour the Mufti would be the most authoritative spokes man for the Arab world. It would then be his task to set off the Arab operations which he had secretly prepared. When that time had come, Germany could also be indifferent to French reaction to such a declaration.

Once Germany had forced open the road to Iran and Iraq through Rostov, it would be also the beginning of the end of the British world empire, He (the Führer) hoped that the coming year would make it possible for Germany to thrust open the Caucasian gate to the Middle East, For the good of their common cause, it would be better if the Arab proclamation were put off for a few more months than if Germany were to create difficulties for herself without being able thereby to help the Arabs.

He (the Führer) fully appreciated the eagerness of the Arabs for a public declaration of the sort requested by the Grand Mufti. But he would beg him to consider that he (the Führer) himself was the Chief of State of the German Reich for 5 long years during which he was unable to make to his own homeland the announcement of its liberation. He had to wait with that until the announcement could be made on the basis of a situation brought about by the force of arms that the Anschluss had been carried out.

The moment that Germany's tank divisions and air squadrons had made their appearance south of the Caucasus, the public appeal requested by the Grand Mufti could go out to the Arab world.

The Grand Mufti replied that it was his view that everything would come to pass just as the Führer had indicated. He was fully reassured and satisfied by the words he had just heard from the Chief of the German State. He asked, however, whether it would not be possible, secretly at least, to enter into an agreement with Germany of the kind that the Führer had just outlined.

The Führer replied that he had just now given the Grand Mufti precisely that confidential declaration.

The Grand Mufti thanked him for it and stated in conclusion that he was taking his leave from the Führer in full confidence and with the reiterated thanks for the interest shown in the Arab cause.

SCHMIDT

Part IV

1942

TABLE TALK

April 23, 1942, at dinner

[From *Hitler's Table Talk,* edited by H. R. Trevor-Roper (New York: Enigma Books, 2008).]

My opinion of the Duce—The man who best understood the Bolshevik menace—The fate awaiting Europe—The Duce's difficulties with the Italian aristocracy—In praise of Edda Mussolini.

It will give me very great pleasure to see the Duce again and to discuss with him all the military and political problems of the day. I hold the Duce in the highest esteem, because I regard him as an incomparable statesman. On the ruins of a ravished Italy he has succeeded in building a new State which is a rallying point for the whole of his people. The struggles of the Fascists bear a close resemblance to our own struggles Did they not have, for example, six thousand six hundred dead at Verona?

The Duce is one of the people who appreciated the full measure of the Bolshevik menace, and for this reason he has sent to our Eastern front divisions of real military merit. He told me himself that he had no illusions as to the fate of Europe if the motorized hordes of the Russian armies were allowed to sweep unchecked over the Continent, and he is quite convinced that, but for my intervention, the hour of decline was approaching for Western Europe.

It is always painful to me, when I meet the Duce in Italy, to see him relegated to the rear rank whenever any of the Court entourage are about. The joy is always taken out of the reception he arranges for me by the fact that I am compelled to submit to contact with the arrogant idlers of the aristocracy. On one occasion these morons tried to ruin my pleasure at the spectacle of a dance given by the most lovely young maids from the Florence Academy, by criticizing the dancing in most contemptuous terms. I rounded on them with such fury, however, that I was left to enjoy the rest of the program in peace!

It was certainly no pleasure to me to find myself continually in the company of the Court hangers-on, particularly as I could not forget all the difficulties which the king's entourage had put in the Duce's way from the very beginning. And now they think they are being tremendously cunning in flirting with Britain.

Nothing, to my mind, is more typical of the ineptitude of these aristocratic loafers than the fact that not once did the Crown Princess of Italy succeed in offering me a hot and decently cooked meal! When a German hostess offers me hospitality she makes it a point of honor, however humble she may be, not only to give me an excellent meal but also to see that it is decently hot. These degenerates of the Italian aristocracy give proof of their futility in even the most elementary things in life. What a pleasure it was, in contrast, to talk to an intelligent and charming woman like Edda Mussolini! A woman of this kind shows the stuff she is made of by volunteering to be a nurse with the divisions serving on the Eastern front—and that is just what she is doing at the present moment.

Hitler and Mussolini
Klessheim: April 29–30, 1942

[From Santi Corvaja, *Hitler and Mussolini: The Secret Meetings 1934-1944.*]

On the morning of April 28, 1942, Mussolini's special train arrived at Puch, near Salzburg. The Duce and his staff, Ciano, Cavallero, and diplomat Mario Luciolli were to have accommodations in one of the wings of Klessheim Castle, the former residence of the Prince Archbishop of Salzburg and now refurbished as a luxurious hunting lodge for the Führer's most illustrious guests. Ciano was convinced that the Germans were using art treasures stolen in France to decorate the castle.

Hitler was six paces in front of the rest of the German welcoming party waiting on the platform. Mussolini stepped off the train, quite curious to discover the reasons for such an urgent meeting. Right after the effusive greetings, the groups left for the castle, where the first discussions began at once. Hitler and Mussolini were alone at first, while Ribbentrop and Ciano, and Cavallero and Keitel, met separately. Military matters were on top of the agenda with three major issues on the table: the Italian contribution in Russia, operations in Cirenaica, and the Malta operation. On the first issue, after attempting to keep the Italian effort as low as possible with the CSIR at 60,000 men, Cavallero in the end had to accept Mussolini's position to increase the number of divisions for political reasons. But as a final, desperate argument, Cavallero had insisted that there was hardly any transportation, which made the problem of supplies all the more acute.

This final attempt to stall the operation was immediately broken down in the conference next door between Hitler and Mussolini. Hitler at first began by praising the German soldier during the awful winter just passed on the Russian front. He also congratulated himself for his own strategic and tactical intuitions and was asking the Duce about the Italian divisions the OKW could count on in view of the renewed offensive on the Russian front. Hitler also talked about the courage displayed by the Romanians and the Hungarians who had committed 27 and 12 divisions, respectively. Mussolini answered that, as he had repeatedly promised, the brave CSIR would grow during the coming summer to a total of 227,000 men.

There would be several crack Italian divisions in the new army corps that would bear the name "Armir": three Alpine divisions, the Tridentina, Julia, and Cunense, those very troops, Mussolini pointed out, that the Führer admired. To these would be added three infantry divisions of the Second Army Corps: Ravenna, Cosseria, and Sforzesca, plus the reserve division Vicenza. The CSIR of General Messe with its divisions, Pasubio, Torino, and Celere, which included the Bersaglieri and Savoia cavalry, would stay in place as the Thirty-fifth Army Corps. Finally, the Black Shirt Legion was to be formed out of four groups: Leonessa, Valle Scrivia, Tagliamento, and Montello. Even after requisitioning everything available, the Italian army still came short of vehicles. The Führer immediately replied that the German logistical services would make up the difference. The fate of tens of thousands of men was quickly decided, and by August

10, as planned, they would be deployed in the bloody Russian tragedy according to the plans Adolf Hitler had prepared.

The Malta problem dominated the discussions because it was closely tied to the question of Egypt. Cavallero, with General Gandin at his side, as well as military attaché to Berlin General Marras, repeated his point of view that the operation should take place as soon as possible. The Italian chief of staff sent a message to Keitel prior to the meeting in which he stated: "We must make some sacrifices to eliminate this threat. Combined with possible enemy actions in 1942 and, more realistically, in 1943, its continued presence could seriously damage Axis operations. While it is obvious that the heavy bombardment of the naval and air bases on the island has given positive results, these must be exploited before the enemy has a chance to recover or before sudden changes on the ground could alter the balance of the forces facing us."

Cavallero's analysis was correct. During the month of March alone, Axis bombers pounded Malta with ten times more bomb tonnage than the city of Coventry, destroyed in 1940. Churchill was aware of the threat looming over the island. In his diary he wrote: "Malta was up for grabs." Cavallero, sensing a favorable reaction from his listeners, spent some time detailing "Esigenza C.3," the operational plan that would lead to the occupation of Malta. The plan had been written by General Gandin, with Admiral Girosi and air force General Cappa. German and even Japanese technicians specialized in island landings had also participated in its elaboration.

Kesselring spoke right after Cavallero, confirming his support for the C.3 plan (renamed "Hercules" after its approval). Keitel, still uncertain about Hitler's final decisions, answered that he would not be able "to immediately provide the required naval landing crafts and paratroop units." Only the Führer could unlock the situation. Kesselring repeated to Hitler: "Malta has been neutralized by my bombers, but until it is occupied by the Italians we will be unable to stop the British air force. Our plan is now complete and has the approval of both Italians and Germans. We need your final approval." Hitler, always sensitive to requests coming from his admirers, approved Hercules on condition that it be synchronized with Rommel. A final compromise was then reached: in May, Rommel would be given the green light in Cirenaica. Once certain Axis objectives had been reached, such as the taking of Tobruk, Hercules would begin in mid-July, after the full moon on the thirteenth. The units that would be part of Hercules were the Italian fleet under the command of Admirals Iachino,

Tur, and Barone. The air force would deploy 1,506 aircraft, 666 of which would be German. General Vecchiarelli, the supreme commander, would have under him Generals Sogno and Cesare Rossi, as well as German Generals Student and Ramcke, who specialized in paratrooper and other types of airborne units. Right after the Klesseheim meeting, all units intended for the Malta operation began their transfer to Sicily. The operational plan required that it begin immediately, to be ready at day X plus 20. Naval and air attacks on the island were progressively increased.

But Hercules was destined to never see the light of day, and Malta was spared complete destruction, thanks to Rommel. On June 29, Rommel occupied Tobruk and took 35,000 British prisoners, including seven generals. He was convinced that the British Eighth Army was practically destroyed, since it had lost over seventy-five percent of its strength. Cavallero was well aware of the professional weaknesses of the Afrika Korps commander and, on the evening of the great victory in Tobruk, quickly submitted the following letter addressed to Hitler, for Mussolini's signature:

Führer: in the naval and air offensive just completed, the enemy has endured a major defeat. The same can be said for operations in Marmarica that are about to reach a positive conclusion.

It is my opinion and certainly also yours, Führer, that we must consolidate the current results as quickly as possible. At the center of our strategic picture, there is Malta, which we have previously settled. I wish to tell you that preparations for the Malta operation are very advanced. It becomes more urgent than ever before. To make the most of the results we have achieved in the Marmarica and to prepare for future requirements, we must be able to channel our supplies in complete security. The occupation of Malta, besides solving the transportation problems in the Mediterranean, would give us full use of our air forces, now stationed and committed to the Mediterranean theater as long as Malta is controlled by the enemy. The freeing of the air force, along with the other advantages stemming from the occupation of Malta (for instance, the problem of fuel), would allow us to regain freedom of movement, a crucially important factor to achieve victory. The problem of fuel for the Italian Air Force must be examined in relation to the Malta operation, and discussions on the issue are taking place within the Italian high command. The occupation of Malta will create opportunities in this area that we will best examine once the operation is completed.

I have every reason to believe, Führer, that in spite of the considerable difficulties that I can imagine, your personal intervention will also ensure a favorable solution, since it is of vital importance for our position in the Mediterranean and its future developments. Mussolini.

The naval and air battle Mussolini was referring to was known as the "mid-June" operation and was in fact the swan song of the Italian navy. Two months later, as historian Aldo Fraccaroli pointed out, during the mid-August operation, in the middle of another and larger effort by the enemy to occupy Malta, the Italian battleships were unable to sail because of lack of fuel. Many people claimed to have led the Italian forces during the victorious battle of mid-June, Mussolini among them.

Italian forces had been successfully engaged, as evidenced by a rare British admission at the time: "Only two ships of the eastern convoy reached Malta, while the western convoy had to turn back to Alexandria after losing a destroyer, three cruisers, a support ship, and three merchant men." This battle saw the one and only sinking of a British warship by an Italian torpedo plane. The destroyer *Bedouin*, after being heavily shelled by Italian destroyers, was sunk by a torpedo fired by an S.79 plane. During the "mid-August" battle, Axis success was even greater in spite of the absence of large caliber guns; the Allies lost an aircraft carrier, two cruisers, a destroyer, and nine merchant ships, while another aircraft carrier, two cruisers, and seven more ships were heavily damaged.

The letter from Mussolini and Cavallero was sent to Berlin on the evening of the Axis victory at Tobruk, and was preceded by a message from Rommel requesting permission to continue his advance to the Nile and the Pyramids, following in the steps of Napoleon. Hitler examined the entire matter for two days, and on June 23 he answered Mussolini with one of the most crucial documents of the entire war.

Duce, at this time, when militarily historic events are in the offing, I would like to explain my thoughts to you as concisely as possible regarding a decision that may have decisive impact on the course of the war. Destiny, Duce, has given us an opening that will never again become available in the same theater of operations. The fastest and most totalitarian exploitation of this advantage is our best military opportunity at this time. Up to this moment, I have always ordered our forces to pursue a defeated enemy in retreat for the longest possible time as our troop strength would allow. The British Eighth army is virtually destroyed.

At Tobruk, with its practically intact harbor and piers, you have, Duce, an auxiliary base that is all the more important in that the British themselves have built a railroad line all the way to Egypt. If we fail to pursue the remains

of this British army now with the utmost effort of each soldier, we will follow
a fate identical to that of the British when they lost their advantage very close
to Tripoli because they diverted troops into Greece. Only this capital mistake
of the British high command made our effort in reconquering Cirenaica a
success.

If our forces do not march forward to the extreme limit, into the heart of
Egypt, we will be faced with new, long-range American bombers able to
reach Italy. At the same time, British and American forces can link together
from all sides. In a short time, the situation would turn against us. But the
continued pursuit of the enemy will provoke its disintegration. This time,
Egypt can, under certain conditions, be taken from England. The consequences of such an event will have repercussions all over the world. Our own
offensive, helped by the occupation of Sebastopol, will determine the fall of
the entire eastern structure of the British Empire.

If I, Duce, can give you, in this historic moment which will not be
repeated, my most heartfelt advice, it would be this: order the continuation of
operations to seek the complete destruction of British forces to the very limits
of what your high command and Marshal Rommel think is militarily possible
with their existing troops. The goddess of fortune in battle comes to
commanders only once, and he who fails to seize the opportunity at such a
moment will never be given a second chance. The fact that the British,
contrary to every rule of the art of war, decided to interrupt their advance on
Tripoli and divert their units to another battlefield was enough to save us . . .
Please, Duce, accept this request only as the advice of a friend, who has considered for many years that his fate is tied to your own and is acting in consequence. In faithful comradeship, Adolf Hitler.

Mussolini read and reread the letter. Between the lines, it ironically
tried to be provocative. But in substance, it was an out-and-out order.
Unsure how to react, the Duce summoned Cavallero for advice. The Italian
commander arrived at the Palazzo Venezia with Kesselring. They both
remained unmoved by Hitler's prose and begged Mussolini not to make
any decision before they both had a chance to inspect the front in
Cirenaica. The next day they flew to Africa.

Concerning this event, Carlo Cavallero, son of the Italian military
leader, wrote:

At a meeting in Derna, on June 25, 1942, Kesselring and my father
attempted to convince Rommel that because of the long distance separating
them from their objectives, an advance under such conditions would not
allow the Axis to fully take advantage of its success. In fact, Rommel would

face a refreshed enemy, close to his bases, with a reduced and ragged Axis army that would be dangerously low in supplies.

Kesselring pointed to the difficulty of effectively supporting the Axis ground forces with the few planes he had, hundreds of kilometers from their bases. The enemy would have the advantage of being very close to his own bases. He concluded by stating: "I am very skeptical of a deep advance. If I am given the order, I shall obey, but the end result of the battle in this case is very much in doubt."

Rommel told Mussolini's two envoys that it was now too late to alter the battle plans. He said he had already given the green light to the units to take Marsa Matruh. However, he continued, given the very persuasive points he had heard, he would consider each of his movements nothing more than a series of "jumps" forward; he was not willing to become engaged in a "deep operation." Rommel only spoke this way to get rid of the emissaries sent by Rome to upset his plans. Rommel also knew that the Führer was definitely on his side, so much so that from Berlin, he had been forewarned that the OKW was preparing an underhanded slap at the Duce.

On the evening of June 25, with typical Nazi arrogance, Keitel phoned the Italian high command to inform them: "The German high command cannot furnish the minimum fuel requirements which have been requested for the Malta operation." Without even waiting for the return of Cavallero and Kesselring, Mussolini, with this piece of information, cabled Rommel that he had a free hand to move forward. The Duce was now beginning to dream of the Nile and the Pyramids. The shelving of the Hercules plan was a German decision and must rest with Marshal Rommel himself. In this entire matter, Mussolini only played a cameo role but perhaps he already saw himself on a white horse, making his own triumphant entrance into Cairo.

General von Rintelen, German military attaché in Rome, confirmed that at the Salzburg conference, Cavallero had termed the occupation of Malta a prerequisite to any successful campaign in Africa, but the Führer, after Operation Merkur over Crete, had become skeptical about paratroop landings into enemy camps that were well protected and well armed. For Hitler the supply of bridgeheads was the most difficult of all military operations. For this reason, he concluded that it was preferable to let the British stay in Malta so that the Axis could inflict even greater damage to the merchant shipping tonnage of the enemy engaged in supplying the island. Based on this analysis, confirmed by the recent victories in Africa and the Mediterranean, Hitler approved Rommel's plan. The Field

Marshal, well aware of Hitler's views, had told him, before resuming his march toward El Alamein, that in taking Tobruk he had seized enough vehicles and fuel to reach the Nile at the enemy's expense.

The field marshal's enthusiasm effectively convinced Mussolini, who went to North Africa on June 29 and remained there until July 20, waiting in vain to make his own triumphant entry into Alexandria. This was to be one of most humiliating episodes in Mussolini's life. Rommel virtually ignored the Duce's presence in Cirenaica even though he had been invited more than once to report in person to the man who was nominally his direct commander in the Mediterranean. Cavallero, even though he cut a rather understated presence, consoled himself with his promotion to marshal of Italy.

Vittorio Mussolini was at Derna at the time and wrote about the Duce's trip: "I reached Berta on July 1 and went straight to the small villa where my father was staying. He was in a sitting room. I hugged him affectionately and he smiled without interrupting his work. I asked him how he felt, because I saw him push his belt below his waistline and assume his usual slumped position, resting deep into the back of the chair. 'Not too well, but maybe it's the change of climate. If Professor Castellani were here, he'd say that I have amoebae. He specializes in diagnosing the amoebae bacteria in anyone who has visited Africa.' At that time, Mussolini would answer questions about his health this way: 'My ulcers are the convoys that leave Italy and never reach Libya.'

"He was in a bad mood," wrote Vittorio, "because he had to cancel his flight to Tobruk due to the weather. I asked about his impressions of the prisoners: "Impressive looking soldiers, tall and strong, almost all of them Australians and New Zealanders, with a few British and South African units. I also saw a lot of Hindus, blacks—a few thousand in all. The commander of the camp told me he had to separate the colored troops at the request of the whites. And then *we* are the ones accused of being racists.'

"Something was bothering him, and in harsh tones he asked me: 'Why is it that our command is located in positions so far removed from the front line? There are some 600 kilometers separating the fighting from the first commanding general. It's good to be cautious, but I think they are exaggerating . . . 'The advance came faster than they could move the command post.' I replied, in attempting to justify the situation. 'You're probably right, but the troops want to see the faces of their generals, and that's why I admire Rommel, who is always extremely active up on the front lines. He may be stubborn, rude, and gross, but he's always among the soldiers and they appreciate it.'

"Of the situation on the front, Mussolini said: 'Rommel has assured me that we will soon be in sight of the Nile. You know how much I hate silly optimism, but this time I want to believe it. Cavallero also thinks we're not doing so badly even though we're losing precious time due to transportation problems. Rommel is insisting on taking advantage as much as possible of the initial success even if it means reaching Alexandria with only one *panzer*. Kesselring and Bastico, the Italian supreme commander in Libya, are much more cautious; they feel we must consolidate our positions in the El Alamein depression.'

The next day the Duce received at his villa headquarters not Rommel, who was still avoiding him, but Minister Plenipotentiary Serafino Mazzolini, who was to become civilian high commissioner of Egypt once the Axis forces had taken Alexandria. This was a premature appointment, as events were to show. Mussolini justified this move ahead of time: "The Germans will be full of Teutonic pride when they reach the Pyramids, like Napoleon. The presence of the Duce in the area will serve to demonstrate that on these shores we are the ones in command." Then Mussolini said: "I didn't come here to be confined to this little house and wait. Rommel doesn't show up. He has the good excuse of being engaged in battle on the front. I told Cavallero that I would like to go over there, but he doesn't recommend it because of the rapidly changing lines. I don't like to receive second hand information. And when there is no one around me, it means things are not going so well."

Mussolini's analysis of the situation at the front was far from wrong. To go and seek out Rommel would have been a humiliating gesture for him as the "Duce." Fortunately, Cavallero was able to avoid this with a plausible excuse. Mussolini was killing time by traveling around and handing out decorations and harvesting wheat with the Italian colonists at Barce and Borgo Baracca. He finally visited the bombed-out town of Tobruk. On July 16, he held a military conference in his quarters with Cavallero, Kesselring, and Bastico. Cavallero made a pessimistic assessment: at El Alamein the attacks by Australian and New Zealand infantry had made better progress than expected. Afrika Korps tanks were now reduced to about thirty, as many as the Italian divisions Ariete and Littorio.

The breakthrough that would begin on October 23 with the offensive of General Montgomery's Eighth Army was not far away. After meeting with the generals, Mussolini said to his son: "I have decided to go back to

Italy as soon as possible, possibly tomorrow." The crisis of the Axis had begun.

After Mussolini accepted Hitler's veto to attack Malta, Cavallero, on July 7, transformed the Hercules plan into the C4 plan—the occupation of Tunisia. General Messe wrote about this change: "The cancellation of the occupation of Malta was one of the major mistakes of the war. The materiel and supplies which had been put together at great cost for the operation and were ready at the beginning of July were immediately assigned to other tasks. The excellent paratroop division was thrown into El Alamein and used as an infantry division. The German paratroopers of General Ramcke had the same fate."

At the end of April 1942, during the Klessheim conference these dramatic events were still to come. The atmosphere of the meetings in the Berchtesgaden area was almost idyllic, so much so that Hitler invited the Italians to come and have tea at his residence at the Berghof. Mario Luciolli, aghast at the news that fresh Italian divisions were to go to the Russian front, was part of that group.

"We ran into snow as our cars took the mountain road toward Hitler's residence. The German general who had just returned from the Russian front and was sitting next to me suddenly became angry and cursed the snow. It took him a few minutes to calm down, and then he said: 'You know, when you have seen too much of something . . . ' He was obviously thinking about the eastern front. That ride awakened some poetic memories in my case . . . As we had tea, I noticed that the 'Satan' [Hitler] who was responsible for the bloodiest battles in history, was playing host with the simple courtesy of an Austrian *petit bourgeois* . . . "

Ciano, worried by the excessively friendly atmosphere, became suspicious: "The cordiality of the Germans is always in reverse proportion to their good fortune . . . On the second day, April 30, after lunch, we had said all there was to say—on Great Britain, the United States, Russia, France—Hitler spoke uninterruptedly for one hour and forty minutes. There was not as single topic he did not touch upon: war and peace, religion and philosophy, art and history. Mussolini kept looking at his wristwatch, I was lost in my own thoughts, and only Cavallero, who is a model of servility, pretended to listen in rapture and nodded repeatedly. The Germans were much less able to withstand this than we were. Poor people: they had to listen to this every day, and I'm sure there wasn't a word or gesture they didn't know by heart. General Jodl, after a brave fight to stay awake, fell asleep on the couch. General Keitel was groggy, but he was sitting much too close to Hitler to let himself go as he would have wished."

Cavallero, servile as he needed to be to get ahead, was privately celebrating his success after having obtained from the loquacious gentleman his approval for the operation against Malta. This was worth the small sacrifice of being the Führer's audience for more than an hour. Had Cavallero known that Hitler's promises had no value perhaps he would not have been so compliant. Mussolini was very happy to leave Klessheim, probably because he could see the problems besetting the Führer. He summed up the two days of meetings this way: "The German war machine is still extremely powerful, but it has suffered wear and tear. Now it will make another gigantic effort . . . "

Mussolini left the following note: "Magnificent valor displayed by the Germans in Russia. But strategic difficulties are growing in the east for the Führer. We spoke with him about defensive actions: "We will need only a few forces to defend this front in prepared positions. The mass will be turned toward the west. Perhaps Great Britain will finally become convinced that it cannot win and will ask to negotiate.' These are the Führer's thoughts. For the rest, a stepping up of the submarine war, and containment on other fronts. Some hope about Turkey."

Mussolini further confided to his son Vittorio: "The Führer is fully convinced of victory and is counting on Anglo-American resistance in the face of Stalin, a useful but dangerous ally who keeps on demanding the opening of a second front. As far as we are concerned, soon we will begin our action in Libya, and immediately after that, we will snatch Malta away from the British. The Germans will start their offensive for Leningrad and Sebastopol in June with huge troop and artillery concentrations. The very difficult winter crisis seems to be over now, and the German high command is confident in the success of the coming operations."

On May 1, a joint communiqué was issued: "The Duce and the Führer met in Salzburg on April 29 and 30. The conversations were held in the spirit of close friendship and brotherhood-in-arms of the two peoples and the two leaders. The result has been a complete agreement regarding the situation created by the victories of the powers of the Tripartite Pact and the future course of the war by both nations. Once again, on this occasion the iron-clad decision by Italy and Germany and their allies was reaffirmed to insure the final victory with all the power of their arms."

At the Rome cabinet meeting of May 2, Mussolini gave his version of the "two days in Salzburg" as Bottai noted: "Very long talks, on a single day up to twelve straight hours. There was a polite mention by the Duce about the Führer's loquacity and his fluent oratorical style. The main issue was the Russian campaign where the Germans were experiencing a collapse similar to that of Napoleon. According to Hitler, Russia is the only worthy foe we have been facing. Bolshevism did, in fact, create something serious: an army that can qualitatively compete with that of Germany."

After meeting four times in 1940 and three times in 1941, the Salzburg summit would be the only one in 1942 and marked the end of a certain sense of balance in the relationship between Hitler and Mussolini. The Führer and the Duce would meet one year later on April 7, 1943, once again at Salzburg. This meeting preceded the events of July 25 that were to overthrow Fascism. But before its unstoppable decline, the Axis was to live through the victorious summer of 1942.

Hitler and Mannerheim

Meeting in Finland, June 4, 1942

[Considered to be the only secret recording of Hitler's voice in one-on-one, conversation thanks to the device used by Finnish intelligence, this document is interesting because of its context following the failure of *Barbarossa* to take Moscow and the start of the fateful second year of the war in Russia with the drive south to Stalingrad and the Caucasus. See Gerhard L. Weinberg, *A World At Arms* (New York: Cambridge, 2005-2010); Robert M. Citino, *Death of the Wehrmacht. The German Campaigns of 1942* (Lawrence: Kansas, 2007). Baron Carl Gustav Mannerheim (1867-1951), Finnish military leader and president of Finland from 1944 to 1946.]

Recorded secretly by Finnish intelligence on the railroad dining car where the meeting took place.

Hitler: ...a very serious danger, perhaps the most serious one—its whole extent we can only now judge. We did not ourselves understand—just how strong this state [the USSR] was armed.
Mannerheim: No, we hadn't thought of this.
Hitler: No, I too, no.

Mannerheim: During the Winter War—during the Winter War we had not even thought of this. Of course...

Hitler: (Interrupting) Yes.

Mannerheim: But so, how they—in reality—and now there is no doubt all they had—what they had in their stocks!

Hitler: Absolutely, This is—they had the most immense armaments that, uh, people could imagine. Well—if somebody had told me that a country—with... (Hitler is interrupted by the sound of a door opening and closing.) If somebody had told me a nation could start with 35,000 tanks, then I'd have said: "You are crazy!"

Mannerheim: Thirty-five?

Hitler: Thirty-five thousand tanks.

Another Voice in Background: Thirty-five thousand! Yes!

Hitler: We have destroyed—right now—more than 34,000 tanks. If someone had told me this, I'd have said: "You!" If you are one of my generals had stated that any nation has 35,000 tanks I'd have said: "You, my good sir, you see everything twice or ten times. You are crazy; you see ghosts." This I would have deemed possible. I told you earlier we found factories, one of them at Kramatorskaja, for example, Two years ago there were just a couple hundred [tanks]. We didn't know anything. Today, there is a tank plant, where—during the first shift a little more than 30,000, and 'round the clock a little more than 60,000, workers would have labored—a single tank plant! A gigantic factory! Masses of workers who certainly, lived like animals and...

Another Voice in Background: (Interrupting) In the Donets area?

Hitler: In the Donets area. (Background noises from the rattling of cups and plates over the exchange.)

Mannerheim: Well, if you keep in mind they had almost 20 years, almost 25 years of—freedom to arm themselves...

Hitler: (Interrupting quietly) It was unbelievable.

Mannerheim: And everything—everything spent on armament.

Hitler: Only on armament.

Mannerheim: Only on armament!

Hitler: (Sighs) Only—well, it is—as I told your president [Ryte] before—I had no idea of it. If I had an idea—then I would have been even more difficult for me, but I would have taken the decision [to invade] anyhow, because—there was no other possibility. It was—certain, already in the winter of '39/ '40, that the war had to begin. I had only this nightmare—but there is even more! Because a war on two fronts—would have been impossible—that would have broken us. Today, we see more clearly—than we saw at that time—it would have broken us. And my whole—I originally wanted to—already in the fall of '39 I wanted to conduct the campaign in the west—on the continuously bad weather we experienced hindered us.

Our whole armament—you know, was—is a pure good weather armament. It is very capable, very good, but it is unfortunately just a good-weather armament. We have seen this in the war. Our weapons naturally were made for the west, and we all thought, and this was true 'till that time, uh, it was the opinion from the earliest times: you cannot wage war in winter. And we too, have, the German tanks, they weren't tested, for example, to prepare them for winter war. Instead we conducted trials to prove it was impossible to wage war in winter. That is a different starting point [than the Soviet's]. In the fall of 1939 we always faced the question. I desperately wanted to attack, and I firmly believed we could finish France in six weeks.

However, we faced the question of whether we could move at all—it was raining continuously. And I know the French area myself very well and I too could not ignore the opinions, of many of my generals that, we—probably—would not have had the élan, that our tank arm would not have been, effective, that our air force could not been effective from our air-fields because of the rain.

I know northern France myself. You know, I served in the Great War for four years. And—so the delay happened. If I had in '39 eliminated France, then world history would have changed. But I had to wait 'till 1940, and unfortunately it wasn't possible before May. Only on the 10th of May was the first nice day—and on the 10th of May I immediately attacked. I gave the order to attack on the 10th on the 8th. And—then we had to, conduct this huge transfer of our divisions from the west to the east.

First the occupation of—then we had the task in Norway—at the same time we faced—I can frankly say it today—a grave misfortune, namely the—weakness of, Italy. Because of—first, the situation in North Africa, then, second, because of the situation in Albania and Greece—a very big misfortune. We had to help. This meant for us, with one small stoke, first—the splitting of our air force, splitting our tank force, while at the same time we were preparing, the, tank arm in the east. We had to hand over—with one stroke, two divisions, two whole divisions and a third was then added—and we had to replace continuous, very severe, losses there. It was—bloody fighting in the desert.

This all naturally was inevitable, you see. I had a conversation with Molotov [Soviet Minister] at that time, and it was absolutely certain that Molotov departed with the decision to begin a war, and I dismissed the decision to begin a war, and I dismissed him with the decision to— impossible, to forestall him. There was—this was the only—because the demands that man brought up were clearly aimed to rule, Europe in the end. (Practically whispering here.) Then I have him—not publicly... (fades out).

Already in the fall of 1940 we continuously faced the question, uh: shall we, consider a break up [in relations with the USSR]? At that time, I advised the Finnish government, to—negotiate and, to gain time and, to act dilatory in this matter—because I always feared—that Russia suddenly would attack Romania in the late fall—and occupy the petroleum wells, and we would have not been ready in the late fall of 1940. If Russia indeed had taken Romanian petroleum wells, than Germany would have been lost. It would have required—just 60 Russian divisions to handle that matter.

In Romania we had of course—at that time—no major units. The Romanian government had turned to us only recently—and what we did have there was laughable. They only had to occupy the petroleum wells. Of course, with our weapons I could not start a, war in September or October. That was out of the question. Naturally, the transfer to the east wasn't that far advanced yet. Of course, the units first had to reconsolidate in the west. First the armaments had to be taken care of because we too had— yes, we also had losses in our campaign in the west. It would have been impossible to attack—before the spring of 1941. And if the Russians at that time—in the fall of 1940—had occupied Romania—taken the petroleum wells, then we would have been, helpless in 1941.

Another Voice in Background: Without petroleum...

Hitler: (Interrupting) We had huge German production: however, the demands of the air force, our Panzer divisions—they are really huge. It is level of consumption that surpasses the imagination. And without the addition of four to five million tons of Romanian petroleum, we could not have fought the war—and would have had to let it be—and that was my big worry. Therefore I aspired to, bridge the period of negotiations 'till we would be strong enough to, counter those extortive demands [from Moscow] because—those demands were simply naked extortion's. They were extortion's. The Russians knew we were tied up in the west. They

could really extort everything from us. Only when Molotov visited—
then—I told him frankly that the demands, their numerous demands,
weren't acceptable to us. With that the negotiations came to an abrupt end
that same morning.

There were four topics. The one topic that, involved Finland was, the,
freedom to protect themselves from the Finnish threat, he said. [I said]
You do not want to tell me Finland threatens you! But he said: "In Finland
it is—they who take action against the, friends, of the Soviet Union. They
would [take action] against [our] society, against us—they would continuously, persecute us and, a great power cannot be threatened by a minor
country."

I said: "Your, existence isn't threatened by Finland! That is, you don't
mean to tell me..."

Mannerheim: (Interrupting) Laughable!

Hitler: "...that your existence is threatened by Finland?" Well [he said]
there was a moral—threat being made against a great power, and what
Finland was doing, that was a moral—a threat to their moral existence.
Then I told him we would not accept a further war in the Baltic area as
passive spectators. In reply he asked me how we viewed our position in,
Romania. You know, we had given them a guarantee. [He wanted to
know] if that guarantee was directed against Russia as well? And that time
I told him: "I don't think it is directed at you, because I don't think you
have the intention of attacking Romania. You have always stated that
Bessarabia is yours, but that you have—never stated that you want to
attack Romania!"

"Yes," he told me, but he wanted to know more precisely if this
guarantee... (A door opens and the recording ends.)

TABLE TALK

September 5, 1942

I helped pull down Serrano Suñer—Personality of Alphonso XIII—The
race of Princes—The process of selectivity in reverse—The train of the
Archduke Otto—The art of cultivating idols—Serrano Suñer and the Latin
Union.

Epp has just submitted a paper on the colonial problem to me. I must
say, no colonies which we may obtain elsewhere in the world will compare
with those which we hold in the East.

Serrano Suñer, had he been given the chance, would gradually have engineered the annihilation of the Falange and the restoration of the monarchy. His disgrace has certainly been accelerated by my recent declaration that he was an absolute swine!

Alphonso XIII was certainly a man, yet he, too, brought ruin on himself. Why, I wonder, did he not keep Primo de Rivera? I can understand most things, but I shall never understand why, when once one has seized power, one does not hold it with all one's might!

Princes constitute a race unique in the world for the depth of their stupidity; they are the classic example of the laws of selectivity working in reverse. If the Habsburgs were to return to Hungary, they are so stupid that their presence would immediately give rise to a crisis without parallel. There are circumstances in which an attitude of passivity is absolutely untenable. With each generation, the Princes of Europe become a little more degenerate. In Bavaria this process developed into tragedy, for they eventually became insane. When all is said and done, the whole of the European royal families are descended from the old Frankish nobility, which was founded by Charlemagne and has since withered away through inbreeding. The Austrian Princes had a better chance of survival, for they were allowed to seek their wives amongst commoners.

I cannot but admire the patience of the people who tolerate such fripperies! The practice of kneeling to Royalty had at least this advantage, that it prevented the subjects from contemplating the idiot faces of their rulers!

Efforts for improving the breed of cattle never cease, but in the case of the aristocracy, the reverse obtains. The Hohenzollerns are no exception to the rule; they all have their little idiosyncrasies—not excluding our dear little A. W [Prince August Wilhelm, son of Kaiser Wilhelm II and member of the NSDAP]. There should be a law prohibiting Princes from having any intercourse with anyone, except chauffeurs and grooms!

If the crown of Brazil were offered to the Spanish Pretender, he would accept it unhesitatingly. He would become king of Sweden with the same enthusiasm! He doesn't care a damn what the country is, as long as he is king of it! Are people like that of any real value? To browse through the archives of these families is an edifying experience; the Wittelsbachs wanted to exchange Salzach for Belgium, but the whole thing fell through thanks to a disagreement over sixty-eight acres of land, and thanks, also, to a certain degree, to the intervention of Frederick the Great, who did not wish to see the influence of the Habsburgs spread westwards. The negotiations were conducted by the Minister Kreittmeyer, which is why our friend

Hanfstaengl insisted on the destruction of Kreittmeyer's statue in Munich. I myself was opposed to it. The men of those days did not possess the national sense, as we understand it today. Ludwig I of Bavaria was the first monarch who thought in terms of the whole German Reich. For the others, dynastic interests were predominant.

The journey of Otto, the son of Zita, to Budapest reads like a novel. His suite consisted of a Hungarian nobleman—and a trumpeter, perched on the engine, who from time to time all but burst his lungs with his trumpetings! Horthy did not even deign to receive him. The whole buffoonery had been organized by Zita; its repulse was the work of Madame Horthy. I leave you to imagine for yourselves the dénouement of this grandiose undertaking! The only person whose head it entered to welcome the heroes was the brother of Franz Lehar. In Vienna, Otto would just about have been fitted to become a maître d'hôtel. If the Habsburgs had had an ounce of character they would have defended their heritage or died; as it was, they docilely surrendered their rights—and then tried to recover them by force!

Humanity cannot exist without an idol. The Americans, for instance, need to put their President on a pedestal—for as long as he remains President. The monarchies have shown themselves singularly adept at setting up this particular type of idol, and there is no doubt that the whole performance has a measure of common sense in it. It succeeds splendidly, provided always that it is backed by force and power. The Church, for example, possesses nothing but the outer trappings; its troops consist of inoffensive archers, nice fellows with broken arrows! One has only to see them marching in the Corpus Christi procession to understand why the revolutionaries of 1918 left them in peace!

When Franco appears in public, he is always surrounded by his Moorish Guard. He has assimilated all the mannerisms of Royalty, and when the king returns, he will be the ideal stirrup holder!

I am quite sure that Serrano Suñer was goaded on by the clergy. His plan was to found a Latin Union of France, Italy and Spain, and then to range it at Britain's side—the whole to have the blessing of the Archbishop of Canterbury—and a little spicing of Communism for good measure!

I think one of the best things we ever did was to permit a Spanish Legion to fight at our side. On the first opportunity I shall decorate Muñoz Grandes with the Iron Cross with Oak Leaves and Diamonds. It will pay dividends. Soldiers, whoever they may be, are always enthusiastic about a courageous commander. When the time comes for the Legion to return to Spain, we must reequip it on a regal scale, give it a heap of booty and a handful of Russian Generals as trophies. Then they will have a triumphal entry into Madrid, and their prestige will be unassailable. Taking it all round, the Spanish press is the best in the world!

*****

Hitler and His Generals

Military Conferences

[In September 1942 Hitler instructed stenographers to record the military situation conferences, at which the detailed orders for future operations were issued. Hitler at this time took over command of Army Group A because of disagreements with some of his generals. By then the Russian army had almost cut off the Stalingrad area as a prelude to the capture of the city and the encirclement of the entire Sixth Army commanded by von Paulus. From: Helmut Heiber and David Glantz Eds., *Hitler and His Generals. Military Conferences 1942-1945* (New York: Enigma Books, 2003)]

Midday Situation Conference December 12, 1942, in the Wolfsschanze[1]

[A few hours before the beginning of this conference, Army Group Hoth began operation "Wintergewitter"—relief for Stalingrad—from both sides of Kotel'nikovo, in the southern sector of the Eastern front. Otherwise, the situation in the East has changed very little, except that the Russians are now attacking the German salient of Rzhev from the south as well, between Rzhev and Gzhatsk.]

Beginning: 12:45 p.m.

East

THE FÜHRER: Has something disastrous happened?
ZEITZLER: No, my Führer. Manstein has reached the sector[2] and controls one bridge. The only attacks are against the Italians. This one regiment,

which had been alerted during the night, appeared at the command post at 10 a.m. That was good, because the Italians had already thrown in all their reserve battalions.

THE FÜHRER: I have more sleepless nights because of the action here than because of the South. We don't know what is happening.

BUHLE: They are unreliable.

ZEITZLER: Something has to be done as quickly as possible, just like yesterday evening. If the Russians had taken advantage of it, it could have turned into a catastrophe last night. The army group didn't want to send in the regiment until early morning. So we got it at exactly 10. In the Seventeenth Army area, there wasn't a lot going on. Agent reports are surfacing again regarding a landing in the Crimea[3]—they wanted to have really bad weather with snowstorms, etc.

THE FÜHRER: That is very likely. Is our Navy able to make use of such weather as well?

JODL: You cannot land there.

THE FÜHRER: The Russians do it; they can get through. We would not land in snowstorms and the like. I admit that. But I believe the Russians would do it.

KRANCKE: If it is not too bad. If there is frost and everything is icy, then it is bad. But if there is only snow and it is around freezing, then it will work.

THE FÜHRER: That works fine. That is like with fog—they land while there is fog.

ZEITZLER: Here[4] there were stronger attacks by battalions. For the first time, we have received from here reports of deaths caused by exhaustion—14 cases within 6 days. I asked them to give me the detailed documents on what this bend looks like, in case we have to decide to eliminate it. If we take it away, in my opinion, we could save most of a division. There is a huge number of battalions in there, because they are holding it pretty tightly. However, we cannot attack down here within the next few weeks, and as to supplies, we can always get in the same situation again, so that we will have just as hard a time as we are having right now.

THE FÜHRER: It depends on whether or not they get something final over there—and, secondly, they should build a final position.

ZEITZLER: If the weather was good and we drew this back, we would have a division. I worry a lot about the armored army[5] down there; we need to bring some additional forces in there. We could get these here free for a while. The other thing is that the mountain regiment can't be there before the 20th, and the Luftwaffe even later, so we don't have much available right now.

THE FÜHRER: I'm only afraid that if we draw back now, all the materiel will be lost. Then we won't have anything.

ZEITZLER: No, it will have to be well prepared, of course.

THE FÜHRER: The enemy will probably follow further, if they don't have a position here.

ZEITZLER: It is a huge waste of forces, if one looks at the whole battalion. It's awful.

JODL: All they have in there are mountain guns. Once they brought up one anti-aircraft battery and one heavy battery.

THE FÜHRER: We'll have to see what they have.

ZEITZLER: I think that in the winter the same situation could happen here again.

THE FÜHRER: It is not very nice here in the south.[6] They have to build a position.

ZEITZLER: They definitely have to work on it.

THE FÜHRER: Then we can always take it back again. What I wanted to say about this Georgian battalion or company[7]: I really don't know, to tell the truth; the Georgians are people who are not Muslims. So one cannot call them a Turkish battalion. The Georgians don't belong to the Turkish peoples. The Georgians are a Caucasian tribe that has nothing to do with the Turkish peoples. I regard only the Muslims as safe. All the others I consider unsafe. That can happen to us anywhere, so we have to be incredibly cautious. For the time being, I regard building up battalions of these pure Caucasian nations as quite risky, whereas I don't see a danger in building up a unit consisting of only Muslims. They will always charge.

ZEITZLER: I have sent various questions down, in order to gather some experience. The Baltitz[8] asked a Russian general, who was quite open, about the Georgians. He answered, "We don't have any advantage or disadvantage because of the Georgians, but neither do you."

THE FÜHRER: I believe that. They only think of making themselves available to all sides. Secondly, they are, according to what we hear, quite unreliable to all sides. However, I can imagine that because Stalin himself is a Georgian, quite a lot of people are attracted to the Communists. They had a kind of autonomy. The real Turkish people are Muslims. The Georgians are not a Turkish people, rather a typical Caucasian tribe, probably even with some Nordic blood in them. Despite all explanations— either from Rosenberg or from the military side—I don't trust the

Armenians, either. I consider the Armenian units to be just as unreliable and dangerous. The only ones I consider to be reliable are the pure Muslims, which means the real Turkish nations. Whether or not they are all militarily useful is a different question, which I can't assess. (*Presentation of the Armed Forces report.*[9])

ZEITZLER: He is getting a bit livelier down here near the First Panzer Army. He pushes forward a bit—on this front relatively little. But here there are bridge constructions in progress at seven locations, as if he has something special planned there. I already reported yesterday that the bunker and a company were destroyed here.

THE FÜHRER: Where is this position being built?

ZEITZLER: Here, my Führer. This position will save us some people. This position hardly saves us anything, actually; not a lot will be coming out of it. But this position saves people because of the mountains—according to my feeling, the entire 13th Panzer Division or the SS *Viking* [Panzer Grenadier Division],[10] depending on which of them we want to draw out. Strangely enough, during the night a request from the army and the army group arrived. They are worried because of this thing up here, and they want to pull this in, in order to draw out the 13th Panzer Division and the *Viking* [Division], and to pull them in a more mobile way to Army Group South.[11] I think we have to come to this decision. It is a pity to give it up, but we can take it again. We will save an entire division if they prepare this. Up here there was a surprise, insofar as it was reported in writing that they had entered up to this point. I looked into that matter. It seems that it developed from the impression that the attack up there was not successful and had to retreat. The reasons are as follows: an armored group attacked here with an infantry regiment, and proceeded quite well. A Russian armored attack came from up there against the rear or the flank, so quite a few tanks were lost—18 were destroyed initially, and this morning another 16. Altogether 5 infantry [rifle] divisions, 6 cavalry brigades and 2 tank brigades are in opposition. It seems as if he drew everything together that was here—which I reported several days ago—and that there is an army of riders here that he is putting together. That is the bulk of it. He is relatively strong here. During the night, the order went out to hold this position to the very last man, and that it is forbidden to take a single step backward.

THE FÜHRER: Tell me one more thing. Where are the tanks that were eaten up by mice back then?[12]

ZEITZLER: They were up there with the 22nd Panzer Division. May I now give the order for these preparations?

THE FÜHRER: The decisive thing is that we take this road.

ZEITZLER: The roadblock doesn't do much, since there is a side road here. If we really block this army road, he can use this side road here. But including Schikola, so we have the whole thing.

THE FÜHRER: We have to remain over there, so that we have the road. That is an unpleasant thing.

ZEITZLER: We won't be able to do it. That frees up the only reserves. I have double-checked, and the mountain regiment won't arrive here before the 20th.

THE FÜHRER: Whether or not they will finish the thing by the 20th is also a question. If they don't build themselves in, they will retreat here.

ZEITZLER: I think, though, that it is naturally quite strong.

THE FÜHRER: Whenever they retreat, I always fear that they will leave the materiel behind.[13] Then we have troops but no materiel—leaving aside the issue of morale, because we can't do anything with it then.

ZEITZLER: The preparation has to be divided up over several days; then we will get it back, because there is a position here with not much in it. The 16th Motorized Division has made quite a nice thrust—150 were taken prisoner and they went back with these.[14]

THE FÜHRER: They didn't conduct mobile warfare down there; they left the tanks behind and didn't do anything—position warfare.

ZEITZLER: We could have moved the flanks much further forward. Relatively little on this front. I have settled this thing with the retreat order. It will now be diluted a bit. He wanted to give the order to retreat. (*Presentation.*)

Thrust on Stalingrad

The situation here[15] has developed like this: this morning Field Marshal Manstein phoned me. He holds the bridge at this village. A little bit of pressure is already beginning against the 23rd Panzer Division. That is probably because of the troops that were brought in. The resistance here was not terribly strong. During the course of the day today, though, there was some quite heavy fighting. He took Rychkovskii. That is unfortunate because of the bridge. That was the connection we wanted to make over to this place. The attack has also spread out further to here, while on the whole, it has relaxed. We listened in on a radio message from the 8th Cavalry Corps and heard that they want to shift into defense posture. Up here it is still unclear what he is actually doing. One could regard it as a reaction to our radio operation, since it was especially high during the days before we lined up for the attack. But one could also see it as him wanting to do something. Attacks against the Sixth Army were mainly in this area here. Field Marshal Manstein called today about the coming of this attack,[16] and he put it down on paper as reiteration and sent it. (*Presentation.*[17])

THE FÜHRER: He has 80 kilometers as the crow flies.

ZEITZLER: He sent it as a written document. Perhaps you could read it. The 16th (likely referring to the 6th Panzer Division); is not up for discussion. If we pull the 16th out, the entire Romanian front will collapse, and we'll never get it right again. Maybe he thinks that because there is a gap, the panzer army can send something in there. Otherwise, I'm surprised that he actually came up with this suggestion.

THE FÜHRER: We'll have to wait and see what he has in the way of forces. After all, he has two strong divisions. One of them has 95, the other 138 tanks.

ZEITZLER: Of course, there is a risk, if two divisions are drawn out.

THE FÜHRER: I admit that—without doubt. However, he has Luftwaffe units there as well, and something has to come out here. When is the next infantry division coming?

ZEITZLER: It will be a long time—8 days—before we have them. We had hoped that the 11th Panzer Division would be able to go in there. That would be tolerable. If it can't go there, the two armored divisions[18] will be left behind. This 23rd [Panzer Division] is getting bitten into from the flank and will have to do it. The only one left is the 6th (Panzer). It's particularly difficult when the counterattacks come and the connection is supposed to be maintained. If we take away the 17th [Panzer] from up there, then a risk is created there, too. But the attack of two panzer divisions can wait, and it is possible that we will be forced after 2 days to pull in the 17th [Panzer], and then maybe a day will have been lost.

THE FÜHRER: He wanted to put the 17th [Panzer Division] in here.

ZEITZLER: He wanted to pull this one in here and take this one over here.

THE FÜHRER: Actually, the 17th [Panzer Division] is of no value.

ZEITZLER: If any of them is, then it's the 11th [Panzer Division].

THE FÜHRER: It has only 45 tanks.

ZEITZLER: So far it had 49. Only a few have broken down. It has one detachment located up here, and we could add a regiment of the 306th [Infantry Division] as a temporary measure.

THE FÜHRER: When did the 11th [Panzer] lose so many tanks? It used to have 70 or 80 tanks up there.

ZEITZLER: As far as I know, it came down with 49 tanks.

THE FÜHRER: There are breakdowns again.

ZEITZLER: Of course, there are always short breakdowns, which last for a day. In such weather the number increases again the next day.

HEUSINGER: The 11th Panzer Division once had 57 down here.

THE FÜHRER: They left up there with 73 or 75.

ZEITZLER: I will check it again. I don't know the number by heart. From my experience, in this kind of weather one generally has to count on 10 to 20 missing tanks.

THE FÜHRER: I want to hear the rest of the situation first. I will come back to this matter at the end.

Don front

ZEITZLER: On the whole, nothing else is going on here. With the Italians, it turned out yesterday that they had been in it after all, and dug a hole of 1,200 meters. Afterwards they marched here during the night, arrived at 10 a.m. and are now able to join in if something happens. The situation seems to be more or less under control. If attacks start here during the morning, it will be a good thing that the regiment is located here. He attacked again; yesterday he sought some contact here, and this morning here. Here he entered a bit. In reaction to this, the army group acted quickly and independently. They deployed a regiment of the 385th Infantry Division and gave the 385th the command in this small sector so that the "Cosseria" is free. I think this is right. There were only small thrusts there. He made a small advance west of Svoboda, came in a bit and left again. At the moment, one gets the impression that he is not really done here yet. It is also possible that this is only a holding action somehow. But with the Italians, one never knows what will come out of it. He can make a small tactical attack and be successful after all.

THE FÜHRER: Here they've been driven back everywhere?

ZEITZLER: Only at this spot. A regiment of the 385th [Infantry] Division is deployed here, and the 385th Division took over command.

THE FÜHRER: But there is a steep escarpment.

ZEITZLER: Yes, actually it was safe from tanks. He is not reported to have appeared with tanks.

THE FÜHRER: If we had had 14 days, these units would have been there. I wanted to give these tanks to the Italians. Actually, it is really a loss of 14 days. But on the other hand, to put three more German divisions in here, you know—until the railway functioned better, it would have been difficult to feed this.

ZEITZLER: The supply situation is already starting to get a bit tense. We already had a difficult supply situation back then. Now we have troop transports there. We actually have to juggle with the Quartermaster General every evening, whether to put those trains in there.

THE FÜHRER: Has this branch been completed?

ZEITZLER: The railway is done.

THE FÜHRER: Completely done?

ZEITZLER: Yes.

THE FÜHRER: Over the whole way?

ZEITZLER: Yes, it is already in use. It has some minor defects. It has not been completely graveled. Everything will be pressed out that can possibly be pressed out. I have set up supply trains instead of some troop transports. They will join this rail transport.

THE FÜHRER: If one looks at all the danger points, this front[19] is still the greatest danger. It is our weakest ally, and there is nothing behind it in places. The Schulte brigade is arriving now, and then our escort battalion.[20] The Schulte brigade will be pressed in somehow, in order to hold there, at least. That is a small block. But if they evade infantry attacks without tanks in a territory where they are quite good because of their colossal artillery power, then I have to be pessimistic. How is the "Cosseria," actually?

ZEITZLER: As far as I know, 6 battalions.

JODL: A normal division, which has just arrived today. It has not been in action yet.

THE FÜHRER: And the *Cuneense*?

JODL: That is the Alpine [mountain troops] division.

HEUSINGER: There are three Alpine divisions.

THE FÜHRER: They will be better. [—] And the *Celere*?

JODL: *Celere*, *Torino*, and *Pasubio*[21] are the old ones. The *March 23* division is the Fascists.

ZEITZLER: There is one *January 3* division and one *March 23* division.

JODL: Those are the Fascist divisions.[22]

THE FÜHRER: Have they been taken out, or are they in there at the front?

JODL: They have them as reserves, and here they put the reserve battalion into action.

ZEITZLER: The 27th Panzer Division is not quite complete either. It's not doing a whole lot. It looks better on the map than it does in reality.

THE FÜHRER: I've been thinking about something. Here there is nothing more. If he starts here, then there's nothing left.

ZEITZLER: At most, we could put only a regiment of the 306th [Infantry] Division down there. That is the only way out of it. The army group suggested that they pull this one regiment group down to here. Then there would be something here tomorrow, and here we would have to pull in this regiment to here.

Part V

1943

Beginning: 12:17 p.m.

The East

ZEITZLER: In general it appears that the encirclement along the Don is now starting against the northern wing—a tank group with (numerous) tank corps, up here in this area. Manstein is bringing up the 7th Panzer Division. He is also taking the 3rd and the 11th Panzer Divisions over here. The 3rd Panzer Division is marching toward Rostov. ... Of course, it could get very difficult up there. This thing (with reference to the map): He's making a mistake with a secondary action. It could, of course, be connected—like a collapse. Which is why I came beforehand,[1] because I wanted to speak to you again once more about this important issue.[2] In general, the situation is now such that our offensive group in Khar'kov is being built up. One division will soon be ready, (the other) on the 12th.[3] We formed it here in order to push down here, to clear up this thing here and to (relieve) it. (It may be that we now) have to take it up above, at least one division. That would not be ideal. It totally depends: first, there is a huge amount of fuel required here. ... Now, it depends: if we have to drive them up above, of course, this salient (down below is endangered)…this salient, of course, only temporarily. But then there is also an unpleasant situation up here.

(ZEITZLER): I always worried about that. With the 3rd Panzer Division he has advanced quite well, and everything that is coming in is of extremely high quality.

THE FÜHRER: How is it going now with the 13th [Panzer Division]?[4]

ZEITZLER: Down here it seems that all the movements are going very well and are drawing near relatively quickly. The 3rd [Panzer] should now approach to here, and the 11th [Panzer] will follow. The ... arrives in this area this evening and should come through in one push to this area up here.

THE FÜHRER: We want to make sure that we can still ... them

ZEITZLER: Yes! In any case, I consider it correct to attempt to put them in up here.

THE FÜHRER: Is he going over here with the 7th Panzer Division?

ZEITZLER: Yes, he's going over there with the 7th Panzer Division.

THE FÜHRER: There are now 16 trains of the 335th [Infantry] Division there?

ZEITZLER: Yes! It was a little slower again, because of bomb damage along the way. [—] And now up here the question arises, ... to relieve…the cavalry corps. Then we would have something to provide cover below.

THE FÜHRER: The relief takes longer than the new arrivals.

ZEITZLER: ... But huge tension remains in any case, and I wanted to ask (For this reason,) that the economic program not be affected.[5]

THE FÜHRER: I will think about that. But I can say one thing: Then there would no longer be the possibility of ending the war through offensive action in the East. We have to bear that in mind.

(ZEITZLER: Yes!)

THE FÜHRER: Because I can't do it without the materiel. I can't do it with those people. Then I may have the people, but I have no materiel. The question is: what do we want now? We (now) have a width of 5 km,[6] but I can give the people guns and ammunition. Then I have only a 3 km width, but I have no more guns or ammunition. If you think we can fight at 3 km better without ammunition than at 5 km with ammunition, the calculation is correct.

ZEITZLER: Yes, that's a good question. At the moment it's not important, but it will be later.

THE FÜHRER: No, now as well as later! (At the same time) the whole defense production program becomes invalid. Our whole tank program that is made of electro steel then drops out immediately ... (Also) our gun program. Instead of 600 per month we could then produce only 150 guns. The large ammunition program is (eliminated) immediately as well. At that moment it drops swiftly. (It won't happen gradually); it will happen rapidly. I wouldn't win anything with that. If I were to go back, I would lose the ..., there will be utter confusion, and the enemy would push in behind. We've also had those experiences while retreating.

ZEITZLER: That's quite clear to me. But if we had not conducted the retreat, it would have become even worse. They had to move back there and down here—here by the panzer army.

THE FÜHRER: I've said since the beginning—for me it was completely clear: If the action can't be undertaken here, then there are only the two bridgeheads. That is obvious. If (it had been done like that), as the good Manstein wanted, they would not have been able to withdraw and everything would have fallen to pieces. If I had given in to Manstein, they would (not have returned). ... (He would have) had not more panzer army nor would he have brought a Seventeenth Army back—everything would have collapsed. ... I've always been concerned that he might stay here too long[7] [—]

(ZEITZLER): And now I (thought) we might immediately bring the 337th [Infantry] Division up from France behind the 4th Panzer Division, with some of the 78th [Infantry] Division at the same time, in order to start forming a new block here. And now we have to see what happens with the advance of the SS units. If we take the "Reich" [SS Panzer Division][8] up there, they will surely restore the situation. But that would take a long time. ... I would like to think that we have no other choice but to put them in down there.

THE FÜHRER: We will see. It depends on how it goes with the 4th Panzer Division. If the 4th Panzer Division gets off to a halfway good start [—]

ZEITZLER: There are 15 trains (on their way. Progress is slow) because they have destroyed everything with bombs; 7 trains should arrive today.

THE FÜHRER: When the 4th Panzer Division arrives (one unit will be there). Another unit will be there when the 337th [Infantry] Division comes behind it. And the 78th [Infantry Division] would come as well.

With them, we'll have (a group of forces that might) permit us to take hold of (this thing). We have to wait and see. If we can grab it with that, it's [—] True to form, they surrendered themselves.[9] Because otherwise, you gather yourselves together, build an all-round defense, and shoot yourself with the last cartridge. If you imagine that a woman, after being insulted a few times, has so much pride that she goes out, locks herself in, and shoots herself dead immediately—then I have no respect for a soldier who (shrinks back from it and prefers) going into captivity. There I can only say: (I can understand it in a case) like General Giraud, where we come in, he gets out of the car, and is immediately captured.[10] But [—]

ZEITZLER: I can't understand it either. I still think that (it may not) be true—that he may be seriously wounded.

THE FÜHRER: No, it is true. The Russians will now … immediately … They will go to Moscow immediately, to the GRU [Military Intelligence Directorate], and they will give out orders that the northern pocket should surrender as well.[11] This Schmidt[12] will sign everything. A person who does not have courage at such a moment to take the step that everyone has to take once, will not have the strength to resist. He will develop a martyr complex. (With us) the intellect is cultivated too much and strength of character not enough …

ZEITZLER: One can't actually explain how.

THE FÜHRER: Don't say that! I had a letter [—] Below received the letter.[13] I can show it to you. There he said, "I reached the following judgment about those people"—and then it read: "Paulus[14]: Question mark; Seydlitz[15]: shoot him; Schmidt: shoot him."

ZEITZLER: I have also heard bad things of Seydlitz.

THE FÜHRER: And below them: "Hube[16]—that man!" Of course, (one could say that it might have been) better if Hube had stayed inside and the others had gone out. But because people are still important and because we need the men for the entire war, I am really of the opinion that Hube will go out. In peacetime, 18,000 to 20,000 people chose suicide each year[17] in the German Reich, without being in any such situation. Here a man can see how 50,000 to 60,000 of his soldiers die and defend themselves bravely to the end—how can he then surrender to the Bolsheviks?! Oh, that is [—]!

ZEITZLER: It's something that we really can't understand at all.

THE FÜHRER: But the first (doubt had already arisen earlier). That was the moment when it was said that he asked what he should do now.[18] How can he even ask such a thing? So in the future, whenever a fortification is besieged and the commanding officer receives a demand to surrender, he is going to ask first: What shall I do now? [—][19] How easy he made it for himself![20] Or Becker[21]: He became confused when loading his weapon, made ... and later on he shoots himself.[22] How easy it is to do such a thing! The pistol—that is quite easy. What kind of cowardice it must be to flinch even from that! Ha! Better let yourself be buried alive! And in such a situation where he knows full well that his death is the requirement for holding the next pocket. Because if (he) gives (an example like that), you cannot expect the men to continue fighting.

ZEITZLER: There is no excuse. Then he has to shoot himself before, if the nerves threaten to fail.

THE FÜHRER: If the nerves fail, there is nothing (left but to say:) I couldn't take it any longer—and shoot oneself. There you can also say: The man has to shoot himself, just like (in earlier times the generals) threw themselves onto their swords when they saw that all was lost. That is a matter of course. Even Varus ordered to the slaves: Kill me now!

ZEITZLER: I still think that they might have done it, and (that the Russians only claim) they all gave themselves over into captivity.

THE FÜHRER: No!

ENGEL: The peculiar thing is—if I may say it—that they did not announce (that Paulus was captured seriously wounded.) Then they could say tomorrow he died of his wounds.

THE FÜHRER: Do we have precise news about his wounds?[23] [—]
The tragic thing has happened now. That might be a warning.

ENGEL: The names of the generals can't all be correct.

THE FÜHRER: During this war no one else will become a field marshal. That will all be done after the end of the war. One should not count ones chickens before they hatch.[24]

ZEITZLER: We were so strongly convinced about the end that we ... our last joy ...

THE FÜHRER: We had to assume it would end heroically.

ZEITZLER: One could not imagine anything else.

THE FÜHRER: And in this human environment, how could one act differently?! There I must say that every soldier is an idiot who risks his life, and risks his life again and again. If a little "pussy" is overwhelmed, I can still understand that.

ZEITZLER: The troop commander has it much easier. Everyone looks at him. For him it is simple to shoot himself. It is difficult for the ordinary man.

THE FÜHRER: If the little worm, on which everything is falling, says in such a situation, ... and lets himself be captured, then I can understand that. But I must say: How heroically have the ... One cannot argue with that. Of course, also many Germans! [—] and that we don't achieve it with our intellectually superior command cadre, our high-quality soldiers and our weapons that are still in the end superior to the Russians.' Nevertheless, we were always superior, disregarding Stalingrad. When I heard it tonight, I had Puttkamer find out if the news was already out. If (it had not been announced) via radio broadcast, (I would have) stopped it immediately.[25] It hurts me so much because the heroism of so many soldiers is destroyed by a single spineless weakling—and the man is going to do that now. You have to imagine it: He comes to Moscow, and just imagine the "rat cage"![26] He'll sign everything there. He will make confessions and appeals. You will see: They will walk down the road completely disregarding any principle—to the deepest abyss. In this case one can also say: An evil deed generates new evil again and again.

ENGEL: One thing, tomorrow Major Zitzewitz[27] is scheduled to (speak about Stalingrad) to the domestic and foreign press. Should that be cancelled?

THE FÜHRER: No, ...

ENGEL: I come to that point because there, of course, questions will be asked, among others a question ...The best thing would be to ... only very generally [—]

(THE FÜHRER): ... If somebody knows something, we don't know about; it cannot be determined exactly. But with soldiers, the primary thing is always the matter of principle, and if we cannot cultivate that, if we breed only pure intellectual acrobats and intellectual athletes—mental athletes—then we never will get that species which alone can stand the heavy blows of fate. That is decisive.

ZEITZLER: Yes, also in the General Staff. For the first time, I gave the uniform to an officer[28] who had not gone through general staff officer training because his preparation for the withdrawal of the division was as brilliant as the General Staff does it. It also does not matter that he has been in the course only 8 weeks.[29] It had an immediate effect. I immediately said: as of today, you are a general staff officer.

THE FÜHRER: Yes, we have to take bold, courageous people who are also prepared (to risk their lives), just like every soldier risks his life. What does that mean, "Life"? Life ... people; the individual indeed has to die. What remains alive beyond the individual is the people. But how one can fear this moment—through which he (can free) himself from misery—(if) duty (does not) hold him back in this valley of suffering! Well! [—]

They also reported that Paulus was captured. I want to have it sorted out: captured and missing. If they break in and take it without a fight, everyone knows they've been captured. The others must be reported as missing. ...

ZEITZLER: ...The attacks did not continue today. The report from (Kurzbach[30]) about the withdrawal is very reasonable—the order for it. He's also arranged it very sensibly. To be sure, he has sent a bit too much paper about how they are doing everything, but he did think about all those things. I don't know if it interests you. I can leave it here if it does. He has divided it into different stages. That is definitely good. And he also (planned) the immediate steps (correctly): that the thing here is thoroughly covered, and the ammunition goes in here, and also there—but first, that whatever comes from here, ... does not go in there under any circumstances. [—] Then I can leave it here.

THE FÜHRER: I do not know how to proceed in Paulus' case. (We must give the commander in the northern pocket an order that he must hold it under all circumstances. The pocket must be held until the end. [—])

(ZEITZLER: Then you agree) that I should do it this way?

THE FÜHRER: Yes! I'll come back to that thought again. The Romanian general Lascar fell with his men. I'm glad that I gave him the Oak Leaves.[31] How can such a thing happen? When I heard about that at 2:30 last night—I had gone to bed early—I had Puttkamer come right away in order to find out (if the radio report had gone out already. Because the Russians reported): Marshal Paulus captured with his entire staff. The whole staff surrendered. Now the Russians leave [—]

ZEITZLER: Just what I suspected! I thought they would misuse the dead Paulus ... And now it's even worse.

THE FÜHRER: He will soon speak via radio—you will see that.[32] Seydlitz and Schmidt will speak on the radio. They will lock them into rat cellars, and two days later they will have broken them, and then they will speak immediately. A beautiful woman—who really was a first-rate beauty—is (insulted) with (a single word. She says afterward), because of some trifle: "Then I can go; I am superfluous." ... (replies:) "Then go!" Afterward, the woman leaves, writes farewell letters, (and shoots herself).[33] [—] Did the wounding occur before Jaenecke's[34] departure or afterward?

ZEITZLER: I want to check on that. I'll phone Jaenecke, because he would know if it had happened beforehand.

THE FÜHRER: We have to confirm that! Then we have to take the position that the staff also fought to the last, and that they only gave in to the enemy's superior strength (and were taken into captivity) when they were wounded or overpowered.

ZEITZLER: That is surely what the majority of the staff did.

THE FÜHRER: We have to say that it was not a capitulation but an overpowering.

ZEITZLER: We can also write in: "The Russians will describe it differently"—that way the world press will get it from us first.

THE FÜHRER: (That they) had not received any supplies for months and that (therefore the Russians) succeeded in overwhelming some of them.

ZEITZLER: I agree that this direction is the right one.

THE FÜHRER: It is just the beginning. I would guess that in eight days at the latest [—]

(General Zeitzler excuses himself: 1:02 p.m.)

Continuation of the conference at 1:05 p.m. with the usual circle of participants.)

THE FÜHRER: Can I get Below?

CHRISTIAN: I don't know if he drove to Leipzig today.

Stalingrad

[A relief operation for the Sixth Army, which has been surrounded in Stalingrad since December 23, can no longer be considered. Yesterday, on January 31, Field Marshal Paulus surrendered. Only in the northern pocket is the remainder of the XI Army Corps still holding out.]

February 1, 1943

JODL: Concerning the Russian report, we are now checking carefully to see if there are any mistakes in it. Because a single mistake—a general who could not possibly have been there—would show that the whole thing was made up from a list that they captured somewhere and then published.

THE FÜHRER: (They report) that they captured Paulus, as well as Schmidt and Seydlitz.

JODL: I don't know about Seydlitz. They're not sure whether he's in the northern pocket. That's what will now be determined through a radio inquiry. Which generals exactly are in the northern pocket?

THE FÜHRER: He was surely with Paulus.[35] [—] I want to tell you something: I do not understand a man like (Paulus), who does not prefer death. The heroism of so many tens of thousands of men, officers and generals is wiped out (by a man like that,) who, when the moment comes, does not possess the character to do what a weak woman has done.

JODL: But I'm still not quite sure if that's right. [—]

(THE FÜHRER): ... The man and the woman were together there. Later the man died of his illness. Then I received a letter from that woman; she begged me to care for the children. It was not possible for her to continue living, despite her children. ... Then she shot herself. The woman did that; she found the strength—and soldiers do not find the strength! You will see: It won't take eight days before Seydlitz and Schmidt and also Paulus speak on the radio.

JODL: I am firmly convinced of that.

THE FÜHRER: They are now taken into the Lubyanka, and there rats will eat them. How can somebody be (so cowardly)? I don't understand it.

JODL: I still have doubts.

THE FÜHRER: I don't, unfortunately. Do you know—I also don't believe anymore in the wounds that (Paulus supposedly received). That doesn't seem to be true either. Because they still have to expect that they [—] What should we do then? Personally, it hurts me the most that I still did that—promoted him to field marshal. I wanted to give him the last (happiness). That's the last field marshal I will (make) during (this war). One should not praise the day until it's over. I don't understand that at all. If you see so many (men) die—I really must say how easy it was for our ...; he did not consider anything. That is completely ridiculous. So many men have to die, and then a man like that goes out and besmirches the heroism of so many others at the last minute. (He could have) delivered (himself from every misery) and reached eternity and entered into the national immortality—but he preferred going to Moscow. How can (there even be a choice)? It's just crazy.

JODL: That's why I still have doubts [—]

(THE FÜHRER): ... just as if I were to say today: I'll give a fortification to General Förster. Then I know immediately that he'll be (the first one to) pull down the flag.[36] There are others who wouldn't do that. It's tragic that in such a moment heroism (is defiled) so terribly like that.

JESCHONNEK: I still consider it possible that the Russians (reported) that intentionally. Their work is very refined.

THE FÜHRER: They will speak on the radio in eight days.

JESCHONNEK: The Russians will even manage to get (somebody else) to speak.

THE FÜHRER: No, they will speak personally over the radio. You will hear it right away. No, they will all speak personally on the radio! They will first order the men in the pocket to surrender, and will say the most awful things against the German Armed Forces. You have to bear in mind: (they come) to Moscow, to the Lubyanka, and are being "treated" there. If a person doesn't have the courage in such an hour [—] I also already told Zeitzler that he must give an order to Heitz, telling him to hold the northern pocket.

KEITEL: He was in the southern pocket, and Heitz was not mentioned (in the Russian report).[37]

THE FÜHRER: Then he must be dead if he was not mentioned.

JODL: Yes, and because of that we must also (inquire) and establish who is in the northern pocket now. If there are names in it[38] of people who are in the northern pocket, then it must be a list that they found somewhere and published. On the other hand, (it is already a fact) that they have not mentioned a man who certainly fell—Hartmann—who was in the southern pocket.

KEITEL: He was killed four days ago.[39]

JODL: Yes!

THE FÜHRER: If Heitz was in the southern pocket and was not mentioned ... I am convinced that the whole staff simply surrendered obediently [—]

Weapons for Italy

THE FÜHRER: I spoke to Schmundt to find out (whether we) have the people to do it. We'll give the Italians (weapons), and the weapons will find their way to people who will pass them on to the enemy, and before long we will be attacked with them. It makes no difference whether these are weapons seized from the Russians or others—at any case, the weapons will soon be turned against us. I asked Schmundt whether we have the personnel to do something, if I could propose to the Duce—if I meet with him—to establish 6 Fascist divisions, which he would take out of the M-divisions[40] and we would establish, organize and train in Germany. They should consist of only tried and true Fascists. We could help them with the command and provide them with weapons. I'm thinking here of Italy, too, because to him two such divisions—one in Rome and the other (in northern Italy) are not less than ... God knows what ... Let's see, what the Duce ... thinks. We keep having to (supply) weapons anyway. There is no point in continuing like we have been. I can be quite frank (with the Duce), because he has ... told, that I'm going to tell him the whole truth about (the losses) in the East. I'll tell him: if you ... set up from scratch, you won't achieve anything. Of course, (you could) make up for it, provided you (had a) decent officer corps. If you don't have that (and) if you don't start from scratch, the new formation will be doomed from the very beginning. In that case you would have to begin with (Adam and) Eve, otherwise the work would be useless. He has (good) people among them, of course, but they cannot prevent the whole ... The M-battalions were included in the various divisions, but they are worn down there and don't have any value or impact. This will only change when he himself establishes 6 divisions to start with, and then 8, 10, or 12 divisions. If we have to supply weapons to them, then let's supply them for these units. They will be excellently armed and give him support in his own country. As soon as he has four such divisions at his disposal, he will be in a position to have his way and start disbanding the pathetic army divisions or integrate other officers ... in order to bring about a gradual improvement. (Without them) he can't do it. (This is) in our own interest. If there were Fascist (units) trained by us in North Africa, they would be better than four such divisions, (who because of) their incapable commanders and their ... take off at the first gunshot. ... told me: One sees among the people many wonderful ...; but they did not succeed in ... separating them. They just ... around everywhere ... and don't have any zeal. The officers have no sense of responsibility; their only thought is to go (to) the coffee shop.

Japan

JODL: The military attaché from Tokyo will give you an overview of the distribution of Japanese forces.

THE FÜHRER: The Japanese have had bad luck with this big convoy, if the reports are true. The convoy seems to have been broken up.[41]

JODL: Regarding the overall strength, the military attaché reports the following figures: 63 divisions, 6 infantry brigades, 2 armored divisions, 4 motorized brigades and 18 reserve divisions of the reserve army at home. The Kwantung Army Group has apparently been weakened. At least we had earlier supposed their number to be greater. On the northeastern front there are 15 divisions and 2 armored divisions. There is another army, which includes the Manchurian divisions, further to the south: 2 infantry divisions, 2 infantry brigades, one cavalry division, one motorized brigade.

THE FÜHRER: And these three?

JODL: These three belong to Korea. Well, this … the Korea Army and the Peking Army can be brought in.

THE FÜHRER: Then it adds up to 20 divisions after all.

JODL: Yes. We had assumed there would be more, namely … divisions.

THE FÜHRER: What are the estimates?

JODL: According to estimates, there are 20 infantry divisions, 4 brigades … cavalry divisions, 2 armored brigades and 3 motorized brigades.

THE FÜHRER: Those men are the best the Japanese have.

JODL: These are excellent divisions. There is the China Army Group and the Southern Group with 14 infantry divisions. Some of them are brigades. Then there is the Chinese National Army, which is included at a lower fighting value. Here there are 8 divisions and 2 infantry brigades deployed in the northern part. The Kwantung Army, with 4 infantry divisions and 2 infantry brigades, is also part of the China Army Group. The 1,500,000-man Chunking Force is deployed in the entire area. Next is the Southern Army Group with one army in Rangoon, which used to contain 5 divisions and has now been increased to 6. Then, behind the lines, the covering forces (and) 5 Thai divisions. One division with limited strength is stationed in Indochina, and another division is in Singapore. The forces on other islands are relatively weak. There are two divisions on Sumatra and more than one division of occupying forces on Java. Weak occupation forces on Borneo and Celebes. One army made up of two divisions is stationed in Manila. The new Southeast Army Group has now been established; it is comprised of two armies in Rabaul, which were recruited primarily from these forces and will now be transferred there. [—] The evacuation of Guadalcanal was obviously successful,[42] and a new Eastern Front is being established. To this end they are launching several attacks in order to bring the enemy down on New Guinea. The enemy has two American and two Australian divisions on New Guinea, plus 5 American divisions, one Marine division and a division from New Zealand on the eastern islands. Three American divisions and one from New Zealand are stationed in the New Hebrides.

THE FÜHRER: That makes 14 to 15 American divisions in all.

JODL: He deployed major forces on the Aleutian Islands as well. The Japanese limited themselves to keeping one reinforced regiment up there.

But they don't have an airstrip. The number of aircraft reported for the enemy is not very large either. There are 8 British divisions and some 350 aircraft and 2 Chungking divisions in Burma, and there are some 250 aircraft on the Solomon Islands, 350 aircraft on New Guinea, 500 aircraft in Australia, 200 aircraft in … and 100 in the New Hebrides. The Japanese are convinced that the main action in 1943 will continue to take place in the European theater of operations.

THE FÜHRER: That doesn't please us greatly.

JODL: The evacuation of Guadalcanal was successful.

THE FÜHRER: We must not attach undue importance to what the Japanese say. I don't believe a word.

JODL: One cannot believe them, for they are the only people who intentionally tell you a big lie with an expression of sincerity.

THE FÜHRER: They'll tell you a pack of lies—their reports and representations are calculated on something that proves to be deception later on.

HEWEL: The general public in America believes this to be the main theater of operations.

THE FÜHRER: I read a statement from Dieckhoff.[43] He disputes this. There isn't a bit of truth in it. If you want to win over the Americans, you only need to say the following: First, the war is being waged in America's interests; second, the British Empire will be liquidated; third, the Japanese are the main enemy. With these remarks you will get an overwhelming majority. The Jews are against it, but they[44] have the overwhelming majority. The English are now starting to complain (more and more) about the political developments, as they are afraid that things will turn against their empire.

HEWEL: It would be interesting to learn something about the condition of the American divisions in North Africa. Neurath[45] arrived from Tunis last night. He tells interesting stories. He questioned some American prisoners of war and (says) that they tell crazy stories. Most of them came over in order to earn money or for the excitement and adventure of it to see something different and be a part of it. No trace of political aims. They are just rowdies who will disappear quickly—they will not be able to get through a crisis.[46] He says he talked to hundreds of them. None of them had any political convictions or any great ideas.

THE FÜHRER: They will never become Rome. America will never be the Rome of the future. Rome was a peasants' state.

HEWEL: But the Americans have good human material somewhere.

JODL: That is only an outward appearance.

THE FÜHRER: Not as much as one might imagine. They live in the few regions where the Europeans are dominating. But on no account do they have the large … centers. The farmers are impoverished. I saw photographs. Never before have I seen such pitiful and stunted farmers—nothing but uprooted beings wandering around.[47]

CHRISTIAN: No intellect, no inner (attitude).

JODL: Nothing like that.

HEWEL: You only have to look at the posters they use to publicize the war. They are impossible!

THE FÜHRER: There is no doubt that of all the Anglo-Saxons the English are the best.

JODL: With the English you have the feeling that they fight for their country and empire, but with the Americans, you don't have that feeling.

THE FÜHRER: That might explain why the English say that they can always handle the Americans.

HEWEL: That is a very thoughtless attitude. They cannot "deal with" them, if only because they are economically and in every other respect dependent on them. But they consider themselves superior to the Americans both politically and militarily to such an extent that they say, "We will recapture the lost territory in 10 years." This is what the English are saying. Very thoughtless indeed.

THE FÜHRER: There is one thing, Jodl, that is also clear, when it comes to strength, it is not only the population that counts, but also the size of the territory. Just look at the Chinese empire. The fighting has been going on for five years and part of the country is occupied, but the whole block is still standing.

JODL: And, what is more, with hardly any weapons.

THE FÜHRER: This will definitely be the end, unless we can expand our space. Space is one of the most important military factors. You can only operate if you have space. The wars of the future will be won by those who have space. This is the bad luck of the French. During a single offensive last year we occupied more territory than during all of our Western offensives. So France was finished in 6 weeks, while we are enduring here in a huge territory. If we had experienced such a crisis along the old border on the Oder-Warthe bend, Germany would have been finished. But here in the East we can do something about it. We have a theater enabling us to operate.

JODL: Things have changed. Germany was an expanse during the Roman wars. In the Middle Ages, armies marched through Germany in all directions, and now, in the era of tanks and aircraft [—]

THE FÜHRER: It does not take more than an hour and a quarter to go from one end of the old Reich territory to the other in a fast plane.

JODL: But the Russian space is a space that is impossible even for aircraft, as illustrated by the industrial region in the Urals. You can't get there.

CHRISTIAN: It takes 2½ hours to fly from Cologne to Königsberg.

THE FÜHRER: If the aircraft has a speed of 600 km per hour, it takes 1¼ hour from Stettin to Munich. In the pre-war era, Germany was nothing more than Schleiz-Greiz,* etc., as far as the fragmentation of German territory was concerned. It was ridiculous compared with the rest of the world. Here we speak of entire continents: America, East Asia, or Russia. And Australia! Seven million people have an entire continent to themselves. This was one of the craziest proposals: the Prince of Windsor said back then that the Germans should settle in northern Australia.[48] He always was in favor of our getting that region. But then we would have settled there and one day the English would have taken it.

HEWEL: Australian agriculture is German! The German element has been the most creative one in Australia.[49]

THE FÜHRER: That is precisely why they want the Germans in that region. I told him that we do not attach much importance to it. Australia to the Australians! [—] I don't believe what the Japanese are saying.

JODL: The statements do not specify what they are doing there. On the other hand, they are saying that Vladivostok is unbearable in the long run. To avoid a fragmentation of forces, the Japanese won't attack the Soviet Far East right now, unless American bases were to be set up there or the Soviet Union collapses. In any case, the Japanese war economy is prepared for a long war. According to them, they do not think that 1943 would be the decisive year.

THE FÜHRER: If they are prepared for a long war, then they will have to dig in there, because the Americans will certainly establish bases in that area.

HEWEL: They will have to go to northern Australia.

THE FÜHRER: It is surprising that Stalin recently gave the Americans a slap in the face.[50]

HEWEL: I don't imagine that Churchill congratulated Stalin for it.

---

* [NDT] Tiny principality in 18th-century Germany.

JODL: They must move in here.

HEWEL: Yes, this is the area from which they get their raw materials—their resources and their wealth—and as long as these resources last, they will launch new attacks.

THE FÜHRER: Imagine how much the Japanese have accomplished in so short a period! It is ridiculous to believe that Japan is unable to put up more than 30 infantry divisions. Japan has a larger population than Germany in the territory of the old Reich. They should be able to establish 120 divisions. But we don't really know how many they have in reality. It stands to reason that they don't say how many they have, in order to be on the safe side. Then all of a sudden it turns out that they have not 15 but 30 infantry divisions up there.

JODL: You never know with the Japanese.

HEWEL: If they operate in this area, it is not a fragmentation of their forces. The operations are quite independent.

THE FÜHRER: The only issue for them on which I cannot give an opinion is the issue of tanks. Do they or don't they have a modern tank? What was Oshima's answer? I assume that this question was put to him.

HEWEL: He did not tell me.

THE FÜHRER: I believe he said that they do have modern tanks.

CHRISTIAN: He is not properly informed[51] by his people. Their announcements on tanks are just as sparse as those regarding aircraft.

THE FÜHRER: They did not say anything about ships, either, and then all of a sudden there they were with the heaviest ships on earth.[52] They did not speak about aircraft carriers, and suddenly it turns out that they have the largest number of aircraft carriers.[53] However, after the war, they will have to mothball their large battleships, because then only planes will be used. Even over there all talk centers on aircraft.

HEWEL: The Japanese have been bombed repeatedly; for instance, near the Midway Islands and down there.[54] They came too close.

THE FÜHRER: Nobody dares use such large ships anymore. What would be unpleasant for them would be if they couldn't get control of it quickly, i.e., that it might become a base for submarine warfare. I am convinced that the Japanese will completely establish their base here before they start action. They will probably not engage in maritime traffic, but might start with a blockade. One thing is certain. That is something we most certainly will not find out. These people send an ambassador and another ambassador to Washington to moan there and they themselves have no idea what they're talking about. I can imagine good old Kurusu waddling around there.[55] He has no idea what's going on and when he arrives at the White House, he is shouted at, "You're playing dirty tricks." The little Japanese was dumfounded, as he had no idea that Pearl Harbor had been attacked. They don't say a word.[56] I don't say anything either.

HEWEL: Maybe they realized that it's necessary to build tanks first.

CHRISTIAN: Large tanks are of no use in the jungle.

THE FÜHRER: We don't drive around Yugoslavia in our heaviest tanks. Why should I take a Tiger to finish off a sniper? In view of the incredible Japanese secrecy and cleverness, in this regard, it is entirely conceivable that the Japanese have built heavy tanks, but do not use them for the time being so that the Russians don't notice anything. One day, they will use them.[57] So we should not be too concerned if they have two armored brigades and two armored divisions here because we can imagine what the Russians have there. They have been bled white three to five times already.

JODL: Whereas Japan has first-class troops.

THE FÜHRER: Yes, Russia has been bled white. If it were to start all of a sudden, one would assume it would crackle faster than elsewhere. Maybe they will do it quite differently and will push in this direction.[58]

CHRISTIAN: They got a thrashing in their border conflicts with the Russians.

THE FÜHRER: Only once.[59] Stalin … had … They were encircled.

CHRISTIAN: Their air force also suffered.

THE FÜHRER. I don't know about that. They drove back … all the attacks. There is only this single case, where they were ambushed. Stalin said, "I do not want to wage war against the Japanese, but if they raise a fight with us, they are mistaken, because we are also prepared."

CHRISTIAN: That was at the time of the old Russian Army of the Far East.

THE FÜHRER: That was still one of the best ones. The Japanese have usually defeated the Russians, and they will continue to do so if they have nearly equivalent equipment. In this case, they waged war against the Chinese. The ship sent there was the Itsomu, launched in 1899—an old tub indeed.[60] That was the flagship. They only deployed very old ships and did not attack a single ship. They saved their really good ones. We did not fire on the Westerplatte with our most modern ships, either.

JODL: He describes the armaments as follows: (Text is read.)

THE FÜHRER: If they plan something they will never tell us. And if they draw our attention to the fact that they are planning an operation in the south, one could more likely expect something in the north instead. I told the foreign minister, "Dear Ribbentrop, do whatever you are able to do, and whatever you are able to do, do it. They will take advantage of the time. They would be crazy if they didn't. As long as they notice that forces are being withdrawn, they say ... with Asian cunning. Let him bleed white. But the moment they realize that the situation could become stable here and reinforcements may be moved to the East, you'll see swift action on their part and they will be there in time."

*****

The Conference at Feltre and the Fall of Mussolini

San Fermo-Feltre, near Venice: July 19, 1943

[From S. Corvaja, *Hitler and Mussolini. The Secret Meetings* (New York: Enigma Books, 2008).]

[The German leadership had been well aware of the fragility of Mussolini's position and the growing unpopularity of the Fascist regime since the defeats at El Alamein and Stalingrad. Mussolini had asked Heinrich Himmler for advice in case he was faced with growing unrest and even riots. However the German embassy in Rome and the Gestapo representatives were unable to predict the overthrow of the Duce and Italy's armistice with the Allies. See also: F. W. Deakin, *The Brutal Friendship* (New York: Harper & Row 1962).]

On Monday, July 19, 1943, at 8:30 a.m. Mussolini's plane landed at the airfield at Treviso on a flight from Rimini. Present at the airport were Bastianini, Ambrosio, Alfieri (who had just arrived from Berlin by plane as well), and German ambassador to Rome, von Mackensen. Alfieri approached Bastianini and asked: "What kind of mood is Mussolini in?" The undersecretary for foreign affairs replied: "He looks indifferent. He has wrapped himself in total silence." A short time later, at 8:50 a.m., Field Marshal Keitel and General von Rintelen arrived. Both generals approached Mussolini, who was wearing dark sunglasses, to pay their respects. While the Italians welcomed the Germans, the Führer's Condor aircraft landed at 9:00 a.m. Hitler immediately informed his hosts that his plans for an extended trip of several days had been canceled because he had to return immediately to his eastern headquarters to direct a decisive battle against the Russians.

Mussolini has left a biased and highly selective account of this meeting in his book, *Storia di un anno,*[*] dedicating less than one page to such a crucial conference: "Since the Führer had to return to Germany that afternoon, time was of the essence. Rather than at Feltre, which was located three hours away on a round trip, the talks could have easily taken place in the airport command building or at the municipal building at Treviso. But protocol had established its program, and no power in the world could change it. The Führer, Mussolini, and their staff took a one-hour train ride followed by another hour's ride by car to Villa Gaggia.

A beautiful, shaded park, and a labyrinthine building that made an eerie impression on one's mind. It looked like a crossword puzzle cast in stone. After a few minutes, the meetings began: the participants were the Führer, the Duce, Undersecretary Bastianini, Ambassadors von Mackensen and Alfieri, Italian Chief of Staff Ambrosio, Marshal Keitel, Generals Rintelen and Warlimont, Colonel Montezemolo, and a few other minor officials. The Führer started speaking at 11:00 a.m. He began with a clear and complete description of raw materials and the territories where they were located and the need for them to be defended. He then spoke of the air force, its current engagement, and its present and future capabilities. Regarding the battle unfolding in Sicily, he assured everyone that new reinforcements would be sent, especially artillery and troops.

A private conversation between Mussolini and Hitler then took place, where Mussolini underlined the need to dispatch reinforcements to Italy. They continued talking during the return trip by car and on the train and in parting, Mussolini said to Hitler: "We have a common cause, Führer!"

If the meeting went just as the Duce described, it is difficult to understand why the two dictators did not simply talk over the phone. The proceedings were in fact very different, so much so that it can be considered among the most crucial conferences between the two Axis partners. On the one hand, the Führer revealed his plans for his immediate strategy regarding Italy, while on the other hand, Mussolini simply confirmed through his silence that he was now passively expecting events to provide the solution to the problems that confronted the Fascist regime and Italy itself.

---

[*] The book, *Storia di un anno*, was first published as a series of articles by an "anonymous" author, accounting for the references to Mussolini in the third person. The book was published in 1944 and translated as *The Fall of Mussolini: His Own Story*, edited by Max Ascoli, New York 1948.

Before the string of cars reached San Fermo, General Keitel was able to confide to Rintelen that the real objective of the meeting was "to concentrate all power in the Duce's hands, to erase the influence of the House of Savoy, and to send Nazi reinforcements into Italy to place the country firmly under the control of the German high command." If what Rintelen reported was true, then the Duce showed courage on July 19, 1943, opposing by his passive behavior an absurd threat by Hitler and keeping the entire matter completely secret. According to historian Ruggero Zangrandi, Mussolini's dignified behavior can be explained either by the Duce's devotion to the king or by his long-meditated-on decision to quickly take Italy out of the Axis alliance. These motivations were certainly legitimate, especially the first one, if only because during those very hours the king himself was plotting with Acquarone and Ambrosio to remove Mussolini.

In his memoirs, Bastianini relates that during the train trip, Keitel had a heated argument with Ambrosio concerning German short-term plans on the Eastern Front and in the Mediterranean. The German general could barely restrain himself under a pressing question coming from Ambrosio: "I could see his cheeks redden even more and his hairy hand continuously wiping his forehead and temples, both dripping with perspiration, with a handkerchief. Ambrosio was constantly challenging him: 'You declare that you are not worried by the situation in Russia, that your reserves are fine, that all your losses there have been replaced, and then you say that you do not have the necessary supplies to allow Italian soldiers to defend their own soil from the enemy. The truth is that you do not have those reserves and the Russian front is far from secure.' Keitel had obviously not been authorized by Hitler to deal with the Italians. At one point he cut short the dramatic skirmish and said: 'All these issues will be handled by our leaders among themselves.'

At 11:00 a.m. in the vast ballroom of Villa Gaggia, after a somewhat unfriendly comment; *"Nein, Duze, so geht es nicht"* ("No, Duce, it doesn't work"), the Führer started his customary soliloquy with interpreter Paul Schmidt at his side. His presentation began with a strategic and political premise. The main issue requiring immediate attention was raw materials, without which, of course, no war could be won. For this reason, his priority was to defend all those territories under German military occupation that could deliver the means to bring about victory. The principle of this philosophy was to keep all German lands as far removed from the fighting as possible. It was true that in Germany there were some fearful individuals who would have welcomed an understanding with Russia. "And I," said Hitler vehemently, "will reject their suggestions for the simple reason that not even 300 hundred years from now would Germany produce another leader like myself, capable of solving the eastern problem."

Hitler then went on to examine the question of armaments' supply, arguing that the air force and submarine fleet would have to fulfill decisive tasks in the near future. Germany was about to introduce into the fighting new aircraft having exceptional performance capabilities, as well as U-boats equipped with special instrumentation. There were new tanks soon to appear, the gigantic *Panther* was going into record production and would soon confront the Russians. In the spring of 1944, forty-six newly formed and perfectly trained and equipped divisions would be ready. To further sweeten the good news he was giving his audience, Hitler mentioned two powerful new weapons, which would be used against Great Britain during the winter. The Führer had kept this announcement for the end of his introduction, perhaps to prepare his listeners for some unpleasant remarks concerning the behavior of the Italian army.

His revelations regarding the diabolical weapons were true. The project had progressed since his meeting with Mussolini at Klessheim in April. Twelve days before the conference at San Fermo, there had been a historic meeting at German headquarters that included the Führer, General Walter Dornberger, Dr. Werner von Braun, and the builders of the world's first military missile, known as the V2 rocket. They were the "magicians" of Peenemünde, the ultrasecret base of Usedom on the Baltic. Since May 1937, Peenemünde was the location of the new weapons engineering built and managed by Luftwaffe and Wehrmacht personnel. Suddenly, at 11:30 a.m. on July 7, 1943, the directors of the project were ordered to report to Rastenburg. Dornberger and von Braun quickly boarded a Heinkel III, piloted by another expert from the plant, Commander Ernst Steinhoff. The plane landed near Rastenburg at 1:00 p.m. but the group had to wait seven hours before being introduced into the Führer's study. Von Braun remembered the moment this way:

"Hitler appeared, accompanied by Field Marshal Keitel, General Jodl, General Walter Buhle, the Army Chief of Staff and Armaments Minister Albert Speer. Hitler's physical appearance was frightening. I had last seen him in 1939. He looked tired but still radiated an almost magic strength. His eyes had something diabolical in them, but his face was pale, and he looked like a beaten man. Dornberger was also concerned by Hitler's looks. Stalingrad had taken place just six months earlier. The Don River front had buckled. The Kursk offensive, the Zittadelle plan, which had started two days earlier on July 5, had already stopped. The hit-and-run war in the Atlantic was over. The Allies were fighting in Sicily, and the air war was considered lost."

The program was to show Hitler a film about the successful experiment of October 3, 1942: a thirteen-and-one-half-ton rocket—called "A4"—had effected the trajectory from the ramp to point X in the open sea about 200 kilometers from Peenemünde.

After giving Dornberger and von Braun a warm greeting, Hitler sat in the front row between Keitel and Speer. The documentary described the details of the experiment, and von Braun illustrated the images as they appeared on the screen. When the lights went on, no one spoke for a few minutes; there was absolute silence. Suddenly Hitler jumped out of his seat and went over to the two men from Peenemünde, shook their hands and said as emphatically as possible:

"I thank you. Why did I not believe in the success of your research? Had I had these missiles back in 1939, we would never have gone to war. In the face of such a missile, we can only say that Europe and the world, now and in the future, have both become too small for a war. With such weapons, war will become impossible for humanity."

He then asked the question that was foremost on his mind: "Is it possible to increase the payload of the missiles from one to ten tons?"

Dornberger and von Braun replied that they would need another four years to make a missile such as the Führer described. Hitler was satisfied and after promoting von Braun to "full professor," on July 25, 1943, he signed an order giving Peenemünde absolute precedence over all other armament programs. Four days later, Propaganda Minister Goebbels said in a speech at Heidelberg: "By the end of the war, the German people will have to get on their knees to thank their technicians, builders, inventors, and researchers. The British will be amazed . . ." But the road to success would be very long. The technicians of Peenemünde had to overcome many obstacles, and in those weeks they also became a target of enemy bombers. The first V1 "flying bomb" was scheduled to be fired on London at 4:18 a.m. on June 14, 1944 (eight days after the Allies had landed on the beaches of Normandy during the D-Day invasion). The firing of the missile would take place only fourteen months after the July 7 meeting. The first V2 rocket would be launched on the London suburbs of Chiswick and Epping at 6:43 p.m. on September 8, 1944. But by then Germany had already lost the war.

Hitler was in the middle of his monologue, when in the ballroom of the Villa Gaggia appeared an emotional and very pale De Cesare, who whispered to Mussolini: "Rome is under violent bombardment by the enemy." The Duce gave De Cesare's interruption only a few lines in his own chronicle of that day: "The news was given to Hitler and the other participants by Mussolini himself, and this created a very painful impression. During the rest of the Führer's presentation, more news kept coming about the Allied bombing of Rome."

Mussolini was somewhat disguising the truth. Hitler was not so much displeased by the fact that Rome was being bombed as he was annoyed at having been interrupted during his talk. He had little reason to be unhappy about the fact that the Eternal City was under fire when Berlin and the largest German cities were by now under constant attack and reduced, in many parts, to rubble. The Führer did not react overtly to the Duce's news.

"Probably," as von Plehwe wrote, "Mussolini expected some kind of statement of sympathy from Hitler in the face of extensive destruction of the city. Hitler appeared not to have heard what had been said. He just continued with his instructions on the future conduct of the war."

It was close to noon and the time for reprimands was at hand. Hitler said that according to his information Italian soldiers had not really fought in Africa or Sicily. The Italian high command had not been able to fulfill its mission. The civilian administration had shown itself to be weak. There was defeatism everywhere. The notes made by interpreter Schmidt show that, in spite of these remarks, Hitler gave his Italian allies assurances that the Reich would do its utmost to help on the southern front. Obviously Italian requests for equipment and supplies, said the Führer, were much too great to be satisfied. To transfer two thousand aircraft to the Mediterranean was out of the question. On that issue, he criticized the lack of well-equipped air bases and the atrocious assistance given to units of the Luftwaffe, operating in Italy for some time. The Italian government would have to lengthen the landing strips and expropriate the necessary land without any regard for the owners. The discipline of the troops had to be improved through military courts martial. As for Sicily, he would examine the possibility of sending new reinforcements and other artillery. Hitler then went on to the problem of communications between Sardinia, Corsica, and the islands of the Dodecanesus, overlooking the fact that Italy did not need advice but, rather, merchant ships, warships, and fuel.

Sicily was the most urgent problem demanding a solution. The Führer said that with the necessary supplies, a counterattack could be launched. Should that become impossible, then the best course of action would be to withdraw from the island, even though Hitler was aware of the consequences of such a decision on morale, adding that to protect the influx of reinforcements, Marshal Göring was ready to concentrate a significant number of antiaircraft artillery at the Strait of Messina. A final decision was necessary: should the decisive battle take place on the Italian mainland, therefore making it useless to dispatch more units into Sicily, or was it imperative to hold on to the island with all the consequences it would imply, including a unified command structure? Germany would then transfer other excellent divisions to the south. Finally Hitler concluded: "The struggle of the Fascist revolution and the National Socialist Party for victory is a task that cannot be left to the next generation."

It was by now 1:00 p.m. and Mussolini, up until then, despite his strong resolutions of the day before, had said virtually nothing. He had remained seated, with his legs crossed over the edge of the armchair that was too wide and too deep, listening patiently and impassively to Hitler's endless sermonizing. According to eyewitnesses, he appeared to be indifferent to what was going on in the ballroom. He shifted positions from time to time to avoid sliding with the cushion. He would draw his left hand behind his back and press on a spot that obviously hurt him. He stared at Hitler with a tired and beaten look, while the German dictator, in an increasingly high-pitched voice, continued to shower the Italians with all kinds of recriminations.

Mussolini could only interrupt Hitler's monologue to read the short dispatches that De Cesare would slip him about the bombing of Rome. Like a radio journalist, he would read them in Italian, then translate them into German. One such message made the Duce very anxious: "The violent attack continues. Four hundred bombers are flying at low altitude. Suburbs and buildings in the center are destroyed. Little reaction from the antiaircraft guns."

It was finally time for lunch. Hitler and Mussolini were in a living room alone, with the windows shut. There were no direct witnesses to this lunch, but it appears that the Duce did not eat at all, while the Führer displayed an excellent appetite as he ate white rice with béchamel sauce, cooked vegetables, cake, and fresh fruit. During the meal, Hitler reiterated his decision to pursue the war against Russia, rejecting another attempt by Mussolini to negotiate an armistice or a cease-fire with Moscow. He also spoke about the secret weapons, stating that some could be used as early as the end of next month, and of the new submarines with special equipment that would make it difficult for the enemy to locate them. Hitler concluded with a demand that the Duce liquidate the traitors of Fascism and beware of the king.

Mussolini did not share confidences with his friend and kept silent on the difficult political times he faced in Rome. He did not even mention the promise he had made to the hierarchy of the Fascist party to call a meeting of the Grand Council of Fascism. The German proposal to move all Italian divisions to southern Italy, leaving all the German units to guard the Alps and the Po Valley, was not really touched upon during the Führer's conference or the private meetings with the Duce, and not even during the clashes between Keitel and Ambrosio.

After lunch, the two dictators went to their rooms to rest. Hitler was given the room of the daughter-in-law of the owner, Senator Achille Gaggia. The Duce went to the main bedroom. It was now 2:00 p.m. While Hitler's footsteps could be heard down the marble hall as he went to his room, Mussolini was stopped by Alfieri, Bastianini, and Ambrosio, all three extremely excited by the news from Rome. The Duce stopped them by saying: "I am very unhappy to be away from the capital at this time. I would not like the people of Rome to think . . ."

Alfieri, the ambassador to Berlin, answered: "No one in Rome will give this any thought, because every Italian expects a momentous decision to come out of these meetings. Did you hear what Hitler is saying? It's your turn to counterattack, Duce. How much longer must Italy passively follow Germany and be transformed into a bastion?" "A supporting wall," corrected Mussolini. Alfieri went on: "For this reason you must answer Hitler with the same kind of brutal candor. The situation is serious. And if our army is in no condition to resist effectively, as General Ambrosio says—"

"I can absolutely confirm what you are saying," Mussolini interrupted. "We must have the courage to face reality. If we must break away we should do it immediately. As long as the carabinieri are in control.* Tomorrow could be too late." Mussolini looked at the two men and, after a few moments, continued: "Don't you think I have thought about this problem and it has haunted me for some time now? Behind my mask of apparent indifference, there is a deep, troubling anxiety. I can accept the

---

* In time of war, they are the Italian army's military police. In peacetime, the carabinieri are one of the civilian police forces.

idea: break away from Germany. What would the consequences be? The enemy will rightly demand a capitulation. Are we ready to erase twenty years of this regime? To accept Italy's first military and political defeat? And then what would Hitler's attitude be? Do you really think he would simply give us our freedom of action?"

Alfieri replied: "I know of some neutral countries that would be willing to assist us in opening up discussions." Bastianini concurred: "There are possibilities in this direction. This very night, if I am authorized to do so, I can begin to make contacts. In the next twenty-four hours, I could inform you in detail." But this was not to Mussolini's liking. He turned away from his staff and went into his room.

The meetings were over. An hour later, the Duce had the Führer informed that whenever he was ready, they could return to Treviso. At about 3:00 p.m. the cars went back to the railroad station at Feltre. Hitler's plane left Treviso at about 5:00 p.m. As they said good-bye, Mussolini shouted over the noise of the propellers to Hitler: "Führer, we have a common cause!" Then turning to General Keitel he said: "Send us everything we need, since we are all in the same boat."

Hitler's plane was still in the air when Ambrosio, Bastianini, and Alfieri approached Mussolini, who, as soon he saw them, said: "There was no need for that discussion with Hitler, because this time he promised to send me all the help we requested." The Duce's three assistants at San Fermo had hoped that, having explained their position, and Ambrosio having even spoken of giving the Germans a two-week ultimatum, Mussolini would decide to tell Hitler during the train trip back to Feltre those things he had not said during the morning. A long silence followed Mussolini's words. Ambrosio thought there was no sense in wasting any more time with a man he already considered the "former" head of the Italian government.

According to the German military attaché, Rintelen, the Duce pointed out during the return trip by train the critical situation Italy was in, only to repeat his request for help, since he could not bring himself to admit that the war was now lost. Hitler had reassured him, saying that he would quickly dispatch new divisions because the defense of Italy was in Germany's interest. A conversation that took place in another compartment of the train, between Keitel and Ambrosio, turned out to be more significant. The German general, emboldened by what had been said at San Fermo, declared that Italy could not expect more help if certain conditions were not met: increasing troop strength dedicated to an efficient line of defense, each country to contribute two divisions; using the narrow area between Calabria and Puglia as the best place to stop the enemy; reaching an agreement to effectively control southern Italy militarily. Ambrosio responded evasively. These conditions assumed the complete evacuation of Sicily. Ambrosio told Bastianini: "Mussolini is still harboring illusions and did not take my words seriously. I tell you he's crazy, completely crazy. What I told him is a very serious matter."

Just as the Italians were leaving Treviso, to return to Rome, the city was being hit by a second bombing raid. Mussolini was thoughtful; he was preparing both his coming moves and especially what he would tell the king. Ambrosio was also worried, not just because of the results of the last conference, which actually facilitated the task of those who were planning to rid Italy of Mussolini and Fascism, but because he had been informed of the death, during the bombing raids, of the commander of the carabinieri, General Azzolino Hazon, one of the main conspirators in the anti-Duce plot. Ambrosio was worried that Hazon could accidentally have left sensitive documents in his office, thus compromising the plotters. No one yet knew the name of his successor, a choice for Mussolini to make. These worries turned out to be unfounded because Hazon had not made the kind of mistakes Ambrosio feared and because the chief of staff was able to secure the nomination of the trustworthy General Angelo Cerica as commander of the carabinieri and have him report to Acquarone during the evening of July 22.

In the meantime, the official communiqué of the San Fermo meetings was made public. It turned out to be a very understated and misleading document, given the usual rhetoric used on such occasions: "The Duce and the Führer have held a meeting at a location in northern Italy. The discussions covered military issues." It was said that Mussolini wanted to avoid its publication, but that he changed his mind when he became convinced he had to justify his absence from Rome while the city was being pounded by American bombers. The Duce's plane landed at 7:00 p.m. at the airfield of Centocelle, since the other two airports had been hit that same day. Mussolini wrote in his memoirs:

"Just before flying over Mount Soratte, the city of Rome looked to the crew of the Duce's plane, as if it were covered by a huge black cloud. It was the smoke emanating from hundreds of burning railway cars at the recently bombed Littorio station. The airport hanger had been destroyed and the landing strip was damaged. Flying over Rome, from Littorio to Centocelle, one could see that the attack was a massive one and that the damage was extensive. Few high-ranking officials were at the airport to greet Mussolini. He took his car to the Villa Torlonia. On the streets, were throngs of men, women, and children, in cars, on bicycles, or on foot, burdened with luggage and home necessities, all going toward the suburbs and the countryside. Not just a throng, but rather a river of people."

Rome had been warned by thousands of paper flyers scattered from Allied aircraft over the suburbs and the airports during the night of July 16-17 that a massive air raid was in the making. Italy's capital had been left untouched by bombing raids for over three years of war for a number of reasons. There was the pope and Vatican City, and the fact that British aircraft were unable to cover the range over the Mediterranean. And even when U.S. long-range bombers were finally available, President Roosevelt initially withheld his approval, mostly for electoral reasons relating to the Catholic vote in the United States.

But the changes in the war after the Sicily landings had prompted General Eisenhower to request Roosevelt's approval to hit Axis sanctuaries, such as railroad depots and airports in Rome: those key traffic points for north-south communications in Italy. Eisenhower's thinking was that no monument however beautiful or historically valuable was worth the life of even one of his men. The British had no objection to the American request. The operation included 270 bombers, 158 Flying Fortresses of the Twelfth Allied Air Force stationed in Tunisia, and 112 Liberators from the Ninth Air Force in Benghazi.

According to historian Giorgio Bonacina, Eisenhower gave orders to pick flight crews that would have no anti-Catholic prejudice and exclude any Catholics who wished to be excused from this mission as well as any other bomber crews that did not consider Rome a very special objective. At 11:13 a.m. on July 19, 1943, just as Hitler began his monologue at San Fermo, American bombers began hitting the districts of the Prenestino, the Tiburtino, the university center, some parts of the polyclinic, the cemetery of Verano, and the basilica of San Lorenzo Fuori Le Mura that was bombed into rubble. The railroad stations were also hit and so severely damaged that it took several days to reestablish normal rail traffic. More tragic was the high number of civilian victims: over 1,500 dead and wounded.

During the afternoon there was a second wave of 321 twin-engine bombers, Marauder, Mitchell, and Lightning, that were concentrating their bombing on the airports of Ciampino and Littorio, forcing the Duce's plane, as noted, to land at Centocelle. There were a total of 591 Allied planes engaged over Rome on July 19. During the morning, the Italian fighter planes were almost paralyzed by the surprise attack, but that afternoon some thirty of them took to the air, and a Mitchell and a Marauder were shot down. Galeazzo Ciano followed the scene from his living room, hurrying to pass drinks around to his guests. Filippo Anfuso, on leave from his post as ambassador to Budapest, was present:

"Ciano was staying at home due to 'political' illness with his hands deep into many conspiracies. From the windows of Ciano's apartment, I could see the dark clouds of smoke from the bombing by Eisenhower's planes fade slowly toward the west . . . Ciano made a sweeping gesture at the whole scene and asked me 'Did you see that?', as if accusing me of having somehow been responsible for this particular bombing raid, but also to include those he felt were responsible for the war in general, including myself. Countesses and princesses were walking around the room; Galeazzo never gave up his role as the center of Roman social life.

"The ladies said very little and were amused to see who would be on his blacklist. He began to criticize Mussolini so much that one countess decided to close the windows...Then he turned on me: 'And what would you do now?' The countesses looked to see how I would respond to the challenge. 'Well,' I replied timidly, 'first I would defend Sicily! At all costs. There is nothing else to do.' He laughed heartily at my words. The countesses were also amused, but their laughter was subdued."

The following morning Mussolini went to visit the areas that had been bombed. "I was always received with warmth by the people everywhere I went," he later said. The pope and the king had also made the rounds the day before, right after the raids. The king, as his Adjutant General Paolo Puntoni was to write, was welcomed by insults and boos as he passed through a hostile and silent crowd. Pius XII was much more successful— after invoking God's help for the city of which he was bishop.

The eyewitness accounts of the San Fermo meeting varied, depending upon the participant. Dino Alfieri replied to questions from embassy staff in Berlin:

"We have decided to draw the line in Sicily. But absolutely no breaking away from the Axis. The two leaders spoke to each other cordially like old comrades. Hitler made a complete description of the current situation. He promised to transfer several divisions into Italy. He is certain of victory. All of us, myself, Ambrosio, and Bastianini spoke our minds very clearly with the Duce. I think the Führer told him some important things in confidence, possibly the reasons for his being absolutely certain of victory."

The Reich chancellery also wanted news on the post-"Feltre" meetings, as the San Fermo conference was erroneously being dubbed, because the Germans, always precise and respectful of protocol, were thinking about the Duce's sixtieth birthday celebration on July 29, 1943. The Führer was preparing a valuable gift for Mussolini and planned to be present while Goebbels, knowing it would please Hitler, had prepared an impressive program of events in Germany to honor the founder of Fascism.

The king was briefed in advance about the conference at San Fermo by General Ambrosio and Montezemolo. On the evening of July 19, as soon as he was back in his office, Ambrosio wrote a memorandum of the conference ending with the following words:

"Since the German units will not be ready for about two months, and since the most urgent measures are to reinforce the defense of southern Italy, it becomes necessary to move all the Italian army units in northern Italy to the south, including the Alpine divisions and those divisions that are currently being reorganized. These units will be replaced later with German units as mentioned above."

Ruggero Zangrandi observed correctly: "These proposals by the Italian high command on the evening of July 19 came after the decision had been made to do away with Fascism and to end the relationship with the Germans. Ambrosio already knew his orders from the king, and one may wonder whether the coup d'état could not have had much worse consequences than it did."

Mussolini had also decided to set the final date for the meeting of the Grand Council of Fascism, moving it from July 21 to Saturday, July 24 at 5:00 p.m. The invitation was delivered to the twenty-eight party leaders. A postscript requested that the interested parties wear "...Fascist uniform: black bush jacket and gray-green riding breeches." The Duce's decision was interpreted by some as coming as a result of a meeting with the king, to whom Mussolini had reported that morning about the Feltre conference. A year later, Mussolini would write:

"Mussolini met with the king, who was nervous and in a bad mood. 'A very tense situation,' the king said. 'It cannot last too long. Sicily is by now lost. The Germans will deal us a low blow. Discipline among the troops is deteriorating. The airmen at Ciampino field fled all the way to Velletri during the attack. They call this "spacing out." I followed the attack of the other day from Villa Ada, with bombers flying overhead. I don't believe, as it was said, that there were four hundred planes. The number was half that. They flew in perfect formation. The fiction of the "Holy City" is over with. We must tell the Germans about this."

On August 19, 1943, during his imprisonment under the Badoglio government, under the title "Musings of a Dictator,"* Mussolini wrote the notes which were the raw material for his book, *Storia di un anno,* regarding the Feltre-San Fermo conference:

> My week of sorrows, if I may refer to it in this way, began exactly one month ago during my meeting with the Führer. That meeting was supposed to last four days, just like the preceding one at Salzburg, and Feltre, near the border, had been chosen for security reasons. The date had not been set. Following the events in Sicily, we chose July 19 . . . Right on time, at 9:00 a.m., the Führer landed at Treviso airport, reviewed the troops, and then we left for the railroad station. We took the train, and one hour later we got off before the station at Feltre. From there, we drove in open car under a broiling sun for an hour to the villa owned by Senator Gaggia: a nightmarish labyrinth of large and small rooms. I exchanged only a few meaningless words with the Führer . . . He spoke first for about two hours . . . After his presentation, I had my first meeting alone with him.
>
> He told me two things: The submarine offensive would start anew with updated equipment, and at the end of August, the air force would begin retaliatory raids over London, which would be destroyed within one week. I replied that while we waited for these attacks, Italy's defense had to be greatly reinforced . . . During the hour I spent with the Führer on the return trip by train, I explained to him that Italy had to withstand the power of two empires, Great Britain and the United States, which threatened to crush us. And the bombing of cities not only damaged the morale of the population but war production as well . . . I repeated once again to him that the African campaign would have ended differently if only we had air power at least equal to that of the enemy. I also told him that tension among the population was now very strong and dangerous in the country. Hitler said that, in his view, the Italian crisis was one of a lack of direction and that he would order air reinforcements and new divisions to defend the peninsula . . . The conversation was always very friendly, and we said good-bye like old comrades . . . At 6:00 p.m. I went back to Rome . . .
>
> That evening, from Villa Torlonia, we could still see the lights of the fires in the sky. Rome had just endured a terrible day of fire, and bombing had destroyed what little hope there was and created an unpredictable

---

* Wilhelm Höttl, *The Secret Front* (Praeger 1954).

situation. During the next few days, I visited the worst-hit locations . . . I gave orders not to mention it in the papers. The enemies of the regime were spreading rumors within Rome that the Feltre meeting had been a failure and had yielded no results, that Germany was leaving us in the lurch, and that after taking Sicily, the British could reach Rome with little or no opposition. All this increased the nervous tension that preceded a collapse.

It should be noted that a very superstitious Mussolini had celebrated alone in captivity the first month's anniversary of the July 19 meeting at San Fermo and wrote: "Every time I met Hitler in or near Venice, some disastrous events followed." Actually the first meeting, on June 15, 1934, was followed both by the failed Nazi attempted coup in Vienna and the assassination of Chancellor Dollfuss, his personal friend and ally, and the liquidation of Ernst Röhm. The second meeting in the Veneto region, at San Fermo on July 19, 1943, was followed by Mussolini's own overthrow and the dissolution in a few hours of the Fascist party itself. This anti-Hitler pronouncement could have cost Mussolini dearly. Right after his liberation on September 12, 1943, Mussolini was taken to Vienna. That night, the Gestapo was able to take his personal diaries from his room at the Hotel Continental while he slept. The documents were quickly translated by the SS and transmitted to the Reich chancellery. In the confusion, the Duce had not noticed the theft.

A few months later, through a priest, Don Giusto Pancino, Mussolini would learn the truth just before a meeting with Hitler. It was a bad surprise for the Duce. Shortly before his death, Don Pancino told the author, he remembered that once with bravado, Mussolini had written a very foolish note but actually attributed the anecdote to the king, who in anger had said to the Duce: "Hitler is a jinx: every time he comes to Italy, something awful happens." Mussolini had also written that Bottai called Hitler "a ridiculous mouse." In any case, Hitler never made any mention of all this to Mussolini, due either to lack of time or inclination.

According to Dino Grandi, Mussolini's decision to call a meeting of the Grand Council of Fascism was the result of the conference at San Fermo and not due to the situation in Rome: "It may seem incredible, but it was Hitler himself who pushed Mussolini to call the Grand Council meeting. Hitler said he was convinced the Duce was surrounded by traitors within the government and in the Grand Council. But it was because of the Führer that the Duce, as soon as he returned to Rome, ordered the Fascist party secretary to call a meeting of the Grand Council. It may seem an unlikely story, but it is the truth."

Mussolini received Grandi at 5:00 p.m. Thursday, July 22, for a purely administrative reason. But it was in fact an extreme attempt by the "rebels" to convince Mussolini to withdraw voluntarily and not be voted down by the "Grandi Agenda," which was by now well known in its main points.

Grandi wrote: "Mussolini listened to me without interrupting or objecting, as I anticipated, and without expressing any kind of anger. When I finished, he only said these words that I shall never forget: 'You will repeat everything you just told me at the meeting of the Grand Council. It could be useful to the country if it is in fact true that the war is lost. I cannot reveal to you some extremely important military secrets; but just be aware that very soon Germany will come out with an extremely powerful secret weapon that will completely reverse the course of the war. Germany and Italy will win this war. Everything else we shall discuss at the Grand Council." According to Grandi, Mussolini had been well indoctrinated at San Fermo with information about the V2 missile which was to reverse the course of the war in favor of the Axis once again. That the Führer had asked Mussolini to keep the information secret is proved by the fact that the Duce also withheld this information from the king during their July 21 meeting, when he could easily have hinted at some big new weapon being prepared by the German war machine.

Perhaps the Duce told the truth about San Fermo to his old friend, Manlio Morgagni, president of the Stefani News Agency and the only person to commit suicide at the news of Mussolini's arrest: "The Germans are strong and could very well effectively intervene to plug and possibly resolve the situation in Italy, which has become very difficult. But they don't trust us. Before they come in, they are demanding the command of the entire Italian front, including the home front. This is a precondition that neither the Italian people nor I can accept."

During the afternoon of July 21, Roberto Farinacci, the "leader" of Cremona and one of the extreme pro-German fascist diehards, was given a brief but accurate horoscope of coming events by the retired Marshal: "Be more and more careful. Grandi and his group—Bottai, Ciano, and others—are conspiring to overthrow Mussolini, but their game will not succeed, because the Crown is conducting its own struggle in the same direction with Duke Acquarone." A few hours later, Fascist party secretary Scorza, would be informed by a police detective that during a tapped phone conversation, Marshal Badoglio and Duke Acquarone agreed to "bundle up the Duce as he leaves Villa Savoia." Mussolini became angry when he was told of these conspiracies but said only: "I hate mystery stories," making the mistake of not believing what he felt were alarmist messages that were reaching him. In reality, the king had already agreed to a meeting on Monday, July 26, during the routine visit that took place at the beginning of the week, the second visit would always take place on Thursdays.

Mussolini was confident that his own charisma would be sufficient to overcome any kind of trap that had been set for him, and that he, in a sense, had also set up for himself in calling the meeting of the highest institution of the Fascist party. To Chierici who had just been named to replace Senise as chief of police, he said:

> Believe me . . . these Grand Council members are of low, very low intelligence, wobbly in their convictions, and without much courage. These people live in someone else's shadow: if the source of light should disappear, they too would be cast back into the darkness from whence they came . . . they just want to believe that I can easily bring back to the stable a Grandi, a Bottai, and even Count Ciano, who I feel is being too obvious in his impatience to replace me.

At this time, Grandi was "campaigning" for his agenda in advance of the Grand Council meeting, which would place Mussolini in a minority position after a vote. He enlisted men like Federzoni, De Vecchi, Bastianini, Albini, De Marsico, Bignardi, De Stefani, Balella, and De Bono. The Crown was looking at the post-Mussolini era in much more practical terms. Acquarone was handling the details of a military coup with Generals Ambrosio, Castellano, and Cerica, as well as former Chief of Police Senise, who was to be reinstated in his old job. Had this entire matter not been the most devastating and far-reaching crisis of modern Italian history, it could be described as a light comedy.

The main beneficiary of the coup, Marshal of Italy Pietro Badoglio, was sitting on the sidelines. Everyone was working for his success while he played bridge with friends in his magnificent villa in Rome, built on land donated to him by the city as a gift from the grateful people of Italy for his wartime contributions. The seventy-two-year-old former chief of the general staff was concentrating on the list of names of those who were to be arrested once he replaced Mussolini as head of the government. According to dozens of witnesses, chroniclers, and historians, during the evening of July 19, 1943, the king made the final decision to remove Mussolini, after Rome was bombed and after learning that the summit at

San Fermo had not produced concrete results either for the breakup of the Axis alliance or the serious defense of Italy itself. General Castellano wrote in 1963, even though this was to be contradicted by many other sources: "While the meeting was taking place at Feltre, the big news was that the king had finally made up his mind and lifted the uncertainty we had been living with for so many months. Acquarone told me, since Ambrosio was attending the conference, that the king would replace Mussolini with Marshal Badoglio."

General Castellano's version of these events and their timing places the decision to effect the coup more or less at the same time as the meeting of the Grand Council. Castellano further states that at noon on July 24, five hours before the meeting, Ambrosio, Acquarone, and he himself, all went together to see Marshal Badoglio.

"I was meeting the marshal for the first time. Acquarone told him that the king had finally decided to replace Mussolini and would name [Badoglio] head of the government. He showed him the proclamation, written by former Prime Minister Orlando, that Badoglio would read on radio and asked for the marshal's opinion. Badoglio agreed." The proclamation included the famous phrase: "La guerra continua…" [The war goes on…]

Badoglio showed little interest in all these formalities and relished his nomination to be the next head of the Italian government.

It is therefore surprising at this point that the coup was to be a mystery only to those Germans in Rome, as it appears from a telegram sent by Rintelen from the German embassy to Berlin, commenting upon the Feltre conference: "The Italian high command is very much worried that more German troops are not available to help the front in Italy. It had always been thought that the opening of a second front in the Mediterranean would have triggered the dispatch of a heavy German contingent, especially armored units. The population is constantly depressed. The public doesn't believe in even the minimal chances of victory and rejects any attempt to be influenced by the press or the radio. We have reached the point where the people only hope in the future generosity of the enemy."

The German high command was not satisfied by this report and requested that Rintelen provide more details as to the Italian political situation, a source of concern for the Führer. Rintelen cabled back at noon the next day, while the king was informing Badoglio of his nomination: "After the meeting at Feltre, the main question on the minds of all competent political and military groups is the doubt that Germany will be able to help Italy enough in its defensive battle against the invaders. The Grand Council of Fascism is meeting on July 24. Given the situation, this meeting is to be considered extremely important. There is a rumor that a group within the Grand Council will request a stronger, more energetic government. It is also rumored that the Duce will be invited to give up the direction of all three defense ministries."

For some time, the German embassy in Rome had been undergoing an internal crisis. It started in March 1942, when the Italian secret police, the OVRA, caught one of the embassy's officials, Kurt Sauer, in the act of spying for the Soviet Union. The Germans had reacted badly to being humiliated in the eyes of the Italians, who had decided to apply the letter of the law and promptly executed the traitor by firing squad, over German protests. The German delegation was a microcosm of German society of the times. All social strata were represented: Ambassador von Mackensen was the son of a field marshal; he was seconded by Prince von Bismarck, von Plehwe, and Rintelen, all three of whom were assisted by a group of brilliant and very aristocratic young men from the best families in the country. There was also a very strong group of newly arrived Nazis, including SS Lieutenant Colonel Eugen Dollmann, powerful enough to influence the cautious Prussian, von Mackensen, who was always worrying about painting a picture of Italy that corresponded to the Führer's fantasies. Von Mackensen went overboard when, on the evening of July 25, he sent a cable to Ribbentrop, saying that the situation in Rome was, in the final analysis, under Mussolini's control. Much to the ambassador's bad luck, the message reached Berlin at the same time as the news that the Duce had been arrested. Von Mackensen was to pay for his bad luck thirteen days later during the meeting at Tarvisio, the only post-Mussolini Italian-German meeting. The ambassador was ordered back to Germany by Ribbentrop on the spot. Dollmann wrote:

> On the platform of the railway station at Tarvisio, Dr. Schmidt whispered to me that the true reason for von Mackensen's recall was due to Ribbentrop's outrage at the cable of July 25, where the ambassador used information from Buffarini-Guidi in a conversation that took place in my presence, where he stated that the situation was serious but not really dramatic. Von Mackensen was replaced with Rudolf Rahn, who represented the 'new line' of the Wilhelmstrasse.

At 5:00 p.m. on July 24, 1943, Benito Mussolini was about to make his entrance at the Grand Council meeting. The situation in Rome was complex and confused. Every conspirator was living with the fear that he would suddenly be attacked by the wounded "target." The history of the Grand Council session has been described in great detail by many participants, friends and foes alike.

One of the most important chapters of Mussolini's *Storia di un anno* describes the events as follows: "In Mussolini's mind, the Grand Council was supposed to be a confidential meeting, where everyone could ask for and obtain explanations, a sort of secret committee. Since a long discussion was to be expected, rather than beginning at 10:00 p.m. as usual, the meeting began at 5:00 p.m." After describing the military situation and criticizing the behavior of generals and admirals who had not held the line and defended their positions in Africa, at Pantelleria, and now in Sicily, he went on to say: "I must be the most disobeyed man in Italy."

He did not exempt Rommel from a reprimand for the decisions that had driven the Axis to defeat at El Alamein. Mussolini said the German commander was a brave military leader, always on the front line, and a great tactician, but when it came to strategy, he had nothing to teach the Italian generals. In closing, he posed the dramatic dilemma: war or peace? Mussolini told the Grand Council members the risks they faced in the event of easy, last-minute choices which could not change the situation. Then came a long debate where Grandi, Bottai, and Ciano played the most important roles. An attempt to adjourn the meeting to the next day was rejected and the Council came to a vote. The Grandi Agenda, which, in effect, stripped the Duce of his power and returned it to the king, carried the vote with nineteen in favor, seven against, and two abstentions.

Before the vote was counted, however, Bastianini said that the war could only have a political solution and requested permission to begin talks with the Allies. Alfieri, in support of the proposal coming from the undersecretary for foreign affairs, said: "In Germany, the certainty in victory has been shaken. We will not get a single plane, tank, or gun from the Germans. If Berlin were shown an acceptable way to end the conflict, they wouldn't even think about us and have no further hesitation to seek peace." Offended in his pride, Mussolini replied: "What Alfieri is saying is in direct contradiction with what I was told at Feltre by the Führer himself. However, we must take it into consideration."

Finally, Mussolini commented with some disgust on the point in the Grandi Agenda that said: "We invite the head of the government to ask His

Majesty the king to accept the offer to take effective command of the armed forces that . . ." Mussolini had asked: "What does this sentence mean? Let's assume that the king agrees to resume his command of the armed forces. The question is whether I agree to be decapitated. I am sixty years old, and I know what certain things ultimately mean. It's therefore preferable to speak to each other very clearly!" And, according to Bottai, he uttered the mysterious sentence: "And then I tell you I have in my hand a key that can resolve the military situation. But I shall not tell you what it is." He was clearly referring to the new secret weapons about which Hitler had sworn him to utmost secrecy.

Once the results of the vote had been read, "everyone left in silence," wrote Mussolini. It was 2:40 a.m. on July 25, 1943. The Duce went to his study, where he was quickly joined by the small group who had voted against the Grandi Agenda. At 3:00 a.m. he left the Palazzo Venezia. During the night that went down in history as the "Night of the Grand Council," the discussion lasted ten hours. Almost everyone spoke and some more than once. It is probable that a crisis would have taken place even without the meeting and the related agenda, but impossible to say. Perhaps the cup was full, but it was the famous last drop that made it overflow.

The biggest surprise would be in store for Grandi himself, the first Fascist leader the king would actually remove, even before Mussolini. The king made the decision rather quickly and gave the task to the accommodating Acquarone, who would inform the interested party. Right after the Grand Council meeting Grandi went to his office at Montecitorio, the parliament building, where he presided. He found Acquarone waiting in a car at the gate requesting an immediate meeting, which took place at 4:00 a.m. at the house of the Marquis Zamboni. Grandi was satisfied about his success and handed the representative of the king the text of the Agenda that had ended Mussolini's dictatorship.

"It's the constitutional tool the king had asked me to provide. Now Victor Emmanuel can act directly and freely . . ." Acquarone then asked, not without some cynicism, "What do you think we should do?" The words sounded very positive to Grandi, who thought he understood in Acquarone's question the possible opening for a new political career. Grandi enthusiastically proposed the dissolution of the Fascist parliament and the reconvening of the old parliament that would give a vote of confidence to the new "government of peace." Acquarone then asked who should be prime minister? Grandi answered: "Marshal Caviglia, the only military leader without ties to this regime. As foreign minister, Alberto Pirelli; the other names could be De Gasperi, Cappa, Soleri, Paratore . . ." But Acquarone interrupted him to say that the king had already named Badoglio as prime minister.

The dawn of July 25 was appearing slowly. It was now 6:00 a.m. Grandi understood. He was about to be forever shunted out of power. The king attempted two months later to have Grandi approved as foreign minister by the Allies, but they were opposed to the idea.

At 9:00 a.m. on July 25, Mussolini went to his office as he had done every day for twenty-one years. At 1:00 p.m. he received the Japanese ambassador, to whom he said: "Please tell Tokyo urgently of my decision to send a note to Berlin on Wednesday that will say that if Germany does not furnish all the war materiel Italy has requested, we will be forced to declare that we can no longer fulfill our duties within the alliance. I ask that the Japanese ambassador in Berlin support my request very forcefully. Unfortunately, this is the situation, and Berlin must understand. In order to fight, one must have weapons." In the meantime, upsetting the plans of the Crown, Mussolini requested a meeting with the king that same day, rather than waiting for the next day, Monday, as planned. The meeting was then set for July 25 at 5:00 p.m. at Villa Savoia.

By 5:17 p.m. the royal audience was over; it had taken the king only twenty-one minutes to fire the prime minister who had "managed" his kingdom for twenty-one years. Italy exploded with joy: the Germans would leave, the bombing would end, freedom would return to political life. The only epitaph for Mussolini came from Winston Churchill, his friend turned enemy:

> And so would end the twenty-one years of Mussolini's dictatorship, when he saved the Italian people from Bolshevism . . . to have Italy reach a position in Europe that she had never known before. The country was inspired by a new kind of energy. He founded the Italian Empire. His regime was too expensive for the Italian people, but it must be said that during his moment of success, he did attract a large number of Italians. He was, I had occasion to write to him after the fall of France, the 'legislator of Italy' . . . His greatest mistake was to declare war on Britain and France after Hitler's victories in June 1940. Had he not done so, he could have kept Italy in a position of equilibrium, as she would have been courted and rewarded by all sides, deriving great prosperity and wealth from the struggles of other countries . . .

It is naturally impossible to speculate upon Churchill's *what if* Italy had remained neutral. The words of praise coming from the British statesman for Mussolini long after the war helped place Italy's position in the world in perspective at the outbreak of the World War II.

Mussolini was arrested as he walked to his car following his meeting with the king at Villa Savoia. At 5:25 p.m. he was taken to the carabinieri barracks in Via Legnano in Rome. The only person who complained about the manner in which he was treated that evening was the queen, because Mussolini had been drawn into a trap in the very house of the Savoy family. At 2:00 a.m. on July 27, the Duce was taken aboard the corvette, *Persefone*, to the island of Ponza. Then, on August 7, he was transferred to the island of Maddalena.

The news of the arrest reached the Führer's headquarters like a bolt from the blue. The messages between Rastenburg and the German embassy in Rome became nervous and dramatic. Hitler was screaming betrayal even though the message Badoglio read to the Italian people over the radio gave assurances that the change of government in Italy did not alter the course of the war with the by now historical phrase, "La guerra continua…" [The war goes on . . .] Ambassador von Mackensen saw his patient work to maintain good relations with Italy go up in smoke in a few hours. As Badoglio began his arrests and others approached the Allies to negotiate an armistice that would be as honorable as possible for Italy, Hitler began his hunt—Operation Eiche—to find the Duce. For propaganda and emotional reasons, as well as to avoid retaliation from his enemies, Mussolini had to be liberated. Hitler was also convinced that the Duce would have been very useful to Germany if a new Fascist government could be created and the monarchy abolished. Furthermore, there were many signs that the new Italian government was trying to break away from the Axis.

At 9:30 p.m. on July 25, the Führer told his entourage: "We must prepare everything so that we can quickly grab this crowd, I mean those bastards who dared arrest the Duce. Tomorrow I will give the order to the head of the Third Panzer Grenadier division to enter Rome with a special unit and quickly capture the king, the entire government, the Prince of Piedmont, and Badoglio. Then you'll see them disintegrate and two days later, there will be another change." The next morning the Führer was asked what should be done about the Vatican. "Who cares? I'll go into the Vatican immediately. That's where the whole diplomatic corps is. I don't give damn. That's where the rabble is. We'll apologize afterwards."

This mopping-up operation inside Rome had been code-named "Student," after the general who was to be in charge of the operation. On July 26, von Mackensen was ordered to transmit to the Führer's HQ "a list of the thirty most important persons in the army, politics, and the Crown who are well-known opponents of German policies." Mackensen listed some notorious anti-Nazis, such as Ciano, Grandi, Volpi, Cerruti, Suvich, and Princess Isabella Colonna, none of them being a surprise to the Nazis. As for the generals, he thought it to best consult General Rintelen, the military attaché, who in fact refused to comply with these requests and said that in the higher echelons of the Italian army there were no elements hostile to Germany.

Rintelen had decided to put a stop to Operation Student, which he thought would forever dishonor the German army, and asked for a meeting with the Führer. On August 1, before leaving for Germany, Rintelen, responding to a request, went to see Badoglio, who made the following comments:

> I have called you because we have been friends for seven years and you are a person to whom, soldier to soldier, I can open my thoughts . . . The Fascist government disintegrated by itself . . . On Sunday, July 25 at 5:00 p.m., the king called me in and offered me the position as head of the government. For me it was a spur of the moment decision. At seventy-two years of age, my only wish is to spend the rest of my life in peace and quiet. As an old soldier, I must answer my king's call. Once I accepted, we discussed the proclamation with its main message: 'The war goes on...' This was the precondition to my taking office. On Wednesday, July 28, I sent a message to the Führer, General Marras handed him a proposal for a meeting at Treviso, which would include the Führer, the king, and myself. The Führer rejected the idea because he had just had the meeting at Feltre and was unavailable at the moment.
>
> On August 6, there will be a meeting between the foreign ministers, including Keitel and Ambrosio . . . It is necessary that you let us know what kind of help Germany can provide us with . . . We have made no moves toward the Allies . . . Should the German army attempt to remove the king and myself, it will experience what forty-five million Latin men who are easily excitable can do . . . If I must continue this war I must have the trust of our ally . . . The situation is very serious . . . The bombing of Rome and, even more, of Hamburg has demonstrated the overwhelming superiority of the Anglo-Americans . . . Please let us reestablish a common trust . . .

In the meantime, the Germans were streaming down through the Brenner Pass into Italy in larger numbers. During the morning of August 2, Rintelen left for Rastenburg in a special plane carrying a box of fresh fruit for the Führer, a personal gift from Field Marshal Kesselring. Upon arrival, he was told that he was to be in the dark regarding Operation Student when he spoke with the Führer because Hitler had ordered that very few generals should be in the know. Rintelen found this situation impossible because it was the very reason for his trip. Von Plehwe, Rintelen's number two in Rome, wrote: "Hitler's state of mind was a mixture of outrage, wounded pride, thirst for revenge, and complete mistrust toward the new Italian government. He was also convinced, after a message from Ambassador Oshima, that the Badoglio government had been dealing with the Allies long before the coup . . . Rintelen, with his way of presenting the facts, succeeded in making Hitler think the situation through. . . It is obvious, and much to his honor, that Rintelen's report was instrumental in delaying, then completely canceling, Operation Student. He played all his cards on the professed attachment to the alliance that Badoglio had assured him before he left Rome. He was to pay for this unconditional faith in the word of the aging marshal with his job, since he was to be immediately recalled to Germany.

Hitler had decided to liberate the Duce just two days after the coup d'état in Italy and summoned to Rastenburg five officers trained in special operations. Among them was Captain Otto Skorzeny, a six-foot-four thirty-five-year-old Viennese engineer with a long dueling scar (a "*mensur*") across his face, a sign of virility among German youth. He was given the mission, when in response to the Führer's question about what he thought of the Italians he said simply, "I'm Austrian." The other four candidates had made long speeches about the Axis, loyalty, and the duties of an ally. Once the right man had been picked on July 27, Hitler told him in private: "I have a very important mission for you. Mussolini is under arrest. Italy today is wide open to Allied invasion, and Rome could fall at any moment into enemy hands. The king of Italy plotted with Marshal Badoglio against the Duce. These two are now planning to go to the Anglo-Americans with Mussolini on a silver platter. I cannot and will not abandon the Duce to his fate. He must be freed before those traitors can hand him over to the enemy. You, Skorzeny, will rescue my friend."

Skorzeny, along with General Kurt Student, his direct commanding officer, flew to Rome the next day on a plane piloted by the very experienced Captain Heinrich Gerlach. Three days later, the commando from Germany arrived in Rome to set up the operation that was top secret, even for high-level German circles. Skorzeny realized very quickly that the Italian government was taking new measures every day to throw off any possible attempt to rescue the Duce. In the end, the Germans were able to find out where Mussolini was being hidden: at the Villa Weber on the little island of Maddalena, off Sardinia. On the morning of August 18, Skorzeny, on a reconnaissance flight, flew over the area in a small plane that had to be ditched into the water because of engine trouble. An Italian PT boat rescued the German crew. But on August 28, when negotiations between the Badoglio government and the Allies had reached their final stages, Mussolini boarded a Red Cross sea plane and was first taken to Lake Bracciano and then, on the same afternoon, to the Gran Sasso mountain in an ambulance.

The way Italy reached the point of signing the armistice of September 8, 1943, is well known. Several groups in Italy made various attempts to contact the Allies over time and in different circumstances. The approaches can be divided into two periods: before the fall of Mussolini and after July 25, 1943. There were three different groups: within the first category were the Crown, Badoglio, and the Fascist leaders. The Crown made its first moves in Geneva during the fall of 1942 through Consul General Alessandro Marieni, representing Aimone, Duke of Aosta Spoleto. This overture appeared serious enough to the Allies and was followed by other contacts by Maria José, Princess of Piedmont and wife of the heir to the Italian throne, who succeeded in setting up a meeting on July 21, 1943, in Lisbon between her representative, Alvise Emo Capodilista, and Prime Minister Salazar of Portugal. The monarchist group wanted peace to save the Savoy dynasty.

In December 1942, Badoglio, in agreement with Marshal Caviglia, sent a message to the British via Switzerland, a message that was extremely vague, except for the idea of replacing Mussolini and his regime with a military government. The more moderate Fascists sent two timid signals proposing an armistice under the auspices of Mussolini himself. The first contact took place in Lisbon, with Ciano's agreement, through Italian diplomat Francesco Fransoni, but had not been cleared by Mussolini immediately following the Allied landings in North Africa in November 1942. This overture was rejected by both London and Washington. After the landings in Sicily, Fransoni, in Lisbon, tried again to contact the British on behalf of undersecretary Bastianini, who had Mussolini's agreement. But by that time it was too late.

The peace feelers initiated after July 25 can be divided into two groups: by diplomats and by the military. The diplomatic efforts that took place on August 2, 1943, in Lisbon by Blasco Lanza d'Ajeta and a few days later in Tangier by Alberto Berio, convinced the Badoglio government that the Allies wanted to negotiate first and foremost a military armistice. This was why on August 12, General Giuseppe Castellano left for Madrid and Lisbon. On August 24, General Zanussi was sent to assist Castellano. After many long discussions, the armistice was agreed upon and signed on September 3, 1943, at Santa Teresa Longarini in Sicily, south of Siracusa. This was known as the "short armistice" of Cassibile, erroneously it turns out, because this small village is six kilometers away from the olive grove where the "peace tent" had been set up for the occasion. There still is a commemorative stone bearing an inscription in English: "Armistice signed here. September 3, 1943, Italy-Allies." The stone was stolen by a newspaperman in 1953, who was subsequently caught and convicted by a court in Siracusa a year later.

On the evening of September 3, after a dinner to celebrate the armistice, General Castellano was given the text of the Long Armistice, which explained in detail the points of the Short Armistice that had just been signed a few hours before. It would not be of great interest to follow all the behind-the-scenes details of these two documents, but suffice it to say that they did point to serious disagreements between London and Washington regarding the political conduct of the war. It also demonstrated how Great Britain was, in effect, handing over world leadership to the United States, repeating on a different level, the same subordinate relationship that existed between Italy and Germany. In brief, the Short Armistice was strongly advocated by General Eisenhower because he felt that an immediate Italian surrender would facilitate the landings on Italian soil on September 8 and 9. The Long Armistice was pushed by the British, who wished to quickly humiliate Italy for having declared war on the British Empire. It should be added that the Long Armistice was to be signed in Malta on September 29 could be condensed to even shorter terms than the Short Armistice. The forty-four articles could be summed up in one sentence: from now on Italy no longer existed. But thanks in part, to the Americans, Italy would be able to reintegrate the ranks of free nations slowly. Among the clauses of the Long Armistice, number 29 specified Italy's obligation:

Benito Mussolini, his most important Fascist associates, and all persons suspected of having committed war crimes or similar crimes whose names are on the lists prepared by the United Nations and who are now or will be in territory under the control of the Italian military command, will be immediately arrested and handed over to the forces of the United Nations. All orders issued by the United Nations to this effect will be followed.

The issue of the "Big Devil," as Roosevelt referred to Mussolini, had been the subject of a long correspondence between the president and Churchill, who wanted to know in advance what the Duce's fate would ultimately be. Roosevelt, who had other problems to handle, said at one point that the problem would be decided calmly after Italy's surrender. The British prime minister, dissatisfied with that answer, wrote a letter to his American partner:

The capture of the Big Devil and his most trusted associates must be considered an objective of the greatest importance. We must use all the means at our disposal to reach such an objective . . . It may happen that these criminals will flee to Switzerland or Germany. They could also turn themselves in voluntarily or be handed over to us by the Italian government. In case they should fall into our hands, we will have to decide after consulting with the United States and the Soviet Union . . . Still, some of us will think that an execution without trial would be the best solution, limiting the proceedings to identifying the criminals. Some others will insist that they be kept as prisoners until the end of the war, delaying the decision. Personally I am quite indifferent. Winston Churchill.

The need for retribution had given rise to point 29, which Mussolini learned about on September 11 while he listened to the radio in the evening in the dining room of the hotel at Campo Imperatore on the Gran Sasso mountain, where he had finally been transferred after his stay at the island of Maddalena. One of Mussolini's keepers, captain of the carabinieri, Alberto Faiola, said:

The news made a big impression on Mussolini, who called me that night, since he knew I had been a British prisoner of war. He was very concerned about this and preferred to commit suicide rather than undergo such humiliation. I took it upon myself to inform him that no such order had been given to us and to promise him, and actually swear, that if that were the case, I would have protected him and guided his flight across the mountains. Only after I made such a declaration did he feel able to go to sleep . . .

As a precaution, Faiola took away Mussolini's shaving equipment to prevent a desperate act in a moment of depression.

Skorzeny pursued the mission the Führer had given him. Hitler was pressing even more urgently for his friend's liberation after the announcement of the signing of the armistice at 6:00 p.m. of September 8, 1943. After the failed mission to Maddalena, the Germans quickly discovered the new hiding place where the Duce was a prisoner. At 2:00 p.m. on September 12, Skorzeny, with a few planes and eight gliders, landed on the short flat strip in front of the hotel. The German commando, meeting no resistance, was able to go straight up to Mussolini's room. Skorzeny told him: "The Führer sent me to free you." Mussolini answered: "I knew that my friend Adolf Hitler would not abandon me."

A perilous flight took the three men, the pilot Gerlach, Skorzeny, and Mussolini, from the Gran Sasso to Pratica di Mare in a single-engine Storch. Mussolini then switched to a Heinkel III to fly to Vienna where he was taken to the Continental Hotel. He looked like a ghost and dragged himself to the elevator with difficulty. Ten hours before, he was still Badoglio's prisoner on top of the Gran Sasso. Now he was the guest of the Führer in a warm luxury hotel in the former capital of Austria, whose independence he had once championed. He fell into bed completely dressed, but only for a few minutes because the phone rang almost immediately. The Führer was on the line to congratulate him on his liberation. Mussolini answered: "I'm tired, very, very tired. I need some sleep. Please take care of my wife and children." Hitler had also thought about this and had made sure that Rachele Mussolini and her children were escorted from the house at Rocca delle Caminate to Munich, where they would be safe.

The next day at noon, the Duce was reunited with his family after a hazardous flight from Vienna to Munich. He told Rachele: "I never thought I would see you again. Tomorrow I must visit the Führer at his headquarters." "What will you do next?" his wife asked him. To which Mussolini replied: "I don't know yet. I must speak with Hitler. It's very urgent." A German officer brought some news: "The weather is awful. Flying is not possible. While we wait for some improvement in the weather conditions, you will be accommodated with your family at the palace of Prince Karl. These are the Führer's orders." Germany was on holiday. The liberation of Mussolini was seen as a sort of sports event and met with widespread enthusiasm. The next day, September 14, Mussolini arrived at Rastenburg for his fifteenth meeting with Hitler. He wanted also to thank Hitler for the sixtieth birthday gift. It was a gift that had made him proud as a prisoner and as a man, so much so that he mentioned it specifically in his *Musings* under the date of August 19:

> This morning Admiral Brivonesi returned to La Maddalena. He broke my isolation by bringing me a letter from my wife dated August 13 and a large box containing the complete works of Nietzsche in twenty-four volumes that the Führer had sent me through Kesselring for my sixtieth birthday. The admiral also informed me that my son Vittorio had been declared a deserter, since the end of July he was the guest of the Führer at Rastenburg.

Kesselring wrote the following note to the Duce:

> The Führer will be pleased if this work of German literature will bring you, Duce, a bit of comfort and if you will consider it as the expression of the deepest personal feelings the Führer has for you.

According to what a former high-ranking SS officer told the author, the box of books was the clue that enabled the Germans to trace Mussolini to Maddalena. German agents had never lost track of the box of books ever since it had been given to Badoglio. They spotted it the day it was seen being loaded on board a small truck, which Skorzeny's men then constantly followed.

Hitler and His Generals
Military Conferences

The Italian Crisis
July 26, 1943

[Fascist Italy was Hitler's ally of choice, an alliance he advocated since 1928, before his ascent to power. On the night of July 25th the Grand Council of Fascism voted against Mussolini by a significant majority that included his son-in-law Galeazzo Ciano. Mussolini was then dismissed and arrested by King Victor Emmanuel III. The overthrow of Mussolini reflected on the Axis and the Nazi regime itself and the deep seated doubts expressed by many Nazis about the alliance with Italy surfaced suddenly within Hitler after July 25, 1943. Despite the innumerable Gestapo and Abwehr agents operating in Italy at the time, the Germans were caught by surprise by the Italian crisis and Hitler was about to react violently.]

THE FÜHRER: Have you received anything, Hewel?
HEWEL: Nothing concrete yet. Mackensen[1] just sent a telegram. He said, shall we say, that the Reichsmarshal's trip[2] could possibly be jeopardized because of the incidents. But we're still waiting for the details. So far he knows that the Duce was finally compelled by the Farinacci group to summon the Grand Council.[3] That was planned for yesterday, but was put off until 10 p.m. because no agreement had been reached yet on the program. He has heard from various sides that the meeting was extraordinarily stormy. Because the participants are bound to secrecy, he hasn't heard anything real yet—just rumors. One of the most persistent rumors he has heard says that they want to make the Duce appoint a head of government—a prime minister in the form of a politician: Orlando, who is 83 years old and already played a role in the Great War[4]—and then the Duce is supposed to become the president of the Fascist Grand Council. These are all just rumors; we'll have to wait and see. Then it is to have been said that this morning at 10 o'clock the Duce went to see the king, together with a number of generals, and that he was still there, meeting a continuing

stream of important personages.[5] Buffarini, among others, is said to be with him currently.

THE FÜHRER: Who's that?

HEWEL: Buffarini is a Fascist.[6] [—] I'm still waiting for details from…that this crisis within the party spreads and becomes a crisis of the state. [—] It is also maintained that the Duce, especially as a result of the meeting in northern Italy,[7] is steadfastly determined to continue the fight. [—] That's all that's come through so far. Glaise[8] hopes to hear something concrete this afternoon from Buffarini, who's with the Duce now. Then this afternoon … would—

THE FÜHRER: Good old Farinacci is lucky to have done this in Italy and not with me. If he had done that with me I would have had him hauled off by Himmler at once—immediately. [—] That's the result of such actions. What can be expected from it anyway? [—] Idle talk!

HEWEL: But, as I already said, Mackensen emphasized that these are just rumors. In any case, there is a considerable crisis there, and Mackensen thinks—because the Duce always told him that he would prefer not to have his birthday mentioned at all, and that nothing at all should be done—that we should be very careful in this crisis. But he will inquire there anyway, to find out what they think about it. Having the Reichsmarshal appear down there just now, at this particular moment, would, of course, be—but I'm getting additional details.

THE FÜHRER: That's one of those things. The Reichsmarshal and I have been through many crises together, and he is cold and calculating in crisis situations. In times of crisis one can have no better advisor than the Reichsmarshal. The Reichsmarshal is brutal and ice cold in times of crisis. I've always noticed that when it's do or die, he is a ruthless and iron-hard man. So you won't get a better one—you cannot have a better one at all. He got through all the crises with me—the hardest crises, then he's ice cold. Whenever it got really terrible, he became cold as ice. [—] Well, we'll see.

Distribution of forces (continuation)

JODL: No Italians are included here!

THE FÜHRER: That's good, too.

JODL: But if we manage to do this, the southern European front will not be badly protected—(if) the East permits it.

THE FÜHRER: This must be given away. It's absolutely clear: Here we're dealing with critical decisions. If worse comes to worse, even more must be withdrawn from the East; that must be done. But, of course, I believe that if we do such a thing, a great deal will obviously have to be done by us. Out of all the liquidation materials from the Italian army, we will certainly get 10 or 12 or 15 divisions together quickly.[9] [—] What does this story in Hungary actually mean?

KEITEL: I'm having it investigated.

HEWEL: I've also ordered that it be investigated.

KEITEL: Perhaps it's the introduction of military jurisdiction and the installation of drumhead court-martials. I will have it investigated.

HEWEL: It may be the introduction of military jurisdiction for special offenses. I believe it's the old Austrian procedure.

THE FÜHRER: I want to have a diagram for this matter as well, Jodl—a map. A map is fully adequate for me. So if this could be drawn one more time!

KEITEL: As for the reserve divisions, we must write below: 6 reserve divisions plus two! [—] So review it once again!

Occupied territories (Belgium)

One more report has come in, my Führer, from the area of the Military Commander of Belgium and Northern France. During the last few days, the SD [security service—Gestapo] has thoroughly cleaned out the Belgian Communist Party—the printing press, the national headquarters. By penetrating the matter, they arrested the office, 53 top functionaries and 22 leading men. And the materiel, weapons, ammunition, all the propaganda materials, files—all kinds of things were confiscated. So it was a significant undertaking. It could be called a major strike.[10] The SD believes that in the Belgium-Northern France Command area—this works everywhere now—everything is in order, and that they have finally achieved something. Cooperation is good—very intensive and therefore also productive.

THE FÜHRER: You know, when we came to power, the police force was not up to the mark, of course, and it was for the following reason: pure ideological firmness is, of course, insufficient—although it is certainly very important. Criminal investigation skills are also needed. Criminal know-how and experience, and, unfortunately, part of the criminal know-how went with the former people. Now it was a difficult task to screen and check them to be sure—i.e., to find the decent people—and it was not entirely successful. They found out with this "Rote Kapelle" [Red Orchestra][11] that one rat had been in there since 1933 who had a permanent connection abroad. I have to say that our enemies succeeded in one thing:

even with the dissolution of the control commissions[12] they had already installed a control mechanism in all the state apparatus, the party apparatus, and everywhere in the public apparatus, economy, and administration.

KEITEL: It was already there.

THE FÜHRER: That's why they could leave without trouble—the apparatus continued working, and was in contact with their embassies or consulate-general offices, attachés, etc. It worked splendidly. They didn't need any control commissions any longer—it worked splendidly. These people were also in the police force. In 1933 the police suffered from the fact that they consisted primarily of National Socialists with good will but very minimal knowledge of criminal investigation. They had not been trained in criminal investigation. Now, ten years have passed since that time. Now these people have gradually acquired skills and knowledge, and have gradually reached the level that the state police always had in the Romance countries—also in old Austria or in Russia, France, etc., which always used to have a good state police. That has emerged now. Now successes can be seen as well. There's hardly an issue on which the police are not totally informed. This is a very comprehensive apparatus, of course, which is necessary there and particularly great resources are needed.

HEWEL: Large resources and a lot of young people!

THE FÜHRER: Young people with the spirit of adventure, but also large resources. Paying bonuses of 100 or 200 marks will achieve nothing. To bribe a fellow like that, larger amounts must be spent.

KEITEL: ... young people were in there.

THE FÜHRER: We have to be very careful there. These people always have to be arrested and imprisoned as well, so that the others don't notice what kind of people they are. They are also put on trial and sentenced. In reality they are all agents. The others must never have a clue as to who blew the whistle on them. [—] Do you have anything else?

PUTTKAMER: No.

End: 2:12 p.m.

Italy

THE FÜHRER: Have you already been informed about the developments in Italy?

KEITEL: I just heard the last words.

THE FÜHRER: The Duce has resigned. It is not yet confirmed: Badoglio took over the government and the Duce resigned.

KEITEL: By his own initiative, my Führer?

THE FÜHRER: Probably at the king's wish, because of the royal court's pressure. I already said yesterday what the king's position is.

JODL: Badoglio took over the government.

THE FÜHRER: Badoglio took over the government—our harshest enemy. We must figure out at once how we're going to find a way to bring these people here[13] back to the mainland.

JODL: The decisive question is: will they fight or not?

THE FÜHRER: They say they will fight but it is betrayal! We must be clear among ourselves—it is betrayal, pure and simple! I'm just waiting for the news about what the Duce says. What's-his-name wants to talk to the Duce now. Hopefully he will catch him. I want the Duce to come here immediately if he catches him. I want the Duce to come here to Germany at once.

JODL: If these things are in doubt, there's only one course of action.

THE FÜHRER: I've already thought—my idea would be that the 3rd Panzer Grenadier Division[14] would occupy Rome at once and clean out the whole government.

JODL: These troops here remain there until that is back. ... this whole action here in motion, up here. ... the fighting will cease, for this case ... so that in the region of Rome we combine these forces that we are bringing out with these that are still there, while the other flows together here. [—] This matter here will be difficult.

THE FÜHRER: Here, there is only one thing—that we try to get the people on German ships, leaving the materiel behind. Materiel here or there—it makes no difference. The people are more important.[15] [—] I'm still getting messages from Mackensen. Then we will give orders about the next steps. But this must be taken away immediately!

JODL: Yes, Sir.

CHRISTIAN: My Führer! May I remind you of the order that Colonel General Jeschonnek, who actually didn't want to leave Berlin before tomorrow afternoon, is coming back tomorrow morning?

THE FÜHRER: He must come earlier—as soon as possible![16]

(CHRISTIAN: Yes, my Führer.)

[—] The most critical thing is that we now safeguard the crossings in the Alps at once—that we are prepared to get in touch with the Fourth Italian Army[17] immediately, and that we get the French passes under our control immediately. That's the most important thing. To do that, we must send units down immediately, possibly including the 24th Panzer Division.

KEITEL: Out of all these things, the worst that could happen is that we don't have the passes.

THE FÜHRER: Has Rommel left already?

JODL: Yes, Rommel has gone.

THE FÜHRER: Where is he now? Still in Wiener Neustadt?

KEITEL: We can find out.

THE FÜHRER: Find out right away where Rommel is![18] We have to make sure now that we [—] So in principle, one panzer division—that's the 24th—is ready. The most important thing is that the 24th Panzer Division is brought down into this area at once so that the 34th Panzer Division[19] can be pulled through here immediately on any of the railway lines. That way we can concentrate this here immediately and make sure that the infantry division Feldherrnhalle [Panzer Grenadier Division]—which must be ready—occupies the passes at least. Because we have only a single division here, which is near Rome. [—] Is the entire 3rd Panzer Grenadier Division there near Rome?

JODL: It's there but not fully mobile—only partly mobile.

THE FÜHRER: What weapons and assault guns does it have?

BUHLE: The 3rd Panzer Grenadier Division has 42 assault guns.

JODL: But preparations for taking this sector over from the Fourth Italian Army are underway now.

THE FÜHRER: Thank God we still have the parachute division here.[20] That's why the people here must be saved at all costs. That's of no use here; they must come over, especially the paratroops and also the people from the GÖRING [Parachute Panzer Division]. Their materiel is not important at all. They should blow it up or demolish it. But the people must come over. They are 70,000 men now. If it's possible to fly, they can be over here soon. They must hold a screen here[21] and then take everything back. Only small arms—everything else remains there. They don't need any more than that. We can deal with the Italians even with small arms. It makes no sense to hold this here. If we want to hold something, we could hold it from here on at most, but not from here. We cannot take care of the matter from here, of course. Later we will certainly have to withdraw somewhere here—that's quite obvious … The most important thing is that we get the units in here very soon, and that the Leibstandarte [SS Panzer Grenadier Division] comes out and is transported away!

ZEITZLER: Yes, Sir. I will give the order at once.

KEITEL: In the direction of the former ...

ZEITZLER: We have to prepare first. I have to get the railway materials here. I can go at a tempo of 36 convoys, 36 trains; it will take 2 or 3 days before I get the railway materials here. I will do that now right away.

(General Zeitzler excuses himself.)

JODL: We should really wait for an accurate report to see what's happening.

THE FÜHRER: Of course, but we have to start making deliberations now. There is no doubt about one thing—that they, of course, will declare in their betrayal that they will stick to their guns; that's absolutely clear. But that is a betrayal—they won't stick to their guns anyway.

KEITEL: Has anyone spoken with this Badoglio yet?

THE FÜHRER: Meanwhile we have received the following report: the Duce was in the Grand Council yesterday. There in the Grand Council were Grandi,[22] whom I always called a "pig," Bottai,[23] and above all Ciano. They spoke against Germany in this Grand Council in the following way, "There is no sense anymore in continuing the war; we should try to get Italy out of it somehow." Some of them opposed the idea. Farinacci, etc., seemed to have spoken against it but not as effectively as those who spoke in favor of this movement. The Duce sent word to Mackensen this evening that he will absolutely continue the fight and won't surrender. Then I suddenly received word that Badoglio wanted to speak to Mackensen. Mackensen said he had nothing to discuss with him, but then he insisted even more and eventually Badoglio sent a man—

HEWEL: Mackensen sent one of his men to Badoglio.

THE FÜHRER: He said that the king had just asked him to form a government after the Duce's resignation. [—] What does "resignation" mean? Probably this bum ... I said that the statements of this Phillip ..., one could gather it from that already.

KEITEL: The whole attitude of the royals! The Duce does not hold any means of power in his hands—nothing, no troops.

THE FÜHRER: Nothing! I told him that repeatedly—he has nothing! It is not true that he has nothing. They have also prevented him from obtaining any means of power. Now the minister has ordered Mackensen to go to the Foreign Office first. He will probably be notified of this there. I suppose it must be correct. Second, the minister asked whether I agree that he should go to the Duce at once. I told him that he should go to the Duce at once, and, if possible, prompt the Duce to come to Germany immediately. I would like to assume that he wants to speak with me. If the Duce comes it's good; if he doesn't, I don't know. If the Duce comes to Germany and speaks with me, it's good in principle. If he doesn't come here or cannot leave or resigns because he doesn't feel well again—and that would not be astonishing with such a treacherous rabble—then who knows? But what's-his-name declared immediately that the war goes on; nothing will change in that respect. [—] These people have to do that, because it's betrayal. But we'll go on playing the same game on our side. Everything is prepared; we're ready to catch this whole mob instantly—to clean out all this riffraff. I'll send a man down there tomorrow who will give the order to the commander of the 3rd Panzer Grenadier Division to enter Rome immediately with a special group, and to arrest the entire government, the king, and this whole mob straight away, and especially to arrest the crown prince at once—to seize the riffraff, especially Badoglio and this whole rabble.[24] Then you'll see that they will weaken—down to their bones—and in 2 or 3 days there will be a coup again.

KEITEL: The only formation from the Alarik that's still on the march is the 715th.[25]

THE FÜHRER: Does it have all the assault guns at least? Forty-two?

BUHLE: He must have 42 assault guns; the assault guns were complete when they went.

JODL: Here's the organization. (Presentation.)

THE FÜHRER: How far are they from Rome?

JODL: About 100 km.

THE FÜHRER: 100? 60 km! More will not be necessary. If he starts with motorized troops he can enter and arrest the whole mob immediately.

KEITEL: Two hours!

JODL: 50 to 60 km.

THE FÜHRER: That's no distance at all.

WAIZENEGGER: Forty-two assault guns with the division.

THE FÜHRER: They are down there with the division?

(WAIZENEGGER: Yes, with the division.)

Jodl, draw it up now!

JODL: Six battalions.

KEITEL: Unconditionally ready for action. Conditionally ready for action: five complete ones.

THE FÜHRER: Jodl, draw up the order for the 3rd Panzer Grenadier Division to be sent down right away. An order—without talking to anyone—to enter Rome with assault guns ... and to arrest the government, the king and that whole group.

BUHLE: Perhaps all of the fast-moving units, the two reconnaissance detachments—

THE FÜHRER: Yes, so we have something there, too!

KEITEL: Are they there?

BUHLE: They're there—at least one from the 16th.

JODL: From the 16th.

THE FÜHRER: I want the crown prince in particular.

KEITEL: He's more important than the old man.

BODENSCHATZ: It must be organized in such a way that they are immediately loaded onto the plane and taken away.

THE FÜHRER: Onto the plane and immediately away—away instantly!

BODENSCHATZ: So we don't lose the bambino [baby] on the airfield!

THE FÜHRER: In eight days there will be another collapse here. You will see!

CHRISTIAN: Colonel General Jeschonnek had actually started when he got the call there. He had not intended to come before tomorrow noon, but he has already landed tonight. I haven't been able to speak with him yet. He just landed 10 minutes ago.

THE FÜHRER: How long will it take him to come over here?

BODENSCHATZ: It will take him an hour and a half by car.

THE FÜHRER: When he comes, he should come over here immediately. Tell him that! [—] And then I would really like to speak with the Reichsmarshal!

BODENSCHATZ: I will inform him at once.

THE FÜHRER: Of course, we will have to initiate it when we are ready enough with our forces that they can go over immediately and disarm that whole rabble. The watchword for the whole story must be that the traitorous generals at the top—Ciano is hated anyway—are striking a blow against Fascism.

(Telephone conversation between the Führer and Reichsmarshal GÖRING. The Reichsmarshal's questions and answers were not heard by the stenographers.)

THE FÜHRER: Hello, Göring. I don't know: do you have news yet? [—] So, it's not yet a direct confirmation, but it can hardly be doubted anymore that the Duce has resigned and Badoglio has taken his place. [—] Now, it's not a question of possibilities in Rome but of facts! [—] That's the reality, Göring. There's no doubt about it! [—] What? [—] I don't know; we want to make sure first. [—] That's nonsense, of course. It's carrying on as well, and how! They'll see how we will carry on! [—] So I just wanted to tell you this. Under these circumstances, I believe it would be good for you to come here as soon as possible.[26] [—] What? [—] I don't know! I will inform you about it then. But in any case, be prepared for the possibility that it's correct! (End of telephone call.) We've experienced a mess like this already: that was on the day when the government was overthrown.[27]

(KEITEL: At 10 in the morning in the Great Hall.)

But that turned different then, too. I just hope they haven't detained the Duce! But if they have detained him, it's all the more important that we go there.

JODL: That, of course, would be a different situation. Then we would have to go over at once. Because otherwise the essential thing would be that we can still get units over the passes. Otherwise the traitors could set up elements here, and we wouldn't be able to bring anything over anymore. The most important thing now is that the transports that are stacked up here come over. It was already ordered yesterday that everything should go over there—even if it's only to northern Italy and doesn't go any further from there—so that we still bring forces here to northern Italy. Because in this case—

BUHLE: These here will also be available again for that.

THE FÜHRER: Send those immediately! Just in case, of course, those should go at once!

KEITEL: That's the only reason we didn't pull them in there.

THE FÜHRER: We can do that at once—that's perfectly clear.

KEITEL: The next infantry division.

THE FÜHRER: Wonderful. They should expect something! If they are not deployed there, they would probably—because the betrayal changes everything, of course. I have the feeling that these people[28] here are already aware of the whole thing—this betrayal—and that's why they introduced martial law.

KEITEL: I clarified that. They have the following reason for it: so far, they've had martial law only for looting and robbery after air raids, should they occur. When asked for the date, they said they had already done it during the earlier raid on Budapest,[29] and had now expanded it for daylight raids: anyone who loots or robs during air raids, etc. It's a fine statement. This afternoon they sent me this back.

THE FÜHRER: We must be clear about this: This Badoglio pig was working against us all the time, here in North Africa and here—everywhere. Has Rommel left already?

(… ?): He's being held right now, my Führer.

THE FÜHRER: If he hasn't left yet, we should call him back immediately, of course.

KEITEL: It's possibly that he will still be in Wiener Neustadt tomorrow morning. He wanted to collect his belongings.

THE FÜHRER: Then have him brought here early tomorrow morning in a Condor, and then I'll give him instructions. Once the situation is ripe, everything will be put under the command of Field Marshal Rommel, of course—everyone will accept orders only from him.

JODL: So we have to send Weichs[30] the (order[31]) down there at once.

KEITEL: We can do that.

THE FÜHRER: Make sure Weichs is ready for anything that may happen!

BODENSCHATZ: Will the Commander-in-Chief South be informed?

(KEITEL: Yes.)

THE FÜHRER: Is the Reichsführer here?

DARGES: No, he's out at the moment; he had planned to come back tomorrow.

THE FÜHRER: Find out!

(DARGES: Yes, Sir.)

We have to draw up a list at once. It will, of course, include this Ciano, and Badoglio, and many others. First of all, the whole rabble—and Badoglio, of course, dead or alive!

(HEWEL: Yes, Sir.)

The first measures to be taken: First, we dispatch the units here to the border immediately, so that whatever can come over comes over. But these units here must immediately—Jodl, these units down here must be informed at once about their tasks, so they know that they absolutely must take control of these passes here immediately!

KEITEL: This battalion here in Innsbruck is informed about the secret instructions.

THE FÜHRER: Is it still there?

KEITEL: It's still there. The mountain school, relieved, ... the staff or a group of the Feldherrnhalle [Panzer Grenadier Division] has been instructed, the 715th [Security Division] has also been instructed, and the 3rd Panzer Grenadier Division. These three have been instructed; they received secret instructions at that time from the Commander-in-Chief West regarding the implementation of Alarik. Investigations and such like were forbidden, in order not to draw attention to these things. These three should do this. We had hoped to do it together with the ...

THE FÜHRER: They aren't there?

KEITEL: No, they're not.

V. PUTTKAMER: We should inform the Navy because of the transports. They are spread out everywhere in the ports, among the Italians.

THE FÜHRER: Certainly! But the crossing must still be made here, as far as possible.

GÜNSCHE: Field Marshal Rommel left for Salonika this morning and has arrived there.

THE FÜHRER: Then he can fly back tomorrow—he has his airplane there anyway.

CHRISTIAN: His old 111 crew.

THE FÜHRER: How long will it take him to come from Salonika?

CHRISTIAN: He can be here after 3 or 4 p.m., with one stopover.

THE FÜHRER: So 6 to 7 hours?

BUHLE: Six hours!

JODL: We flew from … to Salonika in two and a half hours in the Heinkel.

SPEER: But he doesn't have my "lame duck"! That is something else!

THE FÜHRER: Your "lame duck"! As if! If good old Mackensen hadn't had it recently, he wouldn't have been able to land. As I heard it, our good man Hewel phoned Mackensen's wife directly and said, "Mackensen's plane is overdue." That's also very "diplomatic"! For that one must be promoted to the position of an ambassador first! [—] All the other things will go forward. So, Jodl, I repeat: First, an order to the 3rd Panzer Grenadier Division, and, if necessary, to these units here in order to support Rome; analogous orders to the Luftwaffe deployed around Rome—whatever is there: anti-aircraft, etc.—so they know right away. That's the one complex. Then immediately moving the other units in. This, of course, must be done in connection with that! The third is immediate preparation for the evacuation of all these areas by German units, which should be brought over here—while retaining the screen in front, of course. All units in the rear are to be removed immediately and brought over here. It doesn't matter at all: Small arms and machine guns should be taken with them, but nothing else—everything else we can let go. We have 70,000 men down there, including the absolute best men there are. We must do it in such a way that the last ones go back in the motor vehicles and embark here. We have enough German ships anyway. There is a great deal of German ship capacity.[32]

JODL: Almost exclusively.

THE FÜHRER: The anti-aircraft artillery will remain here and provide uninterrupted protection. The anti-aircraft artillery that's over there will be the last to go. They will blow up everything and come over last.

CHRISTIAN: But no Italians will come over with the German troops?

THE FÜHRER: It must be done so quickly that they cross over during one night, if possible. If they transport only men, and don't take any equipment or anything with them, they will finish within two days—in one day.

JODL: The normal capacity under normal conditions is 17,000[33] men anyway. That's the standard capacity.

THE FÜHRER: Imagine all of this densely packed. It must be done like it was at Dunkirk back then. It would be ridiculous if they couldn't get the whole company across this narrow strait[34] under the protection of a Luftwaffe like this. What's critical is that they take the guns and machine guns with them. Trench mortars—all the light stuff.

JODL: They should be handed over to the two divisions that are there.

THE FÜHRER: They will immediately come here, to these two divisions. In any case, they will first get normal infantry reinforcements, and we must give them the weapons.

BUHLE: Also here, my Führer, the order ought to be given to the general staff today or tomorrow that from now on the focus in terms of motor vehicles should be shifted to here—meaning everything that is currently being built up and going to the East. Otherwise these units won't get there.

THE FÜHRER: We can still do that tomorrow. Then I have to take precautions about something else. We have to be careful with the Hungarian situation.

JODL: Then the Commander-in-Chief South must get a guard at once.

THE FÜHRER: Yes.

JODL: The 3rd Panzer Grenadier Division must provide a strong guard for the whole headquarters.

THE FÜHRER: Yes.

JODL: Otherwise they will round up the leadership!

THE FÜHRER: Yes, we can do that right away. I'll round up their [the Italian] leadership! They'll get the shock of their lives!

JODL: We should think it over carefully for half an hour first.

BODENSCHATZ: The Italian workforce?!

THE FÜHRER: They haven't arrived yet.

SPEER: We need personnel.

JODL: Don't let any more Italians cross the border—those who are still here in Germany![35]

SPEER: They work very diligently. We could put them to good use for the OT [Todt Organization], etc.

THE FÜHRER: When this thing blows up, I don't need to be concerned about the Belgian any longer either. Then I can lead this fellow away and lock all the relatives up together.[36]

SPEER: The Croatians could become very decent.

THE FÜHRER: Now, but—

SPEER: Better allies than all those Italians. If we could take this opportunity to recruit them, we would have 100,000 men. One day it will happen anyway!

THE FÜHRER: There is a possibility here after all.If they could have the chance to get Fiume on this occasion, it would be a chance to betray the Italians—a chance they would not pass up. They tried it earlier.[37] [—] Has anything else come in?

JODL: The day was relatively quiet. An assembly is reported south of Rivalcuto.[38] Minor attacks against the 15th Panzer Grenadier Division; the attacks were driven back here. And then since this morning an attack—still in progress—along the north coast. [—] Nothing else has been reported yet.

THE FÜHRER: Here, if it becomes necessary, they must retreat quickly and go back here on the roads. The vehicles must be emptied of everything else. All other things must be removed from the vehicles. All tractors, guns, etc., must be blown up! The critical thing is that the people get away.

JODL: A report from informers regarding a secret meeting at the headquarters in Cairo on June 20: the king of England[39] and General Wilson,[40] Commander-in-Chief of the Twelfth Army, which is intended for Greece.

THE FÜHRER: In connection with these people here, with the betrayal!

JODL: Then this message, which might also be connected to that. A controversial person from Switzerland—who, however, has often provided good, sound information—reports, "After stabilizing the situation of the Allies in Sicily ... attack from North Africa against the mainland, in the direction of Rome—with fresh troops—is intended. The occupation of Rome should be regarded as the most important action from a psychological standpoint. They intend to establish a provisional national government in Rome immediately. The Fascist Party would be dissolved, and Italy and Albania liberated from the Fascist dictatorship. Major new contingents of troops and weapons are said to have arrived in Africa from America and Canada."

THE FÜHRER: That's all certainly related to it.

JODL: That takes care of everything else that has been submitted.

THE FÜHRER: What else do you have?

JODL: This was for the Commander-in-Chief West.

KEITEL: The information about the issue you asked about today. The distribution of forces—the overview you asked for. [—] The Palermo port ... already as a motor torpedo boat base by the enemy ...

THE FÜHRER: "Reinforcement for Sardinia"—also outdated.

JODL: According to an aerial photo, the enemy is already using the Palermo port as a motor torpedo base. On the afternoon of the 24th, there were eight motor torpedo boats there.

THE FÜHRER: Shouldn't we prepare the 2nd Parachute Division[41] so they can be put on alert immediately?

JODL: Yes, they might possibly come into consideration as reinforcements in Rome.

THE FÜHRER: Yes, so we throw them in to Rome at once.

BODENSCHATZ: One of the Commander-in-Chief South's companies?!

THE FÜHRER: This is one of the most important things: to be strong here.

JODL: Otherwise, we won't yet be able to tell him anything.

THE FÜHRER: No, nothing else. He should prepare a strong guard. He must not go in person anywhere, either—not to any meetings. He must receive only in his headquarters. The best thing would be to say that he's sick. Or we could also say that he was summoned here to report.

JODL: He must stay there.

KEITEL: I would let him stay there. He is one who can lead and give orders immediately. He holds the apparatus in his hands. He absolutely should not leave his headquarters, and anyone who goes to see him there must have a military escort. He won't receive anyone else or leave his headquarters for any meetings, of course.[42]

THE FÜHRER: ...

HEWEL: No, I only spoke with the minister.

THE FÜHRER: Do you have anything else?

Italy

THE FÜHRER: So, Jodl, take care of the matter now!

JODL: These orders, yes.

THE FÜHRER: We have to go on with this game, of course, as if we believe they will continue!

JODL: We must do that.

THE FÜHRER: We have to do it like [—]

V. PUTTKAMER: The Grand Admiral will be here at the situation conference tomorrow.

End: 10:13 p. m.

Second Evening Situation Report
July 25, 1943

Beginning: 12:25 a.m. (July 26)

Italy

(Presentation of an order[43] by General Jodl.)

THE FÜHRER (after inspection): I don't know if this is possible, Jodl—this item here?

KEITEL: "Withdrawing anti-aircraft equipment"?

THE FÜHRER: Yes. I don't know whether this is feasible. We have to wait until—

JODL: It's just preparation, my Führer.

CHRISTIAN: That won't be possible in all cases because it mostly—

JODL: Just preparation!

THE FÜHRER: " … telephoning strictly forbidden … no order, all these instructions must be given only verbally by couriers or enciphered by telex or code. Telephone conversations—even in a disguised form—about these things is also prohibited, of course."

JODL: Yes, indeed. [—] So this is the border, and that's the border with Croatia. I had this idea in particular because I got hold of the message from the Tarvisio railway command today. For 10 to 14 days the Italians have been running … ammunition transports by … supplied with ammunition of all calibers.

THE FÜHRER: This is a bad story, of course—it's certainly connected to that.

JODL: " … increased alert stand-by." These measures were presumably taken in case of the appearance of airborne troops or partisans.

THE FÜHRER: Then it's connected to that. The betrayal was systematically prepared by these people.

JODL: I think so, too. In addition there is a message from the Commander-in-Chief South: the communication from General Roatta indicates that the Duce, after hearing the report—this was certainly a while ago—renounced his plan to transfer the 3rd Panzer Grenadier Division into the vicinity of Rome as he had wished to do. [—] "Communication from General Roatta"! We have no idea whether all this is true.

THE FÜHRER: I don't believe Roatta is in cahoots with the others.44 They hate each other, Roatta and Badoglio.

JODL: There are still a number of questions, my Führer. The Commander-in-Chief Southeast is asked to report immediately on how he can carry out Operation Konstantin with his forces in the current situation, and the Commander-in-Chief West Operation Alarik. Everything has changed now. But in any case, they have to make suggestions themselves concerning how they can carry this out under the changed conditions, now that some divisions have been taken away. That should come by telex tonight. They knew about the news itself. Nothing further was said. What about the issue of the coal trains to Italy? So far we've left them running.

THE FÜHRER: We will do everything we can to give the impression [—]

JODL: Now there is also the question: shouldn't at least trips to Italy, and private communications, be stopped?

THE FÜHRER: I wouldn't do that yet either.

KEITEL: No, not yet!

THE FÜHRER: All important persons have to give notice of departure anyway; they won't receive permission any longer.

JODL: Then I talked to Kesselring. Now that he has heard the appeal, he wants—he was not contacted, but there is in fact a new supreme commander and a new head of government—to take up contact with the king or Badoglio, which he must indeed do.

THE FÜHRER: Should he? Yes, he must!

JODL: He should do it tomorrow morning, at least to explore the situation.

THE FÜHRER: Good old Hube with his opinion, "Everything is tight here!"[45]

KEITEL: Hube didn't know anything. He only passed on what the—

THE FÜHRER: You see how dangerous it is for "nonpolitical generals" when they get into such a political atmosphere.

JODL: Then the order went out to alert the 2nd Parachute Division immediately, and to prepare for airborne transport, as far as capacity is available.

CHRISTIAN: We are still waiting for the report on what is available. But now another question, my Führer: Second Air Fleet, Field Marshal v. Richthofen, has been using 100 Ju 52 transport planes to supply the 1st Parachute Division in Sicily ... ten shot down again today. Consequently he wanted to withdraw them. The Commander-in-Chief South wanted to confiscate these planes at once, and he apparently also wanted to draw troops from northern Italy to central Italy, according to the developments of this situation. The Second Air Fleet then asked the Commander-in-Chief of the Luftwaffe. Then I said to the Commander-in-Chief of the Luftwaffe, "Any further telephone conversations on this matter are prohibited; from now on they go through the Commander-in-Chief South."

THE FÜHRER: The Commander-in-Chief South has to do all that, to pull everything together. I've just told the Reichsmarshal as well that no telephone calls are allowed.

CHRISTIAN: That came from below, my Führer. It didn't come from the Commander-in-Chief of the Luftwaffe; it came from the Second Air Fleet. [—] But now there is the question whether the 2nd Paratroop Division should have access to these planes?

THE FÜHRER: First the 2nd Paratroop Division. That's the most important—it's absolutely clear ...

KEITEL: The order reads, "If necessary without the heaviest materiel, which is to be destroyed if required. No transmission of orders by phone, not even in disguised form."

THE FÜHRER: No, I would write, "all the heavy materiel."

KEITEL: So, "If necessary without all the heavy materiel, which is to be destroyed if required!"[46] [—] Then here, "No transmission of orders by phone, not even in disguised form; instructions only by courier."

THE FÜHRER: By couriers whose letters must also be enciphered!

HEWEL: My Führer! There's a question of whether we shouldn't perhaps block the telephone connection from the postal service entirely. The postal service just called. That would let them get rid of the press calls. They're probably suggesting that now—that we should just block everything except the military lines.

THE FÜHRER: One could say that it's needed for military purposes, for government calls.

HEWEL: Above all the journalists, who now, of course—

THE FÜHRER: Only for government calls!

HEWEL: Only for ministries?!

THE FÜHRER: Only for ministerial and military government calls!

KEITEL: " ... whose written instructions must be enciphered." [—] So that there's nothing in anything they have with them.

CHRISTIAN: Encoded telex and radio?

THE FÜHRER: Encoded telex and enciphered radio. But this cannot be deciphered?
KEITEL: No, it's done by the Navy as well.
THE FÜHRER: Encoded telex or enciphered radio!
KEITEL: " ... or encoded radio."
THE FÜHRER: Like that!

Sicily

JODL: Then the afternoon reconnaissance identified transport movement today along the northern Sicilian coast from Palermo to the east, consisting of about 50 vessels, including eight large, the rest smaller, probably landing boats. The course was not exactly established—probably eastward.[47] So it may have to do with a landing attempt at the rear of our right wing.
THE FÜHRER: Has all this been planned by the Luftwaffe?
JODL: The Luftwaffe is informed.
CHRISTIAN: Yes, indeed. It comes from the Commander-in-Chief South.
THE FÜHRER: Nevertheless, I think we must send another officer down there at once.
JODL: The aircraft is ready; we should just wait until tomorrow.
THE FÜHRER: An officer must come here, who can tell Hube how to do it: that they transport the rear people back at first, so that they come over, and that those in front have to keep holding and then rush back in one night. They must be pulled out in one night, with just the personnel. The last ones must shoot continually and make a spectacle.

Italy

JODL: This must be communicated verbally in any case—the fall of Rome.
THE FÜHRER: That must happen under all circumstances. That's absolutely clear. We cannot get around it. It must be beaten back, and we must be sure to capture the entire government. The paratrooper division must plan it so that they jump around Rome. Then Rome must be occupied. No one can be allowed to leave Rome, then the 3rd Panzer Grenadier Division must go in.
JODL: And the troops that are on the way—those from the 26th [Panzer Division]

THE FÜHRER: That's not clear in the order in the words: "those being unloaded." It should be worded that they have to be unloaded there.

KEITEL: So let's add: "the troops to be unloaded," i.e., aside from the unloaded ones. I read it twice. I also thought, "Shouldn't we write instead, 'the troops of the 26th Panzer Division that have to be unloaded'"?

JODL: Some of them were unloaded because they couldn't get any further, and were supposed to—marching on land—

THE FÜHRER: That must be added: the unloaded troops and the troops that have to be unloaded. So: "Aside from the already unloaded troops, the rest of the 26th Panzer Division must be unloaded and placed under the command of the 3rd Panzer Grenadier Division."

HEWEL: Shouldn't we say that the Vatican exits must be occupied?

THE FÜHRER: That doesn't matter. I will go into the Vatican immediately. Do you think the Vatican troubles me? It will be seized immediately.[48] First of all, the entire diplomatic corps is in there. I don't care. The rabble is there. We'll take out all the whole herd of swine. … What is already … Then we apologize afterward; that doesn't matter to us. We are waging a war there …

BODENSCHATZ: Most of them are sitting there…believing they are safe.

HEWEL: We will get documents there!

THE FÜHRER: There? [—] Yes, we will get documents; we will bring out something about the betrayal! How long will it take the Foreign Minister—what a pity he isn't here!—to draw up the instructions for Mackensen?

HEWEL: It's probably been sent out.

THE FÜHRER: So there!!

HEWEL: I will find out right away.

THE FÜHRER: Will it be a journalist's work of 12 pages? That's what I'm most afraid of with you; it can be done in two or three lines. [—] Now I have one more idea, Jodl. If he wants to attack tomorrow or the day after tomorrow[49]—I don't know whether the units are already together—I would have them attack in the East once more. Then the Leibstandarte [Panzer Grenadier Division] can strike together with them one more time, because if the materiel is just coming anyway—

KEITEL: The railway materiel!

JODL: They can do that, of course, because it's better if they leave a more consolidated position behind.

THE FÜHRER: That would be good, of course. Then the one division, the Leibstandarte, can be transferred out. That one should go first and can leave its things there. They can leave a lot of materiel over there; they don't need to take the tanks with them. They can leave them over there and bring them in again from here. So they remain over there for now. They will also get the Panthers here, so they're well equipped. It's ridiculous. Until this division gets there, they will have these tanks available as well.

HEWEL: I would like to ask about the Prince of Hesse, who is hanging around all the time. Do you want me to say that we don't need him?[50]

THE FÜHRER: Let him come, and I will say a few words to him.

HEWEL: He goes around asking everyone, of course, and wants to know everything.

THE FÜHRER: That is actually a very good disguise—an iron wall. It's very good. In the past we often had people around us when we were planning something, but they had no clue, and the others were convinced that as long as those people were there, everything was in order. I'm afraid that Göring is overstepping his bounds.

BODENSCHATZ: I told him that very clearly beforehand.

THE FÜHRER: One has to be extremely polite. I would give him all those appeals—they are public anyway—that we've collected. He can read them, this Phillip—that would be totally harmless. But tell them that he's not to be given anything incorrect! I don't know where they are. Take care that they don't take anything incorrect! [—] And the outbound transport? When can it begin, the first one? All at once would be best!

JODL: We haven't received that yet. It's the 305th [Infantry Division] that's standing by.

THE FÜHRER: And the 44th [Infantry Division]?

JODL: It's ready; that depends on the shortages [in materiel]. The 44th will not be released until tomorrow; that depends on the shortage [in materiel]. But I assume that it will begin during the day tomorrow.

THE FÜHRER: Is the 44th motorized?

(JODL: No.)

But it's a triangular division?

KEITEL: A triangular and completely serviceable division. We wanted to bring it down there four weeks ago. Rommel wanted it because it was ready. You refused at the time, so we deployed the Brandenburg there because we didn't want it to become conspicuous.

THE FÜHRER: The Brandenburg is not there either.

KEITEL: It left again as well. It was in Innsbruck; things have gradually changed.

THE FÜHRER: Shouldn't we give these units—which might have to crack open these few bunkers[51]—some things? Either Tigers or something else, if there are difficulties somewhere? [—] Of course, a Tiger like that would shoot these few bunkers to pieces at once—the embrasures?
(KEITEL: No doubt!)
Perhaps we can find out from Buhle what there are in the way of Tigers in the schools, etc.
JODL: Whatever is available should be taken to Innsbruck.
THE FÜHRER: They only need a few to crack these few things open and... down to Krain, ... these few things will be cracked open soon. If a couple of Tigers come and shoot into them, they will go out at once. The concrete they have can be penetrated by the Tiger anyway. We might be able to take Panthers as well. Maybe we can see if it's possible to take something from the schools for this purpose—assault tanks as well, for example.
KEITEL: I will speak with Buhle.
THE FÜHRER: Tell Guderian to come here as well!
End: 12:45 a.m.

Midday Situation Report
July 26, 1943[52]

Beginning: 11:46 a.m.

Italy

THE FÜHRER: Jodl, have any new reports come in?
JODL: No, so far only one meeting with Badoglio has been set down there, at 6 p.m. There was no time before that because he's overloaded ... some shout, "Pace, pace!" [Peace, peace!] while others are hunting Fascists.
THE FÜHRER: That's good.
JODL: But so far it's like the childishness before Ash Wednesday.
THE FÜHRER: But it will in fact become an Ash Wednesday. We've experienced this before ...
JODL: The supreme command has secured itself completely. A discussion took place some minutes ago regarding the fact that because of the danger he ... has secured ... an airfield totally in German hands ...

THE FÜHRER: And another question. Do you have any news yet about when the paratrooper division will be ready to jump?

JODL: It's on alert but there's no news yet about when the additional troops will arrive.

THE FÜHRER: Jeschonnek must know.

JODL: They should come any time.

THE FÜHRER: Has this here been launched?[53] ... Wouldn't it be possible to take the tanks over here at least?

JODL: ... We especially have to take away the most valuable equipment, of course, during the time when no men can be brought back.

THE FÜHRER: Tanks above all! There are 160 tanks there ... according to yesterday's description.

JODL: The new ones have not yet ...

THE FÜHRER: No, they haven't been brought over yet.

JODL: What I received this afternoon is how all the trains are lying on the rails. (Presentation.) They're lying on all the tracks up to the Brenner [Pass]. From the Brenner to the southern wing it's not quite clear yet. But most of what was in last night's telex had already been launched by Kesselring.

THE FÜHRER: We just have to make sure that nothing nasty happens here with the Hungarians.[54] Which tank units can we send in there on short notice if necessary? ... Panther detachments. Is it possible to improvise anything there? If something were to happen there ... Now, I don't know where they are deployed. Where are they? In Döllersheim? That would be lower Austria.

JODL: Döllersheim, yes.

THE FÜHRER: Up here?

JODL: Between Vienna and Brno, to the northwest. The closest place for Hungary is Bruck.

HIMMLER:[55] Bruck on the Mur [River], not Bruck on the Leitha [River].

THE FÜHRER: Here, Untersteinfeld near ... ?

HIMMLER: ... I still don't have a thing ... on the whole, if they haven't closed a lot before ... everything that's sitting inside. There these fellows are sitting directly ...

THE FÜHRER: With the Hungarians it's complicated because we have Hungarian security divisions in the East. They are out of the picture at the moment.

HIMMLER: I have two with me; they participated in the fighting decently this time.

JODL: They have a good commander.

HIMMLER: ... we could really consider how we can manage it.

THE FÜHRER: It would in fact be possible—

HIMMLER: I think it's possible that ...

THE FÜHRER: No, they won't do that.

HIMMLER: My Führer, ...

THE FÜHRER: No, they won't do that. But it would be possible for them to declare—because they know— ...

HIMMLER: But it could ... economically ...

THE FÜHRER: Very much!

HIMMLER: That they stop this with the divisions. I wouldn't put any cowardly stunt beyond them.

(GÖRING: Yes.)

THE FÜHRER: And what can we do with this one here now?[56] How can we get this one out—the people, in particular?

JODL: Yes, I would propose to take them ... to Corsica, if possible, and pull them together there.

GÖRING: That's my opinion as well. Make Corsica as strong as possible.

JODL: The troops would have to give everything away, though, if they're to go to Corsica.

THE FÜHRER: Then we must discuss today how they would get over to Corsica.

JODL: Yes, indeed. Especially if I don't have enough capacity available to get them here. I can take them over here, of course. But there's still something there.

THE FÜHRER: Of course, we'll have to give this up here as well ... bring over here. [—] How is this here, Jodl, with the paratroopers? [—] This here will be given up now!

GÖRING: Why will it be given up if we're holding this?

THE FÜHRER: ... up there the ports, and you cannot occupy everything with two divisions.

JODL: ... the three divisions on the coastal front and the Feldherrnhalle [Panzer Grenadier Division]. But then the unit will come down which is intended for[57]—

THE FÜHRER: Which one is it?

JODL: The 715th [Security Division].

THE FÜHRER: It has arrived?

JODL: It's there.

THE FÜHRER: It's there, but not mobile.

JODL: It's partly motorized, with buses.

THE FÜHRER: We could put them in here.

JODL: Their task is to safeguard Mussolini anyway.

THE FÜHRER: And then perhaps to go on to Turin.

JODL: The next to come now are the 305th [Infantry Division] and the 44th [Infantry Division] by two routes, beginning tomorrow—the 44th into this area and the 305th into this area.

THE FÜHRER: And the 24th Panzer [Division]? When does it arrive?

JODL: It's not in yet.

THE FÜHRER: I believe the 24th Panzer is the most important one. That's the panzer division ...

JODL: It is, of course, the only panzer division that ...

THE FÜHRER: Granted.

JODL: It's just a question of whether we ... in the northern part. [—] He's closer to Italy now, of course. It's just that he has that huge flank. If the Italians ... to here, here from Trieste downward.

GÖRING: As I said outside beforehand, "If we don't get the weapons, the rebels will get them."

THE FÜHRER: Where is the 10th SS [Panzer Grenadier Division]? Is it here?

HIMMLER: It's here.58 It came down there first.

JODL: It's not quite ready yet, but almost.

THE FÜHRER: I heard a very good evaluation of the GÖRING [Parachute Panzer Division]... actually a characteristic, because it's a general evaluation of our youth.

JODL: I read it.

THE FÜHRER: The young people fight fanatically, the ones from the Hitler Youth, ... young German boys, some of them 16 years old.[59] These Hitler Youth usually fight more fanatically then their older comrades. ... report over there that they didn't get them until all of them had fallen— down to the last man. So, if these divisions all fight like these two SS divisions fight—

HIMMLER: They are good divisions now, my Führer.

THE FÜHRER: ... that's how the Hitlerjugend [Hitler Youth] [Panzer Grenadier] Division will fight, and the youth in general. They have already been uniformly trained. They will get the shock of their lives there. These are young boys but they are now ... trained for a long time.

HIMMLER: These two divisions will have been trained from February 15 to August 15.

GÖRING: Fourteen ... were army officers.

HIMMLER: But now they are in very good condition. They were also inspected by Dollmann,[60] Blaskowitz[61] and Rundstedt,[62] and they said they were very satisfied.

THE FÜHRER: Each division has how many men on average? And what's the average age?

HIMMLER: They have 400 officers on average and about 3,000 to 4,000 older non-commissioned officers—"older" meaning also between the ages of 20 and 30. The two divisions have an average age of 18½ years for the whole division, i.e., from the commander to the recruits.

THE FÜHRER: So it can be said that the majority of them are 18?

HIMMLER: Yes, 18 years.

GÖRING: Recently it was said that people between 26 and 30 have proven to be the best fighters.

HIMMLER: On average—purely physically.

THE FÜHRER: If they are trained so long ... earlier the young people were mostly God knows what ... But they are all boys who enlisted already at the age of 17—many of them even earlier ... so that they come in ... But they certainly did fight with unparalleled bravery ... The others were poorly trained— two months' training ... some before April, some after April, some during April, and from the remaining months we have about 14 days ... those were all "wonderful" exercises—meaning exercises on the training grounds in Oberwiesenfeld ... They are certainly better.

HIMMLER: They are well trained, all in all.

THE FÜHRER: So these first five divisions are there now. But then you have the 24th Panzer [Division] ready as well?

JODL: Then the 24th Panzer is also ready.

THE FÜHRER: We must put them in here—that's quite certain. We have to make sure that we get a division down here from the East quickly, and that we pull this in behind.

JODL: Then, my Führer, Field Marshal v. Rundstedt is arriving at the Fourth Italian Army headquarters today.

GÖRING: For a visit.

JODL: Within the framework of these ongoing visits. The relationship has always been very good so far. I think it's quite a good—

GÖRING: Perfect!

THE FÜHRER: But he shouldn't stay there for long. He should leave again as soon as possible. The thing must be done quickly. We must look as quickly as possible—he must get an accurate picture of the situation today already.

GÖRING: What Italian formations are deployed in Rome?

HIMMLER: My Führer! We could try to get this division from the Duce. We gave them 12 assault guns, 12 Panzer IVs and 12 Panzer IIIs. That's 36—

THE FÜHRER: ... division, as much as they get.

JODL: There are people there anyway.

HIMMLER: Obersturmbannführer (Leinert)[63] from my staff is still there.

THE FÜHRER: He ought to make sure that we get the whole division— that it joins us.

GÖRING: At least the guns ...

HIMMLER: Then the training commands are also down there.

JODL: When may I send this order down?

THE FÜHRER: ... can give ...

JODL: I've just transmitted an order to Kesselring.

GÖRING: Are we really giving these orders?

THE FÜHRER: They all come by encoded telex.

JODL: It's perfect.

THE FÜHRER: By encoded telex? What do you want? Otherwise we can't give anything—no orders at all anymore. Otherwise he won't know what we want.

GÖRING: I thought that in this case it could be done with special secret couriers.

THE FÜHRER: Couriers are even more dangerous, if they have anything on them. This must be enciphered again.

GÖRING: Memorized!

THE FÜHRER: But they can't memorize too many things. Besides, they memorize it anyway because ... was also here; that's essentially how it was down there as well.

SCHERFF: Probably here ... in the event of a coup.

HIMMLER: I can send something down to his people by radio.

GÖRING: It would certainly be most disastrous if they gave this here to the English. That would be disastrous, of course. That would be just fantastic. [—] They have the task of disarming them?

SCHERFF: Only very generally: to act if necessary. Then they usually lead them to the possibility—

THE FÜHRER: They are informed about the possibility of a coup, both of them, since in that case—

GÖRING: …

THE FÜHRER: No, they should get a signal. If we communicate it to them, it would cause difficulties. With them we can … radio …

HIMMLER: I can also radio to my division in Rome.

THE FÜHRER: Enciphered?

HIMMLER: Yes, indeed. Enciphered.

THE FÜHRER: And is that completely secure?

HIMMLER: Completely secure. We've agreed on a brand new key. Yesterday we made the last key. I can give them the order that they … with their …

GÖRING: … it must be secure.

JODL: That can only go to Kesselring, because otherwise he won't know what the further intentions are. The news that he then receives … a totally different situation again …

THE FÜHRER: Jodl, so for the march in here … pull in to get in here first or to get across the Brenner?

JODL: I don't see any difficulties in getting across the Brenner [Pass]. The trains simply run through there.

THE FÜHRER: Yes, but if they suddenly occupy this?

JODL: Then there's the other point of view—

HIMMLER: And South Tyrol rebels!64

THE FÜHRER: But there are no South Tyrolese. They've all been called up!

HIMMLER: There are still men there. The Italians are … if we seize them … They have to enter their bunkers anyway. I'm quite sure of that.

THE FÜHRER: … Innsbruck garrison … and makes his Tigers available for this purpose ... have you already spoken with Thomale about the affair? (JODL: Yes.)

Also about that?

SCHERFF: Thomale was here anyway.

JODL: We spoke with him already. At least over there in the east we have—the next closest regiment is there in Tarvisio.

HIMMLER: That's what I was going to say. This regiment came there … this is now undamaged here … this mountain regiment. We can bring it up easily.

THE FÜHRER: What kind of police regiment is this here?

HIMMLER: That's the police regiment that's in Marseilles. My Führer, we could … this with Laibach and Trieste …

JODL: The crossing points that we … from Agram to …

HIMMLER: It is important to me that we hold this in Laibach.

THE FÜHRER: But this we could bring over here.

HIMMLER: I can do that easily.

THE FÜHRER: Shouldn't we do that right away?

JODL: I suppose they will do this anyway because they have the order to safeguard … —we will find that out today—to use increased security. We won't have anything else.

HIMMLER: Here I would get over much easier; we're located here already. So I would reach it more easily if I were to take Tarvisio from here. If I go in there, … and then I have to say, of course: how far should we go up to this point we can … go up.

THE FÜHRER: Well, if the tanks come the whole rabble will run away immediately like cowards. It's just good that I—

HIMMLER: Are our panzer units going down there as well?

GÖRING: They won't fight!

HIMMLER: Where are they going?

THE FÜHRER: Here, but we'll have to see. The Leibstandarte [Panzer Grenadier Division] will leave its tanks behind and get them back here.

GÖRING: I'm not concerned. That these cripples will oppose us at the Brenner [Pass]—that's totally impossible.

THE FÜHRER: If our Panthers come—

GÖRING: I think it's very good, the paratroopers jumping. Himmler's people can do it better than mine. Immediately!

THE FÜHRER: They can't jump. They have to land!

GÖRING: Some of them will land, yes.

KEITEL: … Six o'clock in the morning goes up to …

THE FÜHRER: He should come here!

KEITEL: He will come here at once. Yes, Sir.

THE FÜHRER: …

GÖRING: Yes, that's my opinion as well.

THE FÜHRER: … the Italians mad.

GÖRING: I mean that he did write the letter there!

LINGE: My Führer, Field Marshal Kluge and General Zeitzler have arrived. Would you like the gentlemen to come right away?

THE FÜHRER: Yes.

(Meeting is interrupted by a discussion with Field Marshal v. Kluge.[65])

Italian fleet

DÖNITZ: My Führer! … came back. It's just that there is a constant connection … that 90% of his officers would come with us. I don't know.

THE FÜHRER: That couldn't be right.

DÖNITZ: That's too much. I cannot do anything to prevent … submarines … were in La Spezia and Toulon and that 5 or 6 of them anchor near La Spezia. The right thing would be—if the propaganda did not work—to seize the ships as soon as possible.

THE FÜHRER: They will be … in Toulon …

DÖNITZ: Yes, perhaps they can be seized before. I myself have submarine crews in La Spezia, too.[66] But they have nothing but shotguns or pistols, and they are not equipped with anything else. So if you want to seize the ships, the troops have to be equipped with the appropriate weapons. But I actually believe the Italians will let us seize them.

THE FÜHRER: Do you have any idea [—]?

GÖRING: We have people in there.

DÖNITZ: But they are not mobile—perhaps 300 men. We have 2 submarines in there. With 300 men you cannot do much in the way of propaganda. Obviously, they are not trained for this—they are sailors. I think, my Führer, we should try to prevent these people from putting to sea.

THE FÜHRER: I have said before that a special squadron or troop should be made available for this purpose.

DÖNITZ: Let's wait and see. You never know.

GÖRING: But you are there in front with submarines?

DÖNITZ: I will immediately be there with submarines if they put to sea. We have to wait and see how it develops. It's also possible that there will be a split within the fleet—that the young officers will arrest the old ones.[67]

GÖRING: But keep the group prepared for action!

JUNGE: You can let them know that there are submarines there.

FÜHRER: No, for God's sake, no!

DÖNITZ: That is still premature…

Part VI

1944

Meeting of the Führer with Colonel General Jodl
July 31, 1944, in the Wolfsschanze

[On July 20, 1944, a powerful bomb shattered the conference room where Hitler was discussing military operations. The plot, known as Operation Valkyrie, was meant to overthrow the Nazi regime and facilitate a coup by the German Army. Hitler survived and the plot failed.]

Present:

The Führer
Colonel v. Below
Colonel General Jodl
Lieutenant Colonel v. Amsberg
General Warlimont
Lieutenant Colonel Waizenegger
Gruppenführer Fegelein
Major Büchs
Beginning: 11:53 p.m.

General overview

THE FÜHRER: Jodl, when I look at the big concerns today, there is first the problem of stabilizing the Eastern Front—we can't go beyond that at the moment—and I ask myself with regard to the situation if it really is that bad that our forces are concentrated relatively closely together. Because there are not only disadvantages, but also advantages. If the area that we are occupying now can be held, then this is an area that we can still live in, and we don't have those huge communication zones. Assuming, of course, that we really provide the combat group[1] with what we created in those earlier communication zones. Then it will be a real force. If we don't do this, but the communication zone goes into Germany instead, if we develop an ever-deeper rear army service area, where no army area is necessary, and if we still link this with the idea of executive authority, where no executive authority is necessary, because all people administer authority only in the sense of the army anyway—then in 1939 I would have had to have given up executive authority in the West as far as Hannover, Minden it was all a single deployment area. When we do away with this homegrown but other-worldly ideology—which is not at all soldierly and is not even known in other armies—then the narrowing of the area isn't always a disadvantage, but can also be a gain. But only under one condition: that we really put that which we have developed or consumed in this gigantic area into the fight. If this prerequisite is met, it is my solemn conviction that we can stabilize the thing also in the East. [—] Italy. In Italy I would not remain in the Apennine position. I wouldn't do that because[2] I couldn't contain a large enemy force, which will definitely be brought into action somewhere else. Because he won't pension off the forces if we go back now. But you could seal off Germany, of course, with a minimum of forces, when I go to the Alpine front. But I need the forces elsewhere anyway, and the other one's forces are freed up as well. In any case, it is still better if I lead a battle in a different country than if I bring it close to Germany and I have to draw the forces away when the mobility of the forces is quite limited—because his air force, as we know from experience, will move itself along. [—] In the West, in my view, there is actually one very decisive question. If we lose France as a war theater, we will lose our point of departure for the submarine war.[3] We have to be clear about this. That's the point of departure for the submarine war. We will still get some militarily important things out of this area, including the last tungsten—and the mines probably could be exploited more than they have been so far. We could do even more.[4] But it's also clear that an operation in France—and I believe we must be fully aware of this at all times—is totally impossible in a so-called open field of battle under today's circumstances. We can't do that. We can move with some of our troops, but only in a limited manner. With the other ones we cannot move, not because we do not possess air superiority, but because we can't move the troops themselves: The units are not suited for mobile battle—neither their weapons nor in their other equipment. They can't do it either. They haven't learned that. But the total strength of the forces in France cannot be measured by the number of divisions—which we theoretically have here—but really only by the limited number of units that are actually able to move.[5] That's only a very small fraction. If the territory weren't that important, a decision would be forced upon us—namely to clear the coast without hesitation and to lead the mobile forces immediately back into a line, which, I would like to say, we would defend unyieldingly. But one thing is already obvious now. I have here a certain number of forces. Those forces are hardly enough to defend this narrow front. If we can say that about 75% of all our mobile forces are here and a certain number of our immobile forces, and I transfer them to a line like this—then we can see the complete hopelessness of holding such a line with the forces that are available to us, no matter where I built it up. We have to realize that a change in France could only happen if we managed—even only for a certain time—to establish superiority in the air. That's why it's my opinion that we have to do everything—as hard as it may be right now—to prepare the Luftwaffe units, which we are setting up in the Reich now, to be used as last reserves in the worst possible circumstances. To use them—I can't tell now where the last dice will fall, but to use them where we can possibly create a change again.[6] It's unfortunate that it will still take so many weeks and that we can't manage it faster. Because for me there is no doubt: if we could immediately draw in an additional 800 fighters, to reach 2,000 fighters at once, as we probably could do now, this entire crisis would be overcome immediately; there wouldn't be a crisis anymore. But even later we can only conduct the war here if we manage to rebuild the Luftwaffe to some extent. So I considered the question: what are the most dangerous moments that could occur during the entire war? First, of course, would be a breakthrough in the East with a real threat to the German homeland—whether in the Upper Silesian industrial area or in East Prussia—with the accompanying difficult psychological effects. But I believe that with the forces we are putting up now, which are slowly coming out, we are in a position to stabilize the East—I believe that—and that we will overcome this human crisis, this moral crisis. It can't be separated from the event that took place here.[7] Because the action is not to be taken as an isolated action. But this act which happened here is, I would like to say, just a symptom of an inner circulatory problem, of an inner blood poisoning, that we are suffering from. What do you expect in the end from the front's highest leadership, if behind them (as we can see now) the most important positions are occupied by absolutely destructive people—not defeatists, but destructive people and traitors? Because it is like that. If the communications service and the quartermaster's office are occupied by people who are absolute traitors[8]—and you don't really know how long they have been in contact with the enemy or the people over there—you cannot expect that the necessary initiative to stop such a thing will come from there. Because the Russians certainly did not improve so much in morale within one or two years. That is not the case. They did not improve in a human sense either. But our morale doubtlessly became worse—became worse because we had this place over there, which constantly spread poison over the path of these General Staff organizations, the organizations of the quartermaster general, of the intelligence chiefs,[9] and so on. So we only have to ask ourselves today—or rather, we don't have to ask ourselves anymore: How does the enemy learn about our thinking? Why are so many things neutralized? Why does he react to everything so quickly? [—] It's probably not the perception of the Russians at all, but permanent treason, constantly being carried out by some damned little clique.[10] But even if it weren't possible to put it in concrete form, it would be absolutely enough that people sit here in influential positions, who, instead of constantly radiating power and spreading confidence and especially deepening their understanding of the essence of this battle brought to us by destiny—a battle of destiny that somehow can't be avoided or which can't be bargained away by some clever political or tactical skill, but that it really is a kind of Hun battle, in which you either stand or fall and die: one or the other. When those thoughts are not present in the higher positions, but when those idiots imagine that they are in a better position because the revolution was brought about by generals—instead of by soldiers as in 1918—then everything just comes to a stop. Then an army must gradually be taken apart from top to bottom. I have received so many individual letters from the front—about the Party—from good soldiers, who say, "We don't know at all what's going on; what's happening there can only be treason—it can't be explained in another way." So we also have to say, "Certainly there has been ongoing treason, and it's partly our fault as well. We always acted too late against the traitors, out of consideration for the so-called army, or we did not act at all, although we already knew for a long time—for a year and a half—that they were traitors, again to avoid compromising the army."[11] But the army is rather more compromised when we leave it to the little soldiers to handle the call that the Russians continue to give in the name of German generals—when we leave it to the little worm, to the little front officer, who must gradually come to the conclusion that either the whole thing is true or we are too cowardly to answer to it. [—] It must come to an end. It's not right. We have to repel and drive away those low creatures—the lowest creatures in history ever to wear the soldier's uniform—this riffraff, which managed to save itself from former times. That is our highest duty. When we have overcome this moral crisis, the Russians will not be better than they were previously, and we won't be worse than we were before. And with regard to our equipment and supplies, we're even better than before. Our tanks and our assault guns are better today, whereas the Russians' equipment has likely become worse.[12] [—] In my opinion, we will also be able to fix the thing in the East. The great concern I see is obviously in the Balkans. I have the fundamental conviction: If today the Turks were persuaded—like the Finns—that we can hold out, then they wouldn't lift a finger. Everyone has only the one concern that they might sit on the ground between all the chairs. That's their concern. So if we managed through some act of extremely decisive resistance or even a successful big battle somewhere, if we managed to regain the trust of those people—the trust that we can hold this, and that this withdrawal is only in the end to shorten the front, because otherwise we couldn't do it on all fronts—then I am convinced that we could bring the Turks to a more-or-less waiting attitude, even though they severed the relationship themselves.[13] The Turks are not pleased that the strongest European power opposed to Bolshevism and Russia is being eliminated in favor of a totally unstable counterweight: the Anglo-Saxons—who, furthermore, are questionable in their importance and firmness. They're not pleased. But also in Bulgaria they're slowly coming to the idea: yes, if Germany collapses, then what? We small ones can't do it. If the big one can't do it, we can't do it. There's also something else that depends on the stabilization of the Eastern Front, in my view. In the end the attitude of all the small Balkan states depends on it: the attitude of the Romanians depends on it, the attitude of the Bulgarians depends on it, the attitude of the Hungarians depends on it, and also the attitude of the Turks. Nevertheless, we must meet certain safeguards. The most critical safeguard is and will remain the initial securing of the Hungarian area—the only possible substitute for the sources of food that we lose otherwise, and also a source of many raw materials: bauxite, manganese and so on.[14] But above all for transport purposes—the prerequisite for the Southeast. Securing the Hungarian area is of essential importance to us—so important that we can't overestimate it at all. We first must think about what in terms of new troop arrangements we can either bring in or build up there, to be able at any time, if necessary, to anticipate or prevent a Hungarian coup d'état against Herr Horthy.[15] The second—just as important—is, of course, the attitude of Bulgaria. Because without Bulgaria it's practically impossible for us to secure the Balkan area so that we can get ore from Greece, etc. We need Bulgaria for that no matter what. Also in securing against bands, etc., we need Bulgaria. But it also depends partly on the fact that we really can stand in the East, and, of course, that we don't have a crisis in the rear or in the heart of Europe. So that's why any British landing attempt in the Balkans—in Istria or on the Dalmatian islands—would be very dangerous, because it will immediately affect the Hungarians. We shouldn't be surprised by the Hungarians. When we have such idiots or criminals with us, who say that even if the Russians come in we'll make peace, but if we have the Russians to ourselves not much can happen to us—so what right do we have to complain when some Hungarian idiot or magnate says, "We'll let ourselves be occupied by the British; they will have an interest in making sure that we aren't absorbed, so everything will be fine."

JODL: They might find out from those people.

THE FÜHRER: It's not impossible that they've been incited by those people in that way. So the danger is here, too, that the landing of the British could lead to catastrophic results. In my opinion, a landing on the islands, etc., can hardly be prevented in the long run, if it takes place with huge forces. There's only one question here. In the end I think it is the question of whether or not the Allies really act in agreement. If they act in total agreement, if the Russians say: we agree that you go onto the islands and we Russians in this case take, say, the Dardanelles—we would not be able to prevent it. Because I cannot prevent the landing of four or six divisions on an island with 40,000 men, and even less on a small island. We just can't do that. We don't know if that's the case or not. I would like to doubt it. I don't want to believe that the Russians would leave the Balkans to the British. I would say that in this case a fierce Russian protest would follow. At most something could happen during a period of tension between the Russian Bolsheviks and Allies: that the British might try to get at least the Aegean islands for themselves. That would be theoretically possible. Together they wouldn't do it. [—] The Italian theater is now tying up a large number of forces that would otherwise appear operationally somewhere else. Even if a landing is made here, it would be partial units, though, that come. The great mass of all Allied forces is still concentrated there like before, whether we are in front of or within the Apennine position. One thing we have to be clear about: if we're thrown back in the Apennines, the operation is finished for us. Then it's over. We can't prevent him from coming over the Po plain. We probably can't even really prevent him from breaking up our retreat. So the Apennine position is decisive. If we're defeated there, in my opinion, we won't have the option of staying to fight somewhere in the Po plain. The only possibility left will be total retreat—sensible and accelerated retreat, if it even works—to the Alpine position. I don't see any other option. [—] Here the danger is that this whole position is just as much threatened by a landing from here[16]—because you never know if he's going to turn here the next minute—with a landing from the West or with a breakthrough or with a new landing from Brittany. I've thought everything over now and I've come to the following conclusion, Jodl. If a crisis develops here, we can't leave all the responsibility to the Commander-in-Chief West. The headquarters must be here and we must, under all circumstances, lead from here. It's such a huge responsibility, and a solution can only be found if all forces work together. We may have to make the most difficult decisions. It could be that we'll have to accept a substantial reduction of the German living space again—possibly even to abandon the Balkans, even with the risk that our chromium will be used up within a short time. But it may be the only possibility to get the forces to operate here at all. We may at last have to deploy here, and then also draw back forces from here.[17] And with that, I understand that it will be lost. We might have to retreat into the Alps directly in order to be able to operate here at all. Now I think the most important thing, Jodl, is that a number of orders are given here, which aren't connected to each other but which correspond to a certain plan of ours—but the plan must not be distributed to the army groups at all. You can't keep such thoughts from being immediately transmitted to the enemy these days, considering the lack of security within the inner army services. You can't avoid this. Because we don't know what's here in Paris. Stülpnagel[18] was here. He took part in this mess. We don't know what

relationships people have among themselves. We don't know which operational plans that we transmit here will immediately leak through and be in
the hands of the British by tomorrow. Basically that's why I would say the
following: first, we have to make it clear to the army group that, come
what may, they have to lead the fight here with absolute fanaticism,
because movement—or mobile combat—is totally impossible. We just
have to imagine this in practice: if I turn back the whole front there, then it
will go up to there. That's the same front. So I don't even cover a tenth or
a sixth of the entire developing Western Front. You actually couldn't do
that. Now you may say: let's take other forces. These other forces I
couldn't really get here in time. In practice, that's impossible. We could
bring some in here maybe, but it's not actually possible. I'm convinced a
total collapse would happen. I'm not yet quite sure about which position is
the best: if a Seine line—

JODL: No, that one is practically out of the question. Only this[19] one could
be considered. That's the best one. It is well reconnoitered, too.

THE FÜHRER: As I said before, that's the question anyway.

JODL: It's only for the start, because it's a clear line.

THE FÜHRER: Because it's a "break." The Seine line is very dangerous
for us because he can destroy all the bridges over the Seine and can hinder
all of our movements. That applies to every river that's in the way of a
German retreat. In the long run, with the forces we have now in the
West—with 50 or 60 divisions—we wouldn't be able to hold either this
line or that line, but at best this line.

JODL: Because it's improved.

THE FÜHRER: It's partially improved. We could prepare it further here.
Then we have another line in the back, so it's questionable if he will
interfere here at all, because he has to say to himself, "I can't get in too
deep." He will likely lead his attack where it's the weakest—probably up
here, where he assumes he can get into our industrial area[20] the fastest. We
have the connection here. Here it's the most decisive. Primarily he would
also be in this area here, so we have a shorter line, and we have to secure
this region to protect the industrial area. These are such wide-ranging
thoughts that if I were to tell them to an army group today, then the men
would be horrified. That's why I think it necessary that we set up a very
small staff of ours here,[21] which, if a crisis occurs, is prepared [to work] as
an operations staff. The staff would be educated about the potential
problems that could arise, and would, from the headquarters—we will
probably have to relocate the headquarters here, too, or into the Black

Forest;[22] I have to discuss that with our Below again, where we would put it[23]—but the Commander-in-Chief West can't carry the responsibility anymore. That is absolutely impossible. It's the fate of Germany. We couldn't sit up here—I assume that we will stabilize the Eastern Front— we can't sit up here while the fate of Germany is being decided. That is impossible. But in any case certain steps must be taken, and I would do this by giving out orders that are totally independent from each other, so that nothing points in any way to any intention or any particular direction. First, we must be clear about this among ourselves, Jodl. Which places do we want to hold under any circumstances, because they provide additional opportunities for the enemy? Because the only thing that can stop the enemy from obtaining an unlimited supply of materiel, troops and units is the number of airstrips available to him. So if he does not get a number of harbors, or ones that are efficient, then that's the only brake on his otherwise unlimited mobility.[24] That's the only thing we can tell for sure, so we will simply have to decide to sacrifice certain troops in order to save other things. We have to do this ourselves. We have to identify these harbors in collaboration with the Navy. Their efficiency must be secured. And other harbors—which brings me to something else as well—must be handled in such a way [assuming] that the entire railway system is destroyed. And maybe it's more important to destroy all the engines, all the railway installations, all the pumps—everything—not just the rail lines. That might be even more important. Those are the only things that could buy us some time in the end. I can't operate myself, but by doing that I can make it immensely difficult for the enemy to operate deep into the area. I lead him into a war—I would like to say a scorched-earth war—that's different from the German one. But we must actually carry it out here then, and ruthlessly. [—] The one thing is the establishment of the harbors that must be held at all cost—without regard for the people there, so that it's impossible for the enemy to send in unlimited reinforcements. If he can send in unlimited reinforcements, then we absolutely have to give up the idea of withdrawing here with only our essential forces. We can't do that. Because you can see that a breakthrough like this can happen quickly! We can't do that at all. [—] This is the second point: now we have to demand from the Commander-in-Chief West that units which are not intended for fixed positions be made mobile—temporarily mobile—and that he report all of this. We must receive a report regarding each unit's degree of mobility and the quantity of weapons it can carry while mobilized. We also need to secure the destruction of the intermediate units in this whole front. When I have harbors, the intermediate units are not necessary. In fact, I have to give them up, because I would rather draw those people into the harbors and establish a solid defence there. Then we should be able to hold the harbor for, let's say, 6 or 8 or 10 weeks—and those 6 or 8 or 10 weeks will mean a lot in the months of August, September, and October. Then we might be able to gain some time. That's the second step that he has to make independently from this. [—] Third: the line command, Jodl, must be established here by a senior officer, in my opinion. We can't leave it to the Commander-in-Chief West. We have to put in a staff that will set up this last possible line command, based on the entire battle experience that has been gained up to now.

JODL: It happened once already, my Führer, on your order.

THE FÜHRER: That happened once.

JODL: There's a fairly detailed report about that. Of course, we still aren't fully aware of all the effects of the carpet-bombing efforts, but the disadvantages of all the open and unprotected sectors are pointed out in the report. They don't have enough protection from the enemy's superiority in the air. That's the case in some areas. He already took that into consideration. He also discussed the various possibilities here. It's mostly wooded and covered terrain. It's excellent down there. The main problems begin here.

THE FÜHRER: That is the object?

JODL: That's the object.

THE FÜHRER: In those days it was meant as a pivot, as a kind of fortress.

JODL: That's why this line here is relocated forward. It's not only shorter, but it also occupies better terrain, because it's not so open as it is back there by the Somme [River] at Péronne.

THE FÜHRER: I would do just one thing, Jodl: I would set up your own development staff to improve this thing. Because it doesn't matter at all. Even if we managed it here, I would still come back to the idea—despite everything—that we should gradually reduce the further development of the coast and proceed with the development of this land front instead.

JODL: That's too much for the Commander-in-Chief West because he's an army group leader at the same time. He's not in Paris at all. He's leading the army group. They never see him any more—his army group has been abandoned anyway. Everything calls for another Commander-in-Chief. They want to have Rundstedt back, because Kluge is hardly accessible to them.[25] There should be a dedicated staff here for these assignments anyway.

THE FÜHRER: And, Jodl, even in that case I come back to my previous opinion—even if we drive back all the attacks, even if fate changes, if we really could deploy more aircraft within 2 or 3 weeks, favored by the weather conditions that are gradually worsening and assisted by the Navy, and if the enemy develops problems replenishing his units, and if he has difficulties with the landings because he doesn't have any efficient harbors anymore—even if all that is the case, we need to have this line improved by the OT [Todt Organization]. It would be better to postpone other land missions and improve this line—in collaboration with the coastal defense from here northward, of course—because in the end it will be the most significant line for us.

JODL: The majority of the OT forces, aside from those building in advance of the Nineteenth and First Army, are now involved in the reconstruction of railways and roads.

THE FÜHRER: We'll have to see what we can pull out from there, especially what we can get in the way of cement. Because a position that isn't equipped with concrete bunkers—as we have seen—is worthless; it will be destroyed immediately. That works in terrain like they have in Italy. But it's not feasible elsewhere. This position seems important to me regardless, so we have to build this thing, no matter what happens. I would not call political units for the construction, because they really can't do this, but we have to establish a little shell organization here, which in fact consists of the OT. The political units can't do this. We could at most put political units in Lothringen, in Alsace, for those rear positions, and for the possible restoration of our German matter.[26] But not much can be done except mining at the Western Wall. Except for wire, we don't need to do much. What's bad at the Western Wall is the antitank defense, because back then it was built for the 3.7-cm antitank gun. Now we have to see if the heavy gun will even fit at all. We need to investigate immediately to find out how much can be done. [—] I would say the following, Jodl: we have to establish a very small operational staff now. This operational staff must deal with the different problems that could occur if a successful landing is made—either in the West, in Italian territory, or in Brittany or further north, which would be even more tragic. But this in itself shows that it can't be done by the Commander-in-Chief West by himself anymore. Finally, we must also consider the Italian matter, because a crisis could happen there as well. In my opinion, only our central staff can do that, because the Commander-in-Chief West by himself can't make the necessary resources available for such a purpose. In fact, one thing will happen right away: we will in fact establish such a thing—that will be decided—to arm certain positions that are not tank-secure from the beginning. That will happen very shortly, as we cannot count on the returning units to arm them. It can only come from a central point—only from a point that is available to us. So again, I am convinced that it's wrong to give away 1,200 or 2,000 old Russian 7.6-cm or 12.2-cm weapons. Instead we should remodel them again—like we converted the Russian guns to split-trail carriages—and then we have to give them hollow shells, to add an extra level of antitank defense to our general anti-tank defense.[27] But the operations staff has to think about all those problems carefully, so that we can in fact give clear direction to the Commander-in-Chief West right from the beginning—and on an ongoing basis. Also, we need to establish a headquarters immediately. It can't be too far away—preferably in the Vosges, and if that's not possible, within the Black Forest. In the Vosges would be best of all.

V. BELOW: The one at Diedenhofen is finished.[28]

THE FÜHRER: Is it more-or-less secure against today's bombs?

V. BELOW: Against the 6,000s, I don't think so, my Führer.

THE FÜHRER: I don't think so either. [—] Is it camouflaged, so no one can see it?

V. BELOW: It's not at all visible from above because it's completely underground. It's located in some of the old forts on the Maginot Line, which are not visible from above.

THE FÜHRER: Can I see pictures of it right away?!

V. BELOW: We just have to take something that already exists. We couldn't build it anymore in that amount of time.

THE FÜHRER: I would like to have a foundation there again.

V. BELOW: Yes, Sir. Of course, I also consider this best. [—] Then, as mentioned, a OT construction staff to do the work. Then, I would like to say, establish a demolition organization early, again with the help of the OT, because we have destroyed nothing so far. That's ridiculous. Then we need to work out general orders that will be made available to the army group, of course, and to the Commander-in-Chief West and others who would be affected. Also the concern that it's based upon—and we have to tell this to the Commander-in-Chief West instantly: he has to make the units mobile. We'll tell him which units we need, and he must make sure that they reach a certain level of mobility within the shortest possible time. The units that we plan to pull out are to be made mobile. He doesn't need to know the purpose, because if he knows the purpose and it somehow goes through Paris, and if some Frenchwoman or Frenchman learns it the next day and the whole story immediately—

FEGELEIN: Rothacker[29] was here 2 or 3 days before the attack—the Chief of Staff—and he helped plan the whole attack. He came from Paris.

THE FÜHRER: So it's impossible. We must play it safe. They don't need to know that—we'll simply tell them: this and this and this unit must be made mobile—improvised if need be. The army group, or rather the Commander-in-Chief West, hands in suggestions of his army groups, then we'll see to what degree they are mobile. Or better: he has to report to what degree they are mobile, how they're made mobile, and, especially, what they can carry in the way of weapons. That's the decisive factor. [—] And we determine the locations. We can't leave it to him; we'll determine them based on higher insight. We'll have to discuss that with the Grand Admiral and all the naval experts first thing tomorrow. This harbor will be defended at all cost, this harbor will be defended at all cost, this harbor will be defended. From here on out, the OT will provide everything for the defense of those harbors! [—] One thing became clear recently. It would have meant failure here at this little peninsula near Cherbourg if we had blocked this here, and there were some concrete-protected batteries that could always shoot into everything and into the harbor.[30] It is not so much about the fact that we get harbors under all circumstances, but that we have a secure position from which we can shoot into a harbor constantly. Those few batteries must be put in concrete so that they can't be destroyed by the air force, and they must be supplied with ammunition so that we can shoot into the harbor no matter what. First we have to defend the harbor itself anyway, then finally destroy it—that is the most important thing. [—] But, as mentioned earlier, if we send out such an order in the usual form, it means that the enemy will be involved in everything we do. He is in it from the beginning and can neutralize the whole thing. We achieve no more this way than we achieve if we say that the Commander-in-Chief West doesn't need to know any more than necessary. First, he must know that he has to fight here in any case; second, that this battle is decisive; third, that the idea of operating freely in a free area is nonsense. He must know that he has to bring together all the forces that can possibly be brought together using human judgment. [—] That's one thing. Furthermore, he must know that certain units must absolutely be made mobile. That's also important. The third is that we ourselves, with the staff, must consider different contingencies right from the beginning—maybe without arranging everything in detail, but just for the sake of clarifying the

exchange of units and determining the routes by which the units will be
brought back. [—] It's totally clear that if he breaks through here,[31] the
railway system will still work for some time, but we must not risk that—
we must not wait until it's too late. Then we'll have to make a decision.
We'll turn one part back toward the Italian Alpine front, block that here,
and pull the other part up from the Southern front right away. Then it's
important that we transport those forces, which we'll bring up here, as far
as possible by railway, and get them right into the planned reception areas,
so that there are at least units there that are equipped with a lot of antitank
guns, tank defense, assault guns, etc. That way we can immediately break
up any advance we see, also from American units, and make it impossible.
We can also let mobile units go further ahead—they will always return—
and they can catch something like that and win some time, so that the
enemy doesn't run right into our line immediately. That must be done from
the very beginning. It will be crucial to set up a staff of ours that can deal
with this under clear orders. The moment the height of the crisis is
reached, the main emphasis of the entire leadership shifts to the West
again—as it once was, when, in the end, we led the way and the army
groups received orders. It has to shift because it impinges immediately on
the Italian theater. It just can't be done any other way. I have to turn one
part down toward Italy at once to establish the front here. We can hold not
only the Alpine front with those units, but with those units we can hold the
whole Italian front, and maybe get one or two divisions free for the whole
Ligurian front. That could be possible under some circumstances, so that
we're at least totally secure here. The rest we would lead up here then.
Positions that are key to our ability to continue the war, and which could
fall into the enemy's hands right away,[32] must be determined by a senior
officer. Nonetheless, the Commander-in-Chief West himself will get the
instructions to improve the positions. This and this position must be
improved, this one is to be completed, this one is to be completed. He will
also get instructions from us. He must in any case report which units he
can shift into those areas. It's always presented as if they can't be moved
at all. He has to make sure that the bravest officers get into those positions,
not talkers like this character who went into Cherbourg and made a
glorious appeal, who went ahead into the bunker at the very front and
waited until the others approached, and then raised the white flag
immediately. When the other one said then, "How can you reconcile this
with your honor after you gave such an appeal?" he just shrugged his
shoulders.[33] [—] But we must find such officers. And so I've also come to

the decision now that I don't care about this damned hierarchy at all. Here it's about men, nothing else! If I imagine what men we have—like this little major in Berlin who made such a hard decision. If I put a man like him into such a position, instead of some lieutenant general or commanding general, he's worth ten times as much. It really depends on one man, and the others are bastards. We raise them so they consider it to be obvious that others sacrifice themselves, but they don't even consider it themselves. They already have one eye squinting over here: what can happen to us? If we're imprisoned, we'll be treated according to our rank, especially those of us from noble families, so we'll be dealt with in keeping with our station and won't be put together with all the plebian masses. [—] Well, that's unbearable, and that's why we have to check all the commanders again. The Cherbourg case must be a warning. It cannot be like that—it's a disgrace! It won't do to keep saying that we must not write about something like that in order to avoid damaging the army, and that it's better to praise such a person. [—] We do exactly the same thing that we have criticized in the Italians for years. Cowards are praised as heroes—characterless swine, who really behave worse than some Communist pig, because at least he's an idealist and is fighting for something. They're not mentioned, or they're even praised somewhere eventually, so that in the end this whole mess is camouflaged. I'm convinced that we can't do this! [—] I would put the staff together immediately; maybe you can bring some suggestions tomorrow, Jodl. Also concerning the fortress, so that we go over here if a crisis really occurs. I can't leave the Western campaign to Kluge. That's absolutely impossible because everything depends on it. The troops would not understand that either, if we sit in East Prussia while the decisive actions are taking place here. One can't know if we are here or here, or behind. Here are the most valuable parts, and behind it is the Ruhr area!

JODL: The one thing that concerns me is that in case something happens here[34] within three, four or five days, we haven't yet ordered anything—

THE FÜHRER: You can't give any orders—or rather, you can order something, but nothing will be done.

JODL: Nothing has been prepared yet!

THE FÜHRER: You can give some orders, since we have to take on the responsibility anyway. That would be of no use. We would have to take it on anyway, if something happened within the next three, four or five days. We can order anything we want, but nothing can be done in the meantime. [—] So I can't leave the responsibility to Kluge even then. That's not possible. But orders regarding preparations that would be important in that case (in three, four or five days) can be given out right now. Mobilization of those and those units, determination of the harbors that are important to us, choice of commanders for those positions. And the people we bring here must know about a German officer's honor—not like those 16 people who handed over the Prussian fortresses one after the other in 1806,[35] but like the one who held his fortress until the end!

JODL: That is the question, if General Warlimont should present verbally what was intended. He wanted to go there tomorrow[36] because they wanted to have someone from us.

THE FÜHRER: I would only bring up those few things that don't have anything to do with the big story, but that have to be done anyway. We must not give these people the slightest hint, and we can't prevent that otherwise in this pigsty. It's as bad here as anywhere else. If I imagine that a man[37] sits here for two years, who has done nothing in those two years but help to undermine the German front! Furthermore, the whole base in Paris is this man's fault. It's a fiasco! I didn't want him back then—you know that. A short time would have been enough. That man in the armistice commission and Mr. Abetz[38] in Paris as our German representative—those two together would have given it all away within a few months. Everything that we had gained in our glorious six-week victory would have been gone within a few months! That was the best teamwork one could imagine: the one in the armistice commission and the other one in Paris. He is a totally incapable man, and besides he has taken his revenge. We should be able to find, say, 30 officers in the German Army that are heroes! It would be sad! But then I must not look at their insignias—I can put the insignias on them. I can do that. When I think of such people having received insignias—people who have become generals when they in fact deserved to be hung upside down—why shouldn't I name a good courageous front officer who has limited duties?! He doesn't need to operate tactically; I don't need a general who has proven to me that he led gloriously in the sandbox or on the troop training grounds somewhere! And by the way, I have seen myself what our generals have done on the troop training grounds, and how terribly they operate. They prove what they are capable of in organizational achievement, if they want to do something like this—a man like the Chief of the General Staff, Beck,[39] who wanted to do this. That man has done nothing else in his life but busy himself with ridiculous little plans. How do I establish an army that, without ever provoking an enemy, is always in a position to take over the entire executive authority at home, without confronting the enemy at all? [—] This man does not travel to Paris without reason. He admired Gamelin.[40] When he came back, he shook his head ceremoniously.[41] I said that I don't even consider Gamelin to be clever. If he had been a genius, he would not have watched while I armed! [—] It's interesting to read the assessment of Gamelin and Beck: those two big heroes of mankind met there! But if I imagine a scamp like Tito compared to a Gamelin or a Beck! But we have those people here, too, and if I want to defend a fortress here, you can't say, "My Führer, that doesn't work—the seniority of rank!" [—] I don't care about that at all! Here we need to bring in brave men who are willing to die if necessary, and we do have them! If we didn't have them in the German Armed Forces anymore—they are there among the German people—it would only be proof that the Armed Forces had made a totally negative selection. But that is not the case; they are there! Now, I've received letters from generals, etc., who are finally coming out and saying, "We saw this coming the whole time—it couldn't have turned out differently!" [—] So such people exist, and if the form is good enough, we still can do something. We'll go there in the name of God and promote the people! I'll do that with lightening speed because it absolutely does not matter. If a Napoleon could become a First Consul at the age of 27, I don't see why a 30-year-old man here can't be a general or a lieutenant general—that's ridiculous! We lead a revolutionary war! It is absolutely correct when they call Tito a marshal. A man who, with nothing, keeps an entire enemy war force constantly on the jump and continually recovers again, deserves the title of marshal more than anyone here deserves the title of Colonel General or field marshal who is not able to operate skillfully even with the best instrument that has ever existed. Such a man deserves this, and why shouldn't I treat good, brave officers in the same way here? We only have to give them the opportunity. [—] But looking at the big picture, we can't make any preparations from one day to the next that will be decisive in 5 days, or in 10 or 14 days. If it goes the normal military way, Jodl, absolutely nothing will happen. If it goes the normal way, only conferences will take place. I just spoke with a man who once again looked into the Apennine position. He says that it's a great fallacy if someone imagines that this is a position. This is no position at all![42] [—] An expert who was down there—also an officer—says the same thing: this is no position at all; it's a big fallacy! [—] You know, in every position you have a display example that is presented. Now you wrote once yourself, Jodl, that a position is as strong as its weakest spot, because the enemy will discover its weakest spot and attack there, not at the strongest one.

JODL: See the Western Wall; see the Atlantic Wall!

THE FÜHRER: See the Atlantic Wall!! [—] Now the display examples are shown. They wanted to do it the same way with me. Had I had myself been in command at the Western Wall, I would have seen only the display examples: between Bingen and the Pfälzer Forest, the drilling area at Zweibrücken, Saarbrücken—a few spots. I didn't want that. I went everywhere—the entire wall, up and down—and looked at the weak spots. Then this fellow[43] came and said, "There are only 5 emplacements per kilometer here because it's not an attack area anyway." [—] I asked, "How can it not be an attack area?" [—] He said, "Tank-proof!" [—] But tank-proof is absolutely out of the question." [—] So if I hadn't pushed back there, there would have been nothing in those spots. But then it was put in! Something must happen here, too. I can't leave it to the army group, who can't do it at all. They have other things on their minds and can't do anything. So if we leave it to the army group the same thing will happen as what we experienced in the East. I should have taken Kitzinger then—he offered himself. He would do that. He had the people and would round them all up. But then the Army was indignant at such an idea. That wouldn't work—it could only be done by the army group; the army groups should rule in their rear territory. This is what we were told, with the result that nothing—absolutely nothing—happened. Not a single spade thrust. And the positions that supposedly existed between Melitopol' and Zaporozh'e were faked.[44] I was simply lied to—nothing had ever been there. In the fall of 1941 a few minor efforts were made there. That was all. It was a pure swindle, and it would be the same here. I've seen on a large scale what happens in reality. The people have had lots of time to develop the Black Forest at least. They know themselves—I don't need to repeat this—what is in the Black Forest: nothing. Absolutely nothing! [—] So we really will have to set up a small staff here, and we need to get Jacob and the OT here. Jacob and Dorsch together must put in a staff which will be in charge of making the developments, without regard for anything else. If we can't make the extension solid here, it will be at most a very short delaying line. A proper defense can only be established where we have either the Western Wall or at least ground conditions to permit this—and that would be the Vosges [Mountains]. There we can organize resistance.

JODL: But it hasn't been reconnoitered yet. That must be done first.

THE FÜHRER: It must be done immediately, and as far out as possible, so that we have the option of going back to a main line—and especially so that we can blow up the streets. Here in this country we can do something, of course. There must not be a single bridge that isn't prepared for demolition—not one bridge! It doesn't matter if the enemy blows it up or we do.

JODL: Quite a few are already destroyed here.

THE FÜHRER: Many have been destroyed already, but also the last that remain! The tracks must be destroyed. Those are all general orders; it must all be prepared. Of course, it can't be done by a central staff; the local authorities should destroy all the track in such a situation. Everything must be prepared so that we can destroy at least the most critical sections of each track. We won't be able to destroy all the lines. That will be a problem because we need, for example, to provide rail cutters. Here's a question. Some time ago I ordered rail cutters to be made for usual railway tracks and also for steel posts. These were rejected—some agency has forbidden further construction! We ask ourselves how an idiot like that could dare to do such a thing? I give Speer the order to build these things, and a different department comes along and just says, "Not for steel tracks!"[45] [—] That means I can't demolish anything in the West because almost all the tracks are steel. But that's no problem. We can give the order right now to carry it out. [—] But in the basic combat instructions,[46] the first part has to be agreed to absolutely, and we have to make it clear to him. That it must be held at any cost! If he loses this he cannot operate. That's the decisive factor—we must take away from him every thought of being able to operate. The forces are ridiculous for that, of course.

JODL: He doesn't mean that. He's absolutely determined to hold it.

THE FÜHRER: Maybe tomorrow we can already—think about it!—put together a staff of some equally intelligent and inventive heads. Because if we really want to transport this back, it's not so much systematic work—nothing happens systematically, because the enemy is able to destroy everything systematically—but it must be intelligent work. If we don't do it intelligently, the whole thing will be lost. Then we can't do anything about it. Then, as mentioned before, the second point: I have to push the Luftwaffe so that these 12 or 15 groups will be finished, which initially, I would like to say, must be led in an informal and flexible manner. We can't make a long-term plan because it might have to be thrown out in the next few days. All we need is for a revolt to break out in Hungary or something like that. So what we need to secure we must secure now! So I would think about what we can still pump into Hungary.

JODL: Replacement formations, except for those two brigades.

THE FÜHRER: Yes, put them in there, so that at least something is in the country.

FEGELEIN: There are still two cavalry divisions in there, and they're also getting stronger.[47]

THE FÜHRER: What do they look like? What do they consist of?

FEGELEIN: They have three regiments.

THE FÜHRER: And the people?

FEGELEIN: Ethnic Germans [Volksdeutschen] and Reich Germans [Reichsdeutschen].

THE FÜHRER: There are Reich Germans?

FEGELEIN: Yes, Sir. One division has about 60% Reich Germans right now. The other division, the volunteers, also has 30% Reich Germans—all the commanders and so on. But there are three strong cavalry regiments, one artillery regiment with three detachments (two heavy and one light), one engineer battalion with two companies, one intelligence detachment with one radio company, one reconnaissance detachment with a Volkswagen reconnaissance detachment.

THE FÜHRER: They are already mostly mobile?!

FEGELEIN: Yes, Sir, with three squadrons. [—] Then they also have one assault gun detachment.

JODL: Readiness for action?

FEGELEIN: Two were made out of the one—that's why it will take until October 1 for them to be ready. But if we have a revolt within the country they can be used right away. The one has to pull up the other one, though, or it won't work.

THE FÜHRER: And to what extent are they still mobile at this time? Can we at least everywhere—

FEGELEIN: It always works in Hungary because they can make themselves mobile in the customary manner.

THE FÜHRER: I really wanted to go over here to the West, but I can't do it now, as much as I would like to. For at least the next eight days, I won't be able to fly because of my ears.[48] It is also questionable for the second one, but when one is completely better, then I don't care anymore—then I would risk it. But if I get into an airplane now with the roaring and all those changes in pressure, it could be catastrophic. And what would happen if I suddenly got a middle-ear infection? I would have to be treated. The risk of an infection is there as long as the wound is open. It didn't go off without affecting my head, either.

FEGELEIN: Everybody suffered from a light concussion.

THE FÜHRER: Of course, I can stand and I can also talk for a certain length of time, but then I have to sit down suddenly. Today I would not dare speak to 10,000 people. A speech like the one I held at the Obersalzberg recently[49] I would not dare to hold today, because I might suddenly get a dizzy spell and collapse. A moment like that can even occur while walking, and I have to pull myself together in order not to make a false step. But, of course, if all else fails, I'll do anything; then I don't care at all. Then I will go in a single-engine aircraft and be the target shooter up front, so I get there quickly. I don't care at all. Of course, it would be better if I were well again. [—] Only we have to lead very flexibly within the next few days. So I consider it necessary that the Reich Foreign Minister comes over here more frequently, since you50 don't go to the Reich Foreign Minister. I really would like to talk through everything with him myself, but it's too long for me, and I can only tell him what you would tell him anyway. You are also exhausted, no doubt, but I get so many matters all the time that deal with other things, including absolutely critical ones. Normally I would have stayed in bed for 10 or 14 days, but altogether I have worked at least 8 hours every day, not counting reading the dispatches. Eight hours went by anyway, reading memoranda and other things. So in my current state of health I do about the same amount of work as our gentlemen in their stressful offices in Paris, etc. But if it is not necessary I don't want to push it and possibly cause a collapse; that's not necessary. [—] Otherwise, the amazing thing is that this blow seems to have caused my nerve problem to almost disappear. I still have some shaking in my left leg, if the meeting takes too long, but this leg used to shake in bed. It has suddenly disappeared almost entirely because of the blow, though I don't want to say that this is the best cure.[51]

End: 12:58 a.m.

* * * * *

Meeting of the Führer with Lieutenant General Westphal[52] and Lieutenant General Krebs[53]

August 31, 1944, at the Wolfsschanze[54]

Also present: Field Marshal Keitel

Beginning: 3:35 p.m.

THE FÜHRER: You know that Field Marshal Kluge has committed suicide.[55] There are very strong suspicions that if he had not committed suicide, he would have been arrested immediately anyway. Yesterday the trial at the People's Law Court was interrupted.[56] Unfamiliar with this (procedure, the chairman) turned to Field Marshal (Kluge) [—] (It is to be assumed that the thing failed due to an enemy fighter-bomber) attack. He sent away his General Staff officer. The action did not succeed then, though. British-American patrols advanced forward, but apparently no connection could be established. He also sent his son into the pocket. The British have reported that they are in contact with a German general, and the officer, who was probably the contact, has been arrested.[57] It is claimed that he was exchanged out of British captivity because of malingering. But he was arrested for other reasons. That was the man who was supposed to mediate in this thing, who was, in those people's opinion, supposed to bring about a change of fate. The idea was that we would surrender to the British and then join together with them against Russia—a totally idiotic concept. Especially with the criminal abandonment of German territory in the East! They thought we would have to (abandon) up to the Vistula [River] anyway, maybe up to the Oder … up to the Elbe [—] August 15 was the worst day of my life. Thanks to a coincidence, this plan was not fulfilled. All the army group's measures can only be explained under those circumstances; otherwise, they would be absolutely inexplicable. The staff of the Seventh Army—I must also tell you—is not in good shape.[58] It would be good if you, General Krebs, could take all the men you think are worth your trust, and give the orders necessary to clean up this staff entirely. Unfortunately, Field Marshal Rommel[59] is a very great and enthusiastic leader in successful times, but he is an absolute pessimist when the slightest difficulties arise. Before, I faced the difficult question of whether I should send Kesselring's staff there or if I should hand the task over to Rommel.[60] Before, I always blamed (Kesselring) for (seeing things) too optimistically [—] North Africa totally lost his nerves, so that after the abandonment of El Alamein he got worked up about an idea that could not be accomplished. He had to stay out front—that was the only possibility to save everything.[61] Because the enemy's superiority was not balanced out when he went into the wide-open area—it made it even more effective. At this narrow spot, 60 km wide, an attack could possibly be withstood. Once pushed out of there, and without the coverage of Schott on the left side,[62] then, based on desert warfare experience, there was the possibility of constant overtaking, and then he was not able to maneuver, but the enemy could maneuver. When I was informed about the decision that night—unfortunately I learned about it only the next morning—I ordered right away that it shouldn't happen. As a result of the unfortunate tangle of circumstances, the matter remained here and was handed over to me too late, and my order to cancel (the thing) immediately[63] [—] he did the worst that could be done in such a case for a soldier: He looked for non-military solutions.[64] In Italy back then, he also predicted that the collapse would come very soon. It hasn't happened yet. In fact, it was totally disproved by those events, and I have been justified in my decision to keep Field Marshal Kesselring there. I see in him an unbelievable political idealist, but also a military optimist, and I think that one can't lead militarily at all without optimism. I consider Rommel in certain circumstances to be an extraordinary bold and also clever leader. But I don't consider him tenacious, and that that is also the opinion of all the others.

KEITEL: Yes, that has become more and more obvious.

THE FÜHRER: As long as things (go) well, (he) is shouting for joy. When the first [—] imagined the further development at all. I said right away: It's not yet time for a political decision. I think I have proven enough in my life that I am able to gain political successes. I don't have to explain to anybody that I wouldn't let an opportunity like this pass by. But it is, of course, childish and naive to hope for a convenient political moment to do anything during this time of heavy military defeat. Such moments can arise if we have successes. I have proven that I (have done) everything possible to deal with the British. In 1940, after the French campaign, I offered my hand to the British and renounced (everything). I did not want anything from them. On September 1, 1939, (I) made a suggestion to the British—rather, I repeated a suggestion, which had been transmitted by Ribbentrop already in (1936)—the offer of (a) union, whereby Germany would (guarantee the British) Empire[65] [—] recommended. Churchill, in particular, and that entire circle of hatred around Vansittart,[66] opposed all those suggestions; they wanted the war and can't go back now. They are staggering toward their ruin. But there will come moments in which the tension between the Allies will become so great that the break will happen then nevertheless. Coalitions in world history have always been ruined at some point. We must only wait for the moment, no matter how hard it is. It is my duty, especially since 1941, (not to) lose my nerve under any circumstances, but if there is a (collapse) somewhere, to (find) a way out and a means to repair the mess somehow. I could (well say): you can't imagine a bigger crisis than the one we have experienced already in the East this (year). When Field Marshal Model came, Army Group Center was in fact only a hole.[67] There was more hole than front, and then finally there was more front than hole [—] has, to say that those divisions were completely immobile, that they didn't have any German materiel, that they were equipped with God knows what kind of guns, that we sent all the prepared divisions into the East, that there were only training divisions in the West, that we had the panzer divisions in the West only to fill them up, and once they were ready we sent them to the East.[68] If I had had the (9th) and 10th SS Panzer Divisions in the West, the (thing) probably would not have happened at all. But this was not done, due to a—I must say—(criminal) urge[69] to (cause) an overthrow here. The people imagined they could go either with the British against the Russians or—in the second, (Schulenburg,) direction[70]—with the Russians against the British or—in the third and stupidest direction—to play one off against the other. Pretty naïve![71] (The judgment) of all the people who have (seen) the guilty in court now goes as far as a shocking [—] continue the fight, until the opportunity for a reasonable peace arises—one that is acceptable to Germany and that can secure the life of later generations. Then I will do it. Because everyone can imagine that this war is not comfortable for me. I've been cut off from the outside world for five years now; I haven't visited a theater, listened to a concert, (seen) a film.[72] I live only for the single task of (leading) this battle, because I know that if there is no strong will (behind) it, the war cannot be won. I reproach the General Staff, because instead of always exuding (this) iron will, it weakened front officers who (came here), or spread (pessimism) from the General Staff to the rest of the forces, when (General Staff) officers came to the front. It is tragic when the young officers, who face sentencing now, declare in front of the court: [—] department of the General Staff, in which the chief was absolutely fine, namely with Gehrcke,[73] where not a single man has been found so far who is involved in this thing,[74] while in the other departments, the quartermaster general, the organization departments, foreign armies, etc., the leaders supported this base action. What happened here was directed against me. If it had been successful, it would have (been) a catastrophe for Germany. The fact that it didn't succeed gives us the possibility to finally get rid of this abscess (inside) our organization. We can't foresee, though, how badly it may have damaged our foreign policy—with (the Romanians), the Bulgarians, the Turks, the Finns, the other neutrals, and so on. How it has hurt the German people—(now), of course, the speech restrictions have been loosened, and things have come to light that are hair-raising. Until now the German people were silent, but now everyone is speaking out. [—] have experienced. The fact that we've had to experience terrible things here with Army Group Center, which are just now slowly becoming clear[75]—the disgrace that German officers can be found, who deliver speeches over there, and that German officers and generals capitulate—all that cannot be compared with what happened in the West. That's the most outrageous of all.[76] I believe that you, Westphal, are joining a (staff that) is basically sound. First of all, Field Marshal Rundstedt (is) absolutely clean and a man of integrity. (Further), Blumentritt[77] is very sound and personally (decent; I) just think he lacks a bit of experience to command (such a staff) and that he was heavily affected by this whole (thing). But absolutely (nothing) has been submitted against him.

KEITEL: The only one in this staff was the quarter(master, who) had been sent there a few weeks before, Colonel Fink.[78] He was one of (Wagner's[79]) men [—]

THE FÜHRER: [—] thought very highly of. I promoted him twice myself, gave him the highest awards, gave him a great gift to help him get settled, and gave him a large bonus in addition to his salary as field marshal.[80] So for me, this is the most bitter and disappointing thing of all. The way he came here, it (might) have been tragic. Maybe he slipped into it by accident—I don't know—and maybe (then he) couldn't (see) any way out anymore. He saw a number of (officers) being arrested, and he feared their statements. His nephew is blamed the most, who stated this in front of the court,[81] and, as a result, President Freisler[82]—which was correct—interrupted the trial immediately to (get proof) of this and to hear the field marshal. But he (was no) longer alive. Freisler also said, of course: there is a limit; all (trust) in the German Armed Forces command will collapse. [—] It is like a Western. When you look at the people—Stief[83] and all those people—the level is really shocking. I got rid of a man like Colonel General Höppner[84] back then not only because he disobeyed a command but (because) he was really a small character. Kluge himself[85] (was also) convinced that he had to go. Now I've been (justified). The trial showed everyone (in the courtroom) how little they were. The observers said, "How could those (people ever) become officers at all?!" Yes, how could they? I had to take what was available, and I've tried to make the most of it. [—] (The staff) that you, Krebs, are taking over, is no doubt (messed up)—we have to be clear about that. I can only (tell) you: take care that you (clean up) this lot as fast as (possible), that you ... Field Marshal Model the [—] We will fight—if necessary even at the Rhine. That doesn't matter at all. We'll keep fighting this battle at all costs, until, like

Frederick the Great said, one of our damned enemies gets tired of fighting, and until we (get) a peace that will secure life for the German nation for the next 50 or (100 years) and that (does not) damage our honor a second time the way it (happened) in 1918. Because this time we would not (be silent) anymore. (Back then) we were silent about it.[86] (Destiny) could have gone in a different direction. If my life had ended, personally, for me—(I can say)—it would only have been a relief from worries, sleepless (nights and a) serious nervous disease. It's only (a fraction) of a second, then you are freed from all of this (and have) everlasting peace and quiet. But I nevertheless thank providence that I (survived), because I believe [–] I don't want to spread it any further. I don't want to disgrace the German Armed Forces by talking about this thing any longer. If it became public knowledge that Field Marshal Kluge wanted to lead the entire Western army to capitulation and go over to the enemy himself, it might not lead to a collapse of (morale) in the German nation, but at least to (contempt) for the Army. That's why I want to (be silent) about it (now). We have informed only the generals that he has committed suicide.[87] He did commit suicide. The (things that) were said before were wrong. That was … It was said that he had already earlier … and had suffered from a stroke. In (reality), he was waiting for the British patrol, which … They missed each other. He lost his … in the fighter-bomber attack. Now he was (in the area), could not get any further, and (drove back) again. [—]

The Führer's Speech to Division Commanders,

December 12, 1944, at Adlerhorst[88]

[This talk preceded the Battle of the Bulge and was meant to instill optimism and fighting spirit into the officer corps.]

Beginning: 6 p.m.

THE FÜHRER: Gentlemen! A fight like the struggle in which we find ourselves right now, which is being fought with such unlimited bitterness, obviously has different aims than the quarrels of the 17th or 18th Centuries, which might have concerned minor inheritances or royal dynastic conflicts. People and nations do not start a long war of life and death without deeper reasons. One cannot deny that the German nation, in terms of size and value, has (earned the claim) in central Europe to become the leader of the European continent. Politically, however, especially since the Thirty Years' War, Germany has not been able to realize this claim, as it was the goal of the peace of Münster and Osnabrück to prevent the German nation from unifying and regaining the German Reich's dominant position in Europe. Political disunity kept the power of the German people from coming together, and is responsible for allowing the establishment of the British world empire, for the American continent being English instead of German, and for the predominance of France on the continent itself. Likewise, only political impotence can be blamed for...[89]

Both states have taken every opportunity to resist a German political recovery—meaning a union of individual states and tribes or even the formation of a German empire in the sense of a unified state. The attempts to bring about this unification are very old. Whenever Germany breaks up, many German rulers and leaders—princes as well as generals—as well as politicians, writers, artists, economists, and so on, feel the necessity of reestablishing a unified (Reich of all Germans. All these attempts to erect a unified German Empire have been fought) relentlessly by these opponents. The peace of Münster in 1648 almost achieved the status of a European Magna Carta. It was said that the so-called balance of power thus created, and the impossibility of one nation achieving predominance in Europe—and this could only be Germany—corresponded to a more or less divine order and served a general human legal order as well, and that the attempt to change this situation was a crime against human rights, against the freedom of the people, and later against democracy, the parliamentary democracy, and so on. Nothing but words! The foundation (for this argument was the attempt to prevent a German union under any circumstances. They recognized), as this war proves once again, based on the cultural history and the general history of man's development, that the unification of 85 million people of this quality would certainly have solved the problem of hegemony right away. They realized this and defended themselves against it by all possible means.

Bismarck suffered from it. When, let us say, especially after the age of Bismarckian union, the power of this unifying thought spread and—in part economically, in part also politically—inevitably brought the unified Reich into being, (they started a policy of uniting against Germany, and the war against Germany) was seen and proclaimed as a sort of holy war. The father of this idea was Churchill, but one has to admit that international world Jewry stood behind it, for obvious reasons.

Now, today, this battle is being fought as a continuation, not only, as it sometimes is said in the press, of the World War of 1914 to 1918, but really as a continuation of the wars of 1870-71, 1866, 1864. Because the so-called unification wars were different from the liberation wars, as they had the aim of unifying the German nation once again, it was a natural requirement that this aim be reached only in stages, and not completed right from the start. But the goal was clear. In the end, the goal could only be—even if this was not obvious (to everybody)—the complete unification of all Germans. I have made it part of my lifework to reach this goal. This goal has to be reached, not because of any (theory) or political will, which can also be changed or postponed, but because of the recognition that otherwise the requirements of a people of millions cannot be adequately pursued. Life without *Lebensraum* [living space] is unthinkable. *Lebensraum* can only be secured by a corresponding political power. The deployment of political force is again required by the organization of the factors from which the political power can or should arise. Germany can only realize its right to existence in this world if all Germans are unified and (defend this right to exist. This became very clear to the others when they saw in National Socialism) also the ideological possibility of unifying all the German tribes. That is why National Socialist Germany has been fought so fiercely—right from the start, when we first took over of power, and even before—again supported by international Jewry.

So today we are facing a fight that was inevitable—it had to come, sooner or later. The only question is whether it is the appropriate time. I showed yesterday[90] that the first objection can be eliminated easily—the objection that we've acted in too preventive a manner.[91] All of man's successful wars, gentlemen, have been preventive wars. Whoever recognizes that a battle cannot be avoided and does not ... the (best moment), in his view ... The political situation (is always changing, and there is—if one wants to reach a political goal that is recognized as necessary—no stability) guaranteeing the achievement of such a goal. Such stability does not exist politically because likes or dislikes in the life of the people are constantly changing concepts. I read a memorandum this year, which I wrote in 1939 right after the Polish campaign. I could publish it even today. In the meantime, reality has proven its truth not once but ten times over. It showed that the theoretically positive situation of 1938-39 did not have to remain stable, but, on the contrary, it was dependent on many factors that could change at any moment.[92] (It is like this) ... as long as one is not convinced that they have a certain lifespan, but that the death of a single person can bring about a complete change in the political situation, and that the changing of a regime can turn the political goals completely upside down. In other words, one cannot say that in six or ten or twelve or twenty years there an especially fortunate situation will exist to carry out, let us say, a political union or the attempt to achieve a union, which is recognized as necessary.

But the military factor also supports this. There is no moment in which a weapon can be seen (as final). Once we were lucky enough, because of a gigantic effort following the previous lack of armaments—I spent 92 billion up to 1939[93]—to create complete predominance in most armament areas. But it was obvious that this predominance could not last. Because at the same moment in which we—to name just one example—introduced the new heavy field howitzer, other countries were already poised to move from the construction of a gun with a range of 15 km to a range of 17 km. The Russians already had a gun with a range of 18 km. At the same moment in which we introduced a certain type of tank, the Russian KV 1 and 2 tanks—but especially the T 34 type were already designed and under construction.[94] In other words, this war has already shown us after one or two years that some of our models, which were the state of the art when we started the war, were already outdated in the course of the first two years.

In war it is possible to catch up again because there is complete disregard for the usual economic conditions. In peacetime, one can never completely overtake other nations year after year in the technical aspects of one area of armament or the other. Not to mention the tactical perceptions, the training, etc., not even the leadership. Because no armed force can swear that it now has the best training or the best leadership. That won't be proven until the war. One cannot claim it beforehand. And regarding the fortunes of war, one can be completely silent in this context.
...

It was impossible to achieve such technical superiority in five or ten years. There could not have been a luckier moment than we found in 1939. It was very clear—right from the moment in 1936 when the 2 billion pound [sterling] credit was granted in England and they converted to practically universal conscription[95]—that the Tories in England, together with the Jewish underworld, were determined to return to their old policy of gagging Germany, and that because of this, sooner or later it would come to a fight.

But there was another moment to be considered, and that was decisive for me personally. I have had to make hard—infinitely hard—decisions in my life. (Such decisions can only be made by a person who is willing, by sacrificing all personal life, etc.,) to offer himself to one thing alone and to devote himself to it completely. I was convinced that in Germany, in the coming ten, twenty, thirty, maybe fifty years, no man would come with more authority, more possibilities to influence the nation, and more decisiveness than myself. I also believe that after I am gone, time will prove that I assessed things correctly.

That is why I thought it personally correct to clarify—even in my younger years—after evaluating the situation, the conditions that were necessary, not to create the war, but to bring about the security that would be necessary if Germany were attacked. That security was based on: 1. Immediately introducing universal conscription and total armament of the nation; 2. Restoring German sovereignty by occupying the Rhineland and regaining sovereignty in the west, through measures that included the construction of fortifications; 3. Immediately annexing Austria, settling the Czechoslovak issue, and finally settling the question of Poland, to bring the German Reich territory into a defensible condition. These were the prerequisites for maintaining peace in the future. Because even peace can only be maintained if one is armed. And there is not only military armament, but also, I would say, a territorial armament, which, with our infinitely small *Lebensraum* is very difficult to achieve.[96] You can see that today's bombers can (fly from England to the heart of Germany) in less than two hours ... Additional problems arose: (the impossibility for the German people to) exist (in such a restricted *Lebensraum*) in the long term, and the impossibility of feeding the German people without a sufficient agricultural base.

And, finally, there were psychological factors—namely in the mobilization of the power of the German people. You cannot put enthusiasm and the willingness to sacrifice oneself into bottles and just save them. This happens once in the course of a revolution and will slowly fade away again. The gray weekday and the comforts of life will captivate men and turn them into *petit bourgeois* again. What we were able to achieve by National Socialist education, by the immense wave that (took hold of) our people, (we could not let pass.) ...

But even if (the circumstances were fortunate), some conditions had to be carefully fulfilled in any case: the restoration of German sovereignty, the armament of the nation, the reintroduction of universal conscription— but also the occupation of the Rhineland, the freeing of the states annexed by the treaty of Versailles and the treaty of Trianon, etc., and the creation of a unified territory went in that direction. If this led to war, we had to accept this war. Because it is better to accept it right away, at a time when we were armed like never before. (Otherwise we might have had to) accept it at a time when this arming had been lost again. The Great War proved in the end that one cannot avoid a war by not striking. Because starting in 1898-99, when the right moments for initiating a conflict arose, we let years pass, always expecting to keep the peace through flexibility and compliance, or to achieve even better armaments by waiting, until finally—in spite of all attempts to maintain peace—the war was imposed on the German Empire. Anyone today who examines the wishes of Moltke in the years 1876, 1877 and 1878—when he wanted to strike against France once again, to nip the newly strong France in the bud[97]—and the political arguments that were brought up against it, (will recognize clearly how wrong it was not to fulfill Moltke's wishes at that time. Instead,) based on political factors resulting from the internal German parliamentary situation and from other difficulties within the country, they held back— and then finally got mixed up in it anyway, at the most inopportune time.

It is very clear, gentlemen, that such a conflict is now progressing like a grand historical struggle, with its ups and downs. Anyone who believes that the great epochs of world history are nothing but a series of successes has never understood history, or has perhaps not even read it properly; it is very clear that success and failure come and go. In the end, the one who gains the laurels of victory is not just the most capable one, but, most importantly—and I want to emphasize this—(the boldest). The building of states—no matter whether it is the Roman Empire, the British Empire or Prussia—has always been achieved by toughness, stubbornness and durability. Not so much by a single blaze of genius or by a burst of energy that flares up once and then vanishes, but much more by stubborn tenacity, which is the greatest help in overcoming all crises. Rome could not have been imagined without the Second Punic War. England would not be imaginable if crises had not been overcome within England itself. Prussia would be unimaginable without the Seven Years' War. And the greatness of the leading personalities, as well as of the people themselves, was not born in times of fortune but is always confirmed in times of ill fortune. People who can endure good luck are quite common. People who do not become weak when faced with bad luck are rare. (There are) few people (of this kind). History has always awarded success to these few.

So it is understandable that this type of struggle—which is really about bringing up a new world power, which is very necessary if Europe is not to fade away—can't progress like, let us say, a short battle over a minor conflict such as an inheritance or something. In this case the war might last years, with high points and low points, and in the end the winner will be the one who survives all this with the most stubborn tenacity. The objection that there might be moments when technical superiority could decide the final outcome is totally invalid. Because even in technical matters there is no superiority that remains with one side right from the start. Rather, there is (superiority first on one side, then again on the other. Our current situation) is connected with a temporary decline in our armaments in certain technical areas—not in quantity, but in value, due to new inventions that have also been useful to our opponents. I only have to point out that one single invention, which was not made by the English, but which they unfortunately developed better than we did—I am talking about the invention of electric locating [NDT: radar]—in a matter of a few months practically wiped out our prospering submarine war. And now we have unfortunately lost valuable bases at a time when we were just about to make this invention obsolete through the construction of new submarines, which are now ready and being launched. I hope they will be deployed again in the course of the winter, and then they might change the course of fate substantially.

(The war is certainly) an endurance test for all participants. The longer the war lasts, the (harder) this endurance test becomes. This endurance test will be withstood as long as there is still hope for success. Without hope of victory, endurance tests are usually not undertaken with the same strong will with which, for example, a fortress might fight as long as there is hope for relief. So it is important to rob the enemy of his certainty of victory from time to time, and to show him through offensive strikes that his plans are doomed to fail anyway, right from the start. This is never achieved as effectively by successful defensive as by successful offensive strikes. Long term, then, one can't believe in the principle that defense is the stronger part of the fight. It might ... be useful to others. One cannot forget that the total sum of men deployed on our side is just as great as on our opponents' side of. And we must not forget that some of the enemy forces are tied up in East Asia against Japan—against one state that, excluding China, contains well over 100 million people and represents a valuable force in technical armament.

Nevertheless, one has to recognize that too much time spent strictly defending will undermine one's endurance, and that these periods must be relieved by successful strikes. So I attempted to lead this war in an offensive way, whenever possible, right from the beginning—to lead it in an operational way, and not get pushed into any kind of world war situation. When this happened anyway, it was only in connection with the defection of our allies,[98] which naturally had operational effects. ...

But wars are finally decided by the recognition on one side or the other that the war can't be won anymore. Thus, the most important task is to bring the enemy to this realization. The fastest way to do this is to destroy his strength by occupying territory. If we ourselves are forced into defense, our job is to teach the enemy by ruthless strikes that he has not yet won, and that the war will continue without interruption. It is just as important to strengthen these psychological moments by not letting a moment pass without showing the enemy that no matter what he might do, he can never count on a capitulation—never, ever. This is crucial. The smallest sign of such a (mood for capitulation will raise the enemy's hope of victory again) and will fill a generally hopeless mass with new hope, causing them to willingly take on all burdens and sacrifices again. That is why publishing defeatist memoranda is so dangerous, as it happened in 1917, and the danger of files, as we saw that year—which, although known to the enemy for years, still helped maintain the hope that a miracle might happen that would suddenly change the situation.[99] The enemy must know that he won't be successful under any circumstances. If this is made clear to him by the attitude of people, by the Armed Forces, and even more by the severe setbacks he experiences, his nerve will break in the end. The same thing will happen as Frederick the Great experienced in the seventh year of war, and which he could (count as his biggest success in life). One cannot say afterward, "Yes, then (the situation was different." It was not different), gentlemen; rather, at that time almost all the generals, including his own brother ..., almost despairing of possible success. His government presidents, his ministers in Berlin, appeared in delegations and asked him to stop the war right away—this war could not be won anymore. The steadfastness of one man enabled the fight to continue, and in the end the miracle of a turning point did occur.

Also, the objection that this would never have happened without the accession to the throne of a new tsar in Russia is of no importance at all. Because if the capitulation had happened in the fifth year of war, then the succession to the throne in the seventh year, i.e., two years later, would have been completely insignificant. One has to bide one's time.

And the following must also be considered, gentlemen. (Never in the history of the world) has a coalition existed like that of our opponents, which has been assembled from such heterogeneous elements with such extremely different and conflicting goals. What we have as opponents are the greatest extremes that can be imagined in this world: ultra-capitalist states on one side and ultra-Marxist states on the other; on one side a dying world empire, Britain, and on the other side a colony seeking an inheritance, the USA. These are states whose aims are now diverging even more every day. And the one who recognizes this development, let us say, like a spider sitting in its web, can see how these oppositions develop by the hour. If a few heavy strikes were to succeed here, this artificially maintained united front could collapse at any moment with a huge clap of thunder. (Each of the partners joined the coalition in the hope of) realizing (its political aims this way), ... to be able to dupe the others or to win something: the USA trying to be heir to England; Russia attempting to win the Balkans, the straits, Persian oil, Iran, and the Persian Gulf; England attempting to hold its position and to strengthen its Mediterranean position. In other words, someday—and it could be any moment, because on the other side history is also shaped by mortal human beings—this coalition will break up, but always with the prerequisite that this battle should under no circumstances lead to a moment of weakness by Germany.

Of course, we also had great weaknesses, right from the start of the war—weaknesses that lay primarily (in our allies. For us it was a very significant weakness that we did not) have very strong states, (but) very weak states as allies. But at least they ... fulfilled their duty for a while. We cannot complain and lament about it; rather, we have to thankfully acknowledge that at least for a time these states fulfilled their purpose. We were able to conduct the war for years at the periphery of the Reich. Now we have been partly pushed back to the borders of the Reich, and partly we are still far from the old Reich borders. In any case, we are still fighting this war from a position that gives us every opportunity to get through and to survive, especially if we are able to eliminate the danger here in the West.

Now, gentlemen, I have accepted sacrifices on other fronts—which were not necessary—to create the necessary conditions that will allow us to move forward offensively. If I speak about an offensive here, the one who is in the thick of battle, suffering especially from the total air supremacy of the enemy, might be a bit concerned and might say right from the start, "How can one even think about something like that?" The situation in 1939 or 1940 was also not to convince nearly everyone that the battle in the West could be decided by taking the offensive. Just the opposite, gentlemen! I have not written memoranda in order to run through open doors, but to open up closed doors. It would not have been necessary back then, in countless and repetitive meetings, to present my ideas about the required offensive means of conducting warfare[100] ...

(Conducting a defensive war was) the official position that I argued against in those years. They accepted the idea of an offensive war against Poland, but an offensive war against France and England was considered insane—a crime, a Utopia, a hopeless pursuit. The fact demonstrated the opposite. Today, we can hardly imagine where we would be if we hadn't conquered France back then. ...

One could object that the difference between 1940 and today (was in a certain view) immense. At that time we faced an unproven enemy army, and now we face an army that is known to us already and is engaged in war. That is true, gentlemen. But where strength is concerned, not much has changed—with the exception of the Luftwaffe, which is a very critical factor, and I will come back to that point. Concerning strength: at that time, in the West, we lined up for the offensive with a total of about 100 divisions—110 divisions, 86 of which were deployed offensively. Not all of them were first-class divisions; some were improvised and hastily assembled in only a few months, and only some could really be called first-class. ...

(Also for the upcoming offensive we do not have only first-class units available.) But on the enemy side (they are not all first-class) units either. We have many worn-out troops, and the enemy has many worn-out troops as well, and has suffered severe losses. We now have the first official report from the Americans, and they really have lost about 240,000 men in just three weeks.[101] These numbers are just gigantic—far higher than what we thought they might lose. So he is also worn out. Technically, we are about equal on both sides. With regard to tank weapons, the enemy might have more tanks, but with our newest types, ours are better.
(*End of the fragment.*)

Meeting of the Führer with Colonel General Blaskowitz, December 28, 1944, at Adlerhorst

Present:

The Führer	*Lieutenant General v. Obstfelder*[102]
Colonel General Blaskowitz	*Lieutenant General Westphal*
Field Marshal Keitel	*Major General Scherff*
Field Marshal v. Rundstedt	*Colonel v. Below*

Colonel General Jodl   *Colonel Meyer-Detring*
...   *Major Johannmeyer*

Later: Reichsführer SS Himmler

Beginning: 6:02 p.m.

The West

BLASKOWITZ: According to the directive, the advance has now been ordered as follows. The right [flank] assault group on the outermost right wing: the 36th Volksgrenadier Division, next to it, the 17th SS [Panzer Division]; Command: the SS Corps. Orders: break through, disregarding the fortifications, in a straight southerly direction. The 36th Division should then begin, when they arrive here, ... veer off. This part ... by the left wing ... Volksgrenadier Division. Then ... must ... first the further ... Then I want to ... army engineer battalion ... is weak. That should ... be strengthened, so it ..., the right pushed in ... the 17th SS later freed up ... through, then (followed) ... both panzer grenadier (divisions) ready for action, (first the) 25th, then the 21st, but the 25th ... is very weak. The 21st is in good condition at the moment. The 21st Panzer Division is on the left wing at the moment. I wanted to let it stay there until late afternoon on the 31st—because the left wing is very weak, as there are very weak forces there—so a safety coefficient will be there until the very last moment; then in a night march they will pass by here, so they arrive on time here. The two divisions will then be able to go through behind there, in the direction of Pfalzburg and Zabern, and take Pfalzburg as well as Zabern.[103] [—] The 2nd Assault Group is composed of four divisions: the 559, 257, 361 and 256. The advance: the inner division turns around the south edge of Bitsch and then turns in the direction of ... should then ... the remaining free ... roll up from the back ... 257 and 361 will initially stay ...

THE FÜHRER: ... Are they the ones here in front? ...

BLASKOWITZ: As they said recently, the ... there are a lot (of small roads), ... more or less to the side ..., in assault units up to battalion strength ... only what they have with them. They are (not allowed to take more) with them. They are in a ... line, so behind our position, which cannot be crossed without the permission of the Army. They have to leave everything behind.

V. RUNDSTEDT: The 361st [Infantry] Division is the one that fought its way back through this whole thing. They know every inch of ground around there.

BLASKOWITZ: That's the division that is now clearing the same path that they made there.

V. RUNDSTEDT: While roads come out everywhere around here.

BLASKOWITZ: The left division, the 256th [Infantry], will first make the flanking movement to the southeast, then go along this through road while the spearhead turns in here; ... if the forces are insufficient ... further: when we have reached...with the lead elements of the 257th and 361st, we will have the report (that the) divisions are (through), and a clarification (has been made) as to whether a threat to the flanks has developed, (then) it will be time for the heads of the 257th and 361st to turn, ... initially the 361st.

THE FÜHRER: Here there is just one question to be asked. In principle ..., how it is possible, so that ... for their part are still in the woods the ... otherwise we can't get here at all ..., unless we refrain right from the start from going in here, and only go here. But that is a decision I would not make until after we've really seen it. Because it could also happen that—if the further, deeper advance fails—if we then stay too deep in here, he might be able to put a block across it immediately with very few forces. That's why it's still desirable to push it back as far as possible. But if faced with a superior attack, we move back.

V. RUNDSTEDT: I believe that if the enemy recognizes the attack, he will never push out here. Instead, he will come out here to reach the open area, especially if he still has some tanks, to press into these points. That he might ... in this difficult terrain ... But I am of the same ... : if the forces ... to the exit routes from the mountains ... for barriers, for min(ing operations) ... directs himself ... So it must be ... with a certain ...

THE FÜHRER: (I have) the feeling that he ... with ... our forces ... advance offensively, can ... on his side ... him ... carry out mining operations ... finally (make) them stop ... but run into him here. But it could be ... possible that we might have difficulties here. We have to ... take into account that we might not be able to support a long covering front, and that we might possibly have to push through to Ingweiler earlier, so that this would be the outermost border we reach. Also, we should not leave too many units here to provide cover. Otherwise we won't get in here anymore. Then it would be good to be near the exit route. Then we have to turn a few units out here right from the start, to push into here. One or two panzer units should be pulled through here. We would have to see, then, that we carry out a much tighter pincer movement. That would not be the ... for the ... but good, if we ... until we see what ... can, that we back ... in case of a ... to hold.

(BLASKOWITZ): ... Division is also with ...

(V. RUNDSTEDT): ... they should then ... with ... will be launched, and, if ... go. If the ... the direction of the march in ... should. I wanted them ... bring, thinking of the best case, so they can build a pivot here.

THE FÜHRER: We could also use them for that at first, if difficulties arise anywhere. We assume he lies somewhere in front here, and the normal divisions can't just move cross-country, so we could use them to create an opening. So I would keep them totally mobile. But certainly we could set a final goal.

V. RUNDSTEDT: That belongs in the area of the 361st. That's the plan.

BLASKOWITZ: This is the plan. This here is the favorable area. ... in all (directions) ...

THE FÜHRER: ... another case: first ... tough. Here is a ... the 100th Division.

BLASKOWITZ: ... along quite a broad (front). ... That is the 100th Division that (has) spread itself out.

THE FÜHRER: Does anybody know how he has organized (his defense)?

(BLASKOWITZ): He has pulled (back), ... pulled very far back. He has ... set cover out front. Otherwise (he has) recently pulled back quite far.

V. RUNDSTEDT: Defense of bases! If the resistance here in front is very tough and heavy, and I come along here maybe with the 559th, I just take the 21st Panzer Division behind it and shut the door from behind. Don't attack it from the front; that makes no sense. There are enough roads everywhere.

BLASKOWITZ: The territory is not too rough.

V. RUNDSTEDT: It only looks wild because woods are marked here. It's not that hard.

KEITEL: The valleys are narrow, though, and we have to be prepared for barriers.

(BLASKOWITZ): One battery has already gone ahead. ... if the thing is set free ...

(KEITEL): There are plenty of (roads) in here. Here ...

(V. RUNDSTEDT): The center, the 361st, is the most difficult (one) ...

THE FÜHRER: The decisive factor is that they (don't) ... and block the way with stuff that ... they don't even need.

(BLASKOWITZ): No, it's very strict.

(V. RUNDSTEDT): After what we unfortunately had to experience up there, there is now a flood of unneeded vehicles standing around.[104] (They) came along—empty cars to carry captured materiel.

THE FÜHRER: Then in the north[105] something else has proven necessary. We can't push the covering forces far enough away from the main fighting line. What we can do in the beginning in an open space with comparably modest forces, we cannot achieve later. Because when the enemy arrives, it's too late. So if we could just set up small barriers everywhere [—]

V. RUNDSTEDT: This sector offers itself. Besides, he is so weak around here. He cannot risk, with the few tiny divisions he still (has) there on the left ... doing ... He will ... everywhere ...

(THE FÜHRER): (I believe) also, that the threat to the (flanks) ... will ...

(BLASKOWITZ): The only thing he has in the ... is the ... Armored Division. If it will still be there, ... is questionable.

(V. RUNDSTEDT): I ... that it will stay, ... It is unlikely that ... away.

(THE FÜHRER): ... deploy them. If ... panzer units are entirely adequate, ... He can ... the whole thing here ... leave the mobile forces in this area. We don't need to pull the 559th in here if this is cleared out; in that case, it can be pulled out and used here for cover.

BLASKOWITZ: We had thought, once they cleared this out, that we would first bring them together and pull them over here to see how it looks, and where I might need them.

THE FÜHRER: In the most extreme case, we could pull them out to cover the flanks, so that we would come out here with the 36th and the 559th—two infantry divisions—and one panzer unit. The two other units we could ... with the forces that ... can bring down here. ... then in here ...

(BLASKOWITZ: Two) panzer divisions and four in(fantry divisions) ...

THE FÜHRER: ... we could also make ... available to settle this affair.

BLASKOWITZ: ... being led after: ... coming after.

THE FÜHRER: ... We want to rush them.

BLASKOWITZ: No, I mean that it comes from ... (I believe that) this moment will be the decisive one for us. (If this) starts, he will now gain the impression that all the pressure will be against the southwest at first—

THE FÜHRER: He won't believe that.

BLASKOWITZ: —and that later we will hook around.

THE FÜHRER: He will never believe that we are going to the southwest. If everything works out and stays secret, he will not expect us to attack

here. Or do you have some indication that he is concerned about some-
thing here? He ...
(BLASKOWITZ): No.
(JODL): We hope that the attack (plan) won't be (taken along) to the front
line, like in every other (operation).
(V. RUNDSTEDT): It's not planned, according to the distribution list.
THE FÜHRER: (If it doesn't) come up by accident, (he) won't (expect it).
He thinks (it's impossible that we) would line up against him there. He
won't guess (that we are lining up again.[106] The deciding factor is) that we
have to (arrive) down here so early that he can't move away to the south
under any circumstances. The one thing that must not happen is that we are
forced to follow him onto the Rhine plain. If he starts pulling down right
away and goes to the south, we will have to turn in as fast as possible, so
he can't get away. Otherwise, there is a great danger that this guy will go
down here.[107] We don't know to what degree this bridgehead will really be
successful, and how deep it will become. I told Himmler[108] that he should
make himself a few very small commands—with only a few assault guns,
armored personnel carriers and Volkswagens, which he should be able to
scratch together—and drive them ahead ruthlessly to blow up bridges.
Here is a line, which, if everything turns out well, we won't cross. That
would be this line here. If we push through here, we'll be north of ... north
of the railway. So we could ... the cros(sings, which) are ... all easily
blocked over the ..., so he won't be able to (escape to the south) ... and if
there are only a (few) ... (that) cause confusion (for him), so he ... It is
still possible (that he) could pull through the forest via Hagenau to (try) to
get into Strasbourg. We (have) to be prepared for the worst. That would be
(the) moment (then), when he could force (us), if we ... get the street,
around Ingweiler ..., that we turn in with ... as fast as possible.
V. RUNDSTEDT: If the thing comes out right and the (tanks) turn off and
the infantry turns off, then I will still have the mountain division. I will
chase them forward to the south and block the pass that goes through here
from Strasbourg.
BLASKOWOTZ: The Schirmeck valley!
V. RUNDSTEDT: Right down here, from Zabern to the south.
THE FÜHRER: That is not a great distance.
V. RUNDSTEDT: No, and the territory is not very rough for a mountain
troop. That's on condition that this works out well. Then he'll say to
himself, "What shall I do? So out with that stuff, especially with the
French!" But ... just keep it in mind.

(THE FÜHRER): ... the 361st [Infantry Division] comes cross-country?

(V. RUNDSTEDT): Yes, Sir.

(THE FÜHRER): ... the condition of the roads ... There one cannot ...

V. RUNDSTEDT: I have to point out again and again. (That division has, in the) battles from here ... fought back (up to this line), and (they know) every step and stone (in this area). That's (why it is important that we) relieve them of the things (that they don't) absolutely need [—]

KEITEL: They will probably find roads around here.

V. RUNDSTEDT: There are roads everywhere. It's not a high mountain area.

THE FÜHRER: The northern Vosges are flat.

BLASKOWITZ: Attack beginning at 11 p.m., sneaking in without a sound, so at first he won't know if they are raiding party operations. We are very clear about this: without artillery support in the moonlight. The moon is up from 7 p.m. until 7 a.m.; the moon is full for two days. There are only a few assault guns along. With artillery support we (could not work) in this (situation). ... batteries everywhere out front ... no artillery behind ...

(THE FÜHRER: How did he react) to raiding party (operations) ... in the area of the First Army?

(BLASKOWITZ: It was) different ... That time there were ... there were predominant ...

(V. RUNDSTEDT): Everywhere where we are still standing in front of the Saar, the (action) has turned out fine. ... our raiding parties had these difficulties. (At) ... or whatever it's called, it worked out well. Where the salient still extends forward around Forbach, everything worked well.

BLASKOWITZ: Yes, there they always get through.

V. RUNDTSTEDT: Now, all of this is still in front of the Maginot Line. The difficulty arises only when our attack hits up against the Maginot Line.

THE FÜHRER: Now this heaviest 653rd Tank Destroyer Detachment should come here.[109] It would be desirable, of course, if they could come here for the attack, because they, working together with any ... (unit)—if any engineer battalion could (join—) would be invincible. That is ... with the 12.8 cm and armor (of 250 mm) ..., maybe has a (speed of) 12 to 15 km, not (more). But it is very durable ... if the other ... with his ..., he will position himself in front of the bunkers ... after which he ... places himself 30 to 40 m in front of the bunkers and shoots them to pieces. (It) will shoot every bunker from a distance of 2,000 to 3,000 m, (guaran)teed.

The heaviest bunkers lie deep, the ... (The French have) no works that are (stronger than) 1.60 m from the back. In general he has 1.20 m. But it usually shoots through 2.40 m with a concrete shell from 2,000 m. It has armor plating of 250 mm. Against this he has no weapon. We've already seen how his weapons fared facing the Königstiger. This is the assault gun designed to completely eliminate the heaviest obstacles. If difficulties arise anywhere along the Maginot Line—he does not have any artillery inside the Maginot Line, because we took the artillery out back then.[110] I hope that the few batteries that were in there—that we destroyed those few barrels at least, and that the breech locks were taken out. He does not have anything in the towers—as far as the towers that are still there. So he can't defend the Maginot Line in front at all. It is in fact an (installation) that is mostly underground. (There are a few) machine gun emplacements and a few armored (cupolas). But these (works) are damaged. (Back then) we ... (removed) the electrical installations, the ventilation systems ... electrical machines, and especially ..., because we needed them elsewhere, ... One can ... the towers, ... not lift ... I also don't (believe) that he has learned to manage the (works) in this short time. I don't think it's (possible). So (he places) himself (in) several in-between installations, which one can reach from the rear. (These things) deployed here will, in my opinion, have the greatest effect. [—] Where is the detachment (now)?

WESTPHAL: I already reported that it is doubtful that they will arrive in time. The commander has already reached the First Army. He doesn't help too much. He claimed that one train had left.

THE FÜHRER: It would have been better if he had stayed with his detachment and led it here.

WESTPHAL: He has been sent back to bring them here. They are at several railway stations.

THE FÜHRER: It doesn't matter. That is such a valuable weapon, that three or four pieces are of more value than ... (takes others. But I have to) point out that (they can't) cross (weak bridges). The vehicles have (a weight) ... about 90 tons.[111] So (they are immense) hunks of metal.

(V. RUNDSTEDT): Everything has been done to (bring) the (detachment) in ... on time.

THE FÜHRER: Especially if it concerns clearing out individual installations afterward, where the enemy (still resists)—at the 559th—that would be (the best weapon) imaginable.

BLASKOWITZ: The 559th in this line!

THE FÜHRER: I don't know if it might not be easier to pull through in this terrain. We will have to see. Bitsch is here. I believe that what comes through east of Bitsch will be easier, because here the Maginot Line is still in our possession, while here the Maginot Line is not in our possession anymore. I just don't know how it works in these sectors here. I cannot judge. It can't climb very steep slopes. It's not a weapon that can take on very steep slopes like other tanks. At most, it can climb slopes of 20%. It's best to take only 15%.

(… ?): …the mobility … the very best on the barrel…that we have, and …

(THE FÜHRER: Even if he) builds himself an antitank-gun blocking position, (it can) eliminate it. (It is) also wonderful against antitank-gun blocking positions. The moment they fire, they're (given away, and when they're) given away, they can't do anything against (this weapon). If the 12.8 (fires at the antitank-gun position) with high-explosive shells, every round from 2,000 to (3,000 meters is a hit). So every antitank-gun position is (worthless. How are the people) outfitted in terms of footwear?

WESTPHAL: The footwear is not first-class, of course. But we have now brought in quite a lot and are also working on resoling them.

V. RUNDSTEDT: The question of clothing is a very dark chapter anyway. One has to ask if it might not be possible to take something away from the good Luftwaffe, which is sitting around on the airfields. The head doctor visited me recently, and he said that when an airman is being deloused, he brings along three changes of clothes. We could take boots away from them as well.

(THE FÜHRER: There are) several different possibilities. (One possibility is) that I first find out, (from all the storehouses of the three) branches of the Armed Forces in Germany, what exactly it is that they have.

(KEITEL: That has been) prepared: (Confiscation—initial) inspection, taking in and (confiscation).

(THE FÜHRER: The) second possibility is that because (so many things) are kept secret (anyway), the (different branches of the Armed Forces) won't get anything new (until they) report their supplies very thoroughly, and also very thoroughly …

KEITEL: We know the storehouses.

THE FÜHRER: How many storehouses are there? I heard the number today.

KEITEL: There are thousands of storehouses.

THE FÜHRER: It's very clear that it has deteriorated significantly because of the of the air defense measures. Before we regulated it very closely, but now it is out of control because of the air defense measures.

HIMMLER: Dispersing and hiding!

KEITEL: It was a hard battle, to break up the clothing depots.

THE FÜHRER: The infantryman is still the poor (devil. He has to) carry everything along. He only has (what he carries with him.)

(HIMMLER: Because I) could not equip the Volkssturm [peoples' militia] on the Upper Rhine ... or my ... either, (I have) ... confiscated ... the supplies of the customs (border guard) in Württem(berg and in Baden), which I have taken over.[112] (There were) thousands of boots and (uni-forms).

V. RUNDSTEDT: In the little village where (I am located, there is a) storehouse with hundreds of police uniforms.

HIMMLER: Wonderful! Send it on over!

KEITEL: You gave Reich Minister Speer the authority to dispose of all resources in the Armed Forces' stores.[113] Now I've seen an order—it was delivered to me—for the confiscation of all Armed Forces' supplies of fabrics and leather. It was delivered to me, because at that time it was said: in agreement with the Chief of the OKW. Minister Speer signed the order on December 16 or 17 and it is now being carried out.

THE FÜHRER: I'm afraid, if Speer has signed it—did I sign it?

(KEITEL: The basis of the) order! It was an (authorization) at that time.

(THE FÜHRER: The) authorization will be denied (for this matter) imme-diately. (It was only a very) general authorization: (Reich Minister Speer) was authorized to take the measures necessary to continue to wage war.

(KEITEL): We can do it again right away.

(THE FÜHRER:) I just spoke with Frank.[114] (He said: The) Navy has (large stores), of course. (There) every man has three or four shirts. [—]

WESTPHAL: With us everyone has only one set of underwear.

THE FÜHRER: [—] If I take away one set from everyone there, I'd gain at least one to one and a half million sets of underwear for the Army. That would certainly satisfy the most urgent needs. [—] That's one measure. But then another measure has to be taken—he also said that things have to be done more economically. It's strange, but there's a continual loop. In Germany we take up a fabric collection, while things are constantly coming home from the front. It is a constant (loop. Today you can) go into tens of thousands or (hundreds of thousands) of households and you will find (Armed Forces things everywhere).

(HIMMLER): … millions of blankets since …

THE FÜHRER: With what? The bombed-out men (say to themselves, "I have to) care (for) my wife"—and send the (blankets home. Or) they take three blankets on leave (and come) back (with only two). Everyone turns a blind eye (because he says to himself: We've) done the same thing … On the other side, I have to make a fabric collection in order to get hold of the stuff.

HIMMLER: The measure requiring them to pay ten times the price—270 marks—is of no value either. Everyone is happy to pay that. He says, "270 marks—that's cheap; I'd have to pay more on the black market."

THE FÜHRER: For a blanket they pay more than 270 marks at home. So he doesn't lose anything. He then buys two blankets and sells one on the black market. So he still has one for himself, and with what he gets for the one on the black market he easily pays what the second one cost him.

KEITEL: At least we've managed, (from the stocks) … of the (Navy and the Luftwaffe) … especially the Luft(waffe)—to give more to the Army) in many areas.

(THE FÜHRER: If someone) has not (reported in more) than a year, (it's proof) that he has huge (supplies in his depot). We just have to go after that.

(KEITEL): The Navy and Luftwaffe have much lower (consumption. What) wear and tear on clothing (they) have, and what (wear) and tear the man in the trench has!

THE FÜHRER: We can say that the man in the infantry gets one to two sets a year, and the man in the Navy and the man in the Luftwaffe also get one to two sets a year. But the men in the Navy and Luftwaffe collect them. It's clear that the men in the Luftwaffe paratroop divisions have the same consumption as the infantry, but the others—the ground staff, for example—don't. We have to bring some things out, just like we brought men out—even though it's getting harder, since everyone clings to them, for a thousand reasons. I assume that all the commanders-in-chief say only what they think is true. (The commanders-in-chief report what) has been reported to them as true. (But many things that are) reported to them as true are (not true. If I'm given a) report saying that we can … (not) give it out … (No) one wants to be the one who wrote (it. It is said: That) is a careless, stupid (remark, that I) need (half a year) to train a female Luft(waffe assistant, who) does nothing but (operate a searchlight).

(KEITEL: It was said that they) also had to be (trained to radio). … also in the Army…

THE FÜHRER: Only a small amount is reported by radio. They don't need to radio—only to (illuminate). But these gentlemen expected that I wouldn't look at it or read it.

BLASKOWITZ: So can it be carried out this way?

THE FÜHRER: Yes! Hopefully you'll get through.

BLASKOWITZ: We'll get through.

THE FÜHRER: I have the feeling that not much more can happen during that operation, if it doesn't get stuck right at the start or experience unusually bad luck. Because the other one doesn't have anything. He has a few (divisions) here. (What can he do with them?) Here he also has ... has (pulled) away anyway. (It's possible that he) will suddenly bring something back. (But it's ... un)likely that he would (do it). ... we will also ... him ... That could (lead) to a (major success—that we might possibly (destroy) five divisions. (That) would eliminate (one) piece, and then we (could be sure to get another) piece out (with a second strike).

(V. RUNDSTEDT: At least) no danger could (result) from it ... could never (become a danger for us).

HIMMLER: That's what happened near Hagenau, where I'm forming a bridgehead.

THE FÜHRER: I said this before: Go ahead with the forces you have, and place them in front everywhere, even if many are lost. That doesn't matter—they'll hold for several days, especially if they have a few assault guns. [—] Another important thing is that if we build an all-round defense anywhere, we have to spread the assault guns out and dig them in immediately, as far as possible, even if that means they aren't as mobile. We have to set them up in an all-around defense position. But when they're dug in, they're almost unreachable. If the 38-ton[115] is in the ground, dug in well, it can't be (hit) at all.[116] [—]

(HIMMLER): ... of the Rhine-Marne (channel [canal?].) ...

(THE FÜHRER: ...Zabern,) to ... push ... to here ... (If), as mentioned earlier, (we) meet difficulties here—and (we) move away too much there, so that sealing it off here is impossible—there would still be the possibility to pull in here. But we also have to block it to the south. We can't stay on the road. That would still be a possibility as a last concession. But it's not ideal. It would be ideal, of course, if we could get Zabern—and even more ideal if we could pull through the 6th SS Mountain Division to block off the Schirmeck valley so he can't move out here anymore either.

HIMMLER: The American divisions are located in here. This here is a relatively empty space. There (is not much in here).

(THE FÜHRER: Here) there are still two ...

(HIMMLER): ... American divisions ... pull out first ... still in the area of ... so that he ... in the current ... these units ...

(THE FÜHRER: They will) certainly be picked apart ... available ...

HIMMLER: That's not of much value (either). (It) has company strengths of 40 to (50) men. For American proportions that's quite weak.

THE FÜHRER: The Americans are writing now that they could save 6 divisions if they'd cut back their rear services. That improves the troops' morale unbelievably, if one takes out the rear services and puts them in the front! We know this ourselves. Anyone who has not really tested the procedure will be greatly surprised here.

HIMMLER: The engineer battalion was deployed with the 36th, and it was said that it (had not been deployed) since Nettuno. (Now) they are (supposedly) deploy(ing) it again ... because the infantry (had such great losses.)

(THE FÜHRER: It must) be going poorly for them. Otherwise (there would not be such extensive) new conscription.[117] (One only has to calculate). They have an air force (of 3 million men; they have a) navy of 3 million (men. That already makes 6 million) men that the Americans ... have, today (even more, probably.) ... (Then) in East (Asia) they have ... have 40 or ... (divisions).

HIMMLER: The Americans certainly do not have a higher conscription rate (than 10%) of their population. (That) makes 13 million out of 130 million people. They certainly don't have more than that yet.[118]

THE FÜHRER: But that is a great deal for democratic states. They can't do it with the industry, either. Everything starts to get squeezed.

KEITEL: They are supposed to have an army of 7 million men, plus 6 million men in the air force and navy—that makes all in all only 13 million men.

THE FÜHRER: Now they do have big rear services. They have a completely motorized army. It is ... (their situation is anything) but perfect. (In America) criticism of the whole (way of conducting the war is starting, so that one ..., instead of concentrating on *one* thing,) divides it along the whole front ...

(End of the meeting.)

Part VII

1945

Endgame

Hitler's Situation Reports,
April 23, 25, and 27[*]

Monday, April 23, 1945

[Marshal Zhukov's 1st Belorussian Front and Marshal Koniev's 1st Ukrainian Front—with 2.5 million soldiers, 41,600 guns, 6,250 tanks, 7,560 aircraft—are tightening the screws on the Reich capital. On this day, Red Army units occupy Potsdam and Döberitz west of the city. Fighting is already taking place in the northern and eastern city districts of Frohnau, Friedrichshain, Tegel, Pankow, and Köpenick. Underground (subway) lines C, D and E cease operating, and in Kantstrasse the inhabitants hang the first white flags out of their windows. In the Führer bunker under the Reich Chancellery, not far from Potsdamer Platz, Adolf Hitler appoints Artillery General Helmuth Weidling as commanding officer of the Berlin defense area. Using random units—44,630 soldiers, 42,531 Volkssturm men, 3,532 Hitler Youth, Labor Service men, and members of the Todt Organization—General Weidling is supposed to withstand the pressure of

---

[*][NDT: In these final transcripts, Hitler is identified by name, rather than as "The Führer."]

the 2.5 million Soviet soldiers; only one of every two German defenders has a rifle. Wenck's "army" (three weak divisions)—ordered by Hitler to carry out a relief operation on behalf of the capital—still remains 60 kilometers southwest of Berlin. To the south of the Reich, American and French troops reach the Danube River on this day, in the area of Donaueschingen; to the northwest and north, British and Canadian forces attack Delmenhorst and Hamburg; and in the east, Soviet troops are fighting in the Lausitz and in East Prussia. From Berchtesgaden, Reichsmarshal Göring telegraphs to Führer Headquarters that if no other order is issued, he will take over governmental responsibilities. At 9 a.m. Hitler orders—in vain—that Göring be arrested.]

* * * * *

Present (April 23):
Adolf Hitler
Field Marshal Wilhelm Keitel, Chief of the Armed Forces High Command
  (OKW)
General Hans Krebs, Provisional Chief of the Army General Staff
General Wilhelm Burgdorf, Chief Adjutant of the Armed Forces
SS Gruppenführer Hermann Fegelein, Deputy to the Reichsführer SS at
  the Führer Headquarters
Colonel Ernst Kaether, from April 22 to 23 commanding officer of the
  Berlin Defense Area

HITLER: When can we expect the auxiliaries to arrive?
KREBS: That issue is still unresolved. Except for the two promised battalions, additional forces are not immediately available. Whatever we could get has been brought in here.
KEITEL: The two battalions won't be here before tomorrow morning, even if everything runs smoothly.
HITLER: It's very late. By then he [the Russian] could already be standing in the city center. There can be no discussion of a real defense if no troops are there. [—] I heard shocking news again: in one area the troops withdrew. The Volkssturm and Hitler Youth repaired the thing again. The troops had received withdrawal orders from someone.

KREBS: There was action there. The thing was brought under control again at the cost of numerous and bloody losses. Except for the Nordland Division, there are no units of foreign origin on any part of the front.

HITLER: An entire corps has disappeared completely. Only the SS Division Nordland is there. Everything else has disappeared, including the corps commander. The only unit that didn't follow that is Nordland. That's so disgraceful! If I think about it all, why then still live at all!

KEITEL: The Wenck unit must throw something in the way of motorized vehicles into Berlin immediately.

BURGDORF: Wenck has four German Labor Service Divisions and no weapons!

HITLER: Then naval units must come as well.

KREBS: The enemy's general offensive is becoming dangerous, because, for the moment, he's still making no attempt to go into Berlin, but instead to seal it off.

HITLER: All available reserves must be provided to Wenck, even if they're poorly armed, in order to fill in the gap. No additional reinforcements are to be given to Steiner.[1] Keitel, find out what battalions are still coming in.

KEITEL: Yes, my Führer, everything will be done.

SECOND SITUATION REPORT,
April 23, 1945

HITLER: Forces must be brought into Berlin by all possible means in order to cover the Grunewald. Berlin is now the main point of attraction for the enemy. The enemy knows I am here. The enemy will do everything in order to concentrate here. That could provide the best opportunity for us to lead him into a trap here. But that presupposes that we finally recognize the significance of this hour on our side, and work very obediently according to the plan ordered from above. Everyone must work honestly! This up here [indicating Army Group Steiner, which was to line up from the north for a relief attack on Berlin] is not honest! Steiner has too many doubts in view of the defensive front standing before of him.

KREBS: I believe we still have four days' time.

HITLER: In four days the thing will have been decided

Third Situation Report,
April 23, 1945

HITLER: The following should be brought in during the course of the afternoon, if at all possible: two battalions of the Grossdeutschland Division. It may be possible to add some other battalion to that. In the government quarter, there are the following reserves: the Führer Escort Company, except for two platoons that are already employed; a Volkssturm battalion from the Propaganda Ministry with three companies; and a Volkssturm company of the Reich Chancellery. Together a strength of around 3,500 men. The Reichsführer SS wanted to send his battalion over here as a last reserve as well.

KREBS: Volunteer soldiers and SS men have strengthened the forces manning the innermost defensive ring in the government quarter.

HITLER: We have to watch out that Seydlitz's soldiers and officers don't come in here as well.[2] Up here on the Havel [northwest of Berlin] a difficult situation arose. If this threatens to collapse, it will be a mess and a serious mistake on the part of the command. Everything that comes in should be employed against that now. We also have to pull everything out from here. The 7th Panzer Division must be employed here in order to eliminate this mess. [—] The current enemy pressure indicates that the enemy's initial intention is to encircle Berlin and thus cut off the supply lines to Berlin. The Luftwaffe must take absolutely everything they still have and concentrate it up here, and quickly! We're dealing with minutes. Also here between Treuenbrietzen and Schwielowsee, everything must be thrown forward in order to cut this off here. The thing up on the Havel must also be brought under control as quickly as possible.

FEGELEIN: The important thing is to clear the street system.

HITLER: In Potsdam we must hold at all cost. Group Steiner has to move down the Havel [River].

KAETHER: New reports just arrived. There are ten to twelve very heavy enemy tanks on Landsberger Strasse east of the main fighting line, supposedly Stalin models. Behind that, innumerable additional tanks. Therefore, [they are] considerably stronger than originally reported. Not only the stated 40, but considerably more. As far as the eye can see. Luftwaffe support was ordered, and engagement has been announced. Artillery commands were ordered to act against that with concentrated fire.

HITLER: We have to go down low with bombers and really destroy them. Our assault guns are a bit too weak when faced with these things.

Wednesday, April 25, 1945

[The Soviet ring around Berlin closes. At around 1 p.m., the attacking spearheads of the 4th Guards Tank Army, advancing from the south, and the units of the Soviet 47th Army advancing from the north, link up at Ketzin, twelve kilometers northwest of Potsdam. In the Reich capital, the Soviets push forward from the south to the Neubabelsberg-Zehlendorf-Neukölln line. In Spandau, Hitler Youth under the leadership of National Political Education Institute chief, SS Gruppenführer Heissmeyer, are encircled. Weidling, the city commander, explains to Hitler with the help of a standard city map that the German front is being systematically pushed back to the city center. Acting against a Führer order, General Busse's Ninth Army does not fight its way through to Berlin from the southeast of the German capital, but instead attempts to break through to the west into American captivity. On the front east of Berlin, the Soviets reach Görlitz, Bautzen and Kamenz, and, in the southeast, Brünn. The British reach a line between Bremen on the Weser and Horneburg on the Elbe. The Americans advance through the Bavarian forest to the south; in central Germany they meet the Soviets' western advancing spearheads at Torgau; the remainder of the Reich is cut in half.]

* * * * *

HITLER: The English and the Americans are being quiet on the Elbe [River]. They've probably agreed on some kind of demarcation line. In Berlin it looks worse than it really is. The Berlin area must be cleared, emptied of people, in so far as possible. The 12th [Wenck] and 9th [Busse] Armies, which are forming fixed fronts in the west and east, must be pulled into Berlin. The divisions in Berlin must be filled up, however possible, using the local population. Recruiting columns must be set up in order to bring everyone in. In Berlin, General Weidling has the central command; Colonel Kaether is his deputy. One division staff or another will still come in. The cadre units will be put in order and replenished again, so we'll have divisions. Everything else that comes in will be integrated into these divisions so that a real order will develop. [—] Southwestern Germany is fragile. Even my influence from Berchtesgaden couldn't have prevented that. The defeatist mood was there [even] earlier. The three men responsible are no longer alive. They have poisoned the whole Western Front from the beginning—a society corrupted by its luxury. [—] I can achieve success here alone. If I do achieve a success, even if it's only a moral one, at least it's an opportunity to save face and gain time. One thing I do know. It's totally useless to go south, because I have no influence and no armies there. I would be there with just my staff. I could only hold a southern German Ostmärk mountain block, even though Italy could also be maintained as a war theater. But there as well, total defeatism dominates the leadership, which is devoured from the top down.

GOEBBELS: In Berlin we can achieve a moral success on a global scale. This success can only be achieved here, where the eyes of the entire world are directed. The fact that the Russians are marching into Brandenburg won't be regretted as much as if Berlin were to be taken into their possession. But if they are driven back in front of Berlin, then that would be the basis for a great example for the world.

HITLER: If it's really true. I received news that the talks between Eden and Molotov apparently did not reach a compromise. The Russians demand the whole area. That would mean the whole war would be lost for the British. England started this war because I demanded a corridor to East Prussia and Danzig, with approval under Allied control. And now they're supposed to allow a power that now dominates practically the whole of Europe already and extends into East Asia to advance even further? [—] I believe that the moment has come when the instinct for self-preservation will cause the others to stand up anyway against this immoderate and proletarian-Bolshevist colossus and Moloch [Devil]. If I were to run away from here today like a coward, the result would be that the others would try to erect in southern Germany a kind of neutral line, and that would be all. Then National Socialism would be eliminated and the German Reich as well. If I strike here successfully and hold the capital, then the hope might grow among the British and the Americans that they might possibly be able to oppose this danger with a Nazi Germany after all. And I am the only man for this.

GOEBBELS: If such a conception is possible at all, which is debatable, then it would only be possible through you and only in this place. If you leave this city, you lose everything else as well. You can't give up Berlin with the idea that you can defend yourself here or somewhere else.

HITLER: I have said that to the gentlemen as well. I said, "The situation is not such that I have a completely stable front down here in southern Germany and have a buffer zone and don't want to leave Berlin out of sheer obstinacy." I see where the development is going. All my attempts to influence the tactics are simply useless. Insane and catastrophic mistakes were made during the defense of the Rhineland as well as in other places. All the plans I worked out failed simply because the ground was pulled out from under them through the arbitrary acts of junior commanders.

KREBS: Field Marshal Keitel has issued the following orders. The combat group of the 7th Panzer Division goes to Nauen and then to Berlin. One of our assault gun groups will go to Berlin immediately. The command structure according to Jodl's proposal. Subordination of Army Group Vistula under the Armed Forces Operations Staff in Rheinsberg, as of this evening. Wenck will take over the command as soon he has influence over Group Holste. The thrust to the south from Löwenberg will start this evening.

GOEBBELS: The war situation is such today that only a visible symbol can achieve something.

HITLER: As an inglorious refugee from Berlin, I would have no authority in either northern or southern Germany, and in Berchtesgaden even less.

GOEBBELS: In 1933 the party was so weakened that without your personal action only further failure would have come. Only by means of your personal effort was everything else swept along. If you had left Berlin on Sunday, Berlin would not be in our hands today.

HITLER: With what was I then supposed to hold the south against the west? You see, it's like that everywhere: A name guarantees a certain order. Wherever there's a name, a personality, there's order. As long as there was a personality in Italy, there was a certain order here. Under Vietinghoff, the demoralizing influences again became stronger.[3] [—] It was those smart-asses that Clausewitz warned of—people who always see the easier way as more intelligent. Actually, the easier way is stupider. And then the false cleverness on top of that. For me there's no doubt: The battle has reached a climax here. [—] If it's really true that differences will arise among the Allies in San Francisco—and they will arise—then a change can only come about if I strike at the Bolshevik colossus at one point. Then the others might come to the conclusion after all that there is only one who is in a position to stop the Bolshevik colossus, and that is I and the party and today's German state. [—] If fate decides differently, then I would vanish from the stage of world history as an inglorious refugee. But I would consider it a thousand times more cowardly to commit suicide at the Obersalzberg than to stand here and fall. [—] One shouldn't say, "You, as the Führer..." [—] I am the Führer as long I can really lead. I can't lead by setting myself on a mountain somewhere; I must have authority over armies that obey. Let me achieve a victory here, and even though it may still be difficult and hard, then I will have the right again to eliminate the lazy elements that are constantly creating obstructions; then I will work with the generals who have proven their worth. Only a heroic attitude can enable us to stand this difficult time. [—] Also earlier in history, the Asian assault was not broken by the fact that everyone surrendered; somewhere he must be stopped. We experienced ourselves once, how difficult it is to negotiate with Molotov. We were at the height of our power then. Here stands the Asian khan, who wants to conquer Europe. England realizes quite clearly that Bolshevism will continue to devour beyond the points already reached today. This is now the decisive battle. [—] If I win this battle, then I expect nothing from it for my personal name. But then I will be rehabilitated. Then I can eliminate a number of generals and lower officers, including in the SS, who have failed at decisive points. But for all those I accuse of withdrawing, I have to provide an example, so that I don't withdraw myself. [—] It's also possible that I will fall here. But then I will have perished in a decent way. But that would be still better than if I would sit as an inglorious refugee to Berchtesgaden, giving orders from there that are of no use. This so-called southern fortress is not self-sufficient. That's an illusion. The armies down there are fragile. There's just nothing that can be done in the south. [—] I can see the possibility of repairing the thing only if I achieve a success in some place. Bear in mind the repercussions on the British. If we defend Berlin successfully today—and certain signs of an anti-Russian mood are emerging—then they will see that the people who possess the appropriate farsightedness will again take a bit of courage in the face of this colossus. These people might then say to themselves: if we were to go with Nazi Germany, then maybe we could hold our ground against this colossus after all.

GOEBBELS: It would also be encouraging for the other side. If Stalin sees this development in the Western States that's based on a German victory in Berlin, then he would say to himself, "I won't get the Europe that I had in mind. I'm only bringing the Germans and the British together. So I will strike a balance with the Germans and make some sort of agreement." Frederick the Great was once in a similar situation. He also got all of his authority back after the Battle of Leuthen. If the Führer proves that it can be done—that one can stay, and that one can win a battle by staying—then these executions will have an educational meaning and not a crushing effect.

HITLER: It's simply unbearable for me personally to have other people shot for things that I do myself. I wasn't born just to defend my Berghof alone.

GOEBBELS: If the thing in the south and west had been different, and if it had just been about a Battle for Berlin—like, for example, for Breslau— then I would have strongly protested against your coming to Berlin and making a prestige issue out of it. But the developments have now made this Battle for Berlin into a prestige case after all. The Führer has decided to oppose the Russian enemy in this place, and has appealed to the German people of Berlin to follow him one last time. This situation must be fought through now, in one way or another.

HITLER: There was no problem for me here at all. It's the only possibility at all to restore my personal reputation. Somewhere, the power of the Greater Asian Khan must be broken. Back then it was the Battle of Vienna [1683]. Now it's the Battle for Berlin. When Vienna was freed, the entire Turkish power wasn't broken instantly. It took years still. But it was a signal. If the Viennese had surrendered like cowards at that time, then Turkish power would have continued to advance.

GOEBBELS: It seems important to me that as long as we're not getting any relief from the outside, we have to keep our defense area around Berlin as large as possible.

HITLER: The narrower we are, the worse it is. [—] The Allies will have created a demarcation line on the basis of diplomatic agreements. But the Russians certainly aren't thinking about observing it. I know how it was in the winter of 1940. I didn't go to war against Moscow out of carelessness, but because, on the basis of certain information, I knew that an alliance between England and Russia was being prepared. The question was whether we should begin to strike ourselves or whether we should wait and be crushed to death sometime. [—] Now, I became acquainted with Molotov at that time. The Russians had not achieved any overwhelming international successes at that time. They were defeated in Finland. Then they occupied a few areas. In the Polish campaign they waited too long— until we were well past the agreed demarcation line. Then came our campaign in the West, in which we achieved a huge victory. The Russians hadn't expected that at all. It was the biggest victory in the history of the world. Then came the various demonstrations by our Luftwaffe against England. And in this whole situation, Molotov demanded things from us in Berlin that were outrageous. [—] He demanded from us that we withdraw from bases on Danish territory at the exit to the North Sea. He had already announced a claim to that back then. He demanded Constantinople, Romania, Bulgaria, Finland—and we were the winners at that time! How will this Molotov act now toward the British and the Americans with such victories and after these catastrophic failures of the Allies. [—] Now this Asian conflict is added to that. In America, sober thinkers will say: what do we want here anyway? Capital investment, perhaps? But we won't gain markets here. There are resources for us in China. On the other hand, they don't want Russia to enter the war against Japan. They say: we'll handle Japan alone.

GOEBBELS: If the Soviets advance up to the Elbe, including the Protectorate [of Bohemia], then the Americans will disappear from here. Only 20 to 25 British divisions will remain. Pacifist and salon Bolshevik propaganda will begin among the British troops. Stalin will militarize his area, including the German area. He will fight with propaganda against the Western forces because they destroyed the cities. He's a better propagandist than the British. [—] The Soviets can play on all pianos. A conflict will arise here in a very short time. I can't imagine that there are intelligent Englishmen who don't see that.

HITLER: Now it's going to happen. What Lloyd George[4] once told me: the provisional peace treaty. Back then Lloyd George declared in a memorandum, "The Peace of Versailles cannot be maintained and is insane. England is destroying the European balance." It was a classic prophetic memorandum by Lloyd George. [—] If we were to leave the world stage so disgracefully, then we would have lived in vain. It's completely unimportant if we continue to live for a while still or not. Better to end the battle honorably than to go on living in shame and dishonor for a few more months or years.

GOEBBELS: If the thing goes well, it's fine anyway. If it doesn't go well and the Führer were to find an honorable death in Berlin and Europe were to become Bolshevik, in five years at the latest the Führer would be a legendary personality and National Socialism a myth. He would be hallowed by his last great action, and everything human that they criticize in him today would be swept away in one stroke.

HITLER: That's the decision: to save everything here and only here, and to put the last man into action—that's our duty.

Second Situation Report,
April 25, 1945

HITLER: There's a formal denial from TASS, which implies that the demarcation line is definitely fixed. [—] I've thought about the situation in East Asia. If the Americans have any interest in winning something from this war now, then the war must prove useful for them in some way. It can only be useful if they

1. Destroy as much as possible in Europe. European industry will then need the next ten years to build itself back up again, and won't provide any competition during that time.

2. America must maintain East Asia as a permanent market. And the Americans are now supposed to fight so that the Dutch and British colonies will become free—only so that the others can make deals and the Soviets can sit in China and Manchuria. [—] It's all madness! The Americans can calculate, too. The change that has taken place now is a far-reaching change of regime.[5] [—] If the thing comes to a halt here, what will the result be? The result will be, under the precondition that we really persist and that we really strike the Russian and give him a blow somewhere and don't collapse—the result will be that the Americans will say, "We want to concentrate on East Asia and secure ourselves a gigantic, lasting market in this enormous area of half a billion people, including Korea, the Philippines, and Manchuria."

GOEBBELS: It's a political development that is striking, but which needs an external impulse to become virulent—like the Great War, for example. They themselves admit that the enemy coalition is ready to break. They talk of the Third World War, etc. The notion of a Third World War is a set formulation of the Anglo-American press. The death of Roosevelt was one of the impulses, but that still wasn't sufficient. If a second impulse comes along here—if Germany proves somewhere that it's capable of action—then that could be the second impulse needed to break up this hostile coalition.

HITLER: It could happen that the isolationists say: American boys can only fight for American interests. Why should the Americans die for non-American purposes? In all those countries there's no democracy at all—for example, Romania, Bulgaria, Finland. The Americans could withdraw here and throw themselves against East Asia alone, thereby binding the Russian here at the same time—because they would free us—so that the Russian can't engage himself so much in East Asia.

Friday, April 27, 1945

Soviet soldiers cut the Reich capital off from its last connections with the outside world; they occupy the airports of Tempelhof and Gatow. Now Berlin can no longer be supplied by air either. On both sides of the Hohenzollerndamm, after strong artillery preparation, the offensive against the city center begins at five o'clock in the morning. Soviet units encircle Potsdam and occupy Spandau; they fight in the Schöneberg and Kreuzberg districts. In Mariendorf the occupation power sets up the first mayor's office. Soviet war reporter Guss observes on this day: "The Germans run from one street to another: they search for underground storehouses and pull out women's handbags, hats, gloves…The 'master race' covers huge distances on foot in order to loot." The center of the battles in the northwest of the Reich is at Bremen. In southern Germany, the Americans push against the Danube line at Deggendorf and march into the northern part of Ulm. The Soviets take Pillau (East Prussia), break through to the west at Prenzlau, and push forward to the Lychen-Templin line. On this day it is revealed that Reichsführer SS Heinrich Himmler had offered the Western Allies surrender negotiations through the Swedish Count Folke Bernadotte. Berlin defender Weidling states, "The moment had come to settle the bill for the sins of the past years."

Present (April 27):

Adolf Hitler

Joseph Goebbels, Reich Propaganda Minister and Reich Defense Commissioner

Arthur Axmann, Reich Youth Leader

General Hans Krebs, Provisional Chief of the Army General Staff

General Helmuth Weidling, Commanding Officer of the Berlin Defense Area

SS Brigadeführer and Major General of the Waffen SS Wilhelm Mohnke, combat commander of the Berlin government quarter "Zitadelle"

Colonel Nikolaus von Below, Hitler's adjutant (Luftwaffe)

Vice Admiral Hans-Erich Voss, Representative of the Commander-in-Chief of the Navy in the Führer Headquarters

KREBS: Brünn is lost. [—] Schörner is now starting to advance in a northerly direction.[6] Strong attack against the Ninth Army from the south by the Russian 28th Army, which had been pulled out of East Prussia.

HITLER: The best relief for that would be the thrust by Schörner now.

KREBS: Wenck has reached the southern corner of the Schwielowsee. The Potsdam Defense Area wants to create a bridgehead at Caputh. Very strong attacks against the southern group of the Ninth Army [General Busse]. The enemy broke through and turned in to the east. We reached Müggendorf in an attack to the west, but we're being attacked in the deep flank by the enemy. Serious supply difficulties, no fuel. Fuel will be brought in today by the Sixth Air Fleet. Stronger enemy attack from the northeast and east.

HITLER: I don't understand the direction of the attack. He [General Busse] is pushing into completely empty space.

KREBS: The freedom to move has diminished considerably.

HITLER: He's pushing into the void. If he had pushed forward to the northwest and had reached the same as now, then he would be considerably further west now.

GOEBBELS: The Gau just reported that Group Wenck has linked up with the Potsdam bridgehead.

HITLER: If an energetic thrust really does take place here, this whole thing here will come into motion, because the enemy has only rear units here.

KREBS: No further enemy progress toward the west. Keitel reports that Group Holste has won ground with weaker assault groups at Nauen and Kremmen, and that these groups will be reinforced by units from the 199th [Infantry] Division.[7]

HITLER: It is getting very urgent that they start.

KREBS: If that were to happen, the prospect of establishing a connection would certainly be possible.

HITLER: I repeat once again how much better the Ninth Army would have been able to operate. The connection between Wenck and the Ninth Army would already have been established by now.

KREBS: It's very unpleasant in the Third Panzer Army's sector. Relatively thin front lines have been penetrated in depth at Prenzlau. It has been ordered that a new line be formed and defended. No reports about Stettin. The enemy has set foot on the island across from Kammin. No change along the Elbe.

HITLER: It almost supports the idea that they have a demarcation line. They're not appearing in the air either.

KREBS: Wenck has three divisions: Körner, Hutten, and Scharnhorst. He's pulling additional forces in behind him. Report from Wenck: "The significance of the task is understood. Proceeding with all forces against ordered objectives." [—] By tomorrow morning considerable reinforcement should have arrived in the northwest. The last units of the 7th Panzer Division, the Schlageter division, and some units of the 199th Division, of which the first units supposedly already arrived in Kyritz yesterday, without a regiment. General Holste will command that then. [—] In Wannsee the 20th Panzer Grenadier Division is holding. No new reports from Gatow, but it probably held. The bridges are being held. The connection has been interrupted.

HITLER: If Wenck really comes up, he'll immediately connect with the Wannsee group.

KREBS: If that happens tomorrow, the group could face the enemy with 40 tanks and assault guns.

HITLER: The thrust to the Schwielowsee should take effect soon.

KREBS: In Berlin the enemy has advanced far to the north. He supposedly pushed forward across Bülowstrasse up to the corner of Lützowstrasse. On the bridge at the Halleschen Tor there are supposedly two enemy tanks on fire. Three companies that made the counterattack are encircled at Moritzplatz. Jannowitz Bridge is unchanged. The enemy came closer to Alexanderplatz. In general, it held in the northeast. Unpleasant penetration at the Humboldthain railway station. Flak towers encircled here. Back-and-forth battles at the western harbor. The enemy supposedly drove around with assault boats. Supposedly enemy tanks north of the Witzleben railway station. A panzer thrust is in progress against it. In the Grunewald, the Reich Labor Service is holding out with assault guns and is connected with the right and left. The bridges of Pichelsdorf and Stössensee are holding. The enemy advanced at the Ruhleben Race Track but was stopped to the south.

HITLER: A city of millions can't be occupied by 400 tanks. That will crumble.

KREBS: In general, it has been confirmed that the intention of the enemy in the past six days must have been the following:

1. Encirclement in general;
2. Isolation in small parts, which succeeded in the west;

3. Now he will push against Potsdamer Platz, Alexanderplatz, and the Charlottenburg railway station, in order to try to divide the city center into individual parts.

HITLER: We must hold a number of assault guns ready here in the middle, as a central reserve. [—] The only thing crippling us is the fact that we don't know exactly what's happening and that we don't have precise data and are dependent on chance news. We have to push again and again.

BELOW: Air supply should start now with the help of He 111s and Ju 87s. At […] the Jus should come with the rest of the SS battalion and the units of Navy soldiers.

VOSS: The Luftwaffe must free at least one airfieldwhere we can fly the people in. But without an airfield it's bad. One hundred men are coming in on the east-west axis today for your personal protection. Those are fellows who will help us here. If Wenck frees the Gatow airfield, then there's no problem at all.

HITLER: The decisive thing is the attack from north to south, and now also from the northwest. We have to tackle it from all sides so we can achieve a success somewhere again.

KREBS: It looks like the Russian didn't send such strong forces against the Elbe as was first assumed. Perhaps he turned in because he hoped to be able to take Berlin with weaker forces.

HITLER: If the thing goes well here—if action is taken from all sides, and if everything available is committed to the operation we're planning—then it's critical that not everyone believes it necessary to still secure a rear cover for himself, as does Steiner, unfortunately. If we can hold two, three or four days here, then it's possible that Wenck's Army will arrive and possibly also Busse's army. Otherwise, it would have been better if Busse had lined up further to the north.

KREBS: A withdrawal of forces from Berlin still cannot be identified. It should have started to become noticeable against Wenck as of today—in the Grunewald area, which is very awkward for us. Wenck is moving with tremendous speed, which is also due to the fact that the enemy is relatively weak.

HITLER: And to that fact that Wenck himself is a man.

KREBS: If Holste gets it in motion in the same way, then I would consider it possible that this relief could come from the northwest and southwest and allow us to establish connections right in those locations where the enemy broke through to the west. We'll have to wait and see to what degree a relief attack materializes on the eastern front.

HITLER: If only we could get a completely accurate picture! I am very worried that Busse's Army is blocking itself off. Colonel General Hube of the First Panzer Army, for example, always kept his situation wide back then, if he was encircled. [—] Wenck can't do it either with only three divisions. That's sufficient to clear out Potsdam and to establish a connection somewhere with the forces that have come out of Berlin. But it's not sufficient to crush the Russian tank forces. But Busse has the panzer forces necessary for that. The panzers that Wenck is bringing are too few. Wenck isn't really motorized. He has three assault gun detachments with 38 T. He has two assault gun training regiments employed as infantry units. Of his three divisions, he'll need at least half to cover the south block. It depends how fast we take away the forces from the east and seal off the opponent at the place where he has to come out.

GOEBBELS: God grant that Wenck comes! I imagine a horrible situation: Wenck is near Potsdam and here the Soviets are pushing on Potsdamer Platz!

HITLER: And I'm not in Potsdam, but at Potsdamer Platz! The only thing that makes me nervous in all this tension is the fact that we want to do something and can't do anything after all. I can't sleep anymore; if I ever really fall asleep, then comes the bombing. [—] The decisive thing is that someone who attacks first and then gets slower and slower doesn't advance! The one who advances is the one who attacks with concentrated power and starts attacking immediately like an idiot. It's a question of disposition.

VOSS: Wenck is coming, my Führer! The only question is if he can manage it alone.

HITLER: You have to imagine. That will spread through Berlin like wildfire when it is said, "A German army broke in from the west and made connection with the fortress." The Russian won't be able do anything but throw in new things again and again in an attempt to hold his widely scattered positions. There will be a first-rate focal point here. The Russian has used up much of his strength crossing the Oder, especially the northern army group. Second, he's using up a large number forces in the house-to-house combat. If up to 50 T 34 or Stalin [tanks] are knocked out every day, then in ten days that's 500 to 600 tanks destroyed. [—] Today I will lie down a bit more at ease, and I only want to be awakened if a Russian tank is standing in front of my room, so I have time to make my preparations. [—] With all this back and forth, there's no other possible way we can cause the opponent real damage other than by the method we're using. We had to hold Berlin because here the Russian can be forced to bleed to death. What else is supposed to stop the Russian if he can even march straight through here? [—] Richelieu once said, "Give me five lines written by a man! What have I lost! Dearest memories!" But what does that all mean? Eventually you have to leave it all behind anyway.

Second Situation Report
April 27, 1945

MOHNKE: Four enemy tanks and two Czech tanks advanced to the Wilhelmplatz. They were knocked out by tank destroyer troops. The tanks had Swastika pennants. We captured the crew of one tank.

HITLER: The identification order must be scrupulously maintained.

MOHNKE: The main battle line still runs across the Moritzplatz. The battalion at the Moritzplatz has been fought free again. Behind the block we want to form small intervention forces everywhere, so that if any penetration should occur, they can eliminate it again in a counterattack. I've brought 10.5-cm light field howitzers into position at the Gendarmenmarkt, aimed in the direction of the Belle-Alliance-Platz, and to the Pariser Platz, aimed in the direction of the Unter-Den-Linden-Palace, also in Leipziger Strasse, aimed in the direction of the Spittelmarkt. Every gun has twelve rounds. As soon as these are fired, the crews will fight like infantry. The enemy firing has decreased somewhat for the moment. An 8.8-cm self-propelled gun came back from Adolf-Hitler-Platz. It stayed there until 14:00 and didn't see a single enemy tank.

GOEBBELS: The Soviets really are motorized robot people. A deadly danger! [—] If the western harbor is lost, we still have individual supply stores in the subway tunnels. The western harbor was the last major reserve. During the last few days, we brought materiel out of the western harbor under artillery fire. But there are 24 tons of grain stored there.

HITLER: By assaulting a city of 4.5 million, the Russian has brought a colossal load upon himself. How many wounded do we have every day?

GOEBBELS: We have 9,000 wounded in the hospitals; so maybe 1,500 wounded every day. [—] If relief actually comes to Berlin, then the supply won't create huge difficulties for us. Because the Russian won't be in a position to transport away such huge amounts in a few days. The supply in Berlin is sufficient for ten weeks. The Russian can't devour in four days what three million are supposed to eat up in ten weeks.

HITLER: If I were ever to be in a position to build government buildings again, then I might equip them with appropriate precautionary measures.

GOEBBELS: I believe every one of us resolved some things for his life.

MOHNKE: What we wanted in 1933 we have not completely achieved, my Führer!

HITLER: You know, I said recently, "It might have been better if I had waited another year to a year and a half."

GOEBBELS: In 1932 you only wanted to come to power as Reich president.

HITLER: I said at that time. The time has not come yet, because I had the conviction that if such a total revolution comes, everything else will be completely ruined. If someone is still there, there's always someone else in the background—for example, Hugenberg or Schleicher.[8] If I had waited still longer, the death of Reich President Hindenburg would have come. He would have died half a year earlier because I would have upset him so much in the opposition. If anyone was called to be German Reich president, it was I…. Then I could have stepped in without being hindered by anything. If you don't settle such accounts immediately, you become sympathetic and don't settle them at all.

GOEBBELS: That happened because you had to make a number of personnel compromises. If, for example, you had received power as Reich president, then you would never have made Admiral Levetzow police president of Berlin. The fact that such a huge number of elements came from abroad at that time can be traced back to the fact that we had such idiots as police presidents.

HITLER: I had to work my way through from one compromise to the next. That lasted until Hindenburg's death. I had intended beforehand to ruthlessly call to account people like Colonel General Hammerstein, Schleicher and others, and the whole bunch around that scum. But after a year and a half, this resolve gradually became weaker. The big building-up work came. Otherwise thousands would have been eliminated at that time. In the meantime, they were assimilated.

GOEBBELS: I know how back in March [1933] so many of these "March casualties" got into the party. There was real fury about that at the time. When we didn't want to accept those elements then, we were asked if we didn't want reconciliation. It would have been better to close the party and say: no one else can join anymore.

HITLER: We could have done that if I had come to power by an explicit act of popular will or by a coup d'état. We regret afterward that we're so good.

GOEBBELS: All the Austrian Gauleiters also said at that time that the revolution had a cosmetic defect. It would have been better if Vienna had resisted [in 1938 during the Anschluss of Austria to the Reich] and we could have destroyed everything.

MOHNKE: Those are two examples: 1933 and 1938. And if it goes well now, my Führer, we shall not let this hour pass by again.

HITLER: That's also why I'm staying here, so that I have a bit more moral right to take action against weakness. Otherwise I wouldn't have the moral right. I can't keep threatening others if I myself run away from the Reich capital in the critical hour. We have to introduce certain codes of honor into the entire Armed Forces. A basic principle that the Navy has always followed must be brought into the party and must apply to every individual: in this city I've had the right to give orders; now I must also obey the orders of fate. Even if I could save myself, I won't do it. A captain also goes down with his ship.

VOSS: Here in the Reich chancellery it's just the same as on the bridge of a ship. One thing is true for everyone. We don't want to go away either. We belong together. It's just important that we are a decent community. The people who are together with us must be decent fellows.

HITLER: It is possible to educate people to have an attitude like that. It's not true that the Japanese are supposed to be better soldiers then we are. They're just better educated. If we hear today that the Americans captured a total of seven Japanese officers who were all seriously wounded, and that all seven committed hara-kiri immediately after their capture, then you can see what kind of heroism can be created through systematic education.

KREBS: I told Jodl that we have only 24 to 26 hours; by then the link up between the armies of Wenck and Busse must be completed. Assuming, of course, that we succeed in receiving the announced transmissions this evening. [—] The situation with the Third Panzer Army is considered serious. Keitel wanted to turn in from the south to the north. I said that was impossible. We first have to free Berlin. I said that the enemy attacks must be parried, of course. Grand Admiral Dönitz is with Keitel today. Everything seems to be coming together so that the Navy forces can be flown in to Berlin. In the northwestern area a stronger panzer group is to be formed, whose task it is to work toward Wenck's Army.

HITLER: I have two concerns. We no longer have any oil areas. As long as we had them, anything could be done. The two oil areas in Austria provided us with a total of 120,000 tons. That could be increased to 180,000 tons. That is catastrophic because it makes large-scale operations impossible. Once I finish this thing here, we'll have to make sure that we get the oil areas back again. The others are fighting using oil areas that are far away across the oceans. We have them right in front of our gates.

Third Situation Report
April 27, 1945

KREBS: In contrast to yesterday evening, a consolidation of the situation and an absolutely cohesive front can be identified. Overall picture: primary pressure right now from the east and north. Relatively stable in the southwest. To that extent, a different picture from yesterday. That could be associated with the fact that the enemy has achieved his aim—to close off—here. But it could also be related to the withdrawal of forces to the southwest. [—] Regarding the situation in detail: Situation of the Reich Sports Field unclear. Smaller German groups are still holding without connection to each other. South of Pichelsdorf Bridge, a larger bridgehead is being held. Individual vehicles came through from there to here. Cohesive front along Bismarckstrasse, including the radio tower and the Grunewald quarter, where the Reich Labor Service, under the command of General Labor Leader Decker, is particularly distinguishing itself. Only a very thin communication line to Bülowstrasse via the Wilmersdorf railway station and the ring railway to the Schöneberg station. The enemy penetration up to the corner of Lützowstrasse no longer exists. There's a penetration in the direction of Spittelmarkt that has not been cleared. The eastern front has held despite the heaviest pressure now. The battle for Friedrichshain has been influenced especially positively by the commander of the anti-aircraft artillery, who is supporting the land battle extraordinarily well from the flak tower. This front has already held like this for several days. Pressure against the Wedding railway station driven back. The details of the situation in the western harbor are unclear; part of it is still in our hands.

AXMANN: The bridgehead south of Pichelsdorf Bridge was strengthened by a company. Attack on Heerstrasse driven back.

KREBS: The Russian will probably come with his main pressure from the east, north and south now. We have to expect an attempt at a surprise breakthrough from various sides tonight, especially if the enemy assesses the threat from the southwest as stronger.

AXMANN: The Russians are in the Charlottenburg Palace as well now.

MOHNKE: Individual Russian snipers appeared at Potsdamer Platz.

HITLER: The shafts of the subway and city trains are a danger.

KREBS: We assume that the connection has been made at Schwielowsee. The connection with Potsdam has been interrupted. In Wannsee a combat group is holding the bridgehead. The Gatow airfield is still in our hands. Fighting with tanks for barracks north of the airfield.

HITLER: The catastrophic mistake of the Ninth Army was to begin the attack to the west and not to the northwest. The army allowed itself to be forced away from its real objective.

KREBS: Our attacks in the northwest are continuing now. Regarding the attack by Group Steiner: The 7th Panzer Division has stepped in and the attack is underway. Plus there will be a regiment of the 199th Division, regiments of the Schlageter Division and an additional division—so a considerable numerical reinforcement. The enemy to the west hasn't concentrated to attack from the Elbe bridgehead so far. Strong pressure against Wittenberg has been identified from the east. As of tomorrow, we can expect pressure from Schörner toward the north, in the direction of Senftenberg.

HITLER: The Ninth Army did the worst thing possible. If there's no radio activity for a fairly long time, that's always the sign of a bad development. Is it possible that something could come into Berlin tonight?

VOSS: A company commander just reported from the escort company of the Grand Admiral. He fought his way through from Bernau to the Tirpitzufer [bank of the Tirpitz] in Berlin with approximately 120 men. He's in the Bendler block now and will then come here.

BELOW: The supply should have started at 21:30.

HITLER: I haven't been able to understand why the Ninth Army pulled itself into such a narrow area and why they lined up to the west and not to the northwest. It's impossible to lead if every plan that's made is changed by every army commander according to his pleasure.

KREBS: Busse probably can't move. He reported supply difficulties. He's starting to attack again now. As a result, forces that otherwise could have turned against Wenck's rear will now be diverted by Busse.

HITLER: If something like that isn't done quickly, it's over. The other one always reacts faster to that. The Ninth Army was one of the best armies we still had: eleven divisions! If he had placed the main force to the northwest, he could have made the thrust. I just want to state how impossible it is to lead if every army commander or corps general does what he believes to be right without concerning himself with the overall plan. Such disobedience never existed in the party. Not following one of my orders meant, for a party leader, immediate destruction and being thrust into nothingness. It's the same with the Russians. If someone there acts against an order, then it's no different. Now, it's come to what I said about taking up an all-around defense position in the narrowest space. [—] On the entire front, only one man has proven to be a real field strategist. The one who has to endure the worst attacks has the most orderly front: Schörner. Schörner had terrible equipment; he put it in order again. With every assignment he was given, Schörner achieved excellent results. Schörner together with Wenck—that was the best team I could imagine. And Schörner, within a few weeks, made a front out of a mess—and he didn't just built it up, but filled it with a new spirit and held the front. When he left it disappeared again. It's all just a leadership problem. You can't lead with a disobedient and high-handed organization. In a company it doesn't work without obedience either. But in general this happens continuously. In contrast to that stands the fantastic achievements of individuals. [—] If you lived through these surprises again and again for twelve years, you'd find it difficult. Many can't understand my bitterness. I can't imagine that a party leader to whom I had given an order would dare to refuse to carry it out. The overall result is damaged by that, and the individual suffers again under the overall result. The bigger the individual's sphere of responsibility, the more obedience must be practiced.

GOEBBELS: Stalin introduced a mechanical obedience. With us, obedience should be more of a moral principle.

HITLER: Blomberg[9] already said to me that obedience only goes as far as the general. It was a mechanism that made it possible to avoid an action through false reports, etc., if difficulties arose. [—] We must establish a connection with the Ninth Army after all. We still have radio communication for half an hour a day. Tito and his partisans radio across the whole Balkan area with short-wave transmitters.

WEIDLING: In the southwest: the 18th Panzer Grenadier Division gave up only limited ground in mobile combat. The connection with the Hitler Youth and Reich Labor Service was established at the Westkreuz railway station. Fortunately, the Russian was stopped here to a certain degree. We've found out that some of the Russian units in the northwest were pulled out, probably due to the relief attacks from the outside. Charlottenburg Palace was lost. Western harbor still in our hands. In the northeast the main battle line held for the most part, with support from the encircled flak tower. In the east, strong attacks in which the opponent advanced to the Spittelmarkt. At the Spittelmarkt the enemy was thrown back again, but later pressed forward again. [—] Two hours ago the alert report arrived that hostile tanks were advancing across Belle-Alliance-Platz into Wilhelmstrasse. The situation was cleared again. The Grossgörschenstrasse railway station is in our hands. In the last four days, 230 enemy tanks have been knocked out; today, according to partial reports, another 40 to 50. So up to this evening, a total of 280 to 300 enemy tanks, which certainly doesn't include all enemy tanks destroyed. Today was a day of "Tatar" [frightening] reports. During this war I've kept nerves that are thick as ropes. But the kinds of reports that came in from the various sides today were terrible.

HITLER: Communists always work with false slogans. [—] I must have absolute certainty that I will not be taken out of here by some clever trick by a Russian tank. This security consists in the fact that here in the city center is a unit that's in the hands of a man who knows me personally, and who's then also a bit stronger in the end. It's not a regular unit either, but an improvisation. [—] The whole defense is a bit peculiar. A city is being held which previously gave away its entire defensive strength. One part was pushed in, not through the fault of the sector commander, but by means of enemy pressure. If I leave a central reserve in the hands of a single man, then in a few days there will simply be nothing left. [—] I had this unit placed under my command because I see in it a kind of central reserve that's there to hold the "Zitadelle." So now I keep giving away the Zitadelle crew, just like earlier the 20 battalions of the Volkssturm. It has turned out well that I receive reports from numerous places, because that gives me an accurate assessment. Either we'll stand this test or we won't stand it.

KREBS: Basis for the solution: The Mohnke Defense Area remains under the command and responsibility of Mohnke, with the exclusive assignment of protecting this main battle line against every attack. If this main battle line were to be pulled into the area of the fortress, as is the case on the southern front, then Mohnke would take over this sector and withdrawn units would be placed under his command. Mohnke's duties remain unchanged. Mohnke must report all observations from his area of command to Commanding Officer Weidling. But we would probably have to step back from the current radical division of the defense districts, since

Defense Commander Weidling must, under all circumstances, be guaranteed freedom of movement in the southwest area, in consideration of the relief attempts.

HITLER: Grand Admiral Dönitz has detached Navy soldiers for the personal protection of the Führer. They are the bravest men he has. He wants to make a certain number of them available to me. This offer comes from Dönitz himself. He'll bring them in at any cost. When I have them, it will be a certain relief for you, because it's the highest elite of a commander-in-chief of one of the branches of the Armed Forces. Of the 600,000 men in the Navy, Dönitz will give the bravest 150 men for my personal protection. The moment could come when extreme steadfastness is everything. With the calibers he's shooting now, the Russian can't destroy us. But the Russian has already announced that he's bringing in 40.6-cm guns and 37-cm mortars. It's just a problem of the speed with which he brings it in. It will take some time, but he'll do it. Then it will come to the heroic battle for a last small island. For this, only very few people can be used. Otherwise it would be a Taubenschlag [Waterloo situation]. [—] I can imagine that the few men who are then standing by me as last protection will all move in here as well, and if the relief doesn't come, we must understand: It's not a bad end to a life if one falls during the battle for the capital of one's Reich. If it were different, within a few years we would be unable to find a single musketeer who would die within the Reich for his Reich. I can't demand of anyone that he fight outside if I myself don't even want to fight in the center of the Reich. [—] The decisive thing will be that you, Weidling, try to balance out the difficulties among the various kinds of units without losing sight of the operational aims in the west and southwest. [—] We have to obtain the maximum possible from every force we have. The important thing is that we always hold back a sufficient panzer reserve for the city center. The whole defensive zone of the inner Zitadelle [Citadel] of Berlin has become larger, so the value of the troops inside is therefore less.

WEIDLING: We have to change the defensive zone according to the situation on the main battle line.

MOHNKE: No, I have to maintain the inner area.

HITLER: Two complete infantry regiments from the Grossdeutschland Division should arrive. The Navy wanted to send in 2,000 men every night for three or four days. The Luftwaffe also wanted to send some very good units. Some of them should be held back for the central reserve. A guard battalion should come from the Reichsführer SS. If I want to hold Berlin to the end, I must also have the best means here. I can't carry out the last resistance with the worst things; I need the best. For example, it's wrong that 300 Frenchmen still have to help to defend the Reich capital as well.

MOHNKE: I would like to have whatever else is flown in.

WEIDLING: We have huge difficulties because of the water shortage. That's an enormous burden on the troops. It's very important that we hold the Tiergarten.

HITLER: Who would have believed that the connection with the west would be ripped out because a well-meaning act took 7,000 to 8,000 of the best soldiers away from me? A completely thoughtless document that they gave out. We had to order: Whatever has been ordered into Berlin must come in! Everything that wants out must be caught. Fifty aircraft with one and a half tons each are announced for tonight.

BELOW: The first drops have already been reported. Landings are still expected.

HITLER: The things that have been dropped must be transported instantly to the focal points.

WEIDLING: Provisions must be improvised.

[Adolf Hitler committed suicide at 3:30 p.m. on April 30, 1945, in the bunker under the Reich Chancellery in Berlin.]

Notes

Hitler and His Generals—1942

1. No record of such a conversation has been found and it seems extremely doubtful that one took place on the date and in the manner described by Hitler. The only meetings between Hitler and Coulondre immediately before the outbreak of the war were on August 25 and 26, 1939. See Robert Coulondre, *De Staline à Hitler* (Paris: Hachette, 1950), pp. 287-292.
2. This is a reference to a speech by Lord Halifax in Atlanta, Ga., on Apr. 23, 1941; see Royal Institute of International Affairs, *Bulletin of International News*, vol. XVIII (1941), pp. 607-608.
3. General Vogl was Chairman of the German Armistice Commission in Wiesbaden.
4. In telegram No. 1468 of May 14 Abctz reported that Darlan had suggested that the German supply material for Libya be brought to the French army arsenal at Toulon and from there be shipped to the arsenal at Bizerte.
5. In French in the original.
6. For Benoist-Méchin's role at the Hitler-Darlan meeting, see Jean-Louis Aujol, *Le Procès Benoist-Méchin: Compte rendu, sténographique avec un Avant-propos et une lettre d'inculpé à son défenseur*, pp. 149 fl.

Hitler and His Generals—1942

1. Transcript number unknown—Fragment No. 8—A partially burned short-hand record, the transcription of which was only possible with gaps.
2. Aksai sector.
3. The year before, during the siege of Sevastopol', the Russians had attempted two landings in the Crimea, which were thought to be relief efforts: on December 29, 1941, at Kerch and Feodosiia, where the Kerch Peninsula was lost until May 1942, and on January 5, 1942, at Evpatoriia, where the attacking Russian forces were thrown back into the sea after a three-day fight. Later, especially during this Stalingrad winter, no Russian landings occurred.—Source: *Tippelskirch*, pp. 276 ff.
4. Probably in the western Caucasus.
5. First Panzer Army.
6. Meaning the First Panzer Army again.
7. Already at the end of 1941, Professor von Mende from the Reich Ministry for the Occupied Eastern Territories had created commissions with Turkestani and Caucasian emigrants and had given orders to search for Turkestanis and Caucasians in the prisoner-of-war camps—of whom the great majority, however, had already been "specially treated as Asians" by

the SD Einsatzcommandos. Under the code name "Bergmann units," Captain Prof. Oberländer formed units with the people who had been collected; these units were supposed to support the German forces in their home territories during the following campaign. In the spring of 1942, the Armed Forces High Command finally give permission to set up regular legions of Turkestanis, North Caucasians, Armenians, Azerbaijanis, Georgians and Volga Tatars, after military command posts had already started doing so on their own. Like all the other "Eastern troops," these units were under German commanders; however, they were also interspersed from the position of company commander down with non-commissioned officers of the concerned nationalities. These minorities from the Eastern areas always had the support of the Ministry for the East, as the ministry wished to weaken the dangerous numerical superiority of the Russian military areas. Initially, however, all attempts to use people from the Eastern nations met with stiff opposition from Hitler. But due to the developments of the war, eventually more and more of these units were set up within the Wehrmacht as well as the Waffen SS. Altogether, approximately 100,000 Caucasians were armed by 1945, of which 48,700 were in the legions and field battalions, 21,500 in building and supply units, 25,000 in German units and 7,000 in the Waffen SS and Luftwaffe.— Source: *Thornwald: Wen sie..., passim; as well as the material collected by Thornwald, which was stored in the IfZ (particularly the Caucasian Committee report of March 26, 1945); NOKW-1604 and further numerous Nbg. [Nuremberg?] documents.*

8. Cannot be identified. Colonel von Pannwitz could possibly be meant here.

9. The Armed Forces report was prepared by the Press and Propaganda Department of the Armed Forces Operations Staff, and was regularly checked by Hitler before being released for publication.

10. The 5th SS Panzer Division *Viking* (until the summer of 1942 a panzer grenadier division) was the first SS unit with European volunteers. In November 1940 the division was established—under Steiner, who would later be SS Obergruppenführer—out of the *Germania* regiment of the SS Support Division and troops from other sources. Up to half of its members were Dutch, Danish, Norwegian and Flemish. From June 1941 on, the division was deployed in the southern part of the Eastern front.—Source: *Order of Battle,* p. 389; *Hausser,* pp. 41 and 46.

11. A transcription error occurred here. There was no Army Group South at that time, as Manstein's Army Group Don was not renamed "South" until February 14, 1943. This part had been corrected in the text; originally it said, "to the south." The stenographers probably corrected it erroneously.

12. Allusion to the supposedly belated intervention (claimed by Hitler and also pursued in legal action) of a German panzer division during a Russian attack on the Romanian Third Army on November 19-20, 1942.

13. Hitler's fear of losing a great deal of materiel during a retreat was not without merit. Aside from the fact that materiel always gets lost in retreats that are not planned far in advance; this danger was considerably increased

due to motorization. Tanks and motorized vehicles that could not be driven had to be abandoned in great numbers, as they often could not be transported back. These vehicles were especially hard to replace, however, as this type of production was affected by the German war economy bottleneck. Bad weather—for example, periods of mud—considerably increased the losses. On top of that, propaganda exaggeration of German armaments had relaxed the troops' attitude toward materiel losses, which had initially been quite careful. Aside from such considerations, Hitler was also in principle opposed to backward movements—especially since he succeeded, through a draconian order, in stopping the German front from continuing its retreat from Moscow during the Russian winter of 1941-42, and probably prevented a collapse of even greater proportions. He applied this experience equally and increasingly to all situations, all seasons, and all theaters of war. In reality, however, the constantly changing assumptions and the refusal to allow any retreat—and the resulting repeated encirclement of entire armies—led to heavy losses of both men and materiel during the course of the war, not to mention the effect on morale.

14. The 16th Motorized Division supported the deep northern flank of the 1st Panzer Division in the Kalmyk steppe at Elista in the northern Caucasus.—Source: *Manstein,* p. 358.

15. The thrust of Army Group Hoth (Fourth Panzer Army and the remains of the Romanian Fourth Army) in the direction of Stalingrad. On November 24, Hitler forbade the Sixth Army from breaking out of Stalingrad, which it was already prepared to do. The following day, Field Marshal von Manstein was taken away from Leningrad and moved to the south, together with his Army Headquarters. There, the Fourth Panzer Army, the Sixth Army (which was encircled at Stalingrad), and the remains of the Romanian Third and Fourth Armies were assembled together in the newly created "Army Group Don" and placed under his command. While the General Staff was arguing with Hitler for permission for the Sixth Army to break out, Manstein put together an attack group in the area of both sides of Kotel'nikovo, 150 km south of Stalingrad, under the command of General Hoth. This group consisted—in addition to the mostly useless remains of the Romanian VII and VI Army Corps—initially only of the LVII Panzer Corps with the 6th Panzer Division brought in from France, and also the 23rd Panzer Division, which had slowly been moving there from the Caucasus since December 1. Later, the 17th Panzer Division was also added. Originally, Hoth's forces east of the Don and Hollidt's forces west of the river were supposed to lead the relief attack. The beginning of the attack was delayed, however, because of the weather—rain and a few degrees above freezing—because of the slow arrival of the 23rd [Panzer], and because of the uncertainty about the 17th Panzer Division. Because of the situation in Stalingrad, Hoth decided to line up on December 12. At the same time, according to Manstein's plan, General Hollidt was supposed to attack in a generally eastward direction from the small Chir bridgehead at Verkhne-Chirskii, turning the Russians away and holding up some of their

forces. The Sixth Army was to line up for an attack at its southern front in order to establish a connection with the Army Group Hoth, once this group had approached within 30 kilometers—to the outer defense ring—since the stores of fuel available in the Pocket wouldn't allow the tanks to operate extensively. By establishing the "corridor," the Sixth Army was supposed to receive reinforcements and supplies, allowing the ring around Stalingrad to be completely destroyed under double pressure from inside and outside. Stalingrad and the Volga position would still remain under German control. For all practical purposes, however—as Manstein and the Army General Staff acknowledged—breaking out in the direction of the relief army would have involved a direct pursuit of the Russians, and with that the abandonment of Stalingrad. Hitler would basically have to accept that, just as he had done in other cases.—Source: *Tippelskirch,* pp. 314ff.; *Manstein,* pp. 353f. and 359ff.; *Schröter,* pp. 98ff.

16.　This reference is again to the Army Group Hoth attack.

17.　At that time, Manstein often transmitted such situation assessments in short intervals via the teletypewriter, in order to emphatically state his opinion to Führer Headquarters. One such assessment, regarding the situation three days before, on December 9, 1942, was published by Manstein in his *Verlorenen Siegen,* pp. 651ff. He also described the circumstances of the reinforcement for the relief attack on Stalingrad in detail in the following text. The importance of this problem justifies the inclusion of Manstein's statement also, as a comparison:

The second question was the reinforcement of the relief forces. Reinforcement of the Fourth Panzer Army was essential after it became obvious that of the seven divisions originally promised for a relief attack by Army Detachment Hollidt, at most the XXXXVIII Panzer Corps with two divisions would be available for this purpose. It didn't require a long discussion to determine that with only two divisions (the 6th and 23rd Panzer Divisions) it would not reach Stalingrad.

There were two possibilities for reinforcement. The Army Group High Command requested again and again that Army Group A send the III Panzer Corps with its two panzer divisions, which would be out of place in the mountains anyway. This request was always refused ...

The second possibility for a timely reinforcement of the Fourth Panzer Army for its thrust toward Stalingrad consisted of the Army High Command bringing in new forces. The 17th Panzer Division, and behind it the newly established 306th Infantry Division, were approaching Army Group Don. The former could have just managed to line up against Stalingrad, because of the delay suffered by the LVII Panzer Corps at Kotelnikovo. But the Army High Command gave the order to unload the division as a reserve behind the army group's left wing, as it feared—not without good reason—that a crisis would develop in the case of a full-scale enemy attack, which seemed imminent. However, one could not have both things at the same time: success for the 4th Panzer Division and security from a crisis on the left wing of the army group—which the 17th Panzer

Division, if it joined in, would not be able to control anyway. We preferred the success of the Fourth Panzer Army, while Hitler opted for the false security that he hoped to achieve by holding back the 17th Panzer Division. As a result, the division—when Hitler finally released it, after the arrival of the 306th Division, which was following it, joined the Fourth Panzer Army too late for the first part of the relief attack. Perhaps the decisive opportunity was lost there because of this! ...

It was a race to see whether the relief troops—the Fourth Panzer Army—would succeed in holding out their hand to the Sixth Army east of the Don before the enemy forced the break-up of the relief operation. If they were successful in overrunning our weak front at the Chir or the left wing of the army group (Army Detachment Hollidt) or the right wing of Army Group B, it would open up the opportunity to cut off all the rear connections of Army Group Don and Army Group A at Rostov.

Launching and sustaining an attack operation east of the Don in the direction of Stalingrad—with the danger described above posing more and more of a threat—must have meant taking a risk that we had rarely dared to take before. I don't think Hitler recognized the real significance of the risk at that time. Otherwise, he probably would have taken more drastic steps, at least for a reinforcement of the Fourth Panzer Army, in order to bring rapid relief for the Sixth Army. Instead, everything he did, as General Zeitzler himself says, 'was always to throw a monkey-wrench in our plans.' For example, when he held the 17th Panzer Division back for decisive action in the wrong place, or released the 16th Motorized Division far too late, as was already mentioned earlier. Hitler constantly claimed that the General Staff—meaning the generals—could only 'calculate' and not risk. There is probably no better proof against this claim than the risk which the High Command of Army Group Don took when it ordered the thrust of the Fourth Panzer Army on Stalingrad, and when it held out until the very last possible moment in a situation which could have meant the destruction of the entire German southern wing ...

While east of the Don the LVII Panzer Corps, which was intended for the relief attempt, was completing its assembly around Kotelnikovo, the enemy had been attacking our front at the lower Chir, west of the Don, with heavy forces since December 10. It became obvious that the XXXXVIII Panzer Corps would not be freed from this front to move out of the Chir-Don Bridgehead and work together with the LVII Panzer Corps.

Thus, the lining up of the LVII Panzer Corps became even more urgent. After the corps had completed its discharge and assembly around Kotelnikovo—in heavy fights against strong hostile forces, which tried to break up the final linking—and had destroyed the enemy to a great extent, the corps started off for the attack in the direction of Stalingrad on December 12. Its flanks covered the Romanian VII Army Corps to the east along the Volga and the Romanian VI Army Corps to the west up to the Don. It seemed as if the attack came as a surprise to the enemy—at least he probably didn't expect it so early. At first the corps made quite good progress, but the enemy quickly brought up forces from the Stalingrad area. He didn't restrict himself to defense at all, but constantly tried to counterattack and retake the territory that had been won by our two armored divisions, or he tried to encircle parts of them with his tanks, which outnumbered ours by far. The LVII Panzer Corps succeeded again and again in destroying strong groups of enemy forces. In the course of this unpredictable battle, a key decision was not made until December 17— when the 17th Panzer Division east of the Don was finally able to join in the operation. Under constant urging from the Army Group High Command, the Army High Command had finally released the division from its unloading area behind the left wing of the army group. However, the division had quite a long march to the Don Bridge at Potemkinskaya and across, before it could attack east of the Don."—Source: *Manstein,* pp. 357ff.

18.   Army Group Hoth.
19.   The reference is to the front at the Don, which had been taken by the Italians.
20.   It was these two weak "last reserves." The leader of the Schulte brigade, mentioned frequently in the following text, could not be identified. The Führer Escort Battalion was a fully motorized Army battalion. It consisted of selected officers, non-commissioned officers and troops, and it was reinforced by tanks, assault guns, anti-tank guns and light anti-aircraft. Generally they were assigned to protect the Führer Headquarters, but in particularly critical situations, such as in this case, they were also often temporarily sent to the front.
21.   Regarding the Italian divisions on the Eastern front. The Italian divisions were named in part after provinces (for example: *Piemonte, Calabria, Sicilia, Puglie*), in part named after towns (for example: *Roma, Napoli, Como, Cremona, Pavia, Siena, Verona*), and sometimes they also had other names like *Re, Regina, Cacciatori degli Alpi, Lupi di Toscana*, etc. So the names were not synonymous with their places of origin.
22.   During the reorganization of the Italian infantry divisions from three to two infantry regiments in 1938-39, plans called for each division to be assigned two militia battalions in case of mobilization. The reference here is to the so-called Black Shirt battalions, 132 in all at the end, which had been formed by members of the "Fascist Militia," a party organization. This extension of the army divisions was actually carried out at the beginning of the war, but it did not prove effective in the least. The four militia divisions *3 Gennaio, 23 Marzo, 28 Ottobre,* and *Giovani Fascisti* were set up from the spare Black Shirt battalions and all of them were stationed in Africa. The two divisions mentioned first were destroyed during an English attack in December 1940. Both divisions—"March 3" is a mistake it must be "March 23"—were later reestablished and were transferred together with the Italian 8th Army to the Ukraine. A fifth militia division was the Armored Militia Division "M," which was set up in the spring of 1943 in Italy and which was trained by SS staff and received German materiel.

Hitler and Himmler wanted it to be a special Lifeguard unit for Fascism and particularly for Mussolini, but it was not used.—Source: *Martin, p. 70; Rintelen, p. 55.*

Hitler and His Generals—1943

1. Meaning before the start of the actual situation conference, because initially only Hitler, General Zeitzler and Lieutenant Colonel Engel were present.
2. The question was whether or not the Donets area—whose wealth of coal, in Hitler's opinion, would be of decisive importance for either the German or Soviet war effort—could be held. On January 18, Zeitzler had suggested to Hitler for the first time the possibility of evacuating the area, as there was the danger of a huge gap developing in the front between Voronezh and Voroschilovgrad after the collapse of the Hungarian Second Army, and Army Group Don was thus threatened with encirclement. In a long-distance call with Zeitzler the following day, Manstein identified timely relief from the direction of Khar'kov as a prerequisite for holding onto the Donets area. If forces for this purpose could not be freed up in time from the Armed Forces High Command theaters, from Army Groups North and Center or through new call ups at home, or if the railway systems did not permit such a rapid assembly of forces, the district could not be held, and the attempt to remain anyway—isolated on the lower Don and on the Donets—would be an operational mistake. In a teletype message to the Army High Command the day before this conference, Manstein had expressed his opinion once more: the timely defeat of the enemy northeast of Khar'kov, before the beginning of the muddy period, or—if, as unfortunately might be assumed, the forces were insufficient for that—the abandonment of at least the eastern part of the Donets region.—Source: *Manstein,* pp. 430ff.
3. The SS Panzer Corps' divisions assembled in Khar'kov to push into the rear of the enemy forces advancing on the German Donets] front. So far, however, only the General Command, the 2nd SS Panzer Division *Das Reich*, and parts of the First SS Panzer Division *Leibstandarte Adolf Hitler* had arrived. The rapid advance of the Soviets and the threat it posed to the assembly area, however, frustrated the planned concentrated counterattack by the corps.—Source: *Manstein, p. 435; Hausser, p. 82.*
4. The 13th Panzer Division belonged in principle to the First Panzer Army, whose withdrawal to Rostov, in order to strengthen the threatened Army Group Don, was finally agreed to by Hitler on January 24. But the 50th Infantry Division—which was also under the command of the First Panzer Army—could no longer make the connection as a result of this hesitation, and had to join the unit of the Seventeenth Army that was withdrawing to the Kuban. After much vacillation, Hitler then decided that the 13th Panzer Division should go with Army Group A back to the isolated Kuban bridgehead, which Hitler considered particularly important due to the Crimea's influence on the attitude of Turkey.—Source: *Manstein, p. 429.*

5.   The following discussion applies to the suggestion to pull the front back in the southern sector, thus abandoning the Donets area. Hitler had strongly emphasized the need to significantly increase German armament production, because he realized—to a certain extent—that from the beginning of 1943, American armament production would accelerate dramatically. Because the production increase seemed possible in the long term only with the help of the Donets area, extensive production programs had been planned for the region; these programs would disappear if the area were evacuated. But one has to bear in mind that the discussion refers to plans only, because in reality—and this was also indicated in a memorandum by Speer written at this time, possibly as a result of this meeting—successful economic use of the Donets area had not been achieved thus far, because the destruction was too extensive and repairs were therefore very difficult. Only in the coal mining sector were some successes achieved; however, after the ore mining and steel production did not materialize, a grotesque situation arose that—because of the great distances—the locomotives transporting the coal away were using almost as much coal as they were pulling.

6.   Meaning per battalion sector.

7.   In the context of this discussion about the clearance of the Don River's mouth and the eastern Donets basin to the Mius River—requested by Manstein in order to reinforce the west wing of Army Group Don, which was continually threatened by encirclement—Hitler refers here to the previous disagreements concerning the withdrawal of Army Group A from the Caucasus after the collapse of the southern sector of the Eastern Front. The First Panzer Army and the Seventeenth Army constituted Army Group A; the former retreated past Rostov and reinforced the defense of the Fourth Panzer Army and Army Detachment Hollidt, while the latter withdrew to the Kuban bridgehead. Although Hitler claims here to have saved Army Group v. Kleist, that is not quite in accordance with the facts, as it required several requests—and took literally until the last minute—to obtain permission from him to withdraw from the Caucasus. Thus, the last incomplete sentence is particularly unclear.—Source: *Manstein,* pp. 379ff.; *Tippelskirch,* pp. 320ff.

8.   The *Reich* Division (Second SS Panzer Division) was an SS support division, formed in 1939 from the SS support troops after the end of the Polish campaign. After the Western campaign, the division received the sobriquet *Reich,* and later *Das Reich.* The division fought under Küchler in France, was among the first German units to invade Belgrade a year later, and was deployed until March 1942 in Russia with Army Group Center. After being refitted in France, the unit was transferred again to the East and in March 1943 took part in the battles in the Ukraine (Khar'kov), after June 1944 on the invasion front, and in Hungary in 1945.—Source: *Hausser, passim; Order of Battle,* p. 337.

9.   The following discussion refers to the Russian report that Field Marshal Paulus and other generals, including v. Seydlitz and Schmidt, were captured in the southern pocket of Stalingrad.

10.   General Giraud—who had already been in German captivity during World War I, and escaped from a field hospital—on May 19, 1940, drove into the headquarters of the Ninth Army, which he had taken over, without knowing that it was already occupied by German troops. He was captured by German officers and imprisoned. Later, through his successful escape from the Königstein fortress, he added considerably to the strain of the Berlin-Vichy relations.—Source: *Aron,* p. 513 and others*; Abetz,* p. 235*; Munzinger Archive.*

11.   On January 26, the Soviets had attacked the pocket at Stalingrad—which was stretched the furthest in the north-south direction—in the middle, and finally divided it in two. After January 27 at 2 a.m., there was no further connection between the main pocket and the troops of the XI Army Corps under General of Infantry Strecker, which were pushed together around the tractor factory in the north of Stalingrad. On February 2 at 11 a.m., the Russians lined up for the final attack on the tractor factory, after the main pocket had surrendered two days before. Three hours later a German reconnaissance aircraft reported: "No further combat action in Stalingrad."—Source: *Schroter,* pp. 196 and 231ff.

12.   Arthur Schmidt; born October 25, 1895; studied architecture at Karlsruhe Technical College; 1914 war volunteer, 26th Infantry Regiment; activated and taken into the Reichswehr; 1937 Lieutenant Colonel and Ia [Operations officer], VI Army Corps; 1939 Ia, Fifth Army (after November Eighteenth Army); 1940 Colonel and Chief of the General Staff, V Army Corps; June 1942 Major General and Chief of the General Staff, Sixth Army; and January 17, 1943 Lieutenant General. Contrary to Hitler's fears, Schmidt did not cooperate with the Soviets and also did not join the National Committee later. He returned to Germany in 1955 from Soviet imprisonment.—Source: *DNB of Jan. 14, 1943; Order of Battle,* p. 620; *Das deutsche Heer,* p. 118; *Rangliste 1944-45,* p. 24; *Manstein,* p. 365; *Keilig 211/297.*

13.   Hitler's Luftwaffe Adjutant v. Below had received this letter from a relative who had been a general staff officer in a unit in Stalingrad.

14.   Friedrich Paulus; born September 23, 1890; 1911 Second Lieutenant; during World War I mostly in adjutancy and general staff; 1918 Captain, Reichswehr; 1931 Major in RWM; 1933 Lieutenant Colonel; 1934 Commander, Motor Transport Detachment, Wünsdorf; 1935 Colonel and Chief of General Staff, Armored Troops Command; 1939 Major General and Chief of Staff, Fourth Army Group (later Sixth Army); 1940 Lieutenant General and 1st Senior Quartermaster in the Army General Staff; January 1942, General of Panzer Troops and Commander-in-Chief, Sixth Army; November 30, 1942 Colonel General; and January 30, 1943 Field Marshal. On the following day capitulated in Stalingrad. Paulus declared after the execution of the July assassins that he had joined the National

Committee to Liberate Germany. He was released in November 1953 from Soviet captivity and took up residence in Dresden, where he died on February 1, 1957.—Source: *Army High Command staff files (Nbg. Dok. NOKW-141); Munzinger Archive.*

15. Walter v. Seydlitz-Kurzbach; born August 22, 1888; 1910 Second Lieutenant; 1930 Major and Adjutant to the Chief of the Army Weapons Office; 1936 Colonel and Commander, 22nd Artillery Regiment; Major General; 1940 Commander, 12th Infantry Division; 1941 Lieutenant General; spring 1942 Commander, Special Corps Demiansk; May 1942 Commanding General, LI Army Corps; and June 1942, General of Artillery. In Soviet captivity, Seydlitz became president of the German Officers' Association and vice president of the National Committee to Liberate Germany, but he refused after the dissolution of the committee to take a position in the German Soviet zone. In October 1955 he was released from captivity.— Source: *Munzinger Archive; Seemen; Order of Battle,* p. 626; *Das deutsche Heer,* p. 479; *Keilig 211/317.*

16. Hans Hube; born October 29, 1890; 1910 Second Lieutenant, 26th Infantry Regiment; lost an arm during World War I; Reichswehr; 1936 Colonel and Commander of an infantry school; October 1939 Commander, 3rd Infantry Regiment; 1940 Major General and Commander, 16th Panzer Division; 1942 General of Panzer Troops and Commanding General, XIV Panzer Corps; summer 1943 in Sicily as commander of Group Hube; and after November 1943 Commander-in-Chief, First Panzer Army in the East. On April 21, 1944, after being promoted to Colonel General and being awarded the Diamonds, Hube was killed in a fatal accident—which he himself caused—on a return flight from the Führer Headquarters (Berchtesgaden). As Commanding General of the XIV Panzer Corps Hube had left the Stalingrad pocket on December 28, 1942, in order to receive the Swords award and had reported to Hitler on this occasion about the situation in Stalingrad. He did return into the pocket, but was flown out again on January 18, 1943, in order to manage the overall supply of Stalingrad.— Source: *Schroter,* pp. 150 and 203; *Manstein,* pp. 382f. and 553; *Seemen; Munzinger Archive; Das deutsche Heer,* p. 804; *Keilig 211/145.*

17. Hitler's information agrees with the suicide statistics published in the statistical yearbooks of the German Reich (1932–1939/40). There, with surprising consistency, the following numbers are given (after 1935 including the Saar area and Austria):

1930 17,880		1935 20,928	
1931 18,625		1936 21,984	
1932 18,934		1937 22,171	
1933 18,723		1938 22,398	
1934 18,801			

18. On January 8, Lieutenant General Rokossovsky had sent Colonel General Paulus, via his representatives, a request for capitulation—which expired

on January 9 at 10 a.m.—promising the Sixth Army life and safety, return to their homeland or to any country after the end of war, normal provisions, and the preservation of their personal belongings, uniforms, badges of rank and decorations. Paulus did not reject this request immediately, but sent it to the Führer Headquarters and asked for freedom to act as he saw fit. Not until the following day was the Soviet ultimatum refused, on Hitler's orders.—Source: *Schroter,* pp. 153ff.

19. As far as it could be deciphered from the individual legible words, Hitler explained further that it must be clear to everyone and impressed upon everyone that a surrounded fortification must fight to the very end. (Note by the stenographer.)

20. These words, according to the recollection of the stenographer, probably refer to Udet, who committed suicide after he failed in his role as the general in charge of aviation production.

21. Karl Becker; born December 14, 1879; 1900 Second Lieutenant; 1908 Instructor at the Berlin-Charlottenburg Military Technical Academy; 1911 Assistant in the Artillery Experimentation Commission; 1914 Captain and Battery Chief (42-cm mortar); 1916 Head of the Ballistics Office of the Artillery Experimentation Commission in the Reichswehr: Army Weapons Office; studied at the Berlin Technical College (1922 Diploma and Doctor of Engineering; 1921 Major in Weapons and Equipment Inspection; 1930 Colonel and Head of the Ballistics and Ammunition Detachment in the Army Weapons Office; instructor and 1932 honorary professor at the University of Berlin; 1933 full professor of Defense Technology, physics and ballistics, and permanent Dean of the Defense Technology Faculty of the Berlin; October 1932 Head of Examination System in the RWM; 1933 Major General; 1934 Lieutenant General; 1936 General of Artillery; 1937 President of the Reich Research Council; and February 4, 1938 Chief of Army Weapons Office in the RKM. Becker was the first active general to be a member of the Prussian Academy of Sciences.—Source: *Berl. Borsen-Ztg. [Berliner Borsen-Zietung] of May 27, 1937; DAZ of Dec. 14, 1939 and April 9, 1940; VB of July 16, 1938 and April 12, 1940.*

22. Becker was a brilliant artillery officer who nevertheless may have been a bit too conservative in carrying out the duties of an office that demanded a great deal of organizational ability, and he may not have been quite equal to the techniques of the defense industry, which it was his task to lead. He also failed in his effort to convince Hitler to establish an operations staff to supervise the three weapons offices, which would be above the various branches of the Armed Forces. Hitler withdrew an order to this effect the same day, at the urging of industry interests that wished to maintain the fragmentation. Instead, Becker suffered the affront that, with the establishment of the Reich Ministry for Armament and Ammunition on March 17, 1940, the new Reich Minister Todt was granted the right to give orders to the Army Weapons Office as well. Added to that was a criminal affair in which the general's son was involved. Becker apparently no longer saw a way out and reached for his pistol on April 8, 1940.—Source: *(regarding*

the Army Weapons Office): Schneider, pp. 241ff.; *Mueller-Hillebrand I,* pp. 101 and 121f.; *Dornberger,* pp. 78 and 87; *Leeb, passim.*

23.   Nothing is known about Paulus being wounded. But the foreign correspondents in Berlin also heard about it that same day, February 1. The transmitter of the Sixth Army, in the GRU [Soviet intelligence service] building in Stalingrad, should have included in his last report that Paulus was heavily wounded.—Source: *NZZ of Feb. 2, 1943 (morning edition).*

24.   Hitler had made General Paulus, who had become Colonel General on December 1, 1942, a field marshal on January 30, 1943. But at the same time he reminded him by telegram to take a pistol in his hand, because—as Hitler wanted it to be understood—a German field marshal had never surrendered before. Hitler did not keep his promise in any case: not only was the promotion of Colonel General v. Kleist, Busch and Baron v. Weichs to field marshal announced that same day, on February 1, 1943, but later Hitler also promoted to field marshal Colonel General Model and Colonel General Schorner, of the Army, on April 1, 1944, and March 1, 1945, respectively, and, from the Luftwaffe, Colonel General Baron von Richthofen on February 16, 1943, and Colonel General Ritter v. Greim on April 25, 1945.

25.   Hitler was badly informed: the promotion of Colonel General Paulus to field marshal was already published, among other places, in the *Morning Mirror* of the previous day, January 31. Puttkamer was probably just an adjutant on duty at the time.

26.   Hitler means Lubyanka, the GRU [Soviet intelligence service] prison.

27.   Major in the General Staff Coelestin v. Zitzewitz (born January 11, 1907) of the Army High Command, who, as liaison officer, was already with the Sixth Army in June/July 1942, and remained, along with his own radio transmitter, in the Stalingrad pocket from November 25, 1942, to January 20, 1943, with the assignment of reporting as quickly and as extensively as possible. After his return he was ordered to report to Hitler for a presentation regarding the question of flying out specialists. Thus, Zitzewitz belonged to the first "pocket flyers" of the Army High Command, who then were called into action more and more frequently later, also to encourage encircled troop leaders.—Source: *Schroter,* pp. 190ff.; *Manstein,* p. 389.

28.   The reference is to a Captain Adam, a son of the former head of the Troop Office [Truppenamt], General of Infantry Wilhelm Adam, who, as an orderly officer, led his division back brilliantly after the loss of the men at the front.

29.   In the old Army at the time of the Kaiser, the next generation of general staff came from voluntary applications. Seeckt, on the contrary, in 1921, after the founding of the Reichswehr, extended the selection principle across the widest base: every officer now had to undergo, during his years as First Lieutenant—i.e., after about ten years of service as an officer—a so-called "Regional Army Examination" (later: "academy examination"), which lasted for a week and took place at the headquarters of the military district [*Wehrkreis*]. This examination determined the officers' suitability

for general staff education, which then consisted of a three-year (temporarily only two-year) visit to the Berlin War Academy, that included approximately 100 to 150 officers per year group. Approximately one-third of the participants were considered suitable for general staff service, which translated to about 5 per cent of a whole officers' age group. Some of these men went into the departments of the Army General Staff, or served as Ic's [intelligence officers] or transport commanders for the general commands, but most were Ib's in the divisions. Those who did not pass the academy examinations still had the opportunity for a career in a ministry or in the higher adjutancy, or as a tactics instructor at a war school. After 1937, a small number of older officers without the military district examination were sent to the academy at the suggestion of their commanders. And finally, during the war, general staff candidates were recruited straight from the troops—also without the examination—after success at the front or through selection by their superiors.—Source: *Teske,* pp. 35ff.; *Erfurth: Generalstab,* pp. 124ff.

30.   The correct name could not be determined.

31.   Hitler's happiness came too soon. But he was not the only one who did not realize that the commander of the Romanian 6th Infantry Division did not die in the Don bend, but, on the contrary, had been captured by the Soviets. Lieutenant General Mihal Lascar was the first foreigner to whom Hitler gave the Oak Leaves, on November 26, 1942. (Then followed: Lieutenant General Muños Grande, Grand Admiral Yamamoto, Major General Teodorini, Colonel General Dimitrescu, Major General Dumitrache, Grand Admiral Koga, Colonel General Lakatos, Marshal Baron v. Mannerheim and SS Sturmbannführer Leon Degrelle.) The Oak Leaves recipient Lascar reappeared at the end of 1943 at Special Camp 20, in Planernaia, near Moscow, as a member of the Communist Romanian Legion and rose to be Romanian Minister of Defense in Groza's second cabinet, from November 1946 to December 1947.—Source: *Manstein,* p. 276; *Schröter,* p. 49; *Puttkamer,* p. 58; *Seemen,* p. 49 (incomplete) and pp. 281f.; *Keesings Archive 1946-47,* p. 937.

32.   Not until a year and a half later, after the execution of the July conspirators and after he had joined the National Committee to Liberate Germany, did Paulus speak via the Moscow radio station—on August 13, 1944.—Source: *NZZ of Aug. 14, 1944 (evening edition).*

33.   According to the recollection of a participant at the meeting, this and the earlier reference to the "proud, beautiful woman" concerned one of Göring's secretaries. She committed suicide after an unjust accusation by the Reichsmarshal, and received as a reward for her heroic attitude a state funeral.

34.   Erwin Jaenecke; born April 22, 1890; 1912 Second Lieutenant, 12th Engineer Battalion; taken into the Reichswehr as a cavalry captain; 1936 Colonel; November 1938 Chief of Staff at the Inspectorate of Fortifications; 1939 Major General and Senior Quartermaster, Eighth Army and Commander-in-Chief, East; July 1940 Senior Quartermaster, West; 1941

Lieutenant General; February 1942 Commander, 389th Infantry Division; November 1942 General of Engineers and Commanding General, IV Army Corps (on January 27, 1943, flown out of Stalingrad); April 1943 Commanding General, LXXXVI Army Corps; June 1943 Commander (October Commander-in-Chief), Seventeenth Army; February 1, 1944, Colonel General; May 1, 1944, Führer Reserves; and January 31, 1945, honorable discharge. While in Soviet captivity, Jaenecke was sentenced to 25 years' imprisonment; he was released in October 1955.—Source: *Army High Command staff files (Nbg. Dok. NOKW-141); Munzinger Archive; Keilig 211/150.*

35.   Hitler assumed correctly. Seydlitz had been with Paulus in the southern pocket.

36.   Otto Förster; born March 16, 1885; 1904 Second Lieutenant, Guard Engineer Battalion; in World War I company commander and General Staff officer; Reichswehr; 1929 Lieutenant Colonel and Commander, 4th Engineer Battalion; 1932 Colonel; 1933-1938 Inspectorate of Engineers and Fortifications (5th Inspectorate); 1934 Major General; 1937 Lieutenant General; April 1938 General of Engineers; and end of 1938 Commanding General, VI Army Corps (Münster). Förster had led this corps in various campaigns until he was suddenly relieved of his command by the Army Commander-in-Chief, Colonel General Strauss, on December 30, 1941, in Staritsa (in the Rzhev area), on Hitler's order. Without bidding farewell to his troops, he was to turn over his responsibilities immediately to his successor, Air General v. Richthofen. The Armed Forces Honor Court initiated investigations into the allegation against Förster—that he had arbitrarily given withdrawal orders. However, with the help of his corps war diary, he was able to prove that this accusation was unfounded, and that he had only recommended such a withdrawal in a situation analysis—which was passed on without his knowledge to Hitler—because the position in his sector had become untenable. The case was dismissed, but Förster received no new assignment; he was honorably discharged in February 1944. The whole affair was related to Hitler's "cleansing action" during the winter of 1941-42, to which also Rundstedt, Guderian, Ritter v. Leeb, Hoepner and others at that time fell victim. On this occasion, of course, Hitler could not overlook Förster, who had been out of favor with him since 1938 (Hitler will again mention General Förster and his alleged failure later on).

37.   Walther Heitz; born December 8, 1878; 1899 Second Lieutenant; 1914 Captain; Reichswehr; 1930 Colonel; 1931 Commander of Königsberg; 1933 Major General; 1934 Lieutenant General; 1936 President of the Reich War Court; 1937 General of Artillery; September 1939 Military Commander of Danzig-West Prussia; and after October 1939 Commanding General, VIII Army Corps. Heitz, surrounded with his corps in the Stalingrad pocket, was separated from the main pocket into a smaller "central" pocket by a Russian advance on January 28, 1943. This pocket was the first to be forced to surrender, on January 31. Heitz—promoted that same day to Colonel General—was taken into Soviet captivity and died there in

February 1944.—Source: *DNB of Jan. 31, 1943; Munzinger Archive; Schröter*, pp. 210 and 221ff.; *Keilig 211/ 127.*

38. Meaning in the Soviet report.

39. Alexander v. Hartmann; born December 11, 1890; 1911 Second Lieutenant; Reichswehr; 1934 Lieutenant Colonel; 1937 Colonel and Commander, 37th Infantry Regiment; 1941 Major General and Commander, 71st Infantry Division; and September 1, 1942 Lieutenant General (subsequently m.W.v. January 1, 1943, General of Infantry). Hartmann died on January 25 in Stalingrad.—Source: *Keilig 211/121; Schröter*, pp. 207f.

40. The militia divisions could not be organized as new Fascist divisions before the collapse of the regime; the only exception was the "M" panzer division of the militia.

41. Reference to the battle in the Bismarck Sea, which took place March 2 to 5, 1943. U.S. B-25 bombers attacked and destroyed a supply convoy sailing from Rabaul to Lae. The convoy was made up of eight ships, and was escorted by eight destroyers under the command of Rear Admiral Kimura. Only four destroyers escaped back to Rabaul. On orders from General MacArthur, the U.S. motor torpedo boat group fired at the survivors floating in the water to prevent them from reaching the coast and reinforcing Japanese garrisons. Immediately after the Japanese attack on Pearl Harbor, the 51 U.S. submarines stationed in the Pacific Ocean launched an all-out submarine war against Japanese ships. Because of the long distance to the target and defective torpedoes (faulty ignition and controls that were too deep), initial success was rather limited. But the Americans soon improved their performance, because until late 1943 the Japanese continued to send out single unescorted ships to increase the utilization of their tonnage. The average monthly tonnage sunk was 50,000 GRT in 1942, 120,000 GRT in 1943, and 200,000 GRT in 1944. U.S. submarines sank a total of 4.9 million GRT, the U.S. Air Force 2.7 million GRT, and surface ships 0.1 million GRT. 0.8 million GRT were destroyed by mines and 0.4 million GRT sank as a result of naval accidents. 52 of 288 submarines were lost. The tonnage of the Japanese commercial fleet—6.1 million GRT at the beginning of the war—was reduced to 5 million GRT at the end of 1943, 2.8 million GRT at the end of 1944, and 1.8 million GRT (of which 1.2 million GRT were operational) at the end of the war. The construction of new ships, which was increased only in 1943 (a total of 260,000 GRT in 1942; close to 800,000 GRT in the first half of 1944), could make up barely half of the huge Japanese losses even in the best of times. The Japanese submarine force, on the other hand, was only occasionally involved in economic warfare and was used almost exclusively in combating enemy battleships, especially the terrifying aircraft carriers. All German attempts to persuade the Japanese to participate more actively in economic warfare failed—including the transfer of two German submarines to the Japanese in hopes that they would be copied.—Source: *Ruge: Seekrieg*, pp. 196, 225, 237f. and 290f.; *Rohwer: Die japanische Ubootswaffe*, passim.

42.   In the spring of 1942, the Japanese, on their way to occupying Australia, had also occupied the Island of Guadalcanar (or, more accurately, Guadalcanal), which is part of the Solomon Islands. On August 7 of that same year, the Americans landed 13,000 men there, but failed to drive the Japanese from the western part of the island. In the following period a number of naval battles were fought for supplies, the climax being two battles involving Japanese convoys on November 13 and 15, 1942. The deployment of an increasing number of U.S. battleships put a strain on Japanese supply lines, eventually forcing the garrison of 30,000 troops to be evacuated. The Japanese evacuated the final 11,700 men during the nights of February 1 and 2, 4 and 5, and 7 and 8, 1943. The retreat could indeed be considered successful, because it was superbly disguised. According to American opinion it was "the most clever evacuation in the history of naval warfare." Not until the morning of February 8, after the last Japanese had left the island (which had been hotly contested for six months), did the enemy realize that the island had been evacuated. The Americans had mistaken the evacuation transports for reinforcements.— Source: *Ruge: Seekrieg,* pp. 240 and 244ff.; *Ruge: Entscheidung,* pp. 129ff.; *Tippelskirch,* pp. 265f.; *Morison: Guadalcanal, passim.*

43.   Dr. Hans-Heinrich Dieckhoff; born December 12, 1884; joined the diplomatic service after his graduation in 1912; 1914-16 cavalry officer; 1916-18 embassy secretary in Constantinople; after being posted in Santiago and Prague, he served from 1922-26 as councilor at the Washington embassy, then later at the London embassy; 1930-36 he was head of Dept. III (England-America) of the Foreign Office; subsequently head of the Political Department; and in the winter of 1936-1937 he temporarily attended to the business of the Undersecretary of State. From March 1937, Dieckhoff served as ambassador to Washington. Because of the violent reaction of many foreign countries to the "Kristallnacht" ["Night of the Broken Crystal"], he, like many other delegation heads, was recalled and did not return to his post. Beginning in April 1943 he represented the Reich in Madrid as the successor to Moltke, and in early September 1944 he was recalled for consultations and was then relieved of his duties. Dieckhoff died in March 1952.—Source: Berliner Börsen-Zeitung *of March 25, 1937;* Frankfurter Zeitung *of April 19, 1943.*

44.   Meaning those who express such opinions. This assessment of American public opinion regarding the primary importance of the Pacific theater of operations was as correct as the above-mentioned Japanese presumption that the Americans would still give priority to the battle against Germany, as had been decided by Washington ("Arcadia") as early as the beginning of 1942 ("Germany first").

45.   Sonderführer Baron von Neurath.

46.   The underestimation of American soldiers revealed in this comment was to have fateful consequences in the battles accompanying the invasion during the summer of the following year. The American part of the landing stage

in Normandy was neglected, and the Americans eventually succeeded in breaking through in France.

47. The naiveté with which Hitler judges the American farmers (based on photographs!) could hardly be surpassed. The man who had led Germany into another world war based his judgment of opponents on these criteria!

48. A statement most likely made during a visit to the Obersalzberg in October 1937. Whether the duke (whose sympathy for Hitler's Germany is well known) actually made this or a similar remark is open to debate.

49. This comment by Hewel does not make sense at all, of course. Although Australians of German descent were the most important component of the non-British population of the country, they amounted to less than 2% of the population before World War II (approximately 90,000 out of a population of 5 million in 1925). Although the cultivation of fruits, vegetables and grain was indeed advanced by the German settlers, the superlatives used by Hewel come from the nationalistic arrogance that was widespread in those circles.—Source: *Lodewyckx, passim; Nowack,* pp. 91ff.

50. Perhaps Hitler is referring to the acerbic statement issued by TASS on March 2, 1943, in reply to the February 25 announcement by the Polish government in exile, stating that the 1939 eastern border of Poland was inviolable and irreversible. The Russian statement, accusing the Poles in London of usurpatory policy, imperialist tendencies and a friendly attitude to the Fascists, read: "Leading Soviet circles hold the view that the Polish government, by denying Ukrainians and Poles the right to unification, gives expression to its imperialist tendencies. Their claim is based on the stipulations of the Atlantic Charter, but in the Soviet view the Atlantic statutes do not contain anything that would support these claims..." Apart from this, no differences between the Western Allies and the Russians are known to have developed during the previous weeks, not even regarding Asian or Pacific issues.—Source: *NZZ of March 2, 1943* (evening edition).

51. General Hirosho Oshima, successor to Togo (who was transferred to Moscow), was promoted to head of the Japanese mission to Berlin on October 8, 1938, after having served as military attaché for four years. He disappeared in late 1939. Probably at German request, he was appointed ambassador on December 23, 1940, to succeed Kurusu, but, because of his extremely pro-German attitude he was sidelined by his government—in particular during the Japanese-U.S. negotiations in 1941, but also afterward, when he was not always informed of things that one would expect someone in his position to know. The then Undersecretary of State in the Foreign Office, Weizsäcker, noted on September 4, 1941: "Oshima was grateful for it [i.e., information on the Japanese-American talks], because his Foreign Minister has left him almost completely in the dark until now. According to him, even private information which he used to get from his Tokyo friends, bypassing the Japanese Foreign Office, has not been available since the beginning of the Russian campaign." Similar information was noted by a representative of the Foreign Office at the Army High Command, VLR v. Etzdorf, on September 22, 1941:

"Ambassador Oshima complained that he was not informed by his home country and had to get information and advice in Berlin." After the collapse of the Reich, Oshima was captured by the Allies but survived the post-war trials.—Source: *Nbg.Dok. NG-4017 and NG-5156; NZZ of May 14, 1945* (morning edition).

52.   The two Japanese super-battleships *Yamamoto* and *Musashi* were, at 63,659 tons, the heaviest units in World War II (in comparison: the *Iowa* was 45,000 tons, *Vanguard* 42,500 tons, *Bismarck* 41,700 tons, *Jean Bart* 39,000 tons). The two ships were put on keel in 1937-38, launched in 1940 and commissioned in December 1941 and August 1942. They were armed with nine 45.7-cm guns in three triple turrets (*Iowa*: nine 40.6-cm, *Vanguard*: eight 38.1-cm, *Bismarck*: eight 38-cm, *Jean Bart*: eight 38-cm guns), plus six 15.2-cm and twenty-four 12.7-cm anti-aircraft guns and 150 2.5-cm guns. In spite of their novel armor, the two battleships were hit and sunk relatively early: *Musashi* on October 24, 1944, and *Yamamoto* on April 7, 1945.—Source: *Hadeler,* passim.

53.   From the beginning of the war the Japanese had ten aircraft carriers compared to a total of seven U.S. carriers, of which only four were operating in the Pacific Ocean. The Japanese completed additional aircraft carriers during the war, but these had little impact, as Japan was unable to provide the required number of planes and, in particular, skilled crews after the losses it sustained in the Battle of Midway. Prior to Midway, the Japanese had lost their four best aircraft carriers on June 4, 1942, so that with the commissioning of the new U.S. carriers built under the "Two Ocean Navy" building program, the American superiority increased constantly from mid-1943.

54.   In the large air-naval battle near the Midway Atoll (west of the Hawaiian Islands), which was decisive for the progress of the Pacific war, the Japanese lost four carriers and one heavy cruiser due to enemy strafing. The Americans, in contrast, lost only one carrier and one destroyer. This compelled Grand Admiral Yamamoto to not attack Hawaii. Hewel's remark about "down there" probably refers to one of the battles in the waters of the Solomon Islands, as details on the complete elimination in the Bismarck Sea of the Japanese convoy headed for Lae (March 2 to 5, 1943) certainly were not available in the Führer Headquarters.—Source: *Ruge: Entscheidung,* pp. 95ff. and elsewhere; *Ruge: Seekrieg,* pp. 241ff. and elsewhere.

55.   Saburo Kurusu; born in March 1886 to an American mother; and a career diplomat from 1910. Kurusu was Japanese Ambassador to Berlin from December 1939 to December 1940 and signed the Tripartite Pact on September 27, 1940. In November 1941, he was sent to Washington to assist Ambassador Admiral Nomura in the negotiations of the peaceful settlement of the Japanese-American differences. When Kurusu, following the destruction of secret papers, handed the declaration of war to Secretary of State Hull on December 7, Pearl Harbor had already been attacked an hour earlier. Although Kurusu later claimed that he had no knowledge of

the attack, Hull believed he did. This remark by Hitler, on the other hand, backs the view that Kurusu, like Nomura (who was considered to be the main advocate of an American-Japanese understanding), was left in the dark about the true intentions of his government until the very end.— Source: *Munzinger Archive; The Memoirs of Cordell Hull II*, p. 1062; *Langer/Gleason, passim (in particular* pp. 932ff.*).*

56. The Japanese disguised their raid against Pearl Harbor, at least in part, based on German advice. For instance, briefly before the action, the Japanese ship *Taturo Maru* left for San Francisco, and the War Ministry invited officers and their ladies to an event on the evening of December 7. On the other hand, foreign radio stations had reported Japanese fleet movements as early as December 6, and British, U.S., and Dutch naval forces were alerted—showing that the attempted disguise had little effect. [NDT: Despite many disputes, most historians have concluded that President Roosevelt was not aware of the specifics of a Japanese attack, although the Pacific forces had been on the alert many times in the months leading up to December 7. It is also agreed that FDR expected and hoped for an incident that would put America at war with Germany, not Japan. See Gordon W. Prange, *At Dawn We Slept*, McGraw Hill, New York 1981.]—Source: *Feis,* passim; *Langer/Gleason, passim; Tansill, passim; Wagner, passim (see further references noted); Rohwer: Zum 15. Jahrestag...,* passim, *Nbg. Dok. NG-4396.*

57. Hitler's hopes were unfounded, as the Japanese never brought out anything spectacular in the development and production of tanks.

58. Following the shelving of operation "Sea Lion" ["Seelöwe"] and after defeat in the Battle of Britain had shown that the war against Great Britain would not end soon, Germany began in the winter of 1940-41 to try to persuade Japan to declare war against England. Beginning in February 1941, the Reich government urged Tokyo to take action against Singapore. However, after careful preparations and Matsuoka's visit to Berlin at the end of March, Wilhelmstrasse changed its course during the summer and requested in late June and early July that Tokyo launch an attack against the Soviet Union. Although Foreign Minister Matsuoka backed this plan, a different decision was reached due to the influence exerted by part of the Japanese armed forces. At the imperial conference on July 2, Japan decided not to take part in the war against the Soviet Union for the time being, but to engage instead in southward expansion, even at the risk of becoming embroiled in armed conflicts with Great Britain and the U.S.A. This decision remained unchanged despite the subsequent diplomatic moves by Wilhelmstrasse, which stuck to its guns and favored Japanese action against Vladivostok, or Singapore if need be, but certainly not what actually came about: an attack against the U.S.A. The German leadership overestimated the Japanese potential, and never lost hope in subsequent years that the Japanese would eventually fight against Russia and thus relieve the German Eastern front. However, peace between the two countries in the Far East continued until the Soviet Union declared war against Japan shortly before

the Japanese capitulation on August 8, 1945, so as to have a say in Japanese affairs.—Source: *Nbg. Dok. NG-1433, NG-1951, NG-3437/38, NG-3459, NG-3825/26, NG-4371, NG-4423/26, NG-4448/51, NG-4640, NG-4657, NG-5156, etc.; Feis,* passim (in particular pp. 213ff.); *Langner/Gleason,* passim (in particular pp. 625ff.).

59.   This is not entirely true. The first armed Japanese-Russian conflict in these border skirmishes took place as early as July and August 1938 on Lake Khasan at the Manchurian-Soviet border, where the Japanese were defeated and had to concede to the evacuation of the disputed no-man's land border strip. They also came off second-best the following year, in the battle for a 20 km-wide border strip east of Khalkhin Gol, on the border between Manchukuo and Inner Mongolia. This was almost a regular campaign, which began in May 1939 and ended with the expulsion of the Japanese from the contested area after a major Soviet attack on August 20, 1939. The War Ministry in Tokyo admitted 18,000 dead, while Moscow even spoke of the elimination of the Japanese 6th Army.—Source: *Jones,* pp. 180f. and 183f.

60.   The old armored cruiser *Izumo,* which was deployed as the flagship of the China fleet.

Hitler and His Generals — The Italian Crisis, July 26, 1943

1.   Hans Georg v. Mackensen; born January 26, 1883 (son of the future field marshal); 1902 Second Lieutenant in active service; 1911 transfer to the reserves to study law; 1919 entry into the diplomatic corps (1919 Copenhagen, 1923 Quirinal [Rome], 1926 Brussels, 1931 Madrid); 1933 envoy to Budapest; March 1937 Undersecretary of State in the Foreign Office; and after April 1938 ambassador at the Quirinal [Italy]. Mackensen was called to the Führer Headquarters on August 2, 1943, i.e., one week after this discussion. The following month, due to a difference of opinion with Hitler regarding the Italian issue, he was relieved from his post, and dismissed in January 1945. Mackensen, who married a daughter of the future Foreign Minister Baron v. Neurath in 1926, died on September 28, 1947.—Source: *Munzinger Archive.*

2.   Göring was supposed to go to Italy for Mussolini's 60th birthday on July 29.

3.   Farinacci was in fact among the initiators of the Grand Council meeting of July 24-25, 1943, but the rebels around Grandi, who had been clever enough to use him as a front, opposed him. The Grandi group wanted to end the war, while Farinacci, on the other hand, wanted to tighten Italy's conduct of war under the Duce and to cooperate more closely with Germany. Farinacci was the first leading Fascist to escape to the Reich in the following days and to report on the incidents that had taken place in Rome. He took an active part in the establishment of the Republic of Salò but was unable to reach the expected leading position because of Mussolini's return. With the title of a state minister without cabinet status,

Farinacci returned to Cremona and to the editorial staff of the *Regime Fascista*. After the collapse, he was executed by a partisan firing squad in Lombardy on April 29, 1945.—Source: *Munzinger Archive; Keesings Archive 1945*, pp. 198f.; *Goebbels Diaries (copy in IfZ archive)*, pp. 2538, 2556 and 2563ff.

4.   Vittorio Emanuele Orlando; born May 19, 1860; 1888 professor of constitutional law in Palermo; 1897 liberal member of parliament; 1903-05 Minister of Education; 1907-09 and 1914-16 Minister of Justice; and 1916-17 Minister of the Interior. In 1919 he was Italy's representative to the Paris Peace Conference and, because he was not able to completely force through Italian claims in the Adriatic, he was ousted in June 1919. Orlando initially established contact with the Fascists, but turned to the opposition in 1925 and retired from parliament in 1928. As Badoglio reported, Orlando was in fact not uninvolved in the change of the Italian regime in 1943; he had, for example, assisted in the drafting of the two proclamations by the king and Badoglio. After the war he became a senator and a member of the Constituent Assembly from June 1946 to August 1947. He died on December 1, 1952.—Source: *Badoglio*, p. 65; *Keesings Archive 1952*, p. 3761.

5.   That Sunday morning (July 25), Mussolini had continued to attend to his daily business in the office as usual, and had received the Japanese ambassador and other persons. At noon he visited, together with Galbiati, the commander of the militia, the areas of Rome that had been bombed during the air raid on July 19. The audience with the king, which had been requested by Mussolini and during which the dictator was deposed and then arrested, did not take place until 4 o'clock in the afternoon.—Source: *Rintelen*, pp. 219f.

6.   Guido Buffarini-Guidi, a friend of the Petacci family, was Undersecretary of the Interior until the "changing of the guard" on the occasion of Ciano's removal on February 6, 1943. At the meeting of the Grand Council on July 24-25, 1943, Buffarini had voted against Grandi's agenda. In the RSI government of Salò, he served as Minister of the Interior until February 23, 1945. According to statements by SD Führer Wilhelm Höttl, Buffarini was an agent of the Supreme Commander of the SS and Police in Italy, SS Obergruppenführer Karl Wolff, and unconditionally devoted to him. After his release by Mussolini, he was supposedly supported by Wolff, and in April 1945 he allegedly submitted a plan to the German security police for playing Mussolini, who was becoming uncomfortable, into the hands of the partisans. With the collapse of the regime in northern Italy, Buffarini, like Mussolini, Pavolini, Starace, Farinacci, and others, was summarily executed by the partisans on April 29, 1945. His party comrade Anfuso characterized him as the "last Italian of the Renaissance."—Source: *Keesings Archive 1943*, pp. 5823 and 6035, as well as 1945, pp. 198f.; *Ciano*, passim; *Anfuso (It.)*, p. 106; *Mellini, passim; Hagen: Die geheime Front*, pp. 468f.

7.   During the discussion in Feltre on July 19, 1943, Mussolini had intended—
      as requested by Ambrosio and others—to point out to Hitler that Italy's
      military strength had been exhausted and that his country was thus no
      longer able to continue the war. In Feltre, however, Hitler—as was his
      custom—delivered a two-hour monologue regarding the necessity of total
      war and his willingness to conduct warfare without limits. Mussolini
      returned to Rome without having dared to utter his concerns. But the
      atmosphere in Feltre was not nearly as warm as it had been during earlier
      meetings.—Source: *Rintelen,* pp. 211f.; *Westphal,* pp. 221f. [NDT: see also
      Corvaja, *Hitler and Mussolini,* pp. 295-330.]

8.   General of the Infantry Reserves Edmund Glaise v. Horstenau; born
      February 27, 1882; Austrian officer; during World War I he was, among
      other things, liaison officer between the Austro-Hungarian and German
      army commands; 1925 director of the Austrian War Archives; 1936 to 1938
      minister without portfolio in the Schuschnigg cabinet; March 1938 to
      March 1940 Vice Chancellor or Minister of the Interior under Seyss-
      Inquart; and subsequently in the Armed Forces High Command (inspector
      of the war graves). From April 12, 1941, to September 7, 1944, Glaise was
      the German deputy general in Croatia. He was in Rome, perhaps by chance,
      at the time of the Italian crisis. Glaise committed suicide in the Langwasser
      camp on July 20, 1946, when he was summoned to Nuremberg as a
      witness.—Source: *Munzinger Archive; Kiszling,* pp. 171, 211 and others.

9.   Later, Hitler became more suspicious of reconstituted Italian formations,
      not to mention the fact that there was less and less material available even
      for the German units. To the indignation of Mussolini and Graziani, his
      minister of war—who wished to have 25 divisions, including 15 panzer and
      panzer grenadier divisions—only 4 infantry divisions of the "Republican
      Fascist Army" and a few battalions of Fascist militia were eventually
      formed.

10.   After careful preparation, the SD had conducted a large-scale action against
      the Belgian Communist Party during the past few weeks. Among the
      functionaries arrested after July 6 were the Secretary General of the Belgian
      Communist Party, Xavier Relecom; the organization leader of the Belgian
      Communist Party, Joseph Leemans; the editor-in-chief of the underground
      newspaper of the Belgian Communist Party, *Drapeau Rouge,* Pierre Joyce;
      and the commander of the Armée Belge des Partisans, Jacques Grippa—
      who, incidentally, all survived the war. In addition, several members of the
      technical staff of the Communist underground press were arrested, and
      typesetting machines and paper stock were confiscated as well. Some non-
      Communist members of the Front de l'Independence also fell into the
      hands of the Germans. The SD believed at the time that it had destroyed the
      illegal Belgian Communist Party, and called upon the Belgian
      Communists—in a forged edition of *Drapeau Rouge*—to give up resistance
      in order to save the lives of their leaders. But the Belgian Communist Party
      recovered surprisingly quickly, and by August a successor to *Drapeau
      Rouge* was being published under the name *La lutte continue.*

11. The "Rote Kapelle" ["Red Orchestra"] complex has thus far not been clarified with complete reliability. This designation is understood to refer to Soviet espionage organizations acting before, during and to some degree even after World War II, but it is not clear whether there were any organizational connections between the individual actions of the "R. K.," or whether this was merely an invention of the Reich Security Head Office [RSHA]. In the narrower sense, one also refers to the Schulze-Boysen/Harnack group as "R.K." This was a circle of Communist-minded or only Bolshevik-influenced people of all kinds surrounding the First Lieutenant in the RLM Harro Schulze-Boysen, the representative in the Reich Economics Ministry, Dr. Arvid Harnack, the author Adam Kuckoff, their wives and others. This group (consisting mainly of convinced resistance fighters but in some cases also persons—like the ambassador v. Scheliha—acting out of self interest) delivered information to the USSR via agents and increasingly after June 22, 1941, by radio. At the end of August 1942, the Gestapo struck against the "R.K." The rounding up of the German organization, most of whose members were executed in Plötzensee in late 1942 and early 1943, was successful; however, because of the premature strike, the main organization in the occupied Western regions was warned in time and was able to evade the Gestapo measures.—Source: *Roeder,* passim; *Flicke,* passim; *Weisenborn,* pp. 203ff.; Numerous newspaper and magazine articles from the years 1950-52 in the *IfZ* archive.

12. The Interallied Control Commissions established under sections 203-06 of the Versailles Treaty were to control the implementation of the military provisions of the treaty. The three commissions (Army, Navy, and Luftwaffe) conducted numerous inspection visits until they were withdrawn from Germany on January 31, 1927, under the Geneva Protocol of December 12, 1926. The so-called military experts at the Berlin embassies of the Allies, who had been assigned to monitor the implementation of the "remaining points" of Germany's disarmament, left the Reich three years later.—Source: *Schwendemann; Berber; Bretton; Ströhle.*

13. From Sicily.

14. Assembling to the north of Rome.

15. Reference to the withdrawal of German troops from Sicily. Hitler's opinion, which he repeated several times here, is in strange contrast to his position during the evacuation of Stalingrad or Tunis, and might be the result of a—however temporary—lesson drawn from those two catastrophes. In addition, he probably regarded the units on Sicily, especially the 1st Parachute Division (assessed by the enemy as "one of the best German divisions"—*Order of Battle, p. 323*) and the 1st Panzer Parachute Division *Hermann Göring*, which consisted entirely of volunteers, as high-value divisions whose men were hand-picked and supposedly reflected the "fanatical" National Socialist approach that he considered so necessary. He had heard favorable estimations of these divisions' personnel, and wanted to rescue them at all costs. The following

day, however, when the first excitement had calmed down, Hitler's position
on this issue was already less strict.

16.   Less than a month later, on August 19, 1943, Jeschonnek committed
suicide in desperation over the failure of the Luftwaffe—a failure for which
he, as a successful advocate of the theory of a short-term war, was partly
responsible.

17.   In southern France.

18.   Rommel had left Wiener Neustadt already at 8 a.m. and was in Salonika at
that moment to meet Colonel General Löhr, whom he was to replace as
Commander-in-Chief of the Southeast, according to a recent decision of
Hitler's. The upheaval in Italy created a new situation, however. Shortly
after 11 p.m., Rommel, in Salonika, received a call from the Armed Forces
High Command, ordering him immediately to the Führer Headquarters,
where he arrived at noon the following day.—Source: *Rommel Papers,* p.
431.

19.   A 34th Panzer Division did not exist; Hitler must have meant either the
24th Panzer Division again or the 44th Infantry Division ("Reichs Panzer
Grenadier Division Hoch- und Deutschmeister"), which, like the 24th
Panzer Division, was transferred from France to northern Italy in August
1943.

20.   The 2nd Parachute Division in southern France.

21.   As a bridgehead near the Straits of Messina.

22.   Dino Grandi; born June 4, 1895; journalist; early Fascist; 1929-32 Foreign
Minister, then ambassador in London; 1932 member of the Fascist Grand
Council; 1937 given the title of count; July 1939 Minister of Justice; and
November 1939 President of the Fasci and Corporations [Parliament]. [—]
During this meeting of the Grand Council on July 24-25, 1943, which
Hitler described here for the most part correctly, the agenda by Grandi—
about whom Mussolini had said only a few hours before, "He is a truly
faithful man!"—was adopted by 19 votes to 7. Grandi, who emigrated to
South America, was sentenced to death *in absentia* during the proceedings
against the members of the Grand Council before a Fascist special court in
Verona in January 1944. He was acquitted by the Supreme Court in Rome
in another political trial in December 1947.—Source: *Munzinger Archive;
Westphal,* p. 211.

23.;   Giuseppe Bottai; born September 3, 1895; early Fascist; author of the
Fascist labor and economic constitution; 1926 Undersecretary of State in
the Ministry of Corporations; 1929-32 Minister of Corporations; 1935
Governor of Rome; and 1936-43 Minister of Education. Bottai voted in
favor of the Grandi resolution in the Grand Council, and was also sentenced
to death in absentia in Verona in January 1944. Bottai later joined the
French Foreign Legion and wrote several volumes of his memoirs before
retiring to Rome, where he died in 1959.

24.   This planned action, in which the members of the Badoglio government
and the royal family were to be arrested in order to reinstall the Fascist
regime, was known by the name operation "Student," after the German

parachute Colonel General. Both Kesselring and Rintelen (who were not originally supposed to be let in on the plans for this action) opposed it. Once Rintelen had given Hitler Badoglio's confirmation of loyalty on August 2, Hitler relented somewhat and halted the "Student" action, which was then never implemented.—Source: *Hagen: Unternehmen Bernhard,* pp. 129ff.; *Rintelen, pp.* 227ff.

25. Code name for the prepared movement of troops to Italy in the event of a defection on the part of the ally. Neither *Alarik* nor similar measures in the Balkan area (*Konstantin*) were implemented, as initially only the Fascist regime was overthrown in Italy while the war continued. In mid-August, when Italy's impending withdrawal from the war became more obvious, planning for the two actions resumed, now under a single code name *Achse.*

26. The following day Goebbels was also summoned to the Führer Headquarters. He and Göring were received by Hitler for a first discussion on July 27 at 10 a.m., as Hitler wanted to "check the situation with his closest assistants." That day Hitler conferred nonstop—with individual midday discussions with Göring, Goebbels, Ribbentrop, Rommel, Dönitz, Speer, Keitel and Bormann, and with as many as 35 persons attending the situation conference in the evening.—Source: *Lochner,* pp. 406-416.

27. In March 1941, after a long hesitation, Prince Regent Paul of Yugoslavia and the Zvetković government gave in to German pressure and joined the Tripartite Pact when German troops marched into Bulgaria and Hitler conceded that Yugoslavia would not be obligated to let troop transports pass through its territory. On March 27, two days after the signing of the treaty in Vienna, the former Chief of the General Staff Dusan Simović revolted against this change in Yugoslavia's policy. King Peter was declared to be of age and ascended the throne, the prince regent fled to Greece, the Zvetković government was forced to resign (some members were arrested), and all over the country—except in Croatia—anti-German demonstrations took place. Ten days later Hitler responded with military actions that soon led to the occupation of the country. [—] With the following aside, Keitel probably just wanted to indicate ironically that it was a palace revolution.

28. The Hungarians.

29. The Soviet air force had attacked Budapest on September 6, 1942. While the Soviets spoke of "extensive and continuous destruction of installations critical to the war effort," "a comprehensive bombing attack" and the occurrence of "33 large fires," the Hungarian denial claimed that only a church, a villa and a house on the outskirts of the city had been destroyed by the "random dropping of 17 bombs."—Source: *Macartney,* pp. 116 and 262; *DNB of Sept. 7, 1942.*

30. Maximilian Baron von Weichs; born November 12, 1881; 1902 Second Lieutenant; 1914 Cavalry Captain; in World War I adjutancy and General Staff positions; Reichswehr; 1923 Major; 1928 Lieutenant Colonel and Commander, 18th Cavalry Regiment; 1930 Colonel; 1933 Infantry Commander III and Major General; December 1933 Commander; 3rd

Cavalry Division; 1935 Lieutenant General and Commander, 1st Panzer Division; 1936 General of the Cavalry; 1937 Commanding General, XIII Army Corps, after October 1939 Commander-in-Chief, Second Army in the West, in the Balkans and in the East; 1940 Colonel General; July 1942 Commander-in-Chief, Army Group B in the East, February 1943 Field Marshal, and July 1943 Führer's Reserves. [—] The following month, on August 25, 1943, Weichs (instead of Rommel) took command over the entire Balkan region as Commander-in-Chief Southeast (Army Group F) until March 22, 1945. Weichs was indicted in the Nuremberg trial against the Southeastern generals, but the proceedings were halted because of the state of his health. In November 1948 he was released from prison, and he died on September 27, 1954.—Source: *Army High Command staff files (Nbg. Dok. NOKW-042); Munzinger Archive; Siegler,* p. 142.

31. Possible correction: "send down to the Balkan" down there, meaning the Balkans.

32. The issue is again the evacuation of Sicily. Available ship capacity included the French steamers captured in southern France in late 1942 and small German-Italian ships and landing craft.

33. Possibly a misunderstanding.

34. The Strait of Messina.

35. In July 1943 nearly 150,000 Italian workers were still in the Reich.

36. By the "fellow" Hitler means Leopold III; born November 3, 1901; since February 23, 1934, king of the Belgians. He had surrendered with his army on May 28, 1940, and had been in the hands of the Germans ever since. One of Leopold's sisters, Princess Marie José, had married Italian Crown Prince Umberto on January 8, 1930. [—] The Belgian king had been extremely reserved after his surrender, aside from occasional interventions in favor of his country's population with the German military commander General v. Falkenhausen, and once with Hitler himself on the occasion of a visit to Berchtesgaden. Despite his earlier consent it disturbed Hitler that the king remained in Laeken Castle near Brussels, i.e., in the middle of the country. Perhaps because he was unable to seize "relatives" [of the king], Hitler abandoned, at least for the time being, the idea of "taking this fellow away." It was not until June 6, 1944, that King Leopold was taken to Germany.—Source: *Fabre-Luce, passim; Munzinger Archive.*

37. When the Austro-Hungarian lands were distributed after World War I, the town of Fiume initially became "independent" during the already bitter border negotiations between Italy and Yugoslavia (Treaty of Rapallo, November 11, 1920)—even though the Italians had raised their claim in a way that could not be ignored (d'Annunzio's coup against Allied-occupied Fiume on September 12, 1919). However, under the agreement concluded by the two neighboring countries on January 27, 1924, it did become part of Italy. The campaign against Yugoslavia in 1941 temporarily provided the Italians with further Dalmatian acquisitions, which greatly angered the Croatians. After Italy's surrender, an administration appointed by Gauleiter Rainer of the Carinthian Gau quarreled with Croatian Undersecretary of

State Turina (who had been appointed by the "Poglavnik" Ante Pavelic) over responsibility for the town. Following World War II, not only Fiume (now Rijeka) but also the whole Istrian peninsula up to the city limits of Trieste became part of Yugoslavia.

38. On Sicily.

39. Churchill mentions a visit by the king of England to North Africa in June 1943. It is probable that the meeting at the Cairo headquarters, reported to Hitler here, took place at that time.—Source: *Churchill* IV/2 p. 456.

40. Henry Maitland Wilson (Baron of Libya and Stowlangtoft after 1946), born in 1881; at the beginning of the war, as a lieutenant general, he commanded the rifle brigade in Egypt. He contributed significantly to the conquest of Cyrenaica in 1940 and, in February 1941, became senior commander of the British troops there and military governor of the province. In 1941 he was commander-in-chief in Palestine, Transjordan and Syria, as well as Commander of the 9th Army. In 1942-43 he commanded in Persia and Iraq, and in 1943 he was commander-in-chief in the Middle East. He succeeded Eisenhower as supreme commander of the entire Mediterranean region at Christmas 1943 and commanded—having been promoted to the rank of a field marshal—the Allied landing operations on the southern French coast in August 1944.—Source: *Who's Who 1950,* p. 3025.

41. In southern France.

42. Because the events in Italy were developing much more slowly and did not result in an immediate defection, Kesselring had no cause to implement a voluntary siege like this. On the contrary, he was received—at his urgent request—by the king as well as by Badoglio the next day.—Source: *Kesselring,* pp. 231f.

43. An order that had been prepared previously and had meanwhile been adapted to the new situation in Rome.

44. The suspicions of the German leadership had been particularly aroused in the past few weeks by Roatta's proposal to divide the German forces in Italy into five counterattack reserves, each consisting of two divisions, located in Sicily and Sardinia, and in southern, central and northern Italy, respectively. In actual and strategic terms this move was justified, and had been evaluated quite positively by Rintelen and Zeitzler at the time. Roatta—unlike the head of the *Comando Supremo,* General Ambrosio— was not among the inner circle of the conspirators because (being unaware of the negotiations being conducted at the highest level) he had unsuccessfully established contact with the Allies through General Zanussi in Lisbon. Thus, it seems plausible that he did repeatedly give his sincere denial to Generals Westphal and Toussaint on the night of Italy's armistice declaration, as he confirmed on his word of honor the following night.— Source: *Kesselring,* p. 242; *Westphal,* p. 228.

45. After the surrender in Tunis, the German general at the *Comando Supremo* was ordered to form three new divisions out of the backlog of units, but only two divisions were actually drawn up. Rintelen was originally supposed to be the commanding general of this corps, but in the end he

remained in his position while General Hube, who had come to Italy recently, went to Sicily in May with his General Command XIV Panzer Corps (Hube group) and essentially served as the head of the operations under the nominal command of the Italian Sixth Army. When he took over this command, Hube was instructed by Hitler not to trust any of the Italian generals and—this was probably meant sarcastically—not to accept any invitations, in order not to be poisoned or otherwise murdered on such an occasion. So Hube was surprised when he realized that the attitude of the Italian generals introduced to him was obviously quite different from that which had been described so clearly to him at the Führer Headquarters. He expressed this in a report—presumably the one quoted here—to the Armed Forces High Command, earning himself a severe rebuke.—Source: *Rintelen,* pp. 201f.; *Kesselring,* pp. 224f.; *Tippelskirch,* pp. 362f.

46.   During the evacuation of Sicily.

47.   The reference is probably to the Allied naval unit off the north coast of Sicily.

48.   Plans to occupy the Vatican, and to kidnap the pope and bring him under secure German influence, were obvious to the National Socialist mentality, of course, and are mentioned repeatedly in the literature. Gisevius moves them to the spring of 1943, where Oster had heard about the plans and Canaris had thwarted them by giving Rome a hint. Rintelen and Abshagen, on the other hand, move these plans to the months between Mussolini's overthrow and the defection of Italy. Another source indicates that Goebbels and Ribbentrop had torpedoed the plan. Weizäcker gives an even later date. After numerous rumors and press reports, he got a hint from the Vatican as late as October 1943. Despite various efforts and explorations, however, he was unable to get a confirmation or a reliable denial of these rumors until the day the Allies entered Rome.—Source: *Gisevius,* p. 470; *Abshagen,* p. 337; *Rintelen,* p. 235; *Gilbert,* p. 71; *Weizsäcker,* pp. 362f.

49.   The reference is to Manstein and his planned relief attack, which is mentioned repeatedly above; "them" refers to the three SS divisions scheduled to be transferred to Italy.

50.   Once Goebbels had arrived at the Führer Headquarters on July 27, he was instructed by Hitler to "take care of the prince" and to keep him away from Italian affairs. The role of the Prince of Hesse did not come to an end until the surrender of his father-in-law.—Source: *Lochner,* p. 413.

51.   Italian fortifications along the passes in the Alps.

52.   Transcript number unknown (presumably 430/43)—Fragment No. 16—Because the preserved shorthand record was heavily charred, the second transcription was possible only with large gaps.

53.   The evacuation of Sicily.

54.   After the first Russian winter, Horthy had appointed Nikolaus v. Kállay the new prime minister on March 10, 1942, under the assumption that he would be the suitable man to "take steps to bring about more friendly relations with the Anglo-Saxons while preserving the foreign relations with Hitler and Germany and without aiding the Soviets." After establishing initial

contact through Polish exile circles, Kállay managed to get in direct contact with the English via Turkey in the summer of 1942. He offered to take active measures against Germany as early as 1943, provided that a way could be found to geographically link the operations of the armed forces of the two countries. On September 9, 1943, a first meeting took place between an official Hungarian representative and the English ambassador in Ankara, Sir Hugh Knatchbull-Hugessen—behind the back of the Hungarian envoy in Turkey, who was unreliable for such purposes. It can be supposed that Hitler was informed about this Hungarian-English entanglement.—Source: *Horthy*, pp. 251ff.; *Kállay*, pp. 369ff.

55. Himmler, Dönitz and Rommel, like Göring and other high-ranking Nazi personalities, were summoned to Rastenburg to discuss the events in Italy.

56. Sardinia.

57. Northern Italy.

58. In France.

59. This judgment was also confirmed many times by other unprejudiced parties. Because these divisions consisted of specially selected young people, their attitude is not surprising. This procedure of gathering together an elite in a few privileged divisions also had a negative side. The military was deprived of young conscripts, as these youth were missing when their age groups were called up. A huge number of these boys died as young soldiers; had they survived until they were somewhat older, they would have provided an outstanding new crop of non-commissioned officers and officers for the whole army.

60. Friedrich Dollmann; born February 2, 1882; 1901 Second Lieutenant; 1914 Captain; Reichswehr; 1930 Colonel; 1931 Commander, 6th Artillery Regiment; 1932 Major General and Artillery Commander, VII; 1933 Lieutenant General; 1934 Commanding General, IV Army Corps; April 1936 General of Artillery; after October 1939 Commander-in-Chief, Seventh Army on the Upper Rhine front and later in northwestern France; and July 1940 Colonel General. On June 27, 1944, during the invasion battles, Dollmann died of heart failure while at his command post.—Source: *VB of July 1, 1944; Seemen; Das deutsche Heer,* p. 144; *Rangliste 1944-45,* p. 14; *Keilig 211/67.*

61. Johannes Blaskowitz; born July 10, 1883; 1902 Second Lieutenant; 1914 Captain; in World War I company commander, battalion commander and General Staff officer; Reichswehr; 1922 Major; 1929 Colonel; 1930 Commander, 14th Infantry Regiment; 1933 inspector of the Arms schools and Lieutenant General; 1935 Commander in Military District [Wehrkreis] II; 1936 General of the Infantry; 1938 Commander-in-Chief, Third Army Group; 1939 Colonel General; in the Polish campaign, Commander-in-Chief, Eighth Army (Kutno, Warsaw); and after October 1939, Commander-in-Chief East. Blaskowitz's memorandum about the excesses of the SS in Poland was taken amiss by Hitler, to the extent that Blaskowitz was given only a reserve command in the French campaign and thus did not receive the marshal's baton. From October 1940 to May 1944 Blaskowitz

was inactive as Commander-in-Chief of the First Army in the West; he subsequently became Commander-in-Chief of Army Group G in Southern France, which, however, was disparagingly designated "Armeegruppe" [Army Group] at first. After the retreat from the mouth of the Rhone to the Vosges mountains, Blaskowitz was—supposedly at the instigation of Himmler, who hadn't forgotten his behavior in Poland, but probably also through Göring's influence—relieved again on September 20, but called back again on December 24. On January 28, 1945, Blaskowitz transferred to the northern wing of the Western front as Commander-in-Chief of Army Group H, and surrendered as Commander-in-Chief Netherlands/Fortress Holland. Blaskowitz, of all people, was accused in the Nuremberg Armed Forces High Command trial; he committed suicide on the way to his first court appearance on February 5, 1948, by jumping into the stairwell.— Source: *Army High Command staff files (Nbg. Dok. NOKW-141); Siegler,* p. 113; *Munzinger Archive.*

62. Gerd v. Rundstedt; born December 12, 1875; 1893 Second Lieutenant, 83rd Infantry Regiment; 1909 Captain in the General Staff; in World War I various positions in the General Staff; 1923 Colonel and Commander, 18th Infantry Regiment; 1927 Major General; 1929 Lieutenant General and Commander, 2nd Cavalry Division; 1932 Commander, 3rd Infantry Division and General of Infantry; 1932 to 1938 Commander-in-Chief, First Command Group (Berlin); March 1938 Colonel General; October 31, 1938 left the service; in the Polish campaign, Commander-in-Chief, Army Group South; in France, Commander-in-Chief, Army Group A and also (after October 25, 1940) Commander-in-Chief, West,; July 19, 1940 Field Marshal; in the Eastern campaign; Commander-in-Chief, Army Group South until December 3, 1941; from March 1942 to July 3, 1944 and again from early September 1944 to March 10, 1945, Commander-in-Chief West; and (until September 10, 1944) Commander-in-Chief Army Group D. Rundstedt presided over the court of honor that expelled the July assassins from the Armed Forces, and he gave the eulogy at Rommel's "state funeral." He died on February 24, 1953.—*Source: Army High Command staff files (Nbg. Dok. NOKW-141); Munzinger Archive; Blumentritt,* passim.

63. The reference is probably to the son-in-law of the KZ [concentration camp] organizer Eicke, SS Obersturmbannführer Karl Leiner, who was born June 14, 1905, later commander of the 2nd Heavy Panzer Detachment in the III SS Panzer Corps.

64. This momentary thought did not need to be considered later because the German troops marching through in the days that followed effectively occupied South Tyrol.

65. Follows as a separate transcript.

66. At this point, La Spezia was still a German submarine base, where boats of the 29th Submarine Flotilla anchored.

67. The Germans settled in Italy in the coming weeks, waiting for the Italian defection. They tried at the end of August (with two divisions) to secure La

Spezia, where the bulk of the Italian fleet was anchored, saying that this port must have particularly strong protection against a potentially hostile landing. However, the Italians saw through this game and moved other forces to La Spezia, declaring the protection of this base by their own forces to be an issue of prestige. Thus, the Italian fleet under Admiral Bergamini, fulfilling the armistice conditions, was able to put to sea during the night of September 8 from La Spezia—joined by other minor elements from Genoa, Taranto, Pola, etc.—and follow a zigzag course to Malta for internment, even though it was part of the German *Achse* (or, previously, the *Alarick*) plan to prevent the Italian units from fleeing in the case of a collapse. The German command authorities, as well as some of the Italian army officers, obviously including Bergamini himself, were misled by messages about putting to sea for an upcoming decisive battle. All in all, the British were able to intern 5 battleships, 8 cruisers, 31 destroyers and torpedo boats, 40 submarines, and numerous small craft, as well as 170,000 GRT in merchant ships. Some units were sunk by the Germans—for instance, the battleship *Roma* was destroyed by a remote-controlled glider bomb. Four warships were interned in Spain and held there until January 1945. Fifty ships were scuttled in ports under the control of the Germans or the Japanese. Only the popular "Decima MAS" midget craft combat unit— the 10th MAS Flotilla (*motoscafi anti-sommergibili*: motor torpedo boats) under the leadership of Prince Valerio Borghese—remained loyal to Mussolini. Some other shipping was taken over by the Germans, mostly after smaller sabotage actions or sinkings in shallow waters, such as the battleships *Cavour* and *Impero*, 2 aircraft carriers, 2 cruisers, and various torpedo boat and destroyer flotillas in the Ligurian Sea, the upper Adriatic and the Aegean. However, practically without the Italian crews, the smaller units (which only the Germans preferred and which only the Germans put into commission) all had to be manned by German crews. Mussolini at Saló was extremely outraged by this inglorious end to "his" fleet.—Source: *Tippelskirch*, pp. 368ff.; *Ruge: Seekrieg*, pp. 256f.; *Anfuso*, pp. 262f.; *Rintelen*, pp. 248f.; *de Belot*, pp. 226ff.; *Westphal*, pp. 226f.; *Moellhausen*, pp. 257ff.; *Trizzino*, pp. 121ff.

Hitler and His Generals—1944

1. Meaning the combat troops—the fighting troops.
2. He no doubt means "if."
3. After the loss of France, the success rate of the German submarine war in the Atlantic in fact decreased to zero in the month of October, but increased again slightly during the last months of war.
4. Tungsten is important for steel production (tools and magnetic steel) and for electrical engineering (filaments and cathodes). The most important European deposits are in Portugal and Spain, with France following at some distance. The French tungsten output was capable of significant development, as was proven by the 56-fold increase from 1938 to 1954

(from 10 tons to 560, while Portugal increased from 1,831 to 2,508 tons during that same time span).

5.   Hitler is constantly criticized by his former military colleagues for his habit of counting the theoretical number of divisions without regard to their mobility or readiness for action. This method of counting (which Hitler himself criticizes here) is seen as one of his cardinal faults. If this is justified (which can hardly be doubted, considering the multitude of statements), then this passage proves the presence of occasional lucid intervals in the mania and delusions of grandeur that have been so reliably testified to.

6.   This happened some months later in the Ardennes offensive and eventually during Operation "Bodenplatte" against enemy airfields in Belgium and northern France on January 1, 1945.

7.   Hitler is referring to the July 20 attempt on his life.

8.   The Communications Inspector, General Fellgiebel, and the Army Quartermaster General, General Wagner, belonged to the circle of the July conspiracy.

9.   Possibly Hitler meant "intelligence" also in a different sense. The military Abwehr [Intelligence Service] (Foreign Intelligence Office of the Armed Forces High Command/Armed Forces Operations Staff) under Admiral Canaris had already been disbanded by Hitler's order of February 12, 1944 regarding the creation of a unified reporting service under the overall direction of Reichsführer SS H. Himmler with Walter Schellenberg as head of the new intelligence structure. Intelligence Sections I and II, namely espionage and sabotage, were first formed as an independent Military Section in the RSHA, and the Intelligence Section III was integrated into its Section IV (Gestapo). Now, after July 20, the Military Section was integrated even more into Section VI (Foreign Security Division.)

10. With his next sentence Hitler already limits the claim again. It is, of course, totally absurd to blame the development and outcome of the war on the information given here and there to the enemy by convinced opponents of the regime. However one wishes to judge such behavior, it has been factually established that the extent and success of those actions could not have been sufficient to justify even a weak connection.

11. By the spring of 1943, a substantial portion of the military conspiracy against Hitler had already been uncovered. The Customs Investigation Office in Prague had arrested two employees of the Munich Intelligence Intelligence Office [Abwehrstelle] on account of totally private foreign exchange affairs. In the hope of clearing themselves, they gave statements regarding an anti-Nazi conspiracy in Intelligence Central [Abwehrzentrale]. On April 4, 1943, the Gestapo arrested Reich legal counsel v. Dohnányi, the closest colleague of Major General Oster, the head of the Central Section in the Foreign Intelligence Office. Oster himself, who imprudently tried to cover for Dohnányi and remove incriminating papers during a search of his office, was suspended immediately. He was removed from office at the end of the year and lived from then on under supervision in a

suburb of Leipzig. Two relatives of Dohnányi, Pastor Dietrich Bonhoeffer and Justus Delbrück, and the Munich lawyer Dr. Josef Müller were also involved in this affair and arrested. The investigations extended until July 20, 1944—on the one hand because of delaying tactics by Admiral Canaris and chief judge Dr. Sack, but on the other hand because of remarkable caution, apparent blind confidence, and a conspicuous lack of interest on the part of Himmler and his Gestapo chief Müller. To this day it remains unclear just how far into the circle of conspiracy Himmler and his people were able to follow the threads—which had fallen into their hands by accident—by July 20. It is widely acknowledged that Himmler's behavior toward the entire military conspiracy was not unequivocal.—Source: *Gisevius II,* pp. 277ff.; *Abshagen,* pp. 356ff.; *Ritter: Goerdeler,* p. 352; *Zeller,* pp. 24ff. and 142.

12. It is correct that German tanks and assault guns had been drastically improved during the war, but it is a pure untruth when Hitler speculates that the quality of the Russians' matériel had decreased. The amount of American materiel alone that went to the Soviet Union within the last few years makes this claim absurd.

13. Turkey broke off diplomatic relations two days later, on August 2.

14. Hungary leads Europe in the output of bauxite; the resources are located in the Bakony Forest, in the Vértes Mountains, and in the area south of Pecs [Fünfkirchen]. Manganese resources are mined in the Bakony Forest.

15. The "coup d'état against Mr. Horthy" was initiated on October 15, 1944, but failed due to German preventive measures.

16. He probably meant at the Strait of Dover [Pas de Calais]; Hitler moves to the West now.

17. Italy.

18. Carl Heinrich v. Stülpnagel; born January 2, 1886; 1906 Second Lieutenant, 115th Infantry Regiment; 1918 Captain in the General Staff; 1932 Colonel and Section head in the Reichswehr Ministry; 1935 Major General and division commander; 1937 Lieutenant General; 1938 Senior Quartermaster II in the Army General Staff; 1939 General of Infantry and (October) Senior Quartermaster I; June 21, 1940 Chairman of the German Armistice Commission for France; February to November 1941 Commander-in-Chief, Seventeenth Army; and February 1942 successor to his distant cousin Otto v. Stülpnagel as Military Commander in France. Stülpnagel had been taking part in the putsch plans since 1938, and became one of the most active members of the military opposition against Hitler. During the night of July 21, 1944, he successfully carried out an overthrow in Paris, eliminating the SD. After the failure of the putsch in Berlin and the refusal of the Commander-in-Chief West v. Kluge to support the mission, he had to withdraw his orders. Stülpnagel was ordered to the Führer Headquarters immediately. He attempted suicide on the way there, at Verdun; however, he only lost his eyesight. He was sentenced to death by the Public Law Court on August 30, 1944, and was executed that same day.—Source: *Zeller,* pp. 22f., 301 and 424; *Ritter: Goerdeler,* pp. 245ff.,

274 and 398ff.; *Schramm (W.), passim; Munzinger Archive; Keiling 211/333.*

19. Somme–Marne–Saône–Jura. This position [Defense Line] had already been reconnoitered by the Commander-in-Chief West in December 1943 on an order from the Armed Forces High Command or Hitler (see below p. 594). Hitler issued the written construction order for the establishment of the field positions on August 2. The speed of the Anglo-American advance in France made all efforts useless.

20. This was in fact Montgomery's plan. Eisenhower's, in contrast, called for regular attacks along a wide front, without establishing any centers, in order to "reach the Rhine along its entire run" before attacking inner Germany. The final decision was made when Eisenhower took over the immediate leadership of the ground operation on September 1, after Montgomery had explained his opinion again on August 23—now directly, but again without effect.—Source: *Wilmot,* pp. 486ff.

21. This idea of a "Special Staff" had already been implemented by Hitler during the Norwegian campaign. Now, in 1944, Jodl was able to prevent the threatened restriction of his authority by establishing a special working group within the Armed Forces Operations Staff for this assignment. Stationed in the Führer Headquarters, this group consisted of a single officer, Lieutenant Colonel Kleyser, and was a pure farce.

22. In the Black Forest, the relevant location was probably the "Tannenburg" headquarters at the Kniebis, west of Freudenstadt. The "Tannenburg" had been used from June 27 until July 1940. Like the "Felsennest" near Münstereifel in the Eifel region (which was occupied from May 10 to June 8, 1940), it was built for the Western campaign. Because of Hitler's state of health and the development of the situation in the East, the Führer Headquarters were not relocated into the West in the summer of 1944. Not until November did Hitler travel to Berlin, from where he moved on December 10 (for about a month) into the West, in order to lead his planned offensive more effectively. This time, however, he was further to the rear—toward Ziegenberg near Bad Nauheim ("Adlerhorst").

23. The establishment of the Führer Headquarters was the responsibility of Hitler's adjutancy.

24. Hitler left behind several harbors as "fortresses" in advance of the weakening front, some of which were able to hold out until the end of the war (see below note 5 on p. 686). In fact, the Allies suffered considerable supply difficulties when their armies advanced into Belgium and eastern France, because all of their supplies still had to be transported via Bayeux and Cherbourg. In October, after they had taken Dieppe and Ostende without a fight, and the "Fortresses" of Le Havre, Boulogne and Calais had been conquered, the desperate supply situation slowly improved. However, the Allies still had to deal with the lack of big dock cranes, which would have been able to unload the heavy equipment arriving directly from the United States. German troops had rendered the cranes in Cherbourg and Le Havre inoperable before the evacuation. The equipment was available only

in the Antwerp harbor, which fell into English hands almost intact on September 4, but it could not be used until the end of November because of German blockades across the mouth of the Schelde.—Source: *Wilmot,* pp. 501ff. and 578f.

25. Kluge had taken over from Rundstedt as Commander-in-Chief West (Army Group D) on July 3, and had also taken charge of Army Group B after Rommel's departure on July 17, as a takeover by SS General Hausser (suggested by Schmundt) was feared. This joint staff arrangement, which Jodl justly attacks here, remained until September. Kluge led from the headquarters of Army Group B in La Roche-Guyon, while the connection to the headquarters of the Commander-in-Chief West in St. Germain, 65 km away, was maintained by telephone calls and trips by staff officers. Model, who initially replaced Kluge on August 18 in both positions, also had to adopt this leadership technique. At the insistence of the staff, and with Model's agreement, Rundstedt returned as Commander-in-Chief West on September 5—this time to Arnberg, near Koblenz.—Source: *Blumentritt,* pp. 240ff.; *Siegler,* pp. 16 and 18; *Speidel,* p. 142.

26. Hitler had already declared on July 23 that he agreed that preparations for a possible reuse of the Western Wall should be initiated.

27. These captured Russian guns were also used in the fall to help build up the antitank defense of the Western Wall. But they were not remodeled into split-trail carriages (as happened earlier, since the old box-trail carriages of those guns had too limited traversing capability). Instead, they now received a specially constructed stationary makeshift carriage with a wider traversing capability. Authorities at that time doubted that there were 1,200-2,000 such captured guns still available and in a functional state.

28. This headquarters was one of the newer facilities. Huge complexes were also built at the Zobten in Silesia and in Ohrdruf. Like Diedenhofen, these had never been used.

29. Fegelein combines the names "Hofacker" and "Rahtgens." He meant Lieutenant Colonel of the Reserves Dr. Caesar v. Hofacker; born March 11, 1896; war volunteer; 1918 First Lieutenant and Squadron Captain; 1921-1925 studied law, various industry positions; after 1936 company secretary [Prokurist] of the United Steelworks; 1940 Luftwaffe Wing Commander; 1941 official in charge of the iron and steel industry in the military administration of France; after October 1943 on Stülpnagel's staff (although he was an officer seconded for special duty and not Chief of Staff—here he is mixed up by Fegelein again, this time with Colonel v. Linstow). Hofacker, who was a cousin of Stauffenberg, provided the connection between the Paris group of the military conspiracy and the Berlin headquarters. He stayed in Berlin for the last time from July 10 to 17, to inform Beck and Stauffenberg about his report to Rommel on July 9. The field marshal had judged the military situation in the West to be very dark, and had emphasized the necessity of concluding an immediate peace treaty detaining Hitler through an action at a central position. Hitler had returned to Rastenburg from Berchtesgaden on July 14, and it is not

impossible that Hofacker was also there on that occasion. Hofacker was arrested on July 24, sentenced to death by the Public Law Court [Volksgerichtshof] on August 30, and executed on December 20.—Source: *Leber,* pp. 259ff.; *Zeller,* pp. 190f*., 222, 233f, and others; Wheeler-Bennett,* pp. 684ff., 706ff. and 761; *Speidel,* p. 133.; *Schramm (W.),* passim.

30.   Hitler either means the large Jobourg Peninsula (Cap de la Hague) north-west of Cherbourg, where the last German bases were located until July 1, or the Cap Lévi Peninsula in front of the harbor in the east—the former location of the "Hamburg" naval battery. Furthermore, it was primarily his fault that Cherbourg was lost sooner than necessary. Although the fall of the fortress was just a question of time after the blockade of the Cotentin Peninsula (considering the increasing enemy superiority and the inadequate fortification on the land side), Hitler repeatedly ordered various advance lines to stop, making it impossible to man the fortifications adequately and in time, and thus hastening the loss of the city.—Source: *Wilmot,* pp. 338ff.; *Hayn,* pp. 41 and 59ff.

31.   Hitler is obviously referring to the breakthrough at Avranches in Brittany, which was practically complete already. There the Americans spread out from the town (which had fallen on the evening of July 30) and won a bridgehead over the Selune at Pountaubault. The next day, Army Group B received the following order from the Führer Headquarters: "The enemy must under no circumstances be allowed to operate in the open. Army Group B prepares a counterattack together with all panzer units, to break through up to Avranches, to cut off the enemy penetration and to destroy it. All available panzer units are to be pulled from their current employment without replacements...The outcome of the campaign in France depends on this attack." When Warlimont arrived at Kluge's headquarters on August 2 (see below note 1 on p. 602) and was received by the field marshal in the early hours of the following morning, he did not in fact deliver—as Wilmot said—"the order from the Führer that the front must be reestablished." At the time of Warlimont's departure from Rastenburg and thus at the time of the present conference, the temporary closure of the breach near Avranches was expected (this passage confirms that) and the staff of the Führer Headquarters were of the opinion that the war in France would continue for the time being with slowly retreating fronts—as had been the case thus far in Normandy.—Source: *Speidel,* pp. 151f.; *Wilmot,* pp. 416 and 423.

32.   Analogously: "...which could fall into the enemy's hands in the case of a breakthrough..."

33.   The commander at Cherbourg had been Lieutenant General Karl Wilhelm v. Schlieben, who, in the usual obituary in the German press, was described as the "brave defender of Cherbourg." According to a German report about those battles, Schlieben was not captured until June 26, during the house-to-house fighting in the inner city. He was captured in his subterranean bunker after having fought for many hours alongside his staff, with infantry weapons, at various bunker exits. Of course, something else was obviously stated in the foreign radio service reports, which Hitler received and to

which he no doubt refers here. The foreign press reported on an order of the day from Schlieben, which the Americans had intercepted on June 24, stating that anyone who did not continue the resistance until the end would be shot. The capture of the German commander was described in a June 27 UP report as follows: "[v. Schlieben and Rear Admiral Hennecke, the Sea Commander Normandy,] were captured when the Americans stormed the entrance of an underground fort. A German lieutenant suddenly appeared in front of the fort, waving a white flag. The officer arrived at the Allies' line and declared that v. Schlieben and Hennecke were inside the fort and were ready to surrender themselves, together with the rest of the occupying forces. A few minutes later the lieutenant returned to the fort, and both officers came out with hands raised, leading a line of more than 300 soldiers. Lieutenant General v. Schlieben, who, in an order of the day a few days before had ordered the garrison to resist until the last, was imprisoned."—Source: *Hayn,* p. 63; *Wilmot,* p. 346; *NZZ* of June 26 (morning edition) and June 28 (midday edition), 1944.

34. At Avranches, where the enemy's strategic breakthrough had not been discovered yet.

35. In 1806 the Prussian fortresses were—following the strategic considerations of those times—neglected, as they were assigned to officers who had become unfit for military field service through age or illness. Not until after the Battle at Jena was the order given to arm the fortresses—and by that time the enemy was already advancing. The moral strength of the commanders collapsed under the impact of the rapid sequence of events. Erfurt, Stettin, Küstrin, Hameln, Neinburg, Plessenburg, Spandau, Magdeburg and Danzig capitulated practically without a fight. In Silesia, Schweidnitz fell after only four days, Breslau and Glogau—heavily armed—capitulated after only 20 days, and the totally neglected Brieg fell as well. The handover of Glatz and Silberberg did not take place because of the peace treaty. Neisse was overwhelmed after 36 days of brave defense. Only three fortresses—Kosel, Graudenz and Kolberg—held up against the enemy until the end of the campaign.—Source: *Alten,* p. 541.

36. In Kluge's headquarters. Warlimont's trip was actually the unofficial reason for the present conference. His visit to Normandy (where so far, since the beginning of the invasion, only junior officers of the Armed Forces Operations Staff—up to major—had looked around), had originally been planned for the days immediately after July 20 and therefore had to be postponed. But now such a project had to be taken on with care. The matter had to be raised delicately with Hitler, as he feared that such journeys brought a defeatist influence to the front. This meeting was therefore planned by Jodl—his manner of speaking shows this—to get Hitler to give Warlimont a general overview of the situation and his opinion, and to a certain extent an oral agreement with Kluge for the discussion of the possible—as was still assumed at this hour—case of an enemy breakout from Normandy. The actual reason, the trip to the West, was then included casually in the discussion. The next day, Hitler toyed with the idea of

recalling Warlimont, who was on his way through Germany. Jodl made a note in his personal diary on August 1: "The Führer has concerns about sending Warlimont into the West. I offered to fly there myself, but the Führer does not want me to. He lets Warlimont travel ahead based on my argument that calling him back would attract attention." As Jodl reported after the end of the war, Hitler had suspected that Warlimont could discuss a new attempt on his life with Kluge. This was probably meant as a joke, as both suspects were hardly suited to revolution.

37.   General Carl Heinrich v. Stülpnagel

38.   Otto Abetz; born March 26, 1903; 1927 art teacher; 1930 founder of the "Sohlberg Circle" (German-French youth meetings); 1933 France Adviser of the Reich Youth Leadership; 1943 French expert for Ribbentrop's office; July 1939 residence prohibition in France; 1940 deputy for the Foreign Office at the Military Commander France; anf from August 1940, German ambassador based in Paris. [—] Despite numerous disagreements regarding the treatment of France and despite the judgment given here by Hitler, Abetz was not relieved until the middle of November 1944 from his position as German representative at the French government-in-exile in Sigmaringen. In 1949 he was sentenced to 20 years of forced labor by a French military tribunal, but was released in April 1954. Abetz died in an accident on May 5, 1958.—Source: *Abetz,* passim*; Munzinger Archive.*

39.   Ludwig Beck; born June 29, 1880; 1899 Second Lieutenant; after 1913 and in World War I in the General Staff; transferred into the Reichswehr as Major; 1931 Major General; 1932 Lieutenant General; October 1933 chief of the Trop Office [Truppenamt] at the Army Command; and 1935 General of Artillery and Army Chief of General Staff. In this position Beck became more and more opposed to Hitler's military policy and pursued, before the Sudetenland mission, a collective step of the generals against Hitler, but he was abandoned by Brauchitsch at the decisive moment. As a consequence, Beck handed in his resignation in August 1938 (effective October 31, 1938, with reassignment to the post of Colonel General in the reserve). He then became a central figure in the conspiracy against Hitler, which reached its climax with the July assassination attempt. After the mission's failure, General Fromm forced him to suicide, which had to be concluded by a coup de grâce.—Source: *Beck,* passim*; Foerster,* passim*; Keilig 211/18.*

40.   Maurice Gamelin; born September 20, 1872; colleague of Joffre in World War I as chief of the Operations Department in the primary French headquarters; 1925-1929 Commander-in-Chief in Syria as Weygand's successor; 1931 Army Chief of General Staff; and 1935 Army Inspector General, Vice President of the Supreme War Council, and thereby also Generalissimo in the event of war. After the French failures in the German Western campaign, Gamelin was relieved by Weygand on May 19, 1940, whose replacement so far had failed due to Daladier's resistance. Vichy France put him—without issuing a verdict—before the National Law Court in Riom. He was held by the French until April 1943, and was then in German custody afterward. In May 1945 he was freed by American troops

in Germany. Gamelin died on April 18, 1958.—Source: *Munzinger Archive.*

41. Beck had been in Paris from June 16 to 20, 1937, officially as a guest of his personal friend, the military attaché Lieutenant General Kühlenthal, and as visitor to the World Fair, and he naturally also took this opportunity to pay a courtesy visit to the leaders of the French army. In reality, however, Beck had four quite extensive talks with Gamelin during those days, and he characterized Gamelin in his official travel report as follows: "After my repeated meetings with General Gamelin, I must say that he gives me an unusually fresh, youthful impression. He is clear, military and highly educated. He says little and keeps his word. His outward behavior is also excellent." Therefore, it is correct that Gamelin impressed Beck. However, Hitler could have known of his supposed enthusiasm only second hand, as the Chief of General Staff had not given him a report on his visit to Paris.— Source: *Beck,* pp. 295ff.; *Foerster,* pp. 63ff.

42. Hitler (or his source) probably exaggerated a bit here, but back then even Kesselring was not satisfied with the development. He had visited the Apennine position at the beginning of July and had noticed some progress and satisfactory results, but considered other parts—in particular the focal point patrols [Schwerpunktstreifen]—to be "far behind."—Source: *Kesselring,* p. 297.

43. He most likely meant General Förster, who was followed by Hitler with almost pathological aversion.

44. In his *Verlorenen Siegen,* Manstein states that the Dnieper Line had initially been improved against Hitler's will, but was later described by him with great exaggeration as the "Eastern Wall." Manstein also described as a "Developed Position" the Melitopol'–Zaporozh'e Line mentioned here. The Sixth Army had withdrawn to this line at the end of September 1943, and, after a Soviet breakthrough at the end of October, the line was "taken back surprisingly quickly toward the West." When Manstein establishes this in his usual careful phrasing, one can easily imagine Hitler's indignation and his search for the guilty parties.—Source: *Manstein,* pp. 537f., 544 and 550.

45. Because there were practically no steel ties in the East, the problem of a suitable rail cutter was not that urgent until the beginning of the retreat from France. Furthermore, no special equipment was needed for steel ties, as they could be ripped out using a standard steel cable wound around the end of the tie. From the 35 possible models that were shown to Hitler in September 1943 in Arys, a reconstruction of a Soviet type was finally selected. It was mass-produced by Schwartzkopf as a "track wolf" for wooden ties.

46. A presentation of the Armed Forces Operations Staff on July 28 regarding the "combat procedure in the event of an enemy breakthrough in Normandy," which suggested to Hitler a retreat from the coastal front.

47. The 8th SS Cavalry Division "Florian Geyer" and the 22nd SS Volunteer Cavalry Division (which had just been built up using parts of the 8th SS Division).—Source: *Order of Battle,* pp. 341 and 347.

48. Damage to both eardrums and an irritation of the auditory canal were the worst effects on Hitler's health resulting from the July 20 bomb explosion. Only after a lengthy period of bed rest did those injuries heal. He also had burns on his leg, a wound on his right elbow, and a bruise on his back from a collapsed ceiling beam.—Source: *Bullock,* pp. 746 and 767; *Görlitz/Quint,* pp. 605 and 613.

49. Hitler had received the attendees of a meeting of "the men responsible for armaments and war production," called by Speer, and had spoken to them. The text of this speech was published by DNB on July 5. According to the recollection of a participant, this meeting had already taken place on June 26 in the Platterhof at the Obersalzberg. The attendees—about 100 armament experts—had been brought by special train from their meeting point at Linz to Freiburg/Berchtesgaden. Hitler had obviously given several other speeches around that time as well, which are also possibilities—for example, a speech before the generals and officers on June 22, also at the Platterhof.

50. The reference here is probably to Sonnleithner, who had joined the meeting in the meantime, though he is not included in the list of participants. Sonnleithner had taken part in the situation report on July 20, when Stauffenberg made the assassination attempt.

51. Today, physicians assume that Hitler's severe nerve problem was *paralysis agitans*, or Parkinson's Disease (not to be confused with the progressive paralysis of syphilitic origin), a degenerative disease of certain brain parts, which manifests itself in serious organic nerve damage and also influences the mental and emotional life, often leading to paranoid and manic delusions. The illness first appeared—probably as a result of the stress of the first Russian winter—at the beginning of 1942, with heavy dizzy spells. At the same time, the stomach problems he had complained about for long time worsened. That same year, or in early 1943 at the latest, he also began to suffer from a shaking of the limbs on the left side of his body (first the arm, later also the leg), which steadily worsened—apart from the temporary improvement mentioned here, which was obviously the result of the shock from the attempted assassination. Hitler's physician, Dr. Morell, treated him with 28 different medications, both pills and injections. These medications, however, did not prevent his illness from worsening toward the end of the war, to the point where he usually had to use a cane for walking, and he attempted to use his right extremities to keep the left ones as still as possible. Physically, Hitler was a sick man after 1943, in the fall of 1944 (September to November), and again even severely ill in April 1945.—Source: *Bullock,* pp. 720 and 767ff.; *Zoller,* pp. 64 and 70; *Trevor-Roper: Hitlers letzte Tage,* pp. 62ff.; *Görlitz/Quint,* pp. 579f.; *Guderian: Erinnerungen,* pp. 402f.

52. Siegfried Westphal; born March 18, 1902; 1922 Second Lieutenant; 1934 Cavalry Captain; 1935-38 in the Operations Branch of the Army General Staff; 1939 Major and Ia, 58th Infantry Division; August 1940 member of the German Armistice Commission; June 1941 Ia German Africa Corps (later: Panzer Group Africa); October 1942 Chief of General Staff, Africa Panzer Army; 1942 Colonel; February 1943 chief of the operations section, Commander-in-Chief, South, and June 1943, Chief of General Staff Commander-in-Chief South; November 21, 1943 to June 5, 1944 Chief of General Staff, Commander-in-Chief, Southwest; April 1944 Lieutenant General; after the beginning of September 1944, Chief of General Staff, Commander-in-Chief, West succeeding Blumentritt (after March 25, 1945: Commander-in-Chief South); and January 1945 General of the Cavalry.—Source: *Westphal,* pp. 331f.; *Siegler* pp. 142f.; *Rangliste 1944-45,* p. 29; *Das deutsche Heer,* p. 430; *Keilig 211/363.*

53. See list of participants. Krebs, General of Infantry as of August 1, 1944, became Chief of General Staff of Army Group B in the West, as the successor to Speidel, at the beginning of September.

54. Record number unknown—Fragment No. 46—A first transcription, of which the lower third was destroyed on the first 15 pages.

55. Since 1942, Kluge—then Commander-in-Chief of Army Group Middle in the East—had been wooed constantly by the conspirators, who thought they needed an active field marshal with troop command to start their actions. The Ia [operations officer] of the army group, Colonel v. Tresckow, who belonged to the resistance group, had meaningful personal influence on Kluge, but was unable to get more from him than an assent in the case of Hitler's death. Kluge stepped down in October 1943 after an accident, and did not receive a new front command for three-quarters of a year. On July 3, 1944, he took over from Rundstedt as Commander-in-Chief West, and then on July 18 also took over from the wounded Rommel as Commander-in-Chief of Army Group B. In these positions he maintained his wait-and-see attitude toward the conspiracy, and gave his final rejection to Stülpnagel only on the evening of July 20, after Hitler's survival had been confirmed. Throughout the course of the following weeks, news filtered into the Führer Headquarters about the ambiguous attitude of the field marshal, who was also incriminated by involuntary or forced statements from those who had been arrested. The statements made by Hitler here indicate that Kluge was finally pulled into the assassination investigation only on August 30—that is, 11 days after his suicide. Another issue in his removal had obviously been the suspicion that Kluge was flirting with the idea of a separate peace in the West, as well as Hitler's anger over the Americans breaking out of their beachhead and the encirclement of the Seventh Army at Falaise. But in a file note from Bormann, dated August 17, 1944, regarding Kluge's discharge, it was already stated that he has been "the commander-in-chief over Tresckow and other traitors." The note said: "Field Marshal Kluge's behavior is not entirely acceptable; according to investigations conducted thus far, Kluge must have known about

individual thoughts and ideas of individual traitors. He did not report these." Because Hitler no longer trusted him completely, he could not remain commander-in-chief. Without prior announcement, Kluge was replaced by Field Marshal Model on August 17 and was ordered to report to headquarters immediately. Kluge wrote a letter to Hitler—in which he emphasized the necessity of signing a peace treaty soon, but which was at the same time a panegyric to Hitler's greatness (see Wilmot, pp. 779ff.)— and got into his car for the trip home on the morning of August 19. Between Clermont-en-Argonnes and Domnâsle he pulled off the road and poisoned himself.—Source: *Bormann's file note of August 17, 1944 (Archive IfZ, Fa 116, Bl.13); Wheeler; Bennett,* pp. 551f., 609, 650, 684ff. and 693ff.; *Wilmot (Engl.),* pp. 420f.; *Zeller, passim; Schramm (W.),* pp. 65, 335ff. and others.

56. The Public Law Court trial concluded on August 30. Accused were the Military Commander in France, General of Infantry Heinrich v. Stülpnagel, his Chief of Staff Colonel v. Linstow, Kluge's Senior Quartermaster, Colonel Finckh, as well as the Lieutenant Colonels v. Hofacker, Rahtgens and Smend. All the accused were sentenced to death and executed that same day, except v. Hofacker (December 20, 1944) and Smend (September 8, 1944).—Source: *Zeller,* p. 427; *Pechel,* pp. 335f.; *Wheeler-Bennett,* pp. 759ff

57. Kluge was without connection to his headquarters for more than twelve hours on August 15, after he left at 9:30 a.m. for a trip into the Falaise pocket. After his return, he reported that he had spent most of the day in a trench because of heavy artillery fire and a fighter-bomber attack. His staff officers considered this claim to be true, and it is supported by Hitler's accusations here, which the Allied side has not yet confirmed. In any case, nothing is known about a released German officer who was supposed to get in touch with Kluge. Despite Schramm's repeated explanation of the escort officer Tangermann, the behavior of the field marshal remains peculiar that day. At this critical moment, the Commander-in-Chief West goes to a front area—which, as no one could know better than he, was made practically impassable by the swarms of enemy fighter-bombers—to seek death on the battlefield, but then, facing death, chose rather to spend the afternoon sleeping in a shelter (see also below pp. 620f.). When the message arrived at the Führer Headquarters on July 16 around 6 o'clock that Kluge had established contact again, Hitler had already called Model back from Russia a few hours before and ordered him to immediately take over of both of Kluge's commands. [—] The field marshal's son, Lieutenant Colonel in the General Staff v. Kluge, had been appointed by his father as head of the Eberbach group, which was located inside the pocket.—Source: *Wilmot,* pp. 444f.; *Liddell Hart: The German Generals,* pp. 246ff.; *Schramm (W.),* pp. 353ff.

58. Hitler's reproaches against the staff of the Seventh Army were probably based mostly on his aversion to the long-time commander-in-chief of this army, Colonel General Dollmann, who died of a heart attack during the

battle in Normandy on June 27 (29?). On August 31, General of Panzer Troops Eberbach had just been replaced by General of Panzer Troops Brandenberger as commander of this army.

59.   The Seventh Army, together with the Fifteenth Army, had been under Field Marshal Rommel until his car accident during the fighter-bomber attack on the afternoon of July 17. It cannot be stated for certain whether Hitler already knew at this point about Rommel's involvement in the July 20 assassination attempt (which forced Rommel to suicide on October 14), as the following text suggests. But it can be assumed that this whole complex was initiated by the proceedings against Stülpnagel and his officers at the end of August. Zeller points out that Rommel's house in Herrlingen, near Ulm, had been under observation by Bormann's representatives long before October 14. Also, his Chief of General Staff, Speidel, had been recalled without explanation on September 5 and arrested September 7—one week after this meeting—and taken into the cellar at Prinz Albrecht Street.—Source: *Speidel,* pp. 170 and 175ff.; *Zeller,* p. 309.

60.   Hitler meant the Italian theater of war, because it had never been considered for the West.

61.   That was Hitler's opinion, but it was less justified after the reserves coming over the Mediterranean failed.

62.   Obviously, Hitler has the picture of the retreat movement in mind, since it should be "on the right side." He is referring to the western Egyptian Qattāra depression, a sand-drift desert of about 20,000 square kilometers, 134 meters below sea level at its lowest point, sprinkled with numerous salt lakes and impassable for motor vehicles. South of El Alamein, the Qattāra comes closest to the coast—within 65 km.

63.   Hitler's claim is a bit bold. On the evening of October 23, 1942, the English prepared to attack the German-Italian Alamein position, after the Axis troops that had reached the Alamein line on June 30 had failed to break through to the Nile 70 km away. The massed Allied forces and English air superiority put such heavy pressure on the German-Italian units (which were suffering from lack of supplies) that on the evening of November 2, Rommel asked the Armed Forces High Command and the *Comando Supremo* for permission to retreat—an action he had already initiated. This report from Rommel is the one referred to by Hitler here. It had in fact been presented to him late due to a mistake by the Armed Forces Operations Staff officer in charge. It arrived on November 3 at 3 a.m., but did not reach Hitler until about 10. (The officer in charge was demoted and put into a penal punishment unit, and General Warlimont fell out of favor for some time.) In response, Hitler, not understanding the seriousness of the situation, ordered Rommel to hold the position and not to give up a single meter of territory: "It would not be the first time in history that the stronger will has ruled over the stronger battalion. You can only show your troops the way to victory or death." Rommel initially obeyed and reversed the retreat movement, under considerable difficulty. But the following day, the English—in addition to breaking through the German lines—were able to

create a 20-km-wide hole in the front after the destruction of the Italian XX Corps. Rommel had no more reserves to fight back the danger, and he ordered a retreat to the Fuka Position on the early afternoon of November 4. This retreat, however, took on an avalanche-like character and really only ended on May 7-12 in Tunis. Hitler agreed to this November 4 retreat command the next day, via radio message. That first order from the Führer, on November 3, actually did reach Rommel belatedly (1:30 p.m.), which resulted in more difficulties, especially in relocating the Italian troops. However, Rommel would have been defeated by the English the following day in any case—after a quiet night.—Source: *Tippelskirch,* pp. 334ff.; *Westphal,* pp. 186f.; *Rommel Papers,* pp. 317ff.; *Rintelen,* pp. 176f.

64. He is probably referring to Rommel's demands to end the war, which the field marshal had presented to Hitler during his visit to the West on June 17 and again during his report in Berchtesgaden on June 29. Otherwise, Hitler could already be speaking about Rommel's contacts with the July men, which militarily could hardly have happened yet, as long as men like Speidel, for example, were still at large.—Source: *Speidel,* pp. 118 and 127; *Blumentritt,* pp. 233ff.

65. In fact, Hitler would rather have avoided war against the "Germanic brother nation" and was never able to understand why England refused to give him continental supremacy. When he speaks here of "renouncing everything," he means only *English* territory and *English* reparations, of course. A renunciation of his conquests so far would never have been considered. The remark about the year 1936 means the appointment of Ribbentrop as German ambassador to London, who was given the explicit command to probe the possibility of a German-English understanding. "Ribbentrop, bring me the English union!" are said to have been Hitler's words of farewell. Further above, Hitler speaks of the "offer" that he made to the English ambassador Henderson on August 25, 1939: He would agree to the British Empire and was willing to commit himself personally to its existence—as well as, if necessary, to use the strength of Germany for its defense—under the preconditions that a) the Danzig corridor problem would be "solved," b) the colonial demands of Germany would be met, and c) his obligations toward Italy and the Soviet Union would not be touched. After the French campaign, Hitler—without mentioning any details—made an "appeal to reason" during his Reichstag speech on July 19, 1940: He had never planned to "destroy or even damage" the British Empire and therefore did not see any reason for the continuation of the war.—Source: *Hofer,* p. 94; *VB* of July 20, 1940; *Ribbentrop,* pp. 91ff.

66. Robert Gilbert Vansittart; born June 25, 1881, and after 1941 Baron of Denham, had entered the British diplomatic service in 1902 and held office from 1928 to 1930 as Assistant Under-Secretary of State for Foreign Affairs; 1930-37 as Permanent Under-Secretary also in the Foreign Office; and 1938-41 as Chief Diplomatic Advisor to the Foreign Secretary. Vansittart was used by Goebbels as a symbol of anti-German behavior and

was constantly attacked. He died on February 14, 1957.—Source: *Who is Who 1950,* pp. 2856; *Vansittart,* passim.

67. Model had taken over the command of Army Group Center on June 28, 1944, from Field Marshal Busch, whose entire front had been torn open by the Soviet attack that started June 22.—Source: *Tippelskirch,* pp. 530ff.; *Siegler,* p. 132.

68. Here Hitler is probably repeating Rommel's statements, which were made during the meeting between Hitler, Rundstedt and Rommel on June 17, 1944, near Soissons.

69. Hitler himself had ordered the transportation of both SS panzer divisions into the East on March 25, 1944; they had been employed in front of Tarnopol. Furthermore, he had been notified several times about materiel and personnel shortages among most of the Western units. In fact, the 700-series of divisions located on the so-called Atlantic Wall were in no shape for a major battle—neither with respect to personnel nor equipment. They were immobile fortress divisions with, in many cases, older age groups, and equipped with captured French, Czech and Russian weapons. All other divisions were only present in the West temporarily—either for initial formation or for rehabilitation before being sent back into the East or to Italy. The latter was true also for the panzer divisions, with the exception of the 21st Panzer Division. This division had been set up 1943 in the West and equipped laboriously with captured French vehicles, but, like the 700-series divisions, it had no battle experience.

70. Of the possible Schulenburgs, the one probably meant here is Friedrich Werner Graf v. d. Schulenburg, born in 1875. Schulenburg, who succeeded Nadolny as ambassador in Moscow from October 1934 until June 1941, had welcomed the German-Soviet rapprochement of 1939 as a resumption of Bismarck's traditional orientation toward the East, and was disturbed by Hitler's attack on the Soviet Union in 1941. After Stalingrad, he joined the conspirators and competed with Ulrich v. Hassell as Stauffenberg's candidate for Foreign Minister in a possible Goerdeler cabinet, as he had asked for an immediate peace with Russia, provided that contact could be made with Stalin. Even though Ritter in his Goerdeler book in no way characterizes Schulenburg as a blind adherent of an "Eastern Solution," his political concept of Hitler's situation at the time is likely presented correctly here. Schulenburg was executed on November 10, 1944.—Source: *Goerdeler,* pp. 364, 379ff., 534f., 542 and 602f.; *Zeller,* pp. 391 and 432; *Wheeler-Bennett,* pp. 352, 637 and 764.

71. With those remarkable words, Hitler judges his own policy during the final years of the war. If he considered it so "stupid" to play the Russians off against the English, his expansion of the war toward Stalingrad and Tunis, and at least up to Avranches, could have the single purpose of lengthening his life and the lifespan of his regime at the expense of the German people—while his propaganda slogans trumpeted that the cause must be more important than anything else, and that even the last German must be willing to give himself up.

72. It is correct that Hitler lived in his headquarters in dangerously unrealistic isolation—in an atmosphere that Jodl in Nuremberg called a cross between a monastery and a concentration camp—and that he gave up all private life. The time span mentioned here is to be taken with a grain of salt, however, as Hitler's isolation was not that intense in the first years of war, and was of quite limited duration. It was not until partway through the war, for instance, that he finally gave up his habit of watching films after dinner.— Source: *IMT XV,* p. 325; *Bullock,* p. 723.

73. Rudolf Gercke; born August 17, 1884; 1904 Second Lieutenant; Reichs-wehr; 1923 left the service as brevet Major; 1933 re-entering as Major and detachment leader in RWM; 1937 Colonel and Chief of the Transportation Department in the Army General Staff; 1939 Major General and head of the Armed Forces Transportation System (in both positions until the end of the war); 1940 Lieutenant General; and 1942 General of Infantry. Gercke died in 1947 in American captivity.—Source: *Keilig 211/98; Seemen,* p. 285; *Order of Battle,* p. 553; *Das deutsche Heer,* p. 11; *Rangliste 1944-45,* p. 16.

74. With the July 20 events.

75. Here he refers to Army Group Center in the East, where, in Hitler's opinion, the collapse of June 1944 was accelerated by the fact that the Soviets used captured German officers to cross back over the line (made possible by the total breakdown of the front), rejoin the command system, and cause confusion. No evidence came to light after the war that could support this claim; the only certain thing is that several of the German generals and officers captured during this Soviet offensive did immediately step over to the side of the National Committee and offer themselves to the Russians.

76. Only in Paris did the conspirators—led by the Military Commander in France, General Carl Heinrich v. Stülpnagel—experience a brief triumph on July 20, despite the first indecisive then negative attitude of the Commander-in-Chief West. At 11 p.m., when everything was already over in Berlin, they had rounded up the senior SS and police commanders in France, including Gruppenführer Oberg and the men from his headquarters on Avenue Foch, and, within half an hour, had secured the vast majority of the 2,000 men (Schramm: 1,200) in the Parisian SS and SD forces, and had put them out of action. At dawn on July 21, the captured men had to be set free again, in consideration of the hopeless general situation and Kluge's attitude.—Source: *Wheeler-Bennett,* pp. 683ff.; *Schramm (W.),* passim.

77. Günther Blumentritt; born February 10, 1892; 1912 Second Lieutenant; Reichswehr; 1933 Major; 1938 Colonel and Chief, 4th Section in the Army General Staff; 1940 Chief of Staff, Fourth Army; 1941 Major General; January 1942 Senior Quartermaster I in the Army High Command; September 1942 Chief of Staff, Army Group D and Lieutenant General; and April 1944 General of Infantry. After this meeting, Blumentritt was replaced by Westphal during the first few days of September. In October 1944 he became Commander, XII SS Corps; January 1945 Commander,

Twenty-Fifth Army; end of March Commander, 1st Parachute Army; and after April 15, Commander-in-Chief, Blumentritt Army. Hitler's opinion about Blumentritt was also shared by his commander-in-chief, Rundstedt, who wrote in his assessment on September 9, 1944: "He deserves special mention for his clear position and his firm measures surrounding the events of July 20, 1944, in the area of the Commander-in-Chief West."—Source: *Army High Command staff files; (Nbg. Dok. NOKW-141); Order of Battle,* p. 530; *Siegler,* p. 113.

78. Eberhard Finckh; born November 7, 1899; came from the 41st Artillery Regiment; 1934 Captain, War Academy; 1938 assigned to the 10th Section of the Army General Staff; November 1942 Colonel in the General Staff Senior Quartermaster for Army Group Don/South; and after April 1944, Senior Quartermaster for the Commander-in-Chief West. On August 30, 1944, as a participant in the July conspiracy, Finckh was sentenced by the Public Law Court to death by hanging and was executed that same day.— Source: *DNB of May 11, 1944; Das deutsche Heer,* p. 12; *Manstein,* p. 326.

79. Wagner, who had been close to Beck and who already agreed with his attitude toward Hitler before the war, had been a participant in the July 20 conspiracy and had committed suicide on July 23 (22?), 1944.—Source: *Wheeler-Bennett,* pp. 481 and 765.

80. Neither Kluge's promotions nor his decorations were particularly unusual. He had been Colonel General for only nine months when he received the marshal's baton during the great field marshal promotion on July 19, 1940. At that time, however, when ranks were even skipped, this quick success was nothing out of the ordinary. The highest award he received was the Schwerter [swords], while Hitler had already awarded the Brillianten [diamonds] to four Army generals (Rommel, Hube, Model and Balck) that same day. But Kluge—like all generals from the army commander rank upward—had, in addition to his field marshal salary of 36,000 Reich Marks [RM] (gross), received special tax-free bonuses from Hitler's private funds. He also received a check from Hitler for more than 250,000 RM for his 60th birthday on October 30, 1942, as well as a building permit for his property in Brandenburg worth about half of that sum. Kluge had accepted the check as well as the building permit.—Source: *Wheeler-Bennett,* pp. 552f.; *Schlabrendorff,* pp. 61f.

81. Karl Ernst Rahtgens, Lieutenant Colonel in the General Staff, was a relative of Kluge, as his mother was born a v. Kluge—probably a cousin of the field marshal.

82. Roland Freisler; born October 30, 1893; law studies; Communist; from Russian war imprisonment Bolshevik commissioner; after his return lawyer in Kassel; after 1925 member of the NSDAP; 1932 Landtag member in Prussia; March 1933 as Ministerial Director head of the Personnel Department in the Prussian Ministry of Justice; in that same year Under-Secretary of State (after the unification of the Reich Ministry of Justice); and Prussian State Council and member of the Reichstag. As Thierack's successor, Freisler became president of the Public Law Court in August

1942, and tried to compensate for this demotion and his politically dubious past by carrying out his duties with extraordinary enthusiasm and an excess of toughness and cruelty. Freisler died during an air raid on Berlin on February 3, 1945, in the cellar of his office building.—Source: *Reichstags-Handbücher; Munzinger Archive; Schlabrendorff,* pp. 213f.

83.   Stieff had contacted the conspirators via Tresckow and was one of the actors in the July 20 assassination attempt. In the main trial, the "smallest and youngest Armed Forces general" was sentenced to death by hanging on August 8, 1944, and executed two hours later.

84.   Erich Hoepner; born September 14, 1886; 1906 Second Lieutenant; Reichswehr; 1933 Colonel; 1936 Major General; 1938 Lieutenant General and Commander, 1st Mobile Division; November 1938 Commanding General, XVI Army Corps (Berlin); 1939 General of Cavalry; with his corps in Poland and France; July 1940 Colonel General; and in the Eastern campaign Commander, Fourth Panzer Group (October 1941 renamed Fourth Panzer Army). On January 8, 1942, Hoepner received his dishonorable discharge from the Army, "for cowardice and disobedience," because he had carried out unauthorized retreat movements and because he had spoken disparagingly—which had reached Hitler's ears—about the "non-professional leadership." At the end of 1943, Hoepner was introduced to the revolt plans by Olbricht, his neighbor in Dahlem, and was tapped for the role of commander-in-chief of the Replacement Army. He was also sentenced to death by hanging by the Public Law Court on August 8, 1944, and executed that same day.—Source: *Munzinger Archive; Siegler,* p. 124; *Keilig 211/139; Zeller,* passim; and others.

85.   At that time (since the end of December 1941) Commander-in-Chief of Army Group Center, to which Hoepner's Fourth Panzer Army belonged.

86.   It is not quite clear what Hitler meant here. He, at least, was certainly not silent "back then."

87.   Kluge's death was not made public; on short notice Hitler prohibited the planned burial ceremony on his [Kluge's] Böhne estate in Altmark. According to Blumentritt's statement, a state funeral was originally planned as well, but was cancelled after the poison was discovered during an examination of the corpse (ordered by Keitel); at first, only a heart attack had been discussed. After the field marshal's corpse had been stored in the Böhne church for nearly two weeks, and tumult was increasing among the population, the propaganda department emphasized via verbal propaganda that Kluge had died of a heart attack. Keitel informed the military district commanders of the death on August 31, and requested that the generals be informed in a "suitable way." This g.Kdos text said: "From a letter Kluge left behind, we read that he obviously acted under the impression that he was heavily responsibility for the outcome of the battle in Normandy." And, in conclusion: "There will be no further discussion of these events." The discussion began, though, at least abroad, as the Allies captured this order at the end of December 1944.—Source: *RdSchr. Parteikanzlei 219/22 gRs.; Report RpropAmt Dessau Sept. 5, 1944 and others (Archive IfZ, Fa*

116, Bl. 18); Files of the Propaganda Department in the German central archives in Potsdam, Bd. 863; Schramm (W.), pp. 376f.; *NZZ* Dec. 29, 1944 (midday edition).

88. Transcript number unknown—Fragment No. 28—During the second transcription in May 1945, the stenographer remarked: "In preparation for the Ardennes offensive starting on December 16, 1944, Hitler spoke on December 11 and 12 to about 20-30 senior officers—army leaders, commanding generals, and division commanders with their staff officers. These officers had been called to the 'Adlerhorst' headquarters for an introduction to their assignments during the attack. This fragment contains the first part—about half—of the speech held on December 12. Hitler spoke without a script; the machine transcription is only a fragment and was made from the stenographic record with only minor stylistic changes. The stenographers who had been responsible for recording the original meeting deciphered the fragment—very poorly preserved, especially the severely burned upper portion of the pages. The parts in parentheses were added based on the meaning and on Hitler's mode of expression." Hitler had arrived at the "Adlerhorst" command post—fitted out for him in Ziegenberg at Bad Nauheim—with a small operations staff on December 10.—Source: *Westphal,* p. 279.

89. A gap of about three lines; the gaps below are generally smaller.

90. A speech of a similar kind had preceded this, on December 11.

91. Hitler tries to justify initiating the war and the moment chosen to initiate it. This means admitting responsibility for a preventative war, which was denied at this time in the official propaganda.

92. This memorandum was printed as document 052-L in the "Blauen Reihe" ["Blue Series"] *Der Prozess gegen die Hauptkriegsverbrecher vor dem Internationalen Militärgerichtshof* [The War Crimes Trial before the International Military Tribunal], vol. XXXVII, pp. 466ff. It is dated October 9, 1939, and is directed to the commanders-in-chief of the Armed Forces branches and the Chief of the Armed Forces High Command, under the title "Denkschrift und Richtlinien über die Führung des Krieges im Westen.[Memorandum and Guidelines for the Conduct of War in the West]" Here Hitler had written quite clear-sightedly on page 7: "Time—in this war, as in the course of all historical events—is not a factor that has inherent value in and of itself, but one which has to be evaluated. In the current situation, under these conditions, time can be seen as an ally of the Western forces rather than an ally of ours." And further below, on page 16 and following, under the headline, "The Dangers of the German Situation": "The first danger for Germany is that in a long war, some states might be drawn to the opposite side, either because of their economic necessity or because special interests have arisen. The second danger is that a long war could alarm states that might in principle wish to join Germany's side— they might remember the last war and take it as a warning, and therefore refrain from joining us. The third danger in a long war is the difficulty of securing nourishment for the people, based on the restricted food and raw-

material base, and getting the means to conduct war. Also, the mental attitude of the people will at least be burdened by it."

93. Already in his speech before the Reichstag on September 1, 1939, Hitler had stated that he had spent "more than 90 billion for the building up of our Armed Forces." This number is in contrast to the statements of Schwerin-Krosigks, who calculated 60 billion Reichsmark for Armed Forces and armament costs between January 1, 1934, and August 1, 1939. This figure is validated by all the documents available today. Hitler might have included all costs that contributed to armament even indirectly—such as railway, canal, and street construction, and similar investments—and he probably rounded up to achieve the desired propaganda effect. That Hitler's statements are not quite correct is evident from the fact that in the time span mentioned, total Reich expenditures were 101.5 billion RM.

94. The KV I was a heavy tank of 43.5 tons, and the famous T 34 a medium tank of initially 26.3 tons (after 1944 T 34-85 of 30 tons), both armed with a 7.62-cm KwK L/30.5 (T 34-85: 8.5-cm KwK L/53). At first, they dominated everything the German attacking armies could bring up and hindered their mobile warfare. A KV II is unknown; Hitler probably meant the KV I S with the 7.62-cm KwK L/41.5.—Source: *Senger-Etterlin,* pp. 120ff. and 240ff.

95. Here Hitler is fantasizing freely. Although Britain did start arming in 1936 as a result of the Ethiopian War and the German conscription measures, neither universal conscription nor a two-billion-pound credit was introduced. On the contrary, after one year, on January 6, 1937, the British Minister of Defense, Sir Thomas Inskip, explicitly declared that the government was not thinking—despite problems with replacements—of introducing universal conscription. The armament credits were 119 million pounds in the fiscal year 1935-36 and 188 million pounds in the fiscal year 1936-37. Not until a white paper was published on February 16, 1937, did the government demand 1.5 billion pounds for armament purposes, to be spent over the next 5 years. Because 400 million of this sum was to be covered by a loan granted on February 18, this meant an increase in the defense budget of only about 220 million pounds per year over the following five years. Perhaps Hitler confused pounds and marks, in which case it would be correct that the English defense budget surpassed 2 billion RM in 1936 for the first time.—Source: *Keesings Archive 1935-37; Times* from Jan. 7, Feb. 17, and Feb. 19, 1937.

96. In this famous, disastrous term—here supplemented by a strange concept of "territorial armament"—Hitler's policy of war lies *in nuce.* Today it seems unbelievable how widely accepted an axiom could have become back then, when—even just considering the unavoidable and significant overlapping of claims—it could only have been valid for a small minority of desperados.

97. Here Hitler was talking about the "war in sight" crisis of 1875, but he confused the facts for his own purposes. It is true that the Prussian General Staff under Moltke had been rattling swords quite heavily and had

approved a preventative war because Moltke thought—which later proved
to be wrong—that France would not be able to support its armament weight
much longer and would have to free itself of it soon through war (the origin
of this crisis was a new French Army organization law, which was quite
overrated in Germany at this time). But the plans for this preventative war
did not fail, as Hitler pretends here, because of the "internal German
parliamentary situation," but because of Bismarck's dislike for preventative
war, at least after 1870—which has been substantiated, even if the
chancellor was using the threat of war to further his political chess game at
that time. Also, this crisis—in which Bismarck tried to halt the French
rearmament program through intimidation and bluffing—was the first time,
as a prelude to later alliances, that England and Russia took France's
side.—Source: *Ritter: Staatskunst,* pp. 289ff.; *Eyck: Bismarck III,* pp.
149ff.; *Herzfeld,* pp. 222f.; *Meyer, A.O.,* pp. 513ff.; *Oncken I,* pp. 145ff;
Jeismann, pp. 91ff.

98.   This is, of course, just the opposite of reality: The allies dropped out when
an offensive war was no longer possible. Hitler expanded on this thought in
his daily order to the Armed Forces on January 1, which included the
following: "If in this immense struggle—which is fought not only for
Germany, but for the future of Europe—we have had to bear setbacks, the
responsibility does not lie with the German people and its Armed Forces,
but with our European allies. From the breakdown of the Romanian-Italian-
Hungarian front along the Don and the subsequent total dispersal due to
sabotage of our joint warfare, to the Italian royalty, to the putsch against the
Fascist Italy of the Duce who was on our side, it is a straight line of
betrayal. It has continued with the dreadful capitulation of the Finnish state
leaders, with the breach of faith by the Romanian king and his circle, with
the self-abandonment of Bulgaria, and with the disgraceful conduct of the
former Hungarian State Administrator. These betrayals had serious effects
on the political and military warfare."—Source: *VB* of Jan. 2, 1945.

99.   This passage is not clear, as there are no known memoranda or files from
the year 1917 to which Hitler's statements could apply. Perhaps he is
referring to the peace resolution of the majority parties, which demanded a
compromise peace and the explicit renunciation of annexations; the
Reichstag accepted the resolution on July 19, 1917, by a margin of 212
votes to 126.

100. The decision to take offensive action in the West had developed in Hitler's
mind as early as during the Polish campaign, where the extent of German
military successes brought up this possibility in answer to the unexpected
entry of the Western forces into the war. Hitler's ideas had met with
immense resistance, especially among Army General Staff. The resistance
was based on various reasons: a general reluctance to engage in war,
concerns about violating the neutrality of Belgium and the Netherlands,
objections against the winter date initially suggested by Hitler, and other
issues. The decisive factor was undoubtedly the fact that the leaders of the
Army High Command obviously did not have the necessary strategic

genius, which was soon found in Hitler and the Chief of General Staff of Army Group "A," Lieutenant General v. Manstein. Only later did the General Staff accept the plan for the attack internally and then—apart from the usual exactness of the composition—expanded the plan significantly [check this whole note...].—Source: *Jacobsen: Fall Gelb,* passim, especially pp. 145ff.

101. In the European and North African theater, American deaths totaled 174,000 in World War II. Even if Hitler here—as was common practice—used the term "losses" to include wounded and imprisoned as well as deaths, his number seems very high for a period of only three weeks.

102. Hans v. Obstfelder, born September 6, 1886; 1906 Second Lieutenant; 1915 Captain; Reichswehr; 1933 Colonel; 1936 Major General and Commander, 28th Infantry Division; 1938 Lieutenant General; 1940 General of Infantry and Commanding General, XXIX Army Corps; August 1943 Commanding General, LXXXVI Army Corps; December 1944 Commander, First Army; and after March 1, 1945, Commander, Nineteenth Army in exchange with Foertsch. From March 26 until the capitulation Obstfelder, commanded the Seventh Army.—Source: Army High Command staff files (Nbg. Dok. NOKW -141); *Siegler,* p. 133; *Seemen; Order of Battle,* p. 601.

103. While the Ardennes offensive was grinding to a halt, Hitler believed he could take advantage of the fact that the American reserves were tied up in the Ardennes region and conduct an operation in lower Alsace (Operation "Nordwind" ["North Wind"]). He wanted to retain the initiative in the West at all costs, and prevent the Anglo-Americans from making a simultaneous attack in conjunction with the expected Soviet winter offensive. On New Year's Eve the eight divisions mentioned here—from the Saar region and the area around Bitsch—attacked during the night in the direction of the Zabern valley. After initial local successes and small penetrations into the Maginot Line, the attack was sauandered by an advance northward from the Colmar bridgehead in upper Alsace, in the direction of Strasbourg. Eisenhower, who in fact did not have any more reserves in this area, considered a temporary evacuation of Strasbourg and a complete retreat to the Vosges, but was initially hindered by French pride. Soon it became evident that the strength of the German attack was waning, well before the defense of Strasbourg became necessary. The outcome of Operation "Nordwind" ["North Wind"] was little more than the forward movement of the front line between Bitsch and the Rhine, which gained some ground in front of the Western Wall in this area and allowed for the building of a useless new small bridgehead on the left bank of the Rhine, north of Strasbourg.—Source: *Tippelskirch,* p. 610; *Görlitz II,* pp. 445f.; *Wilmot,* pp. 650f.; *Supplements to the KTB/WFSt [War Diary of the Armed Forces Operations Staff?]* from Jan. 3 and 4, 1945 *(Nbg. Dok. 1797-PS).*

104. At the site of penetration in the Ardennes.

105. This reference is also to the Ardennes offensive.

106. In contrast to the Ardennes offensive, this attack did not take the Americans by surprise.—Source: *Wilmot,* p. 650.

107. Hitler probably feared that the Americans—as turned out to be true—would
      pull back to the south into the region of Strasbourg, and would thereby
      escape the planned encirclement and destruction. The original plan was
      obviously to conduct this pincer movement only from the Palatinate or the
      Saar against American forces in the northeastern corner of Alsace. Hitler
      obviously did not yet have great faith in the chances of success for
      Himmler's attacks from the south and the newly built bridgehead north of
      Strasbourg—an operation that Hitler, against Rundstedt's resistance, would
      later turn into a main focus.

108. At the climax of the crisis in the West, when their armies were falling back
      hastily onto the Reich's borders, the German leadership faced the problem
      of occupying the Western Wall and the upper Rhine—at least in a
      makeshift manner—in time to take in the stream of returning units there. As
      regards the manning of the actual Western Wall, there were several fortress
      battalions and fortress tank destroyer detachments, etc., while for the upper
      Rhine there were no troops at all except from some training battalions from
      Military District V. In this situation, Hitler named the Reichsführer SS and
      Commander-in-Chief of the Replacement Army as Commander-in-Chief,
      Upper Rhine. He did so, as he once said himself, based on the following
      thoughts: "Himmler always has reserves of police or SS units that no one
      knows about and which he does not give away. If he is responsible for the
      front along the upper Rhein, he will be forced to bring together everything
      that he can get a hold of." And Hitler was right. So for Himmler's first
      employment as a military leader, it was not his military leadership qualities
      that were decisive.

109. The extremely heavy 653rd Tank Destroyer Detachment was the first and
      only "Jägdtiger" ["Hunter-Tiger"] unit. This Tank Destroyer VI was armed
      with a 12.8-cm antitank gun 44 L/55 and was the only German armored
      vehicle with a long weapon of this caliber, which penetrated 202 mm tanks
      from a distance of 1 km. The speed of 12-15 km/h mentioned in the
      following discussion can only be correct for certain difficult terrain
      conditions, as the highest speed of this Hunter-Tiger was 35km/h, although
      it was said to be rather difficult to move. When 250 mm armor is
      mentioned here, it could only be referring to the turret shield, because the
      armor on the nose was 100 mm at a 40° angle (driver's front 150 mm), and
      the sides and rear were armored with 80 mm plating at a 60° angle (the real
      strength of these armor plates measured vertically to the surface was
      accordingly lower). In spite of the fragmentary character of these
      statements by Hitler, and in spite of the contradictions in his statements,
      one can exclude the possibility that at a certain point he was talking about
      his 180-ton monster tank "Maus," which was also supposed to be armed
      with a 12.8-cm gun. For the "Maus," the construction design had actually
      called for 250 mm armor plating; this was achieved if the measurements
      were taken horizontally (actual armor strength on the nose, measured
      vertically to the surface: 200 mm). Two "Mäuse" were built, one of sheet

metal and one with armor plating, both of which fell into the hands of the Russians.—Source: *Senger-Etterlin,* p. 192.

110.   Hitler's assessment of the Maginot Line was probably correct; critical parts such as electrical installations, etc., had been dismantled.

111.   The combat weight of the "Hunter-Tiger" according to Senger-Etterlin: 70.6 tons.

112.   Himmler had already taken control of the border police—whose responsibility was to supervise the German border traffic—in 1937, and in September 1944 he also incorporated the customs border guard into the Amt IV/RSHA, i.e., into the Gestapo. The job of the border guards, who until then had reported to the Reich Ministry of Finance, was to safeguard the financial security of the Reich through border protection measures. The staff was about 55,000 men at that time, but shortly thereafter 10,000 were given to the Waffen SS. It seems, however, that the incorporation into the RSHA had not been fully completed. A few days before the end of the war, the whole organization was moved back into the Reich financial administration.—Source: *IMT I,* p. 297, *XI,* pp. 343f. and *XXII,* p. 578; *Nbg. Dok. Gestapo (A) 31.*

113.   A "decree from the Führer regarding the concentration of armaments and war production," dated June 19, 1944, published in the "News from the Reich Minister for Armaments and War Production," No. 41, says under section II/2 concerning the Armed Forces: "The capacities of the forces employed in the ordnance offices of the Armed Forces branches, and the specialists of all kinds, who until now have been working in business— including businesses owned by the Armed Forces and responsible for new developments for the Armed Forces branches—can be employed by the Reich Minister for Armaments and War Production in the pursuit of revolutionary new developments, as determined by me, without regard to these persons' former obligations to the Armed Forces branches, so that these new developments will come to fruition as soon as possible." As in this case concerning the specialists, Speer probably later obtained authorization concerning the raw materials stored by the Armed Forces. This is quite likely, as it was Speer's usual method of operation to get "Führer orders" for everything possible—even for such things as the confiscation of streetcars in Brussels.

114.   August Frank; born April 5, 1898; commercial apprenticeship; participant in World War I after 1916; 1920-1930 in the Bavarian police service (lastly as police secretary); merchant; after 1933 SS administration; 1935 Sturmbannführer and Hauptabeilungsleiter Haushalt [?] in the SS administration office; 1938 Oberführer and Stabsführer for the head of SS administration; and 1939-42 head of the SS Administrative Offfice and permanent deputy of the chief of the Head Office, Pohl. In addition, after 1940 head of war direction for the Waffen SS, 1943 Gruppenführer and chief of economic administration in the head office of the Ordnungspolizei order police, after August 1944, chief of Army Administration in the Army High Command, and October 1944, Obergruppenführer. At the Nuremberg

Pohl trial, he was sentenced on November 3, 1947, to life im-prisonment; in 1951 the sentence was reduced to 15 years.—Source: *SS staff files (Nbg. Dok. NO-1592); Aff. [?] Frank* from Jan. 17, 1947 *(NO-1576)*.

115. This 38-ton, known as the "Hetzer" ["Hustler"], was a very low—and diffi-cult to locate in open terrain—16-ton tank destroyer with a 7.5-cm antitank gun 39 L/48 and 1 machine gun, and a speed of 38 km/h. The 38-ton was originally a Czech tank, whose production was discontinued in 1942. To use the unexploited production capacity, especially in the Bohemian and Moravian Machine Factory, the model was redesigned as an assault gun or tank destroyer. The prototype was presented in January 1944 in Rasten-burg, and on April 20, 1944, the first 16 38-ton vehicles were ready for action and participated in a tank parade in Klessheim. In July 1944, 83 units were built, and by the end of the year the monthly production had risen to 400 units. Even in the first quarter of 1945, 1,138 pieces were built—all in the protectorate. The very unusual (for the time) increase in production indicates the perceived importance of this weapon. Speer's Führer Protocal of November 29, 1944 (No. 30) says the following about the 38-ton: "The Führer points out again the especially high value of the 38-ton and urges that everything be done to reach the target production rate in the shortest possible time. He considers this vehicle one of the biggest successes of this war in terms of weapons technology and therefore expects that its further production—especially the new type with the air-cooled Tatra diesel engine—will receive every imaginable support." In April 1945, the prototype of a significant improvement in weapons technology was completed: the 38-ton with a recoilless gun (providing more room for ammunition, crew, etc.).—Source: *Die deutsche Industrie,* p. 115; *Lusar,* pp. 34f.; *Senger-Etterlin,* p. 192.

116. This relates to the fact mentioned above, that the 38-ton was built very low (height: 220 cm, compared with Panzer III: 244, Panzer IV: 268, Panzer V: 310 and Panzer VI: 288 cm). On the other hand, however, the rather weak armoring of the 38-ton (nose 60 mm, sides 20 mm, rear 8 mm) argued against the dug-in employment demanded by Hitler.—Source: *Senger-Etterlin,* p. 192.

117. Surprisingly, on December 22, the British government had ordered the conscription of an additional 250,000 men to "strengthen our armies on the front." For the most part, these were men who had turned 18 since the last regular conscription, as well as men released from the armaments industry; some were also transfers from the Navy and RAF to the Army. At that time, it must have been explicitly stated that these conscriptions were in no way related to the significant worsening of the situation in the West, but were to be interpreted as a reflection of the decision to continue the war with all possible means.—Source: *NZZ* of Dec. 24, 1944.

118. Here even Himmler tries—though in vain—to pour cold water on Hitler's ideas. Even in these fragments, one can clearly see how Hitler loses himself more and more in flimsy arguments, blowing the enemy's minimal

difficulties out of proportion and resorting more and more to unfounded wishful thinking.

Hitler and His Generals—1945

1. SS Obergruppenführer Felix Steiner did not carry out Hitler's order to intervene in the Battle of Berlin with "Group Steiner."

2. General Walther von Seydlitz was vice president of the Communist "National Committee for a Free Germany" [Nationalkomitee Freies Deutschland] established by the Soviets in July 1943 in the Krasnogorsk prison camp.

3. In March 1945 Colonel General Heinrich von Vietinghoff was made Commander-in-Chief Southwest, succeeding Field Marshal Albert Kesselring.

4. Lloyd George, British Prime Minister from 1916 to 1922, visited Hitler in September 1936 in Berchtesgaden.

5. After the death of Franklin D. Roosevelt on April 12, 1945, Vice President Harry S. Truman became the new U.S. president.

6. Field Marshal General Ferdinand Schörner was, since January 1945, Commander-in-Chief of Army Group Center, fighting in Czechoslovakia.

7. Lieutenant General Rudolf Holste was, as of April 20, 1945, Commanding General of the XXXXIX Army Corps.

8. Alfred Hugenberg was leader of the extreme right German National Peoples' Party [Deutschnationalen Volkspartei], and belonged to Hitler's government as Reich Economic Minister from January to June 1933. General Schleicher was Hitler's predecessor as Reich Chancellor, from December 1932 to January 1933.

9. Field Marshal General Werner von Blomberg was Reich War Minister from 1933 to 1938.